THE GREENBLATT RE

Praise for *The Greenblatt Reader*

"As a founder of the New Historicism, Stephen Greenblatt has done more than establish a critical school; he has invented a habit of mind for literary criticism, which is indispensable to the temperament of our times, and crucial to the cultural of the past. This admirable anthology represents the subtle play of pleasure and instruction, embodied in writings that move effortlessly between wonder and wisdom."

Homi K. Bhabha, Harvard University

"For three decades Stephen Greenblatt has been the most articulate, thoughtful, and daring voice in early modern studies. The breadth of his reading is vast, the connections he makes are unexpected and often revelatory, and his writing is, quite simply, brilliant. Most of all, his willingness to take chances has made him an exciting and uniquely provocative critic. It is wonderful to have these classic essays in a single collection; and especially to have the most ephemeral of the pieces, the exquisite meditations on his visits to China and Laos, easily available. This is a beautifully conceived, indispensable volume."

Stephen Orgel, Stanford University

THE GREENBLATT READER

Stephen Greenblatt

Edited by Michael Payne

Blackwell
Publishing

BLACKWELL PUBLISHING
350 Main Street, Malden, MA 02148-5020, USA
108 Cowley Road, Oxford OX4 1JF, UK
550 Swanston Street, Carlton, Victoria 3053, Australia

First published 2005 by Blackwell Publishing Ltd

Library of Congress Cataloging-in-Publication Data

Greenblatt, Stephen, 1943–
  The Greenblatt reader / Stephen Greenblatt ; edited by Micheal Payne.
    p. cm.
  Includes bibliographical references and index.
  ISBN 1-4051-1565-3 (hardback) — ISBN 1-4051-1566-1 (pbk.)
  1. Criticism. 2. Historicism. 3. Shakespeare, William, 1564–1616—Criticism and
interpretation. I. Payne, Michael, 1941– II. Title.

PN81.G725 2005
801′.95—dc22

2004055099

A catalogue record for this title is available from the British Library.

Set in 11/13 pt Bembo
by Kolam Information Services Ltd, Pondicherry, India
Printed and bound in the United Kingdom
by MPG Books Ltd, Bodmin, Cornwall

The publisher's policy is to use permanent paper from mills that operate a sustainable
forestry policy, and which has been manufactured from pulp processed using acid-
free and elementary chlorine-free practices. Furthermore, the publisher ensures that
the text paper and cover board used have met acceptable environmental accreditation
standards.

For further information on
Blackwell Publishing, visit our website:
www.blackwellpublishing.com

CONTENTS

ACKNOWLEDGMENTS

The editor wishes to thank, yet again, the remarkable editorial staff at Blackwell Publishing in Oxford; especially, on this occasion, Emma Bennett and Helen Gray. Special thanks are also due to Gustavo P. Secchi, Professor Greenblatt's research assistant at Harvard, for preparing the bibliography of Greenblatt's many publications through 2003. The bibliography was already in proof before the appearance of Greenblatt's *Will in the World: How Shakespeare Became Shakespeare* (Norton, 2004), which brilliantly complements and continues much of what appears in Part III of this book.

Finally, I wish to express special gratitude to the author of these pieces, both for what he has taught us about Shakespeare and the English Renaissance and for his inspiring example of creative scholarship and professional civility.

M. P.

The editor and publisher would like to thank the following for permission to use copyright material:

'Culture' from *Critical Terms for Literary Study*, ed. Thomas McLaughlin and Frank Lentricchia (University of Chicago Press, 1990, pp. 225–32). Reprinted by kind permission of The University of Chicago Press.

'Towards a Poetics of Culture' from *Learning to Curse: Essays in Early Modern Culture* by Stephen Greenblatt (Routledge, 1990, pp. 146–60). Copyright © 1990 by Stephen Greenblatt. Reprinted by permission of Routledge/Taylor & Francis Books, Inc.

'The Touch of the Real' from *Practicing New Historicism* (University of Chicago Press, 2000, pp. 20–48). Reprinted by kind permission of The University of Chicago Press.

'The Wound in the Wall' from *Practicing New Historicism* (University of Chicago Press, 2000, pp. 75–109). Reprinted by kind permission of The University of Chicago Press.

'Marvelous Possessions' excerpt from *Marvelous Possessions: The Wonder of the New World* (University of Chicago Press, 1991, pp. 52–85). Reprinted by kind permission of The University of Chicago Press.

'Invisible Bullets', from *Shakespearean Negotiations* (Oxford University Press, 1988, pp. 21–65). Copyright © 1988 The Regents of the University of California. Reprinted by permission of Oxford University Press and the University of California Press.

'The Improvisation of Power', from *Renaissance Self-Fashioning: From More to Shakespeare* (University of Chicago Press, 1980, pp. 222–54). Reprinted by kind permission of the University of Chicago Press.

'Shakespeare and the Exorcists', from *Shakespearean Negotiations* (Oxford University Press, 1988, pp. 94–128). Copyright © 1988 The Regents of the University of California. Reprinted by permission of Oxford University Press and the University of California Press.

'Martial Law in the Land of Cocaigne', from *Shakespearean Negotiations* (Oxford University Press, 1988, pp. 129–63). Copyright © 1988 The Regents of the University of California. Reprinted by permission of Oxford University Press and the University of California Press.

'Prologue' from *Hamlet in Purgatory* (Princeton University Press, 2001, pp. 3–9). Copyright © 2001 by Princeton University Press. Reprinted by permission of Princeton University Press.

'China: Visiting Rites', first appeared in *Raritan* Vol. 2, No. 4, (Spring, 1983): 1–23. Reprinted by permission.

'China: Visiting Rites II', first appeared in *Raritan* Vol. 4, No. 4 (Spring, 1985): 44–56. Reprinted by permission.

'Laos is Open', from H. Aram Vesser ed. *Confessions of the Critics*, Routledge, 1996, pp. 221–34. Copyright © 1996 from *Confessions of the Critics* by H. Aram Vesser (ed.). Reprinted by permission of Routledge/Taylor and Francis Books, Inc.

'Story–Telling', originally published in *The Threepenny Review* 11, 1990: 23. Reprinted by permission.

Every effort has been made to trace copyright holders and to obtain their permission for the use of copyright material. The authors and publishers will gladly receive any information enabling them to rectify any error or omission in subsequent editions.

INTRODUCTION: GREENBLATT AND NEW HISTORICISM

Stephen Greenblatt is the most influential practitioner of new historicism (or what he sometimes calls cultural poetics). This *Reader* makes available for the first time in one volume his most important writings on culture, Renaissance studies, and Shakespeare. It also features occasional pieces on subjects as diverse as miracles, traveling in Laos and China, and story-telling, which suggest the range of his intellectual and cultural interests and the versatility of his styles as a writer. Taken together, the texts collected here dispel such misconceptions as that new historicism is antithetical to literary and aesthetic value, that it reduces the historical to the literary or the literary to the historical, that it denies human agency and creativity, that it is somehow out to subvert the politics of cultural and critical theory, or that it is anti-theoretical.[1] Such categorical dismissals of new historicism (which is an interdisciplinary and multiplicitous way of knowing) simply do not stand up against a careful reading of these texts. The intended audience for this book includes students of the Renaissance and Shakespeare, those interested primarily in cultural and critical theory, and general readers who have encountered Greenblatt's journalistic writing and who may want to know more about his work.

Admittedly there is a certain irony here in collecting, singling out, and celebrating Greenblatt's writing in an anthology such as this, because much of his scholarship has been determinedly part of a collective project that has included, for example, the members of the Editorial Board of the journal *Representations*,[2] including Catherine Gallagher, with whom he recently coauthored *Practicing New Historicism*,[3] which is a key text for understanding its subject. (Indeed, his notion of authorship, including his own, seems closely allied to Michel Foucault's declaration that "The author's name manifests the appearance of a certain discursive set and indicates the status of this discourse within a society and a culture."[4]) Even the earliest manifesto for a new historicism appeared quite modestly as Greenblatt's introduction to a collection of essays (a reprint of an issue of *Genre* published by the University of Oklahoma Press entitled *The Power of Forms in the English Renaissance*), which included important papers by eleven other scholars.

Greenblatt begins that introduction with Queen Elizabeth's understandably bitter reaction to the revival of Shakespeare's *Richard II* on the eve of the Essex rebellion. On August 4, 1601, she is reported to have said, "I am Richard II. Know ye not that?" The Queen was reacting to the fact that Gelly Meyrick, an officer of Essex's household, paid the Lord Chamberlain's Men (Shakespeare's company) forty shillings to revive a play about the deposing and killing of Richard II. Although the Queen had gone to some lengths to protect the theater against those who thought it had the potential to subvert not only morality but also the authority of the state, on that occasion it must have seemed (in Green-blatt's words) that it indeed had "the power to wrest legitimation from the established ruler and confer it on another" (p. 3).

This is in many ways an apt example of the intersection of the historical and the literary (just to retain those two terms as though they are distinct and unproblematic categories for a moment more) because here an advocate of the theater (Elizabeth) finds herself in a situation in which those who have claimed that the art form she has championed has a potentially subversive power are proven right, even as the members of Shakespeare's company became accom-plices (unwitting or not) in a scheme of rebellion. As messy an event as this was, it is nonetheless exemplary of the mutual permeability of the literary and the historical. Indeed, Sir Philip Sidney a bit earlier (c.1583 in *An Apology for Poetry*) had insisted that the poet performs both the tasks that are particular to the historian and universal to the philosopher.[5] The early modern period (the Renaissance), thus, seems an ideal time on which to reflect concerning the interconnections between history and literature.

Later in the introduction to *The Power of Forms in the English Renaissance* Greenblatt goes on to say that

> The new historicism erodes the firm ground of both criticism and literature. It tends to ask questions about its own methodological assumptions and those of others. . . . Moreover [it] has been less concerned to establish the organic unity of literary works and more open to such works as fields of force, places of dissension and shifting interests, occasions for the jostling of orthodox and subversive impul-ses. . . . Renaissance literary works are [thus] no longer regarded either as a fixed set of texts that are set apart from all other forms of expression and that contain their own determinate meanings or as a stable set of reflections of historical facts that lie beyond them. The critical practice represented in this volume challenges the assumptions that guarantee a secure distinction between "literary foreground" and "political background" or, more generally between artistic production and other kinds of social production. Such distinctions do in fact exist, but they are not intrinsic to the texts; rather they are made up and constantly redrawn by artists, audiences, and readers. These collective social constructions on the one hand define the range of aesthetic possibilities within a given representational mode and, on the other, link that mode to the complex network of institutions, practices, and beliefs that consti-tute the culture as a whole. (pp. 5–6)

Although, understandably, a few details in this program for new historicism have been refined and supplemented during the last twenty years (especially in the Introduction to *Practicing New Historicism*), this is still a fair statement of what it is all about.

While keeping in mind that new historicism is a collection of practices rather than a school or a method, it may be useful to attempt a list of its distinguishing characteristics:

1 New historicists think of culture as a semiotic system, as a network of signs.
2 They, therefore, are resistant to disciplinary hegemony, finding in inter-disciplinarity an important means of generating new knowledge.
3 They are persistently aware that history is both what happened in the past (a set of events) and an account of those events (a story); historical truth arises from a critical reflection on the adequacy of the story that is told.
4 History is, therefore, initially a kind of discourse, which is not a denial that there are real events.
5 A typical new historicist procedure is to begin with a striking event or anecdote, which has the effect of arousing skepticism about grand historical narratives or essentializing descriptions of a historical period such as the Renaissance. Anecdotes also arrest attention and provide what Greenblatt calls "the touch of the real."
6 New historicists are determinedly suspicious of unified, monolithic depictions of cultures or historical periods, insisting that there were countless Elizabethan world views but not a monolithic Elizabethan world picture. Typically such unified myths are created to serve a particular interest in the present, such as the longing for a golden past that Nietzsche calls "antiquarian history."
7 Because it is not possible to transcend one's own historical moment, all histories are themselves historically contingent on the present in which they are constructed.
8 New historicism is implicitly a critique of literary formalism (or "The New Criticism") that treated literary objects as ahistorical icons. The reexamination of the relationship between literature and history is a high priority for new historicists.
9 Just as it is no longer tenable to think of a literary text as a detached object that is independent of its author and readers, so also is it no longer possible to think of the past as an object that is detachable from its textual recon-struction.
10 It is also no longer tenable for students of literature to think of history as some sort of detachable background to iconic works of verbal (or other kinds of) art. History and literature are mutually imbricated.[6]

Two of Greenblatt's texts that readily illustrate these principles and assump-tions are his magisterial *Renaissance Self-Fashioning*, which had a transformative impact on Renaissance studies, and his Introduction to *The Norton Shakespeare*, which is currently his most influential piece of public pedagogy. *Renaissance Self-Fashioning* examines the perception, which has been part of Renaissance histori-ography since Burckhardt and Michelet, that "there is in the early modern period a change in the intellectual, social, psychological, and aesthetic structures that govern the generation of identities" (p. 1).

Whereas Augustine declared in his Sermon 169, "Hands off yourself. . . . Try to build up yourself, and you build a ruin," during the sixteenth century there began to be a widespread self-consciousness about the artful capacity of human beings to fashion their own identity. Thus, for example, Spenser writes that it is his purpose in *The Faerie Queene* "to fashion a gentleman;" and again in the *Amoretti* he uses the word "fashion" to designate the forming of the self. Similarly in his translation of the New Testament and in his own writing Tyndale uses the same verb to refer to purposeful shaping of identity. Drawing on Clifford Geertz's observation that "There is no such thing as human nature independent of culture" (p. 3), Greenblatt adds, "Self-fashioning is in effect the Renaissance version of . . . the cultural system of meanings that creates specific individuals by governing the passage from abstract potential to concrete historical embodiment." Furthermore, literature plays a key role in the self-fashioning cultural system of the time, functioning "in three interlocking ways: as a manifestation of the concrete behavior of its particular author, as itself the expression of the codes by which behavior is shaped, and as a reflection upon those codes" (p. 4).

As he proceeds to elucidate the theoretical foundation – both literary and anthropological – of his book, Greenblatt indirectly provides one of his most succinct statements about the distinctive insight of new historicism:

> Social actions are themselves always embedded in systems of public signification, always grasped, even by their makers, in acts of interpretation. . . . Language, like other sign systems, is a collective construction; our interpretive task must be to grasp more sensitively the consequences of this fact by investigating both the social presence to the world of the literary text and the social presence of the world in the literary text. (p. 5)

There are significant echoes here of both Geertz's *Interpretation of Cultures* and Foucault's *The Order of Things*.

For the epigraph to his excellent "General Introduction" to *The Norton Shakespeare*, Greenblatt takes a familiar line from Ben Jonson's dedicatory poem "To the memory of my beloved, the author Mr William Shakespeare and what he hath left us": "He was not of an age, but for all time!" Earlier in the same poem Jonson seems to have set up something of a contradiction, for beginning at line 17 he addresses Shakespeare as

> Soul of the Age!
> The applause! delight! the wonder of our Stage!
> My Shakespeare, rise; I will not lodge thee by
> Chaucer, or Spenser, or bid Beaumont lie
> A little further, to make thee a room:
> Thou art a Monument, without a tomb,
> And art alive still, while thy Book doth live,
> And we have wits to read, and praise to give.

Indeed, there are at least two possible contradictions (or paradoxes) here. The first is that Shakespeare is addressed as the "Soul of the Age" in which he lived, only later to be declared to be "not of an age, but for all time!" as though he were both the essence of his historical moment and an instance of its transcendence. Here Jonson may be playing with a buried allusion to Hamlet's address to the players who come to Elsinore, when he explains to them the purpose of playing as holding a mirror up to nature. Functioning as such a mirror (into which the audience looks to see certain hitherto unapprehended aspects of themselves), plays (Hamlet says all plays, ancient and modern) have the power "to show virtue her own feature, scorn her own image, and the very age and body of the time his form and pressure" (III.ii.20–2). Perhaps Hamlet means here that one of the three purposes of a play is to convey not only a coherent sense of an age (its form) but also what it feels like to live under its weight (its pressure).

The second Jonsonian contradiction (or paradox) also plays on a buried quotation, this time from the couplet in Sonnet 18:

> So long as men can breathe or eyes can see,
> So long lives this, and this gives life to thee.

Jonson transfers this promise of immortality that Shakespeare makes to the Young Man of the Sonnets back to Shakespeare himself. Shakespeare is not dead, Jonson proclaims, let him rise up and make more burial space for Beaumont. He needs no tomb because he has his own special monument, which is this 1623 Folio that Jonson celebrates; but this book is a monument with special powers because it makes Shakespeare live again whenever the text is read. As to whether Shakespeare is the essence of his age or whether he is not of it but for all time – whether he is historically immanent or historically transcendent – Jonson never tells us; he leaves it to his reader to judge.

Greenblatt brilliantly draws from all of this the thematic energy that charges through his detailed General Introduction, knowing full well, as he does, that introductions to Shakespeare have themselves a complex and troubled history. His opening five paragraphs are, however, yet again a subtle manifesto for new historicism, providing as they do some of the key historiographical themes that are taken up by Greenblatt and his three collaborative editors in their introductions to the plays and poems that follow. In those five paragraphs, Greenblatt takes his readers carefully through three essential points (since the publication of this text in 1997, we may wish to recall, there have already been hundreds of thousands of undergraduates who have studied these words). First, he acknowledges that Shakespeare's "art is the product of peculiar historical circumstances and specific conventions, four centuries distant from our own" (p. 1). Thus, the modern student of Shakespeare can profit from the accounts of life and death, wealth, imports and monopolies, class structure, riots and disorder, the legal status of women, the Reformation in England, Henry VIII's children, the English Bible, Queen Elizabeth, and other such topics. His second point, though, is that the reader should never forget that Shakespeare was an artist and that art, first and last, is about pleasure: "The starting point, and perhaps the ending point as well,

in any encounter with Shakespeare is simply to enjoy him, to savor his imaginative richness, to take pleasure in his infinite delight in language" (p. 1). Third,
Greenblatt stresses Shakespeare's "malleability," which brings us back to the
apparent contradiction or paradox in Jonson's poem: "The fantastic diffusion
and long life of Shakespeare's works depends on their extraordinary malleability,
their protean capacity to elude definition and escape secure possession" (p. 1).
Furthermore, in understanding how Shakespeare has managed (as Jonson anticipated he would) to be alive through the ages, we might admit that "if there is no
clear limit or end point, there is a reasonably clear beginning, the England of the
late sixteenth and early seventeenth centuries, when the plays and
poems...made their first appearance" (pp. 1–2). At last Greenblatt resolves
Jonson's apparent paradox: "An art virtually without end or limit but with an
identifiable, localized, historical origin: Shakespeare's achievement defies the
facile opposition between transcendent and time-bound." This is because "crucial clues to understanding his art's remarkable power to soar beyond its originary
time and place lie in the very soil from which that art sprang" (p. 2).

   In this metaphor of Shakespeare's age as the soil and his art as the aspiring plant,
Greenblatt cuts through such static images from an older historicism as history
serving as "background" to literature (Basil Willey), as "discarded images" (C. S.
Lewis), or as an "Elizabethan world picture" (E. M. W. Tillyard). The metaphor of
the historical soil here brings together the New Testament parable of the sower and
the seed – in which the seed (the word) that flourishes takes root in the self of the one
who receives it with Gilles Deleuze's metaphor of the rhizome, the root of the text.
In "Rhizome Versus Trees" Deleuze wrote, "The world has lost its pivot . . . but the
book remains the image of the world, . . . a book all the more total for being
fragmented. . . . The rhizome itself assumes very diverse forms, from ramified surface extension in all directions to concretion into bulbs and tubers. . . . The rhizome
includes the best and the worst: potato and couchgrass, or the weed."[7]

   Throughout the last twenty-five years Greenblatt's work has displayed a
remarkably dynamic coherence. The signal characteristics of his practice are
remarkably clear and distinct in all that he writes, but his method is sufficiently
elastic – even mercurial – as to insure that each new book, article, and review
offers its own particular surprises. These qualities are not only the sign of a
wonderfully imaginative intelligence at play; they are also distinguishing marks of
a kind of epistemophilia that is determined to find endless pleasure in what it
studies and a constantly renewable source of delight in story-telling and in its
capacity thereby to keep the past alive.

NOTES

1   For a survey of some early critiques of new historicism, see Brook Thomas, *The New
    Historicism* (Princeton: Princeton University Press, 1991), pp. 3–23. There is a more
    recent polemical response to new historicism in Frank Kermode's *Pieces of My Mind*
    (New York: Farrar, Straus and Giroux, 2003), pp. 342–56.
2   The journal was founded by Svetlana Alpers, Greenblatt, and others.

3 For bibliographical details concerning all of Greenblatt's publications, see the bibliography at the end of this book. Page numbers from his books are enclosed in
   parentheses.
4 Michel Foucault, "What Is an Author?" in *The Foucault Reader*, ed. Paul Rabinow
   (New York: Pantheon), p. 107.
5 Sir Philip Sidney, *An Apology for Poetry*, ed. Forrest G. Robinson (New York: The
   Library of Liberal Arts, 1970), p. 27.
6 Cf. H. Aram Veeser's *The New Historicism* (London: Routledge, 1989), p. xi, and
   Raman Selden's *A Reader's Guide to Contemporary Literary Theory* (Hemel Hempstead:
   Harvester Wheatsheaf, 1997), pp. 188–9.
7 Gilles Deleuze, "Rhizome Versus Trees," in *The Deleuze Reader*, ed. Constantin
   V. Boundas (New York: Columbia University Press, 1993), p. 29.

Part I

CULTURE AND NEW HISTORICISM

1

CULTURE

The term "culture" has not always been used in literary studies, and indeed the very concept denoted by the term is fairly recent. "Culture or Civilization," wrote the influential anthropologist Edward B. Tylor in 1871, "taken in its wide ethnographic sense, is that complex whole which includes knowledge, belief, art, morals, law, custom, and any other capabilities and habits acquired by man as a member of society." Why should such a concept be useful to students of literature?

The answer may be that it is not. After all, the term as Tylor uses it is almost impossibly vague and encompassing, and the few things that seem excluded from it are almost immediately reincorporated in the actual use of the word. Hence we may think with a certain relief that at least "culture" does not refer to material objects – tables, or gold, or grain, or spinning wheels – but of course those objects, as used by men and women, are close to the center of any particular society, and we may accordingly speak of such a society's "material culture." Like "ideology" (to which, as a concept, it is closely allied), "culture" is a term that is repeatedly used without meaning much of anything at all, a vague gesture toward a dimly perceived ethos: aristocratic culture, youth culture, human culture. There is nothing especially wrong with such gestures – without them we wouldn't ordinarily be able to get through three consecutive sentences – but they are scarcely the backbone of an innovative critical practice.

How can we get the concept of culture to do more work for us? We might begin by reflecting on the fact that the concept gestures toward what appear to be opposite things: *constraint* and *mobility*. The ensemble of beliefs and practices that form a given culture function as a pervasive technology of control, a set of limits within which social behavior must be contained, a repertoire of models to which individuals must conform. The limits need not be narrow – in certain societies, such as that of the United States, they can seem quite vast – but they are not infinite, and the consequences for straying beyond them can be severe. The most effective disciplinary techniques practiced against those who stray beyond the

This chapter was first published in *Critical Terms for Literary Study* (McLaughlin and Lentricchia (eds), 1990, pp. 225–32).

limits of a given culture are probably not the spectacular punishments reserved for serious offenders – exile, imprisonment in an insane asylum, penal servitude, or execution – but seemingly innocuous responses: a condescending smile, laughter poised between the genial and the sarcastic, a small dose of indulgent pity laced with contempt, cool silence. And we should add that a culture's boundaries are enforced more positively as well: through the system of rewards that range again from the spectacular (grand public honors, glittering prizes) to the apparently modest (a gaze of admiration, a respectful nod, a few words of gratitude).

Here we can make our first tentative move toward the use of culture for the study of literature, for Western literature over a very long period of time has been one of the great institutions for the enforcement of cultural boundaries through praise and blame. This is most obvious in the kinds of literature that are explicity engaged in attack and celebration: satire and panegyric. Works in these genres often seem immensely important when they first appear, but their power begins quickly to fade when the individuals to whom the works refer begin to fade, and the evaporation of literary power continues when the models and limits that the works articulated and enforced have themselves substantially changed. The footnotes in modern editions of these works can give us the names and dates that have been lost, but they cannot in themselves enable us to recover a sense of the stakes that once gave readers pleasure and pain. An awareness of culture as a complex whole can help us to recover that sense by leading us to reconstruct the boundaries upon whose existence the works were predicated.

We can begin to do so simply by a heightened attention to the beliefs and practices implicitly enforced by particular literary acts of praising or blaming. That is, we can ask ourselves a set of cultural questions about the work before us:

> What kinds of behavior, what models of practice, does this work seem to enforce?
> Why might readers at a particular time and place find this work compelling?
> Are there differences between my values and the values implicit in the work I am
> reading?
> Upon what social understandings does the work depend?
> Whose freedom of thought or movement might be constrained implicitly or
> explicitly by this work?
> What are the larger social structures with which these particular acts of praise or
> blame might be connected?

Such questions heighten our attention to features of the literary work that we might not have noticed, and, above all, to connections among elements within the work. Eventually, a full cultural analysis will need to push beyond the boundaries of the text, to establish links between the text and values, institutions, and practices elsewhere in the culture. But these links cannot be a substitute for close reading. Cultural analysis has much to learn from scrupulous formal analysis of literary texts because those texts are not merely cultural by virtue of reference to the world beyond themselves; they are cultural by virtue of social values and contexts that they have themselves successfully absorbed. The world is full of texts, most of which are virtually incomprehensible when they are removed from their immediate surroundings. To recover the meaning of such texts, to make any sense of them at all, we need to reconstruct the situation in which they were produced. Works of art by contrast contain directly or by implication much of this situation within themselves, and it is this sustained absorption that enables many literary works to survive the collapse of the conditions that led to their production.

Cultural analysis then is not by definition an extrinsic analysis, as opposed to an internal formal analysis of works of art. At the same time, cultural analysis must be opposed on principle to the rigid distinction between that which is within a text and that which lies outside. It is necessary to use whatever is available to construct a vision of the "complex whole" to which Tylor referred. And if an exploration of a particular culture will lead to a heightened understanding of a work of literature produced within that culture, so too a careful reading of a work of literature will lead to a heightened understanding of the culture within which it was produced. The organization of this volume makes it appear that the analysis of culture is the servant of literary study, but in a liberal education broadly conceived it is literary study that is the servant of cultural understanding.

I will return to the question of extrinsic as opposed to intrinsic analysis, but first we must continue to pursue the idea of culture as a system of constraints. The functioning of such a system is obvious in poems like Pope's "Epistle to Doctor Arbuthnot" or Marvell's "Horatian Ode" on Cromwell, works that undertake to excoriate dullness as embodied in certain hated individuals and celebrate civic or military virtue as embodied in certain admired individuals. Indeed culture here is close to its earlier sense of "cultivation" – the internalization and practice of a code of manners. And this sense extends well beyond the limits of satire and panegyric, particularly for those periods in which manners were a crucial sign of status difference.

Consider, for example, Shakespeare's *As You Like It*, where Orlando's bitter complaint is not that he has been excluded from his patrimony – Orlando accepts the custom of primogeniture by which his brother, as the eldest son, inherits virtually all the family property – but rather that he is being prevented from learning the manners of his class: "My father charged you in his will to give me a good education: you have train'd me like a peasant, obscuring and hiding from me all gentleman-like qualities." Shakespeare characteristically suggests that Orlando has within him an innate gentility that enables him to rise naturally above his boorish upbringing, but he equally characteristically suggests that Orlando's gentility needs to be shaped and brought to fruition through a series of difficult trials. When in the Forest of Arden the young man roughly demands food for his aged servant Adam, he receives a lesson in courtesy: "Your gentleness shall force/More than your force move us to gentleness." The lesson has a special authority conferred upon it by the fact that it is delivered by the exiled Duke, the figure at the pinnacle of the play's social order. But the entire world of *As You Like It* is engaged in articulating cultural codes of behavior, from the elaborate, ironic training in courtship presided over by Rosalind to the humble but dignified social order by which the shepherds live. Even the simple country wench Audrey receives a lesson in manners from the sophisticated clown Touchstone: "bear your body more seeming, Audrey." This instruction in the management of the body, played no doubt for comic effect, is an enactment in miniature of a process of acculturation occurring everywhere in the play, and occurring most powerfully perhaps on an almost subliminal level, such as the distance we automatically keep from others or the way we position our legs when we sit down. Shakespeare wittily parodies this process – for example, in Touchstone's elaborate rule-book for insults – but he also participates in it, for even as his plays represent characters engaged in negotiating the boundaries of their culture, the plays also help to establish and maintain those boundaries for their audiences.

Art is an important agent then in the transmission of culture. It is one of the ways in which the roles by which men and women are expected to pattern their lives are communicated and passed from generation to generation. Certain artists have been highly self-conscious about this function. The purpose of his vast romance epic, *The Faerie Queene*, writes the Renaissance poet Edmund Spenser, is "to fashion a gentleman or noble person in virtuous and gentle discipline." The depth of our understanding of such a project, extended over a complex plot involving hundreds of allegorical figures, depends upon the extent of our grasp of Spenser's entire culture, from its nuanced Aristotelian conception of moral hierarchies to its apocalyptic fantasies, from exquisite refinement at court to colonial violence in Ireland. More precisely, we need to grasp the way in which this culture of mixed motives and conflicting desires seemed to Spenser to generate an interlocking series of models, a moral order, a set of ethical constraints ranged against the threat of anarchy, rebellion, and chaos.

To speak of *The Faerie Queene* only in terms of the constraints imposed by culture is obviously inadequate, since the poem itself, with its knights and ladies endlessly roaming an imaginary landscape, is so insistent upon mobility. We return to the paradox with which we started: if culture functions as a structure of limits, it also functions as the regulator and guarantor of movement. Indeed the limits are virtually meaningless without movement; it is only through improvisation, experiment, and exchange that cultural boundaries can be established. Obviously, among different cultures there will be a great diversity in the ratio between mobility and constraint. Some cultures dream of imposing an absolute order, a perfect stasis, but even these, if they are to reproduce themselves from one generation to the next, will have to commit themselves, however tentatively or unwillingly, to some minimal measure of movement; conversely, some cultures dream of an absolute mobility, a perfect freedom, but these too have always been compelled, in the interest of survival, to accept some limits.

What is set up, under wildly varying circumstances and with radically divergent consequences, is a structure of improvisation, a set of patterns that have enough elasticity, enough scope for variation, to accommodate most of the participants in a given culture. A life that fails to conform at all, that violates absolutely all the available patterns, will have to be dealt with as an emergency – hence exiled, or killed, or declared a god. But most individuals are content to improvise, and, in the West at least, a great many works of art are centrally concerned with these improvisations. The novel has been particularly sensitive to the diverse ways in which individuals come to terms with the governing patterns of culture; works like Dickens' *Great Expectations* and Eliot's *Middlemarch* brilliantly explore the ironies and pain, as well as the inventiveness, of particular adjustments.

In representing this adjustment as a social, emotional, and intellectual education, these novels in effect thematize their own place in culture, for works of art are themselves educational tools. They do not merely passively reflect the prevailing ratio of mobility and constraint; they help to shape, articulate, and reproduce it through their own improvisatory intelligence. This means that, despite our romantic cult of originality, most artists are themselves gifted creators of variations upon received themes. Even those great writers whom we regard with special awe, and whom we celebrate for their refusal to parrot the clichés of their culture, tend to be particularly brilliant improvisers rather than absolute violaters or pure inventors. Thus Dickens crafted cunning adaptations of the melodramatic potboilers of his times; Shakespeare borrowed most of his plots, and many of his characters, from familiar tales or well-rehearsed historical narratives; and Spenser revised for his own culture stories first told, and told wonderfully, by the Italian poets Ariosto and Tasso.

Such borrowing is not evidence of imaginative parsimony, still less a symptom of creative exhaustion – I am using Dickens, Shakespeare, and Spenser precisely because they are among the most exuberant, generous, and creative literary imaginations in our language. It signals rather a further aspect of the cultural mobility to which I have already pointed. This mobility is not the expression of random motion but of *exchange*. A culture is a particular network of negotiations for the exchange of material goods, ideas, and – through institutions like enslavement, adoption, or marriage – people. Anthropologists are centrally concerned with a culture's kinship system – its conception of family relationships, its prohibitions of certain couplings, its marriage rules – and with its narratives – its myths, folktales, and sacred stories. The two concerns are linked, for a culture's narratives, like its kinship arrangements, are crucial indices of the prevailing codes governing human mobility and constraint. Great writers are precisely masters of these codes, specialists in cultural exchange. The works they create are structures for the accumulation, transformation, representation, and communication of social energies and practices.

In any culture there is a general symbolic economy made up of the myriad signs that excite human desire, fear, and aggression. Through their ability to construct resonant stories, their command of effective imagery, and above all their sensitivity to the greatest collective creation of any culture – language – literary artists are skilled at manipulating this economy. They take symbolic materials from one zone of the culture and move them to another, augmenting their emotional force, altering their significance, linking them with other materials taken from a different zone, changing their place in a larger social design. Take, for example, Shakespeare's *King Lear:* the dramatist borrows an often-told pseudo-historical account of an ancient British king, associates with it his society's most severe anxieties about kinship relations on the one hand and civil strife on the other, infuses a measure of apocalyptic religious expectation mingled paradoxically with an acute skepticism, and returns these materials to his audience, transformed into what is perhaps the most intense experience of tragic pleasure ever created. A nuanced cultural analysis will be concerned with the various matrices from which Shakespeare derives his materials, and hence will be drawn outside the formal boundary of the play – toward the legal arrangements, for example, that elderly parents in the Renaissance made with their children, or toward child-rearing practices in the period, or toward political debates about when, if ever, disobeying a legitimate ruler was justified, or toward predictions of the imminent end of the world.

The current structure of liberal arts education often places obstacles in the way of such an analysis by separating the study of history from the study of literature, as if the two were entirely distinct enterprises, but historians have become increasingly sensitive to the symbolic dimensions of social practice, while literary critics have in recent years turned with growing interest to the social and historical dimensions of symbolic practice. Hence it is more possible, both in terms of individual courses and of overall programs of study, for students to reach toward a sense of the complex whole of a particular culture. But there is much to be done in the way of cultural analysis even without an integrated structure of courses, much that depends primarily on asking fresh questions about the possible social functions of works of art. Indeed even if one begins to achieve a sophis- ticated historical sense of the cultural materials out of which a literary text is constructed, it remains essential to study the ways in which these materials are formally put together and articulated in order to understand the cultural work that the text accomplishes.

For great works of art are not neural relay stations in the circulation of cultural materials. Something happens to objects, beliefs, and practices when they are represented, reimagined, and performed in literary texts, something often un- predictable and disturbing. That "something" is the sign both of the power of art and of the embeddedness of culture in the contingencies of history. I have written at moments as if art always reinforces the dominant beliefs and social structures of its culture, as if culture is always harmonious rather than shifting and conflict-ridden, and as if there necessarily is a mutually affirmative relation between artistic production and the other modes of production and reproduction that make up a society. At times there is precisely such an easy and comfortable conjunction, but it is by no means necessary. The ability of artists to assemble and shape the forces of their culture in novel ways so that elements powerfully interact that rarely have commerce with one another in the general economy has the potential to unsettle this affirmative relation. Indeed in our own time most students of literature reserve their highest admiration for those works that situate themselves on the very edges of what can be said at a particular place and time, that batter against the boundaries of their own culture.

Near the end of his career Shakespeare decided to take advantage of his contemporaries' lively interest in New World exploration. His play *The Tempest* contains many details drawn from the writings of adventurers and colonists, details that are skillfully displaced onto a mysterious Mediterranean island and interwoven with echoes from Virgil's *Aeneid*, from other art forms such as the court masque and pastoral tragicomedy, and from the lore of white magic. The play reiterates the arguments that Europeans made about the legitimacy and civilizing force of their presence in the newly discovered lands; indeed it intensifies those arguments by conferring upon Prospero the power not only of a great prince who has the right to command the forces of this world but of a wizard who has the ability – the "Art" as the play terms it – to command supernatural forces as well. But the intensification has an oddly discordant effect: the magical power is clearly impressive but its legitimacy is less clear.

As magician Prospero resembles no one in the play so much as Sycorax, the hated witch who had preceded him as the island's ruler. The play, to be sure, does not endorse a challenge to Prospero's rule, any more than Shakespeare's culture ever encouraged challenges to legitimate monarchs. And yet out of the uneasy matrix formed by the skillful interweaving of cultural materials comes an odd, discordant voice, the voice of the "savage and deformed slave" Caliban:

> This island's mine, by Sycorax my mother,
> Which thou tak'st from me. When thou cam'st first
> Thou strok'st me, and made much of me; wouldst give me
> Water with berries in't; and teach me how
> To name the bigger light, and how the less,
> That burn by day and night: and then I lov'd thee,
> And show'd thee all the qualities o'th'isle,
> The fresh springs, brine-pits, barren place and fertile:
> Curs'd be I that did so! All the charms
> Of Sycorax, toads, beetles, bats, light on you!
> For I am all the subjects that you have,
> Which first was mine own King: and here you sty me
> In this hard rock, whiles you do keep from me
> The rest o'th'island.

Caliban, of course, does not triumph: it would take different artists from different cultures – the postcolonial Caribbean and African cultures of our own times – to rewrite Shakespeare's play and make good on Caliban's claim. But even within the powerful constraints of Shakespeare's Jacobean culture, the artist's imaginative mobility enables him to display cracks in the glacial front of princely power and to record a voice, the voice of the displaced and oppressed, that is heard scarcely anywhere else in his own time. If it is the task of cultural criticism to decipher the power of Prospero, it is equally its task to hear the accents of Caliban.

2

TOWARDS A POETICS OF CULTURE

I feel in a somewhat false position, which is not a particularly promising way to begin, and I might as well explain why.[1] My own work has always been done with a sense of just having to go about and do it, without establishing first exactly what my theoretical position is. A few years ago I was asked by *Genre* to edit a selection of Renaissance essays, and I said OK. I collected a bunch of essays and then, out of a kind of desperation to get the introduction done, I wrote that the essays represented something I called a "new historicism." I've never been very good at making up advertising phrases of this kind; for reasons that I would be quite interested in exploring at some point, the name stuck much more than other names I'd very carefully tried to invent over the years. In fact I have heard – in the last year or so – quite a lot of talk about the "new historicism" (which for some reason in Australia is called Neohistoricism); there are articles about it, attacks on it, references to it in dissertations: the whole thing makes me quite giddy with amazement. In any case, as part of this peculiar phenomenon I have been asked to say something of a theoretical kind about the work I'm doing. So I shall try if not to define the new historicism, at least to situate it as a practice – a practice rather than a doctrine, since as far as I can tell (and I should be the one to know) it's no doctrine at all.

One of the peculiar characteristics of the "new historicism" in literary studies is precisely how unresolved and in some ways disingenuous it has been – I have been – about the relation to literary theory. On the one hand it seems to me that an openness to the theoretical ferment of the last few years is precisely what distinguishes the new historicism from the positivist historical scholarship of the early twentieth century. Certainly, the presence of Michel Foucault on the Berkeley campus for extended visits during the last five or six years of his life, and more generally the influence in America of European (and especially French) anthropological and social theorists, has helped to shape my own literary critical practice. On the other hand the historicist critics have on the whole been unwilling to enrol themselves in one or the other of the dominant theoretical camps.

This chapter was first published in *Learning to Curse: Essays in Early Modern Culture* (Stephen Greenblatt, 1990, pp. 146–60).

I want to speculate on why this should be so by trying to situate myself in relation to Marxism on the one hand, and poststructuralism on the other. In the 1970s I used to teach courses with names like "Marxist Aesthetics" on the Berkeley campus. This came to an inglorious end when I was giving such a course – it must have been the mid-1970s – and I remember a student getting very angry with me. Now it's true that I tended to like those Marxist figures who were troubled in relation to Marxism – Walter Benjamin, the early rather than the later Lukács, and so forth – and I remember someone finally got up and screamed out in class "You're either a Bolshevik or a Menshevik – make up your fucking mind," and then slammed the door. It was a little unsettling, but I thought about it afterwards and realized that I wasn't sure whether I was a Menshevik, but I certainly wasn't a Bolshevik. After that I started to teach courses with names like "Cultural Poetics." It's true that I'm still more uneasy with a politics and a literary perspective that is untouched by Marxist thought, but that doesn't lead me to endorse propositions or embrace a particular philosophy, politics or rhetoric, *faute de mieux*.

Thus the crucial identifying gestures made by the most distinguished American Marxist aesthetic theorist, Fredric Jameson, seem to me highly problematic. Let us take, for example, the following eloquent passage from *The Political Unconscious*:

> the convenient working distinction between cultural texts that are social and political and those that are not becomes something worse than an error: namely, a symptom and a reinforcement of the reification and privatization of contemporary life. Such a distinction reconfirms that structural, experiential, and conceptual gap between the public and the private, between the social and the psychological, or the political and the poetic, between history or society and the 'individual,' which – the tendential law of social life under capitalism – maims our existence as individual subjects and paralyzes our thinking about time and change just as surely as it alienates us from our speech itself.[2]

A working distinction between cultural texts that are social and political and those that are not – that is, an aesthetic domain that is in some way marked off from the discursive institutions that are operative elsewhere in a culture – becomes for Jameson a malignant symptom of "privatization." Why should the "private" immediately enter into this distinction at all? Does the term refer to private property, that is, to the ownership of the means of production and the regulation of the mode of consumption? If so, what is the historical relation between this mode of economic organization and a working distinction between the political and the poetic? It would seem that in print, let alone in the electronic media, private ownership has led not to "privatization" but to the drastic communalization of all discourse, the constitution of an ever larger mass audience, the organization of a commercial sphere unimagined and certainly unattained by the comparatively modest attempts in pre-capitalist societies to organize public discourse. Moreover, is it not possible to have a communal sphere of art that is distinct from other communal spheres? Is this communal differentiation, sanctioned by the laws of property, not the dominant practice in capitalist society, manifestly in the film and television industries, but also, since the invention of movable type, in the production of poems and novels as well? Would we really find it less alienating to have no distinction at all between the political and the poetic – the situation, let us say, during China's Cultural Revolution? Or, for that matter, do we find it notably liberating to have our own country governed by a film actor who is either cunningly or pathologically indifferent to the traditional differentiation between fantasy and reality?

For *The Political Unconscious* any demarcation of the aesthetic must be aligned with the private which is in turn aligned with the psychological, the poetic, and the individual, as distinct from the public, the social, and the political. All of these interlocking distinctions, none of which seems to me philosophically or even historically bound up with the original "working distinction," are then laid at the door of capitalism with its power to "maim" and "paralyze" us as "individual subjects." Though we may find a differentiation between cultural discourses that are artistic and cultural discourses that are social or political well before the European seventeenth century, and in cultures that seem far removed from the capitalist mode of production, Jameson insists that somehow the perpetrator and agent of the alleged maiming is capitalism. A shadowy opposition is assumed between the "individual" (bad) and the "individual subject" (good); indeed the maiming of the latter creates the former.

The whole passage has the resonance of an allegory of the fall of man: once we were whole, agile, integrated; we were individual subjects but not individuals, we had no psychology distinct from the shared life of the society; politics and poetry were one. Then capitalism arose and shattered this luminous, benign totality. The myth echoes throughout Jameson's book, though by the close it has been eschatologically reoriented so that the totality lies not in a past revealed to have always already fallen but in the classless future. A philosophical claim then appeals to an absent empirical event. And literature is invoked at once as the dark token of fallenness and the shimmering emblem of the absent transfiguration.

But, of course, poststructuralism has raised serious questions about such a vision, challenging both its underlying oppositions and the primal organic unity that it posits as either paradisal origin or utopian, eschatological end.[3] This challenge has already greatly modified, though by no means simply displaced, Marxist discourse. I could exemplify this complex interaction between Marxism and poststructuralism by discussing Jameson's own most recent work in which he finds himself, from the perspective of postmodernism, deploring the loss of those "working distinctions" that at least enabled the left to identify its enemies and articulate a radical program.[4] But to avoid confusions, I want to focus instead on the work of Jean-François Lyotard. Here, as in *The Political Unconscious*, the distinction between discursive fields is once again at stake: for Lyotard the existence of proper names makes possible.

> the co-existence of those worlds that Kant calls fields, territories, and domains – those worlds which of course present the same object, but which also make that object the stakes of heterogenous (or incommensurable) expectations in universes of phrases, none of which can be transformed into any other.[5]

Lyotard's model for these differentiated discourses is the existence of proper names. But now it is the role of capitalism not to demarcate discursive domains but, quite the opposite, to make such domains untenable. "Capital is that which wants a single language and a single network, and it never stops trying to present them" (p. 55). Lyotard's principal exhibit of this attempt by capital to institute a single language – what Bakhtin would call monologism – is Faurisson's denial of the Holocaust, and behind this denial, the Nazis' attempt to obliterate the existence of millions of Jews and other undesirables, an attempt Lyotard characterizes as the will "to strike from history and from the map entire worlds of names."

The immediate problem with this account is that the Nazis did not seem particularly interested in exterminating names along with the persons who possessed those names; on the contrary, they kept, in so far as was compatible with a compaign of mass murder, remarkably full records, and they looked forward to a time in which they could share their accomplishment with a grateful world by establishing a museum dedicated to the culture of the wretches they had destroyed. The Faurisson affair is at bottom not an epistemological dilemma, as Lyotard claims, but an attempt to wish away evidence that is both substantial and verifiable. The issue is not an Epicurean paradox – "if death is there, you are not there; if you are there, death is not there; hence it is impossible for you to prove that death is there" – but a historical problem: what is the evidence of mass murder? How reliable is this evidence? Are there convincing grounds for denying or doubting the documented events? And if there are not such grounds, how may we interpret the motives of those who seek to cast doubt upon the historical record?

There is a further problem in Lyotard's use of the Faurisson affair as an instance of capitalist hostility to names: the conflation of Fascist apologetics and capitalism would seem to be itself an instance of monologism, since it suppresses all the aspects of capitalism that are wedded to the generation and inscription of individual identities and to the demarcation of boundaries separating those identities. We may argue, of course, that the capitalist insistence upon individuality is fraudulent, but it is difficult, I think, to keep the principle of endlessly proliferated, irreducible individuality separate from the market place version against which it is set. For it is capitalism, as Marx suggested, that mounts the West's most powerful and sustained assault upon collective, communal values and identities. And it is in the market place and in the state apparatus linked to the circulation and accumulation of capital that names themselves are forged. Proper names, as distinct from common names, seem less the victims than the products of property – they are bound up not only with the property one has in oneself, that is, with the theory of possessive individualism, but quite literally with the property one possesses, for proper names are insisted upon in the early modern period precisely in order to register them in the official documents that enable the state to calculate and tax personal property.[6]

The difference between Jameson's capitalism, the perpetrator of separate discursive domains, the agent of privacy, psychology, and the individual, and Lyotard's capitalism, the enemy of such domains and the destroyer of privacy, psychology, and the individual, may in part be traced to a difference between the Marxist and poststructuralist projects. Jameson, seeking to expose the fallaciousness of a separate artistic sphere and to celebrate the materialist integration of all discourses, finds capitalism at the root of the false differentiation; Lyotard, seeking to celebrate the differentiation of all discourses and to expose the fallaciousness of monological unity, finds capitalism at the root of the false integration. History functions in both cases as a convenient anecdotal ornament upon a theoretical structure, and capitalism appears not as a complex social and economic development in the West but as a malign philosophical principle.[7]

I propose that the general question addressed by Jameson and Lyotard – what is the historical relation between art and society or between one institutionally demarcated discursive practice and another? – does not lend itself to a single, theoretically satisfactory answer of the kind that Jameson and Lyotard are trying to provide. Or rather theoretical satisfaction here seems to depend upon a utopian vision that collapses the contradictions of history into a moral imperative. The problem is not simply the incompatibility of two theories – Marxist and poststructuralist – with one another, but the inability of either of the theories to come to terms with the apparently contradictory historical effects of capitalism. In principle, of course, both Marxism and poststructuralism seize upon contradictions: for the former they are signs of repressed class conflicts, for the latter they disclose hidden cracks in the spurious certainties of logocentrism. But in practice Jameson treats capitalism as the agent of repressive differentiation, while Lyotard treats it as the agent of monological totalization. And this effacement of contradiction is not the consequence of an accidental lapse but rather the logical outcome of theory's search for the obstacle that blocks the realization of its eschatological vision.

If capitalism is invoked not as a unitary demonic principle, but as a complex historical movement in a world without paradisal origins or chiliastic expectations, then an inquiry into the relation between art and society in capitalist cultures must address both the formation of the working distinction upon which Jameson remarks and the totalizing impulse upon which Lyotard remarks. For capitalism has characteristically generated neither regimes in which all discourses seem coordinated, nor regimes in which they seem radically isolated or discontinuous, but regimes in which the drive towards differentiation and the drive towards monological organization operate simultaneously, or at least oscillate so rapidly as to create the impression of simultaneity.

In a brilliant paper that received unusual attention, elicited a response from a White House speech-writer, and most recently generated a segment on CBS's "Sixty Minutes," the political scientist and historian Michael Rogin recently observed the number of times President Reagan has, at critical moments in his career, quoted lines from his own or other popular films. The President is a man, Rogin remarks, "whose most spontaneous moments – ('Where do we find such men?' about the American D-Day dead; 'I am paying for this microphone, Mr. Green,' during the 1980 New Hampshire primary debate) – are not only preserved and projected on film, but also turn out to be lines from old movies."[8] To a remarkable extent, Ronald Reagan, who made his final Hollywood film, *Hellcats of the Navy*, in 1957, continues to live within the movies; he has been shaped by them, draws much of his cold war rhetoric from them, and cannot or will not distinguish between them and an external reality. Indeed his political career has depended upon an ability to project himself and his mass audience into a realm in which there is no distinction between simulation and reality.

The response from Anthony Dolan, a White House speech-writer who was asked to comment on Rogin's paper, was highly revealing. "What he's really saying," Dolan suggested, "is that all of us are deeply affected by a uniquely American art form: the movies."[9] Rogin had in fact argued that the presidential character "was produced from the convergence of two sets of substitutions which generated Cold War countersubversion in the 1940s and underlie its 1980s revival – the political replacement of Nazism by Communism, from which the national security state was born; and the psychological shift from an embodied self to its simulacrum on film." Both the political and the psychological substitution were intimately bound up with Ronald Reagan's career in the movies. Dolan in response rewrites Rogin's thesis into a celebration of the power of "a uniquely American art form" to shape "all of us." Movies, Dolan told the New York Times reporter, "heighten reality rather than lessen it."

Such a statement appears to welcome the collapse of the working distinction between the aesthetic and the real; the aesthetic is not an alternative realm but a way of intensifying the single realm we all inhabit. But then the spokesman went on to assert that the President "usually credits the films whose lines he uses." That is, at the moment of appropriation, the President acknowledges that he is borrowing from the aesthetic and hence acknowledges the existence of a working distinction. In so doing he respects and even calls attention to the difference between his own presidential discourse and the fictions in which he himself at one time took part; they are differences upon which his own transition from actor to politician in part depends, and they are the signs of the legal and economic system that he represents. For the capitalist aesthetic demands acknowledgments – hence the various marks of property rights that are flashed on the screen or inscribed in a text – and the political arena insists that it is not a fiction. That without acknowledgment the President delivers speeches written by Anthony Dolan or others does not appear to concern anyone; this has long been the standard operating procedure of American politicians. But it would concern people if the President recited speeches that were lifted without acknowledgment from old movies. He would then seem not to know the difference between fantasy and reality. And that might be alarming.

The White House, of course, was not responding to a theoretical problem, but to the implication that somehow the President did not fully recognize that he was quoting, or alternatively that he did realize it and chose to repress the fact in order to make a more powerful impression. In one version he is a kind of sleepwalker, in the other a plagiarist. To avoid these implications the White House spokesman needed in effect to invoke a difference that he had himself a moment before undermined.

The spokesman's remarks were hasty and ad hoc, but it did not take reflection to reproduce the complex dialectic of differentiation and identity that those remarks articulate. That dialectic is powerful precisely because it is by now virtually thoughtless; it takes a substantial intellectual effort to separate the boundaries of art from the subversion of those boundaries, an effort such as that exemplified in the work of Jameson or Lyotard. But the effect of such an effort is to remove itself from the very phenomenon it had proposed to analyze, namely, the relation between art and surrounding discourses in capitalist culture. For the effortless invocation of two apparently contradictory accounts of art is characteristic of American capitalism in the late twentieth century and an outcome of long-term tendencies in the relationship of art and capital: in the same moment a working distinction between the aesthetic and the real is established and abrogated.

We could argue, following Jameson, that the establishment of the distinction is the principal effect, with a view towards alienating us from our own imaginations by isolating fantasies in a private, apolitical realm. Or we could argue, following Lyotard, that the abrogation of the distinction is the principal effect, with a view towards effacing or evading differences by establishing a single, monolithic ideological structure. But if we are asked to choose between these alternatives, we will be drawn away from an analysis of the relation between capitalism and aesthetic production. For from the sixteenth century, when the effects for art of joint-stock company organization first began to be felt, to the present, capitalism has produced a powerful and effective oscillation between the establishment of distinct discursive domains and the collapse of those domains into one another. It is this restless oscillation rather than the securing of a particular fixed position that constitutes the distinct power of capitalism. The individual elements – a range of discontinuous discourses on the one hand, the monological unification of all discourses on the other – may be found fully articulated in other economic and social systems; only capitalism has managed to generate a dizzying, seemingly inexhaustible circulation between the two.

My use of the term *circulation* here is influenced by the work of Derrida, but sensitivity to the practical strategies of negotiation and exchange depends less upon poststructuralist theory than upon the circulatory rhythms of American politics. And the crucial point is that it is not politics alone but the whole structure of production and consumption – the systematic organization of ordinary life and consciousness – that generates the pattern of boundary making and breaking, the oscillation between demarcated objects and monological totality, that I have sketched. If we restrict our focus to the zone of political institutions, we can easily fall into the illusion that everything depends upon the unique talents – if that is the word – of Ronald Reagan, that he alone has managed to generate the enormously effective shuttling between massive, universalizing fantasies and centerlessness that characterizes his administration. This illusion leads in turn to what John Carlos Rowe has called the humanist trivialization of power, a trivialization that finds its local political expression in the belief that the fantasmatics of current American politics are the product of a single man and will pass with him. On the contrary, Ronald Reagan is manifestly the product of a larger and more durable American structure – not only a structure of power, ideological extremism and militarism, but of pleasure, recreation, and interest, a structure that shapes the spaces we construct for ourselves, the way we present "the news," the fantasies we daily consume on television or in the movies, the entertainments that we characteristically make and take.

I am suggesting then that the oscillation between totalization and difference, uniformity and the diversity of names, unitary truth and a proliferation of distinct entities – in short between Lyotard's capitalism and Jameson's – is built into the poetics of everyday behavior in America.[10] Let us consider, for example, not the President's Hollywood career but a far more innocent California pastime, a trip to Yosemite National Park. One of the most popular walks at Yosemite is the Nevada Falls Trail. So popular, indeed, is this walk that the Park Service has had to pave the first miles of the trail in order to keep them from being dug into trenches by the heavy traffic. At a certain point the asphalt stops, and you encounter a sign that tells you that you are entering the wilderness. You have passed then from the National Forests that surround the park – forests that serve principally as state-subsidized nurseries for large timber companies and hence are not visibly distinguishable from the tracts of privately owned forest with which they are contiguous – to the park itself, marked by the payment of admission to the uniformed ranger at the entrance kiosk, and finally to a third and privileged zone of publicly demarcated Nature. This zone, called the wilderness, is marked by the abrupt termination of the asphalt and by a sign that lists the rules of behavior that you must now observe: no dogs, no littering, no fires, no camping without a permit, and so forth. The wilderness then is signaled by an intensification of the rules, an intensification that serves as the condition of an escape from the asphalt.

You can continue on this trail then until you reach a steep cliff onto which the guardians of the wilderness have thoughtfully bolted a cast-iron stairway. The stairway leads to a bridge that spans a rushing torrent, and from the middle of the bridge you are rewarded with a splendid view of Nevada Falls. On the railing that keeps you from falling to your death as you enjoy your vision of the wilderness there are signs – information about the dimensions of the falls, warnings against attempting to climb the treacherous, mist-slickened rocks, trail markers for those who wish to walk further – and an anodyzed aluminum plaque on which are inscribed inspirational, vaguely Wordsworthian sentiments by the California environmentist John Muir. The passage, as best I can recall, assures you that in years to come you will treasure the image you have before you. And next to these words, also etched into the aluminum, is precisely an image: a photograph of Nevada Falls taken from the very spot on which you stand.

The pleasure of this moment – beyond the pleasure of the mountain air and the waterfall and the great boulders and the deep forests of Lodgepole and Jeffrey pine – arises from the unusually candid glimpse of the process of circulation that shapes the whole experience of the park. The wilderness is at once secured and obliterated by the official gestures that establish its boundaries; the natural is set over against the artificial through means that render such an opposition meaningless. The eye passes from the "natural" image of the waterfall to the aluminum image, as if to secure a difference (for why else bother to go to the park at all? Why not simply look at a book of pictures?), even as that difference is effaced. The effacement is by no means complete – on the contrary, parks like Yosemite are one of the ways in which the distinction between nature and artifice is constituted in our society – and yet the Park Service's plaque on the Nevada

Falls bridge conveniently calls attention to the interpenetration of nature and artifice that makes the distinction possible.

What is missing from this exemplary fable of capitalist aesthetics is the question of property relations, since the National Parks exist precisely to suspend or marginalize that question through the ideology of protected public space. Everyone owns the parks. That ideology is somewhat bruised by the actual development of a park like Yosemite, with its expensive hotel, a restaurant that has a dress code, fancy gift shops and the like, but it is not entirely emptied out: even the administration of the right-wing Secretary of the Interior James Watt stopped short of permitting a private golf course to be constructed on park grounds, and there was public outrage when a television production company that had contracted to film a series in Yosemite decided to paint the rocks to make them look more realistic. What we need is an example that combines recreation or entertainment, aesthetics, the public sphere, and private property. The example most compelling to a literary critic like myself is not a political career or a national park but a novel.

In 1976, a convict named Gary Gilmore was released from a federal penitentiary and moved to Provo, Utah. Several months later, he robbed and killed two men, was arrested for the crimes, and convicted of murder. The case became famous when Gilmore demanded that he be executed – a punishment that had not been inflicted in America for some years, due to legal protections – and, over the strenuous objections of the American Civil Liberties Union and the National Association for the Advancement of Colored People, had his way. The legal maneuvers and the eventual firing-squad execution became national media events. Well before the denouement the proceedings had come to the attention of Norman Mailer and his publisher Warner Books which is, as it announces on its title pages, "a Warner Communications Company." Mailer's research assistant, Jere Herzenberg, and a hack writer and interviewer, Lawrence Schiller, conducted extensive interviews and acquired documents, records of court proceedings, and personal papers such as the intimate letters between Gilmore and his girlfriend. Some of these materials were in the public domain but many of them were not; they were purchased, and the details of the purchases themselves become part of the materials that were reworked by Mailer into *The Executioner's Song*,[11] a "true life novel" as it is called, that brilliantly combines documentary realism with Mailer's characteristic romance themes. The novel was a critical and popular success – a success signaled not only by the sheaves of admiring reviews but by the Universal Product Code printed on its paperback cover. It was subsequently made into an NBC-TV mini-series where on successive evenings it helped to sell cars, soap powder, and deodorant.

Mailer's book had further, and less predictable, ramifications. While he was working on *The Executioner's Song*, there was an article on Mailer in *People* magazine. The article caught the attention of a convict named Jack H. Abbott who wrote to offer him first-hand instruction on the conditions of prison life. An exchange of letters began, and Mailer grew increasingly impressed not only with their detailed information but with what he calls their "literary measure." The letters were cut and arranged by a Random House editor, Erroll McDonald, and appeared as a book called *In the Belly of the Beast*. This book too was widely acclaimed and contributed, with Mailer's help, to win a parole for its author.

"As I am writing these words," Mailer wrote in the Introduction to Abbott's book, "it looks like Abbott will be released on parole this summer. It is certainly the time for him to get out."[12] "I have never come into bodily contact with another human being in almost twenty years," wrote Abbott in his book, "except in combat; in acts of struggle, of violence" (p. 63). Shortly after his release, Abbott, now a celebrity, approached a waiter in an all-night restaurant and asked to use the men's room. The waiter – Richard Adan, an aspiring actor and playwright – told Abbott that the restaurant had no men's room and asked him to step outside. When Adan followed him on to the sidewalk, Abbott, apparently thinking that he was being challenged, stabbed Adan in the heart with a kitchen knife. Abbott was arrested and convicted once again of murder. The events have themselves been made into a play, also called *In the Belly of the Beast*, that recently opened to very favorable reviews.

Literary criticism has a familiar set of terms for the relationship between a work of art and the historical events to which it refers: we speak of allusion, symbolization, allegorization, representation, and above all mimesis. Each of these terms has a rich history and is virtually indispensable, and yet they all seem curiously inadequate to the cultural phenomenon which Mailer's book and Abbott's and the television series and the play constitute. And their inadequacy extends to aspects not only of contemporary culture but of the culture of the past. We need to develop terms to describe the ways in which material – here official documents, private papers, newspaper clippings, and so forth – is transferred from one discursive sphere to another and becomes aesthetic property. It would, I think, be a mistake to regard this process as uni-directional – from social discourse to aesthetic discourse – not only because the aesthetic discourse in this case is so entirely bound up with capitalist venture but because the social discourse is already charged with aesthetic energies. Not only was Gilmore explicitly and powerfully moved by the film version of *One Flew Over the Cuckoo's Nest*, but his entire pattern of behavior seems to have been shaped by the characteristic representations of American popular fiction, including Mailer's own.

Michael Baxandall has argued recently that "art and society are analytical concepts from two different kinds of categorization of human experience. ... unhomologous systematic constructions put upon interpenetrating subject-matters." In consequence, he suggests, any attempt to relate the two must first "modify one of the terms till it matches the other, but keeping note of what modification has been necessary since this is a necessary part of one's information."[13] It is imperative that we acknowledge the modification and find a way to measure its degree, for it is only in such measurements that we can hope to chart the relationship between art and society. Such an admonition is important – methodological self-consciousness is one of the distinguishing marks of the new historicism in cultural studies as opposed to a historicism based upon faith in the transparency of signs and interpretive procedures – but it must be supplemented by an understanding that the work of art is not itself a pure flame that lies at the source of our speculations. Rather the work of art is itself the product of a set of

manipulations, some of them our own (most striking in the case of works that
were not originally conceived as "art" at all but rather as something else – votive
objects, propaganda, prayer, and so on), many others undertaken in the construction of the original work. That is, the work of art is the product of a
negotiation between a creator or class of creators, equipped with a complex,
communally shared repertoire of conventions, and the institutions and practices
of society. In order to achieve the negotiation, artists need to create a currency
that is valid for a meaningful, mutually profitable exchange. It is important to
emphasize that the process involves not simply appropriation but exchange, since
the existence of art always implies a return, a return normally measured in
pleasure and interest. I should add that the society's dominant currencies,
money, and prestige, are invariably involved, but I am here using the term
"currency" metaphorically to designate the systematic adjustments, symboliza-
tions and lines of credit necessary to enable an exchange to take place. The terms
"currency" and "negotiation" are the signs of our manipulation and adjustment
of the relative systems.

   Much recent theoretical work must, I think, be understood in the context of a
search for a new set of terms to understand the cultural phenomenon that I have
tried to describe. Hence, for example, Wolfgang Iser writes of the creation of the
aesthetic dimension through the "dynamic oscillation" between two discourses;
the East German Marxist Robert Weimann argues that

> the process of making certain things one's own becomes inseparable from making
> other things (and persons) alien, so that the act of appropriation must be seen
> always already to involve not only self-projection and assimilation but alienation
> through reification and expropriation.

Anthony Giddens proposes that we substitute a concept of textual distanciation
for that of the autonomy of the text, so that we can fruitfully grasp the
"recursive character" of social life and of language.[14] Each of these formulations
– and, of course, there are significant differences among them – pulls away from a
stable, mimetic theory of art and attempts to construct in its stead an interpretive
model that will more adequately account for the unsettling circulation of
materials and discourses that is, I have argued, the heart of modern aesthetic
practice. It is in response to this practice that contemporary theory must situate
itself: not outside interpretation, but in the hidden places of negotiation and
exchange.

NOTES

1   This is the text of a lecture given at the University of Western Australia on
    September 4, 1986. A slightly different version appeared in Murray Krieger, ed.,
    The Aims of Representation: Subject/Text/History (New York: Columbia University
    Press, 1987), pp. 257–73.
2   Fredric Jameson, *The Political Unconscious: Narrative as a Socially Symbolic Act* (Ithaca:
    Cornell University Press, 1981), p. 20.

3   See Mark Poster, "Foucault, Poststructuralism, and the Mode of Information," in *The Aims of Representation*.

4   Jameson himself does not directly account for the sudden reversal in his thinking; he suggests rather that it is not his thinking that has changed but capitalism itself. Following Ernest Mandel, he suggests that we have moved into late capitalism, and in this state cultural production and consumption operate by wholly different rules. In the cultural logic of postmodernism, the working distinctions Jameson earlier found paralyzing and malignant have in fact vanished, giving way to an organization of discourse and perception that is at once dreadful and visionary. Dreadful because the new postmodern condition has obliterated all the place markers – inside and outside, culture and society, orthodoxy and subversion – that made it possible to map the world and hence mount a critique of its power structures. Visionary because this new multi-national world, a world with intensities rather than emotions, elaborated surfaces rather than hidden depths, random, unreadable signs rather than signifiers, intimates a utopian release from the traditional nightmare of traditional history. The doubleness of the postmodern is perfectly figured for Jameson by contemporary architecture, most perfectly by the Bonaventura Hotel in Los Angeles.

The rapidity of the shift between modern and postmodern charted in Jameson's shift from *The Political Unconscious* (1981) to "Postmodernism, or The Cultural Logic of Late Capitalism," *New Left Review*, 146 (July–August 1984), 53–93, is, to say the least, startling.

5   J.-F. Lyotard, "Judiciousness in Dispute or, Kant after Marx," in *The Aims of Representation*, p. 37.

6   See, for example, William E. Tate, *The Parish Chest: A Study in the Records of Parochial Administration in England* (Cambridge: Cambridge University Press, 1946).

7   Alternatively, of course, we can argue, as Jameson in effect does, that there are two capitalisms. The older, industrial capitalism was the agent of distinctions; the new, late capitalism is the effacer of distinctions. The detection of one tendency or the other in the phase of capitalism where it does not theoretically belong can be explained by invoking the distinction between residual and emergent. I find this scholastic saving of the theory infinitely depressing.

8   Michael Rogin, " 'Ronald Reagan': The Movie" and other Episodes in Political Demon-ology* (Berkeley: University of California Press, 1987).

9   Quoted by reporter Michael Tolchin in the *New York Times* account of Rogin's paper, headlined. "How Reagan Always Gets the Best Lines," *New York Times*, September 9, 1985, p. 10.

10 I borrow the phrase "the poetics of everyday behavior" from Iurii M. Lotman. See his essay in *The Semiotics of Russian Cultural History*, ed. A. D. Nakhimovsky and A. S. Nakhimovsky (Cornell: Cornell University Press, 1985).

11 N. Mailer, *The Executioner's Song* (New York: Warner Books, 1979).

12 Introduction to Jack Henry Abbott, *In the Belly of the Beast: Letters from Prison* (New York: Random House, 1981), p. xviii.

13 Michael Baxandall, "Art, Society, and the Bouger Principle," *Representations*, 12 (1985), 40–1.

14 All in *The Aims of Representation*.

3

THE TOUCH OF THE REAL

"Analysis," writes Clifford Geertz in the essay "Thick Description" that opens his celebrated book, *The Interpretation of Cultures* (1973), "is sorting out the structures of signification – what Ryle called established codes, a somewhat misleading expression, for it makes the enterprise sound too much like that of the cipher clerk when it is much more like that of the literary critic – and determining their social ground and import."[1] Small wonder then that Geertz's account of the project of social science rebounded with force upon literary critics like us in the mid-1970s: it made sense of something we were already doing, returning our own professional skills to us as more important, more vital and illuminating, than we had ourselves grasped. We perhaps did not wholly appreciate the scientific ambition lurking in the word "determining," but we were excited to find a sophisticated, intellectually powerful, and wonderfully eloquent anthropologist who could make use of the tools in our disciplinary kit and in so doing renew in us a sense of their value.

Within the contentious discipline of anthropology, Geertz has by now been so routinely accused of one or another form of wickedness – such is the cost of academic success – that it is easy to overlook the liberating effect he had on those who came to him, as we did, from the outside and particularly from literary criticism. He did not attempt, of course, to justify the academic analysis of literature, let alone to find in it the radical politics for which we were longing, but he did something that seemed still more important. He argued that our interpretive strategies provided key means for understanding the complex symbolic systems and life patterns that anthropologists studied. The effect was like touching one wire to another: literary criticism made contact with reality. Or rather, as Geertz quickly observed, it made contact, as always, with pieces of writing. But this was writing with a difference: not poetry or fiction but verbal traces less self-consciously detached from the lives real men and women actually live.

The crucial self-defining move in Geertz's essay on "thick description" comes when the anthropologist pulls away from Gilbert Ryle's distinction between a twitch and a wink (and between both of these and a parody of a wink or even the

This chapter was first published in this form in *Practicing New Historicism* (2000, pp. 20–48).

rehearsal of this parodic wink). "Like so many of the little stories Oxford philosophers like to make up for themselves," Geertz remarks, "all this winking, fake-winking, burlesque-fake-winking, rehearsed-burlesque-fake-winking, may seem a bit artificial" (p. 7). What would be the alternative to such artificiality? How could the distinction between "thin description" and "thick description" (the one merely describing the mute act, the other giving the act its place in a network of framing intentions and cultural meanings) be linked, as Geertz puts it, to something "more empirical"? The answer is still, it turns out, a little story – that is, an anecdote; however, now it is not one of the little stories Oxford philosophers make up for themselves, but rather one of the little stories anthropologists record, or are supposed to record, in their notebooks during the great disciplinary rite of passage known as fieldwork. "Let me give," Geertz writes, "deliberately unpreceded by any prior explanatory comment at all, a not untypical excerpt from my own field journal" (p. 7). There follows, set off in a different typeface, a wonderful short account of an episode of sheep stealing, murder, and justice – a series of events that occurred in central Morocco in 1912 and were related to Geertz in 1968 by one of the participants, an old man named Cohen.

"A not untypical excerpt:" are such recorded stories typical or not of the contents of the anthropologist's field journal? Geertz's delicate double negative enables the text he quotes to have some representative force without being absorbed into a larger whole. If you understand what it means to interpret this excerpt, you will have some idea of what it means to interpret many roughly comparable excerpts, but you will not thereby possess the entire cultural system. That is, you will not be freed of the obligation to ponder each excerpt individually and (as far as possible) on its own terms, nor will you have comprehended anything like the full range of the materials to be pondered. "Deliberately unpreceded by any prior explanatory comment at all:" the excerpt is meant to surprise and to baffle, not to assume a comfortable place in a preexisting analysis of Moroccan culture. It functions then to subvert a programmatic analytical response, a fully systematized methodology, and it helps to call into question, in the midst of a loose allegiance to structuralism, whether either a culture or a method could ever be rendered satisfyingly systematic. The anecdote is, as Geertz puts it, "quoted raw, a note in a bottle." As such, it is meant not only to convey the idea of the "empirical" (as distinct from the philosopher's "artificial" stories) but also to arouse the bafflement, the intense curiosity and interest, that necessitates the interpretation of cultures.

Geertz repeats the image of the note in the bottle twice in the essay on thick description. The image nicely serves to emphasize something at once specific to his sheep-stealing anecdote, since it has bobbed up from 1912 and thus from a Morocco that has by now long vanished over the horizon, and more general, since all cultures that are not one's own are always located beyond one's familiar horizon. It thus underscores the promise, implicit in most ethnographic texts and explicit here, that the excerpt has not been invented by the anthropologist, that it comes from "somewhere else."[2] Moreover, the anecdote has not been carefully cooked up, like Ryle's story of winks and twitches, to exemplify an abstract point; it is not only something found, like a note in a bottle, but also, as Geertz puts it, "raw."

Yet Geertz's link to literary criticism depends upon his immediately qualifying, indeed abandoning, this notion of the "raw." For if it is important for the reader to accept Geertz's claim that he is not making up an exemplary tale but rather quoting something told to him by one of his "informants," it is at least as important for the reader to grasp that the quotation is itself a story, a story that has been written down in the anthropologist's field journal. This insistence on narrative and on textuality helps to justify the appeal to techniques of literary analysis, but it is not quite the same as an insistence that "there is nothing outside the text." Or rather as soon as you collapse everything into something called textuality, you discover that it makes all the difference what kind of text you are talking about. The collapse licenses a certain kind of attention and invites the questions that literary critics characteristically ask, but at the same time it calls for a sharp attention to genre and rhetorical mode, to the text's implicit or explicit reality claims, to the implied link (or distance) between the word and whatever it is – the real, the material, the realm of practice, pain, bodily pleasure, silence, or death – to which the text gestures as that which lies beyond the written word, outside its textual mode of being.

The "raw" excerpt from the field notes makes a stronger claim to reference – it points more directly to a world that has some solidity and resistance – than Ryle's invented example, but the former is no less a textual construction than the latter. The sheep-stealing anecdote has a quality of strangeness or opacity, but not because it is something mute and shapeless, dug up like a potato from an alien soil. What "we" anthropologists call "our data," Geertz writes, "are really our own constructions of other people's constructions of what they and their compatriots are up to." "This little drama" (p. 9), as he calls the passage he quotes from his field notes, is meant to show that there is rather less observation and considerably more explication – *explication de texte* – than anthropologists generally admit to.

Thick description, as Ryle uses the term in his essays on thinking, entails an account of the intentions, expectations, circumstances, settings, and purposes that give actions their meanings.[3] The distinction between a twitch and a wink is secured by the element of volition that is not itself visibly manifest in the contraction of the eyelid; a thin description would miss it altogether. So too with the other layers of framing intentions that Ryle piles on: fake twitches, rehearsals of fake twitches, and so forth. Many of these framing intentions seem to introduce an explicitly aesthetic or representational quality, but such a quality is not essential to the notion of thick description. A thin description of what you are doing when you are pumping up bicycle tires, to cite another of Ryle's examples, would be an account of a series of repetitive physical motions that produce a certain effect. A thick description of those same motions would involve a fuller sense of the significance of what you are doing. If you are pumping up your bicycle tires because you are preparing to go for a bike ride, a thick description of your pumping requires a reference to your intended ride, whether that ride actually occurs or not; if, on the other hand, you are pumping up your bicycle tires because you want to strengthen the muscles of your arms so that bullies will no longer kick sand at you at the beach, the thick description of your pumping would differ accordingly.

Ryle is fascinated by receding planes, a fascination that repeatedly draws him to the game of inventing chains of further complications around what initially seems a simple action: winking (or twitching), clearing your throat, hitting golf balls, playing tennis, cooking, jumping over flower beds. The mental game is not difficult to play: you are not actually intending to go on a bike ride (to continue in Ryle's vein) but only pretending that you are, in order to deceive an observer; or you are rehearsing for a drama in which you will play the part of someone who deceives an observer by pumping up bicycle tires as if in anticipation of a bike ride that your character never really intends to take. And so on. The difficulty lies in accounting persuasively for the relation between these surrounding circumstances and the action as thinly described. Thick description, in Ryle's account, involves two major features: intention-parasitism (the intention with which a person undertakes to pump up bicycle tires is ancillary to and hence parasitical upon his intention to take a bike ride) and circumstance-detachment (the actor rehearsing the part of the tire pumper need not actually have a pump or a bike on hand – a stick and a table will do just fine for the purpose of rehearsal – but the act of rehearsing only makes sense in reference to the intended performance).

For Ryle, thick description is manifestly a quality of the explication rather than of the action or text that is explicated: it is not the object that is thick or thin, but only the description of it. A thick description thus could be exceedingly straightforward or, alternatively, exceedingly complex, depending on the length of the chain of parasitical intentions and circumstantial detachments. A thin description need not be brief or schematic; it could be quite lengthy and complicated – an adequate account of the physiology and pneumatics involved in pumping tires would take many pages – but it would not concern itself with the agent's framing intentions or the culture within which those intentions acquire their significance. Thickness is not in the object; it is in the narrative surroundings, the add-ons, the nested frames.

As Geertz's famous essay deploys the term, however, thickness begins to slide almost imperceptibly from the description to the thing described. For, though Geertz may wish to imply that his excerpt was chosen virtually at random and that one fragment would have been as good as another, some texts seem far more amenable to thick description than others, and consequently some texts seem "thicker" than others. Thickness no longer seems extrinsic to the object, a function solely of the way it is framed. The sheep-stealing narrative is supposed to be nothing more than the ethnographic equivalent of Ryle's winks and twitches, but in fact they seem profoundly different: Ryle's is a purpose-built illustration of a carefully delimited philosophical point; Geertz's supposedly "raw" excerpt from his field notes is a complex narrative in which the motivating intentions seem intrinsic. That is, neither of Ryle's key terms, intention-parasitism and circumstance-detachment, is remotely relevant to Geertz's anecdote, precisely because the intentions and circumstances are not securely situated on the outside of the actions reported.

This slide is not a theoretical proposition, nor is it, in its divergence from Ryle, a mistake; rather, it is part of the disciplinary interest of anthropology. The shift from the philosopher's tale to the "native informant's" tale is for Geertz a shift from the "artificial" toward the "empirical" – that is, toward textual constructions, presented as "raw" data or "evidence," that seem less purpose-built, more resistant to simple appropriation, and hence more nearly autonomous. As the anthropologist interprets his exemplary texts, these texts seem to be increasingly embedded in the cultures from which they come and to possess within themselves more and more of the culture's linked intentions. In practice (that is, in Geertz's interpretive practice), certain constructions of cultural reality appear compressed and hence expandable: "From this simple incident," Geertz remarks about the sheep-stealing anecdote, "one can widen out into enormous complexities of social experience" (p. 19).

Are these complexities actually inscribed in the textual fragments, or are they brought to bear upon them from the outside in the course of interpretation? Part of Geertz's power was his ability to suggest that the multilayered cultural meanings by which he was fascinated were present in the fragments themselves, just as the literary criticism of William Empson or Kenneth Burke managed to suggest that the dense ambiguities and ironies were present in the literary texts themselves and not only in the acts of interpretation.[4] Those acts of interpretation were not completely supplementary – they helped to create as well as to disclose the effect of compression – but the dense networks of meaning charted in an effective thick description had to be traceable back to the anecdote initially held up for scrutiny.

What we are calling the effect of compression enabled a literary historian like Erich Auerbach to move convincingly from a tiny passage to a sprawling, complex text (and, finally, to "Western Literature"). Drawing on literary criticism – Auerbach is cited, along with Samuel Taylor Coleridge, T. S. Eliot, Burke, Empson, R. P. Blackmur, and Cleanth Brooks[5] – Geertz did something similar with cultural fragments, small bits of symbolic behavior from which he could "widen out" into larger social worlds. The techniques of literary analysis thus helped to make possible for Geertzian anthropology something akin to what in optics is called "foveation," the ability to keep an object (here a tiny textualized piece of social behavior) within the high-resolution area of perception. Foveation in cultural interpretation is rather difficult because of problems of both scale and focus. The interpreter must be able to select or to fashion, out of the confused continuum of social existence, units of social action small enough to hold within the fairly narrow boundaries of full analytical attention, and this attention must be unusually intense, nuanced, and sustained.

Geertz grasped that, along with analytic philosophy, literary criticism had for years been honing useful foveation skills. Hence the terms that he uses to describe his piece of thick description not only emphasize its own textuality (in keeping with his insistence that ethnographers are writers), but also repeatedly extend that textuality to the object described: "our sheep story – an assortment of remarks and anecdotes," "a not untypical excerpt from my own field journal," "a note in a bottle," a "passage," "this little drama," "our text," a "social farce," "our pastoral drama," "the rigmarole," a "social discourse" – and moving away from the excerpt and toward what the excerpt is meant to exemplify: "a manuscript – foreign, faded, full of ellipses, incoherencies, suspicious emendations, and tendentious commentaries, but written not in conventionalized graphs of sound but in transient examples of shaped behavior" (p. 10). That is, culture is itself an "acted document," whether it takes the form of "a burlesqued wink or a mock sheep raid" (p. 10). The point is that to understand what people are up to in any culture – and, "leaving our winks and sheep behind for the moment," Geertz takes a Beethoven quartet as his example – you need to be acquainted "with the imaginative universe within which their acts are signs" (p. II).

For the purposes of literary criticism, "imaginative," "drama," "manuscript," and "signs" were reassuringly familiar terms, as was the whole emphasis on symbolic behavior, but the specific force of Geertz's work for new historicism resided in the expansion of these terms to a much broader and less familiar range of texts than literary critics had permitted themselves to analyze. For Geertz this expansion reflected an empowering appropriation of analytical tools, an appropriation that conferred the prestige accorded to the supreme achievements of Western high culture, such as Beethoven quartets, on the flotsam and jetsam in an anthropologist's field notes. At issue was not only prestige – what Pierre Bourdieu famously analyzed as cultural capital – but a transference of the kind of attention paid to canonical works of art to the ordinary and extraordinary behavior of the subjects of anthropology. To construct descriptions, Geertz notes, "of the involvements of a Berber chieftain, a Jewish merchant, and a French soldier with one another in 1912 Morocco is clearly an imaginative act, not all that different from constructing similar descriptions of, say, the involvements with one another of a provincial French doctor, his silly, adulterous wife, and her feckless lover in nineteenth century France" (pp. 15–16). If it is not altogether clear at this moment in Geertz's essay whether it is the anthropologist himself or the anthropologist's informant Cohen who is being likened to Gustave Flaubert, this is because both the informant's discourse and the anthropologist's discourse about that discourse (and, for that matter, the series of actions from 1912) are alike fictions, in the root sense of things *made, composed, fashioned.*

Our goal in response to Geertz was not exactly to reverse the disciplinary appropriation, that is, to apply to literary analysis the terms and concepts developed by anthropologists. (Such an application, of course, was in fact occurring, especially in literary structuralism's use of Claude Lévi-Strauss.) What we wanted was not social science but ethnographic realism, and we wanted it principally for literary purposes. That is, we had no interest in decisively leaving works of literature behind and turning our attention elsewhere; instead, we sought to put literature and literary criticism in touch with that elsewhere. It is a tribute to Geertz that it was not his method that seemed powerful to us (after all, that method was in part borrowed from literary criticism), but rather the lived life that he managed so well to narrate, describe, and clarify. That lived life, at once raw and subtle, coarse and complex, was the thing that had been progressively refined out of the most sophisticated literary studies, or so it seemed to us at the time. By embracing and displacing literary studies, *The Interpretation of Cultures* provided an impetus for recovering what had been lost. Literary criticism could venture out to unfamiliar cultural texts, and these texts – often marginal, odd, fragmentary, unexpected, and crude – in turn could begin to interact in interesting ways with the intimately familiar works of the literary canon.

To Auerbach's powerful ability to conjure up complex life-worlds from tiny fragments, Geertz added the anthropologist's strong claim to a hold on the world. That is, it was crucial, as part of the pleasure and interest of reading Geertz, to believe that he had not made up his Mr Cohen and that Cohen too had not simply made up his story. To be sure, Geertz encourages the reader to grasp that his informant's version of the story is not identical to one that would have been produced by any of the other principals in it and that he may have considerably enhanced the story for rhetorical effect; but Cohen was a real person recounting actual experiences, and his story was *his* story and not the ethnographer's.

"I can call spirits from the vasty deep," claims Owain Glyndwr, the strange Welsh magus in Shakespeare's *I Henry IV*. "Why, so can I, or so can any man" is Hotspur's sardonic reply, "But will they come when you do call for them?"[6] So too an anecdote may conjure up reality, but will reality come when it is called? If it is only a matter of rhetoric – the effect of what the ancient rhetoricians called *enargeia*, or vividness – then only a reality-effect is conjured and nothing more. But something more is at stake. Geertz gestures toward that something when he acknowledges that there are important problems of verification or, as he prefers to term it, appraisal. This process of appraisal is largely internal to a particular discipline – we obviously had no way of testing Geertz's interpretation of Moroccan culture nor could we confirm the authenticity of his field notes – but it is in principle significant for the value anthropology could have for literary studies. For the interest was never to collapse anthropology and literary criticism into each other but to draw upon their particular strengths, strengths that depended at least as much upon the differences between their characteristic texts as upon their surprising similarities. Indeed it is an awareness of how those differences are constituted and what they mean – an understanding of the emergence of the literary and the imaginative force of the nonliterary – that has virtually obsessed not only our own work but that of new historicism in general.

What then should we make of Geertz's claim that an anecdote from the field journal is "not all that different," as an imaginative construction, from *Madame Bovary?* Very little beyond the critical incentive, or rather the imperative, to interpret. To be sure, if it turned out that Geertz's Cohen had taken it upon himself to be the Flaubert of the Maghreb and had made up his entire story, we might still have concluded that we possessed something of ethnographic value: a glimpse of the fantasies of an old man who had been steeped in the symbolic systems of colonial Morocco.[7] If, however, it turned out that Geertz had made up Cohen, we at least would have concluded that as an ethnographer Geertz was not to be trusted, and his work would have immediately lost much of its value. For it is precisely not as a fiction or as a little philosopher's tale that Geertz invites us to read his anecdote; it is as a "raw" sample of his field notes. The frame is crucial, since in this case it helps us to conjure up a "real" as opposed to an "imaginary" world.

Geertz's conjuring of the real seemed to us useful for literary studies not because it insisted upon the primacy of interpretation – that was already the norm in literary criticism – but because it helped to widen the range of imaginative constructions to be interpreted. His thick descriptions of cultural texts strengthened the insistence that the things that draw us to literature are often found in the nonliterary, that the concept of literariness is deeply unstable, that the boundaries between different types of narratives are subject to interrogation and revision. We wanted to argue that human creativity, including narrative and linguistic creativity, only makes sense in the long run because it is a widespread, indeed democratic, possession – a possession that is almost impossible to contain within a small elite or sequester from the sweet, familiar light of the everyday. We wanted also to use the anecdote to show in compressed form the ways in which elements of lived experience enter into literature, the ways in which everyday institutions and bodies get recorded. And we wanted, conversely, to show in compressed form the ways in which poetry, drama, and prose fiction play themselves out in the everyday world, since men and women repeatedly find themselves in effect speaking the language of the literary not only in their public performances, but also in their most intimate or passionate moments.

We sought something beyond this: we wanted to find in the past real bodies and living voices, and if we knew that we could not find these – the bodies having long moldered away and the voices fallen silent – we could at least seize upon those traces that seemed to be close to actual experience. Literature seemed to us, as to many others, almost infinitely precious because its creators had invented techniques for representing this experience with uncanny vividness; but there were other techniques and other texts, outside the conventional boundaries of the literary, that possessed a nearly comparable power. The greatest challenge lay not simply in exploring these other texts – an agreeably imperial expansion of literary criticism beyond its borders – but in making the literary and the nonliterary seem to be each other's thick description. That both the literary work and the anthropological (or historical) anecdote are texts, that both are fictions in the sense of things made, that both are shaped by the imagination and by the available resources of narration and description helped make it possible to conjoin them; but their ineradicable differences – the fact that neither is purpose-built for the other, that they make sharply different claims upon the actual, that they are incommensurable and virtually impossible to foveate simultaneously – made the conjunction powerful and compelling.

We wanted to recover in our literary criticism a confident conviction of reality, without giving up the power of literature to sidestep or evade the quotidian and without giving up a minimally sophisticated understanding that any text depends upon the absence of the bodies and voices that it represents. We wanted the touch of the real in the way that in an earlier period people wanted the touch of the transcendent.

"Readers of the *Odyssey* will remember the well-prepared and touching scene in book 19, when Odysseus has at last come home, the scene in which the old housekeeper Euryclea, who had been his nurse, recognizes him by a scar on his thigh."[8] This is how the text of Erich Auerbach's great book *Mimesis*, both in the German–language original and the English translation, begins: no pages of acknowledgments, no methodological foreword, no theoretical introduction. Between the title (*Mimesis: Dargestellte Wirklichkeit in der Abendländischen Literatur*) and the table of contents, there is only an epigraph in English, to which we will return, from Marvell's "To His Coy Mistress": "Had we but world enough and time. . . . " In the first edition, published in Switzerland by A. Francke AG. Verlag in 1946, there is also along with the copyright information, in very small letters, the words "Mai 1942 bis April 1945." Then we plunge immediately into a close reading of the episode of Odysseus' scar, an analysis meant to bring out "the genius of the Homeric style." This genius, Auerbach writes, "becomes even more apparent when it is compared with an equally ancient and equally epic style from a different world of forms" (p. 7), and thus he moves to an analysis of the biblical account of the sacrifice of Isaac. By the chapter's close, Auerbach has sketched two styles that

> represent basic types: on the one hand fully externalized description, uniform illumination, uninterrupted connection, free expression, all events in the fore-ground, displaying unmistakable meanings, few elements of historical development and of psychological perspective; on the other hand, certain parts brought into high relief, others left obscure, abruptness, suggestive influence of the unexpressed, "background" quality, multiplicity of meanings and the need for interpretation, universal-historical claims, development of the concept of historically becoming, and preoccupation with the problematic. (p. 23)

What is going on here? In some twenty pages, Auerbach has moved from pointillist textual detail – "To the word scar (v. 393) there is first attached a relative clause ('which once long ago a boar . . .'), which enlarges into a voluminous syntactical parenthesis. . . . " (p. 7) – to a huge vista, an overview of the foundational modes for the representation of reality in European culture. It is the literary critical equivalent of one of those canvases – Altdorfer's *Battle of Issus* is the supreme example – where the eye moves from the tiny but legible design on the soldier's button to the curvature of the earth at the horizon. Or rather in *Mimesis* the button, as it were, is made to reveal the shape of the whole wide earth: such is the power of the concept of "representation" in Auerbach's skillful hands. His textual fragments represent the enormous multiauthored texts from which they are drawn – the *Odyssey* and the Bible – and the styles disclosed in those fragments represent historically determined and determining methods by which the world is apprehended, imitated, and reproduced.

The subsequent nineteen chapters of Auerbach's *Mimesis* all begin with short excerpts from a text – a few pages, quoted first in the original and then in translation.[9] Each chapter then proceeds to unpack its excerpt, sometimes in the light of other briefer passages from the same author's work or from that of contemporaries, but more often by intense close reading, that is, by examining very carefully modulations in the level of style, resonances of diction, nuances of tone, rhetorical strategies, latent philosophical and sociological assumptions.

Mimesis does, it emerges, have a grand overarching theme – what Auerbach calls, late in the book, "the history of the literary conquest of modern reality" (p. 331) – along with a series of recurrent preoccupations and motifs, but there is no programmatic statement of purpose, and each of the chapters is discrete and self-contained. Throughout these chapters there is a profound sense of historical process and a rich awareness of complex intertextual relations, but Auerbach makes almost no gestures toward a wholly integrated and sequential account, a history of causes and effects. Even the "basic types" adumbrated in the opening chapter, though they remain available as powerful points of reference, are not insisted upon rigorously, nor is Auerbach's book a sustained history of their rivalry or intertwining.

An immensely ambitious book without a purpose, or at least without a declared purpose: with a lesser book we might assume that this conjunction was a sign that its author took for granted, perhaps fatuously, the importance of his enterprise; or that his ambition lacked an adequate end; or that an elaborate display of learning and interpretive power was, among the community for whom the book was written, an end in itself. But none of these assumptions is correct. Auerbach had been expelled from the academic community for which he had been trained; he writes with a profoundly melancholy sense that the centuries-long project he lovingly chronicles is close to exhaustion, disintegration, or irrelevance; and at the same time his book carries the conviction that it possesses a supremely adequate object. This conviction, never made explicit but pervasive nonetheless, has about it something of an implied religious faith, a faith that seems almost to become manifest in the chapter on the *Divine Comedy*, "Farinata and Cavalcante."[10] Dante wrote, Auerbach observes, in a supremely elevated style, a style that owed everything to his acknowledged master Virgil and to the sublime gravitas of the classical epic, and yet his great work constantly violates the central principle by which classical writers achieved sublimity, the principle of the separation of styles. Paradoxically, the elevated style of the *Comedy* "consists precisely in integrating what is characteristically individual and at times horrible, ugly, grotesque, and vulgar with the dignity of God's judgment – a dignity which transcends the ultimate limits of our earthly conception of the sublime" (p. 194). For all its magnificent gravity and serious-ness and gigantic reach, Dante's style is still, in his own words, a *sermo remissus et humilis*. Hence, in Auerbach's account, Dante's Christianity triumphantly fused the two basic types of represented reality, classical and biblical.

Dante's mixing of styles and his insistence upon the everyday even in the midst of the sacred is linked, Auerbach argues, to figural realism, a mode Auerbach had analyzed at length in a crucially important essay, "Figura," published two years before *Mimesis*. Figura, a concept by which each earthly thing has its fulfillment in the world beyond, allows both for the overarching divine order in which everything that exists is ultimately fulfilled and for the historical specificity of each particular event, phenomenon, and personality. Nothing, no matter how vulgar or grotesque, need be discarded for fear of undermining the elevated style, for the weightiness of Christian representation depends upon the intense appre-hension of an earthly drama whose meaning is fully realized in a timeless eternity. "Conceiving all earthly occurrences through the medium of a mixed style –

without aesthetic restriction in either subject matter or form – as an entity sublimely figural, is Christian in spirit and Christian in origin" (p. 198).

The sublime Christian realism of the *Comedy*, its capacity through the figural power of the *sermo humilis* to integrate the classical and biblical modes of representation, stands at the very center of *Mimesis*. Auerbach's opening chapter posed a riddle – how was it possible for the representation of reality in Western literature to progress from two antithetical and incompatible modes? – that Dante brilliantly solved, plunging "the living world of human action and endurance and more especially of individual deeds and destinies" into the "changeless existence" of life after death. The phrases we have just quoted are not from Auerbach but from Hegel, and they suggest the extent to which *Mimesis* has a buried Hegelian plot.

Yet, as we have already suggested, the plot is not finally realized. To be sure, in Auerbach's vision, Dante's synthesis has its own inherent forward-driving dynamic of a kind we might expect in a Hegelian analysis. The intensity of Dante's realism, its immensely powerful representation of human passions and irreducible individuality, broke the theological scheme from which it derived: "Dante's work made man's Christian-figural being a reality, and destroyed it in the very process of realizing it" (p. 202). But, though Auerbach is fascinated by the secularized representations of human destiny that ensue upon this destruction, he entirely lacks Hegel's confidence in a grand design, a meaningful higher order. Instead, each of the textual worlds that he enters by means of the excerpt has a way of seeming complete in itself, a complex, compelling whole. If there is a hint of a direction in the succession of these isolated representations, it is toward dissolution, but this melancholy intimation of the end of the world as we know it only intensifies Auerbach's commitment to the existential claim of individual, autonomous literary visions.

Those of us who began writing literary history in the 1970s had a strong affinity both with Auerbach's existential pessimism and with his method, a method by which many of us were, from the beginning, influenced and that we self-consciously emulated. The influence is most striking in the adaptation of Auerbach's characteristic opening gambit: the isolation of a resonant textual fragment that is revealed, under the pressure of analysis, to represent the work from which it is drawn and the particular culture in which that work was produced and consumed. That culture in turn renders the fragment explicable, both as something that could have only been written in a moment characterized by a particular set of circumstances, structures, and assumptions and as something that conveys the life-world of that moment. The new historicist anecdote as many of us deployed it is an Auerbachian device. Of course, we typically moved outside of canonical works of art for our anecdotes; we frequently sought an effect of surprise by selecting passages from what looked, in the context of literary criticism, like oddly marginal or eccentric works; and we allowed the analysis of the anecdote to pull away from or alternatively to swamp the explication of the canonical work of art to which it was at least nominally conjoined. We will return to the significance of these differences, but it is important to grasp what was so appealing about Auerbach's strategy.

Its principal appeal is that it enabled critics to illuminate extremely complex and – quite simply but not inconsequentially – long works without exhausting themselves or their readers, without making their audience feel that the task of reading was futile or intolerably boring and repetitive, and without stepping back to a detached distance, a level of generality in which the issues became banal and predictable. Here the epigraph from Marvell finds its meaning: "Had we but world enough and time," Auerbach could examine the entire vast storehouse of Western literary representations of reality, he could grapple with complex questions of periodization, and he could probe every detail of the works on which he has chosen to focus his attention. Above all, he could attempt to explore the concept "realism" around which his whole book turns and that nonetheless he steadfastly refuses to define. But time's wingèd chariot is hurrying near, and here the anecdotal, fragmentary method, which rests on the principle of representation, rescues him. "I could never have written anything in the nature of a history of European realism," Auerbach writes at the close of *Mimesis;* "the material would have swamped me" (p. 548). Moreover, as he explains in the epilogue, he wrote his book in Istanbul, where there was no library suitable for European studies. Auerbach had gone to teach at the Turkish State University after his dismissal in 1935 on racist grounds from his teaching position at Marburg, and after the outbreak of the war there was no possibility of consulting other libraries: hence in part the significance of the dates in the small print at the beginning. So he faced the problem of too few texts as well as too many, and here again he was rescued by the anecdote. Auerbach can say convincing and fresh things about texts like the Bible, the *Odyssey,* the *Inferno, Don Quixote*, Montaigne's *Essays,* and Balzac's *Comédie humaine* because he has liberated himself from the task of writing a full "history," because his analyses have the kind of intensity and detail more typically associated with readings of Shakespeare sonnets or Donne lyrics, and because the fragmentary passages he chooses to analyze seem to represent not only whole works but whole ages.

Auerbach knows perfectly well, of course, that an entire epoch cannot be adequately represented in a single text, let alone in a small textual fragment, but in his work we repeatedly glimpse what we regard as a quasi-magical effect: the conjuring of a complex, dynamic, historically specific spirit of representation out of a few paragraphs. The spirit of representation sometimes corresponds to the boundaries of nation or class or religion or language, but is not consistently linked with any of these, for Auerbach does not assent fully to any of the categories that governed the principal literary histories of the nineteenth and twentieth centuries. He is above all allergic to the nationalism, often racially inflected, that generated most of these histories. National self-consciousness is occasionally granted considerable importance, of course, but *Mimesis* repeatedly absorbs it into the larger project of "Western" literature, where "Western" functions as an antidote to the exclusive claims of a territorial or racial group. (This strategy, we might note in passing, draws Auerbach into the familiar paradox of positing the origins of the "Western" in works from Asia Minor and the Middle East.) The organizational principle, after the opening chapter, is sequentiality, though here too Auerbach is careful to restrict the significance of the chronological order he observes; it is not the link between one age and another that interests him, but rather what we might call a sequence of specters, the specters of mimetic genius.

We suspect that Auerbach would have disliked this characterization of his work. He writes not in the manner of a conjurer but in the sober, solemn manner of a learned literary historian. Nonetheless, in *Mimesis* he does what Francis Bacon in a strange passage from *The Advancement of Learning* (1623) counseled the historian of literature to do:

> For the *manner* of compiling such a history, I particularly advise that the manner and provision of it be not drawn from histories and commentaries alone, but that the principal books written in each century, or perhaps in shorter periods, proceeding in regular order from the earliest ages, be themselves taken into consideration, that so (I do not say by a complete perusal, for that would be an endless labour, but) by tasting them here and there and observing their argument, style, and method, the Literary Spirit [*genius literarius*] of each age may be charmed as it were from the dead.

It is this *genius literarius* – the creative, generative power of language in a particular historical period – that Auerbach repeatedly charms from his fragmentary passages, a conjuring trick that is enhanced, as *Mimesis* proceeds, by what seems to be the increasing arbitrariness with which the passages are chosen. The episode of Odysseus's scar is highly charged, and still more the sacrifice of Isaac: these are fables of identity, to borrow Northrop Frye's phrase, resonant, momentous, and exquisitely shaped. But Alcofribas's brief sojourn in Gargantua's mouth and Prince Hal's expression of weariness to his boon companion Poins are not conspicuously great moments in the works of Rabelais and Shakespeare; and by the time we reach the chapters on the realist classics of the nineteenth century, the passages seem chosen almost by chance, and they begin to proliferate, as if a single resonant anecdote were no longer sufficient. Indeed at moments, in a modern, demystified version of the Virgilian *sortilegium*, Auerbach appears simply to be opening a book – *The Red and the Black* or *Madame Bovary* – at random and starting his analysis wherever his eyes happen to fall. Yet it is precisely in these later chapters, with their analyses of bits of text that no longer tell meaningful stories, that Auerbach's conjuring trick is most striking, and it is here too that Auerbach comes closest to acknowledging that it *is* a conjuring trick.

From Balzac's *Père Goriot*, a novel replete with melodramatic incident, Auerbach selects an almost negligible detail, a passage describing the appearance in the dilapidated pension dining room of its shabby owner, Madame Vauquer. Nothing about this particular appearance of the pension mistress is momentous; on the contrary, Balzac is describing her daily routine, one in keeping with the petty, fetid, claustrophobic triviality of the entire milieu over which she presides. This very ordinariness linking the repulsive, vulgar woman to every corner of her repulsive, vulgar pension fascinates Auerbach, for it perfectly exemplifies the "atmospheric realism" that he finds in Balzac. The hallmark of this kind of realism, he suggests, is the organic unity of the moral, physical, social, and historical environment, so that virtually all details, even those apparently idio-syncratic or marginal or jumbled together in disorder, are clues to the true nature of the whole to which they are structurally bound. Thus there is no need for anecdotes that take the form of miniature narratives, with beginning, middle, and end; the description of a chair, a pair of slippers, or a tablecloth will do.

This atmospheric realism and the disordered, hasty jumble of features through which it is constituted do not bespeak a cool demystification of the world – the leaching out of its narrative glamour – but rather a quality Auerbach proposes to call "demonic." In part the term seems to be elicited by certain details in the text: the arrival of the hideous Madame Vauquer is preceded by that of her cat, the dining room's walls "ooze misfortune," and so forth. But Auerbach characteris-tically employs these local details as a platform on which to construct a far larger structure. The demonic impression does not finally depend upon invocations of witchcraft or the spectral; it is implicit in the organic unity of what Balzac was the first to term the *milieu*, a unity that is "not established rationally but is presented as a striking and immediately apprehended state of things, purely suggestively, without any proof" (p. 471). That is, there is something eerie in the pervasiveness of the moral and physical atmosphere of the dreary lower-bourgeois Parisian pension, impregnating the room, the furniture, the clothing, along with the faces, ideas, dreams, and fates of its inhabitants. And, similarly, there is something eerie in the pervasiveness of the very different atmospheres described in *Père Goriot*'s other milieux, as well as in the unity of the "total atmosphere" that envelops all of them taken together.

Auerbach's close reading of the brief anecdote from Balzac helps us understand how strange the familiar notion of "organic" unity actually is, as if random and apparently autonomous units were revealed to be mysteriously interlinked cells in a monstrous living body. Balzac advanced zoological and sociological theories to explicate his work, but the deepest affinities of his atmospheric realism, Auerbach shows, are to "atmospheric Historism": "his people and his atmo-spheres, contemporary as they may be, are always represented as phenomena sprung from historical events and forces" (p. 480). The power of these historical forces is manifested equally in a tulle bonnet and in a revolution, in a particular style of petticoat and in a stock market crash.

This "historism" that, in Auerbach's view, unifies the fictive worlds of the great French realists, Stendhal and Balzac, also gives Auerbach his own critical method. For the anecdotal technique of *Mimesis* rests on the conviction that tiny details can be made to represent the nature of larger and larger wholes. It is possible for Auerbach to unpack long works and even entire cultures out of a close encounter with a tiny fragment because he is less concerned with sequence and form than he is with "the representation of reality." Hence he does not need to say something about the origin and internal structure of the work so much as he needs to address and explicate its characteristic practice of referring to the world. The paradox here is that it is easier for him to address the representation of reality than it is to address the inner organization of a finite text, an organization resistant to the analysis of short excerpts. The literary work is interesting to Auerbach not for its swerve away from reality – as if reality were something monumental, unchanging, and assured, and as if the literary work needed to make a space for itself, apart from the world – but rather for its claim on the world, its ability to give the reader access to the very condition for perception and action, along with the very condition for textuality, at a given place and time, in a given culture. For Auerbach, textuality – in its specificity, its local know-ledge, its buried network of assumptions – is not a system distinct from lived experience but an imitation of it, and "imitation" (that is, representation) is the principal way human beings come to understand their existence and share it with others.

Auerbach thus does not look for textual traces – anecdotes – that reveal some gap between the work and the world, some sense of tension between life experience and the description of that experience. He is not interested in the ineffable or inexpressible, though he is cannily alert to the significance of silence – for example, all that is unsaid in the account in Genesis of the sacrifice of Isaac. For Auerbach what is unsaid in Genesis is not a sign of tension, a crisis or breakdown in representation, but rather one of the great resources of this particular mode of representation (distinct, as he claims, from the very different resources of Homeric narration). Similarly, Auerbach does not seize on textual traces that disclose some anomaly in the work, something that is not assimilable to the larger conscious design of the author or the dominant values of the period. What principally interests Auerbach, what draws him and what he is brilliant at locating, are moments of representational plenitude: moments in which a cul-ture's apprehension of reality, its experience of reality, and its representation of reality converge.

Auerbach does not believe that there was a single ideal form for this conver-gence.[11] Rather, *Mimesis* begins with two distinct models, equally prestigious, capacious, brilliant. To be sure, as we have seen, Dante's *Comedy* draws upon Christian figural faith to integrate the two, but the integration collapses, in Auerbach's view, under the very weight of its success, and even Dante's genius could not disclose a stable common ground where the classical and biblical modes could meet. On the contrary, Auerbach observes, for example, that the jealousy over election and the promise of blessing that undermines the peace of daily life in the house, in the fields, and among the flocks in the Bible "would be utterly incomprehensible to the Homeric heroes" (p. 22), while we may assume that the patriarchs would be comparably baffled by Odysseus's "reality."

What does it mean that Auerbach and his readers are not similarly baffled and that they do not have to choose one or the other type? It must in some sense mean a loss of the worlds in which these works were originally created: neither the *Odyssey* nor the Bible can make the claim upon us that they must have made on their earliest readers and hearers. But though Auerbach treats texts as inte-grally bound up with the cultures in which they were produced – that is the nature of his own "atmospheric Historism" – he does not assume that these texts could only be read, in the fullest and richest sense, when they were first written.[12] An awareness that there are alternative modes for the representation of reality actually works to heighten the richness of our understanding: we can see features of the Bible that would be virtually impossible to detect did we not know the *Odyssey*. Moreover, *Mimesis* is written with something like figural faith, faith that these great texts are in effect addressed to us and that it is at once our obligation and our pleasure to open and read them. In a dark time Petrarch in desperation wrote letters to the great figures of the past. Auerbach was writing in a still darker time: with a war raging whose outcome was by no means certain and an enemy that would have consigned him to the gas chambers. For Auerbach to read the Western literary canon as a series of letters that the past had sent to him was an act of civility in a vicious world. And his informed appreciation of multiple styles bespeaks a kind of cultural catholicity, an openness to alternative ways of responding to the world.

At the same time, there are distinct limits to what Auerbach could comfortably accept. Ironically, perhaps, it was the texts of his own contemporaries, the letters sent from closest to home, that seemed to him difficult to incorporate in the great capacious vision of literary representation. He responded with some dismay to the modernist attack on representation, to the fascination with distortion, brokenness, failure, and the void. He could find in masterpieces by Proust, Joyce, and Woolf a version of what shaped his study: "confidence that in any random fragment plucked from the course of a life at any time the totality of its fate is contained and can be portrayed" (p. 547). But this confidence was now turned away from the solid exterior world – the material existence that always seemed to him essential to a robust realism – and toward the inward reaches of the psyche. Similarly, he could find in literary modernism the wide range of alternate motifs for the representation of reality that his own philological studies had embraced and illuminated, but these motifs were now intertwined uneasily within single works. That is, Auerbach discovered in the literature of his own time the very "multiple consciousness" that his own work as a critic had brilliantly cultivated, but his encounter with this consciousness was deeply unnerving. *Mimesis* is one of the great literary critical exhibitions in our century of one mind's capacity to grasp "multiple and multivalent reflections of consciousness" (p. 551). How better to describe the power to respond with the deepest sympathetic intelligence to the *Odyssey* and the Bible, Arthurian romance and Shakespearean history, the *Decameron* and *Manon Lescaut*? But the grasp is sequential, a museum effect in which one passes serenely from room to room, each organized neatly by period. Faced with Joyce or Woolf, Auerbach senses in the modern artist's simultaneous grasp of conflicting and/or noncontiguous representation systems something close to nihilistic despair: "We not infrequently find a turning away from the practical will to live," he writes about modern fiction, "or delight in portraying it under its most brutal forms" or "a vague and hopeless sadness" (p. 551).

Mimesis closes with a poignant blend of personal melancholy and impersonal, curiously sour hope. Auerbach sees the murderous violence unleashed in his world as the expression of what he calls, in almost comic understatement, "a crisis of adjustment" to the terrifying acceleration of change in modern existence. This change has forced together into close conjunction peoples, ideas, and forms of existence that had never before been compelled to acknowledge one other's existence, let alone interact. One obvious consequence is armed conflict; less obvious, but crucial in relation to Auerbach's study, is the damage, probably fatal, to the "clearly formulable and recognized community of thought and feeling" upon which any given literary representation of reality had over the centuries been constructed. It is easy to assimilate such a reflection to our own widespread sense of the homogenizing power of certain international technologies and corporate symbols, but in fact Auerbach was thinking about what looked rather like nativist movements, movements that at first glance seemed to appeal to an all too "clearly formulable and recognized community of thought and feeling." But it is precisely here, in what appear to be strident celebrations of cultural particularity, that Auerbach in the late 1930s finds a devastating loss of the individuality, the subtle particularity, of the spirit of representation. In a letter sent from Istanbul to Walter Benjamin, Auerbach reflects on what he calls the "fanatically anti-traditional nationalism" of Kemal Atatürk, "nationalism in the extreme accompanied by the simultaneous destruction of the historical national character."[13] What he witnessed in Turkey seemed to Auerbach a particularly vivid example of what was happening, partially disguised, in countries like Germany, Italy, and Russia: "It is becoming increasingly clear to me," he writes, "that the present international situation is nothing but a ruse of providence, designed to lead us along a bloody and tortuous path to an International of triviality and a culture of Esperanto" (p. 82).

It was to this "ruse of providence" that modern writers, Auerbach understands, were responding. The randomness, the dissolution, the fragmenting of consciousness, the multiplicity of perspectives in modern fiction are, in Auerbach's view, direct expressions of contemporary reality. They are also, he suggests, attempts – by embracing the random, the quotidian, the inward, and the common – to get beyond "the controversial and unstable orders over which men fight and despair" (p. 552). Auerbach had every reason to hope passionately for the resolution of conflict through the lessening of differences between distinct ways of life and forms of thought. But the simple solution toward which he thought the world was tending – "a common life of mankind on earth" – gave him pause: "Perhaps it will be too simple," he writes at the close of his book, "to please those who, despite all its dangers and catastrophes, admire and love our epoch for the sake of its abundance of life and the incomparable historical vantage point which it affords." But, he concludes with a shrug, "they are few in number, and probably they will not live to see much more than the first forewarnings of the approaching unification and simplification" (p. 553).

For Auerbach, surveying European literature from his "incomparable historical vantage point," there was a succession of living monuments to the power of representation, each bound up in the conditions of its time and place, each existentially exigent. The new historicists who adopted his method did not necessarily embrace his vision: they were less inclined to share his distaste for leveling, less suspicious of modernism, and less convinced that the world was tending toward the erasure of difference. If they were also for the most part vastly less learned than Auerbach – he seems indeed from this distance like one of the philological giants who lived before the Flood – they were at the same time grappling with texts that *Mimesis* had confidently ignored or consigned to the margins. We refer not only to works by women – it is notable that Virginia Woolf is virtually the only female author accorded sustained attention in Auerbach's book, and then as an emblem of dissolution and decadence – but also to texts that did not seem to qualify for inclusion in the category of "literature," a category that, like "realism," Auerbach carefully avoided defining. It is clear that the term "literature" functions in part as an honorific; new historicists did not so much doubt the splendors of the monuments as suspect the exclusiveness of the honor roll. For what was the point of claiming, as Auerbach did, the cultural significance of a particular representational practice if that significance did not extend beyond the work in question, that is, if one could not find comparable texts elsewhere? Was not the representation of reality a crucial social and political phenomenon, as well as an aesthetic one? Why did the imagination seem to belong, in Auerbach's view, to such a small community of makers? And why (after the Bible) were the texts almost entirely literary, or, rather, why was the category of the literary left so undisturbed by a text on "the representation of reality"? Auerbach would appeal to a particular ideology to explicate the representational strategies manifested in one of his textual fragments – Christian creaturalism for Montaigne, for example – but what was the relation between Montaigne's unique talent and the surrounding culture that he represented and upon which he drew? Where was the historical reality in which Montaigne was so deeply engaged? Where were the violent struggles that gave his tragic sense of the human condition its specificity?

The point for new historicists was not to assemble a large number of comparable texts, as if to prove statistically the rightness of Auerbach's canon. If anything, the urge Auerbach aroused was something else: to see a vast social process, a life-world, through the lens afforded by a particular passage, a few paragraphs apprehended with sufficient passion, alertness, and sympathetic intelligence. In a sense, as Auerbach said of Dante, the very success of *Mimesis*, the extent to which each chapter seemed not merely a piece of literary history but a conjuring of spirits, fractured the very ethos, the tragic, existential weightiness, that the book was meant to uphold. To be sure, we could continue to acknowledge the special character of each author, and yet the individual author's achievement seemed less monumental, less unique, precisely to the extent that this achievement led to the uncovering of a dense textual and material field. And that field no longer seemed to fit securely within traditional period boundaries.

The spectral effect rather was like that so teasingly depicted in Borges's cunning essay "Precursors of Kafka," where texts that otherwise have nothing to do with one another and were written quite independently of one another are revealed, but only after the fact (which is to say, only after Kafka), to be "precursors." But the Borges example is precisely something that would not be allowed by Auerbach – for he wished to assert something about the fundamental coherence and historical integration of the culture that the literary work represented, the integration assumed by traditional schemes of periodization.

But even on these terms – that is, accepting the premise of periodization that Auerbach assumes and that provides the cultural frame for his individual readings – new historicists writing in his wake felt eager to expand the field, to open criticism to a vast number of texts that needed to be "read," to register conflict and dissent. The fact that Auerbach did not feel obliged to read every moment in his text, that he could concentrate on an anecdote and pressure it to reveal a whole system, in principle liberated the critic to look for fragments scattered across a period's entire textual production.

Nonetheless, how would the choice of any particular text be justified? Auerbach could in effect count on canonicity – that, and the limits placed upon him by his wartime isolation as a Jewish exile in Istanbul. If one abandoned canonicity, what was there beyond a completely arbitrary cut? Arbitrariness, the randomness Auerbach noted in modernist novels, was indeed built into the new anecdotal practice: one made good on one's choice by an act of will, or rather by an act of writing, an act of interpretation whose power was measured by its success in captivating readers. If the attention – one's own and that demanded of one's readers – seemed justified, then it was a successful intervention. But that is not the whole truth: for how would the sense of justification be achieved? The answer seems to be by a sense of resonance for other texts, other readings. In large part – at least in the earliest essays of new historicism – the other texts were canonical literary texts: the anecdote worked if it illuminated a major literary work. There is an obvious problem with this procedure: one chose an anecdote – out of the hundreds of thousands of possibilities – because it "sounded like" a passage in Marlowe or Shakespeare, and then achieved a spurious effect of surprise and confirmation when it turned out to sound like Marlowe or Shakespeare.

Why would you not simply bypass the problem and turn directly to Marlowe or Shakespeare? There were several reasons. In part, it was because the canonical authors had begun to seem exhausted, at least for the close readings that Auerbach performed so brilliantly. One could turn away to other, less heavily worked authors – Thomas Middleton or Elizabeth Carew or Mary Sidney (women authors, long neglected, being particularly ripe for new attention). But the trouble is that the procedure itself – pick a passage from a literary text, examine it closely, and show how an entire representational system is disclosed in its narrow compass – had begun to lose some of its force precisely because it assumed the stability of the literary and because it assumed as well a concept of totality or wholeness that had come into question. It was not the canonical authors then that had begun to seem exhausted but the approach to them and the notion of the boundaries of their achievement. What had promised a new access to the real – Auerbach wrote of represented *Wirklichkeit* – had come to seem curiously detached from anything real, absorbed in the formal identification of modes of literary, high-cultural representation organized by traditional period.

The turn to the historical anecdote in literary study promised both an escape from conventional canonicity and a revival of the canon, both a transgression against the domestic and a safe return to it. The anecdote was not merely background: it demanded attention; it threatened indeed to take over the whole enterprise. But it could somehow be turned toward a revivification of a canonical work, provided that the canonical work lent some of its prestige, its self-justifying importance, to the marginal anecdote. And the anecdote satisfied the desire for something outside the literary, something indeed that would challenge the boundaries of the literary. It offered access to the everyday, the place where things are actually done, the sphere of practice that even in its most awkward and inept articulations makes a claim on the truth that is denied to the most eloquent of literary texts. Or rather the anecdote was a way into the "contact zone," the charmed space where the *genius literarius* could be conjured into existence.

NOTES

1 Clifford Geertz, "Thick Description: Toward an Interpretive Theory of Culture," in *The Interpretation of Cultures* (New York: Basic Books, 1973), p. 9.

2 The promise is conveyed, among other means, by such features as the changed typeface (used, in the case of such a long excerpt, instead of quotation marks) and the brackets that denote the writer's scrupulosity in signaling any additions or alterations to what he had originally written in his journal: "The French [the informant said] had only just arrived." Such printing conventions do a considerable amount of work in establishing the particular nature of the piece of writing.

3 Gilbert Ryle, "Thinking and Reflecting" and "The Thinking of Thoughts: What Is 'Le Penseur' Doing?" in *Collected Papers*, vol. 2 of *Collected Essays, 1929–1968* (London: Hutchinson, 1971), pp. 465–96.

4 For a critique, from the standpoint of social science, of Geertz's way of suggesting the vital presence in the cultural texts themselves of their range of meanings, see Mark A. Schneider, *Culture and Enchantment* (Chicago: University of Chicago Press, 1993), pp. 55–82.

5 "Ideology as a Cultural System," in Geertz, *The Interpretation of Cultures*, p. 208.

6 *1 Henry IV*, 3.1.51–3. All citations to Shakespeare are from *The Norton Shakespeare*, ed. Stephen Greenblatt et al. (New York: W. W. Norton & Company, 1997).

7 It is not the case that Flaubert's novel lacks ethnographic interest, but the level of self-conscious mediation is completely different from what we hope to find in a native informant's narrative.

8 Erich Auerbach, *Mimesis: The Representation of Reality in Western Literature*, trans. Willard R. Trask (Princeton: Princeton University Press, 1953), p. 3.

9 The first German edition had one less chapter, but in the English edition Auerbach added a chapter on *Don Quixote*.

10 *Mimesis* puts in the largest possible frame perceptions that had obsessed Auerbach for his entire career and had been articulated both in his 1929 study of Dante, *Dante als Dichter der irdischen Welt*, and his crucially important 1944 essay "Figura."

11 Auerbach does, however, imply at times that European techniques of representation did in fact "advance" toward an ever greater power:

> The inner history of the last thousand years is the history of mankind achieving self-expression: this is what philology, a historicist discipline, treats. This history contains the records of man's mighty, adventurous advance to a consciousness of his human condition and to the realization of his given potential: and this advance, whose final goal (even in its wholly fragmentary present form) was barely imaginable for a long time, still seems to have proceeded as if according to a plan, in spite of its twisted course.

In "Philology and *Weltliteratur*," trans. Marie and Edward Said, *Centennial Review* (1969): 5.

12   See discussion of this point in Luiz Costa Lima, *The Dark Side of Reason: Fictionality and Power*, trans. Paulo Henriques Britto (Stanford: Stanford University Press, 1992), pp. 483–4.

13   Karlheinz Barck, "Walter Benjamin and Erich Auerbach: Fragments of a Correspondence," *Diacritics* 22 (1992): 82.

Part II

RENAISSANCE STUDIES

4

THE WOUND IN THE WALL

In the Palazzo Ducale in Urbino there is a very large altarpiece by the Flemish painter Joos van Gent of the *Communion of the Apostles*. In a subject relatively common in Byzantine art but unusual in Western painting, Jesus himself administers the holy bread to his kneeling disciples. Though executed on a grand scale, the altarpiece is not likely to strike modern viewers as a particularly memorable work of art. The figures are rather stiff, in the manner of Joos van Gent's teacher, Hugo van der Goes, but without van der Goes's intensity: nothing in the dutiful attitude of the disciples suggests passionate love or awe, while Jesus keeps an oddly formal distance even as he reaches out with his right hand to place the wafer, held delicately between thumb and forefinger, in the mouth of the first communicant. This distance extends to the viewer, who has full access to the scene, without the illusion of being drawn into it or bearing witness to it.[1] Instead of engendering either emotional intensity or mystical remoteness, charismatic presence or sacred awe, the painting makes a doctrinal statement: the narrative of the Last Supper has been almost entirely absorbed into institutional ritual. A table, covered with a white cloth, must allude to the meal Jesus shared with the disciples, but the dishes and food have all but disappeared, leaving only a jeweled chalice and a small heap of holy wafers on the left and, on the right, two pieces of risen bread, a saltcellar, and a bottle of water. The domestic space in which the meal must have taken place has likewise vanished; the table is located in a Romanesque church. Holding a paten in one hand and a wafer of unleavened bread in the other, Jesus stands rather woodenly in front of the table, which has in effect been transformed into an altar, with the spotless tablecloth serving as the "corporale," the cloth spread for the wafers, or any fragments of wafers, to rest on. Augustine believed that when Jesus said, "This is my body," he carried himself in his own hands.[2] Joos van Gent's representation of this unutterably strange moment transforms it into a formal religious service. Assisted by Saint John, who serves as altar boy, Jesus is a priest standing in the crossing of the transept, with the apse behind him, celebrating the Mass.

This chapter was first published in *Practicing New Historicism* (2000, pp. 75–109).

PLATE 1 Joos van Gent (c. 1460/80). *Communion of the Apostles*. Galleria Nazionale delle Marche, Urbino, Italy. Photograph: SCALA, Florence.

This institutionalization of the sacred story is linked, it would appear, with the group of five figures toward the back right, behind the kneeling disciples and the table. Immediately identifiable in this group is the hawk-nosed profile of Federico da Montefeltro, duke of Urbino and patron of the Confraternity of Corpus Domini that commissioned the altarpiece. More than thirty years ago, in an article in *Art Bulletin*, the art historian Marilyn Lavin argued that the turbaned, bearded figure toward whom the duke is gesturing is an ambassador from the Persian court, a Jewish doctor named Isaac, who had come to Italy in 1472 to negotiate on behalf of his master, Uzun Hasan, an alliance against the rival Muslim power, the Turks. Unexpectedly, when in Rome, the ambassador Isaac had been converted to the Catholic faith and had taken the name Sixtus, after the reigning pope, Sixtus IV.[3] If Lavin is correct, this extraordinary event – the conversion of the Jewish representative of a Muslim potentate – is commemorated in Joos van Gent's painting, which may allude to a visit by the ambassador to the court of Urbino. The risen bread and salt on the table in front of Sixtus né Isaac would allude to the Jewish sacrificial meal in which they are essential elements (see Leviticus 2:13 and 24:5–9). This meal has been at once fulfilled and displaced by the Lord's Supper, the sacrificial mystery in which the converted Jew, no longer the enemy of the faith, can now participate.

But the Jew's participation is more implied than represented, more potential than event. The ambassador, the duke, and the others grouped around them are not depicted as waiting with the disciples to receive the Host directly from Jesus. They are witnesses, privileged onlookers of the sacred scene. If the story of the ambassador's conversion is part of the altarpiece's background and occasion, it is not in any sense narrated. Narrative of any kind has been stilled, even the so-called institution narrative – the story of the origin of the Eucharist – that is ostensibly commemorated. For the Gospel recounting of Jesus' Last Supper, a story about particular people at a particular place and time, is of course historically incompatible with the painting's ecclesiastical setting. The confounding of temporal logic is a central element in Christian thought and representation, closely bound up with the way in which Christianity had understood its relation to the Judaism it appropriated and hoped to supplant.[4] "Abraham and other holy fathers did eat" Christ, writes archbishop Cranmer, echoing centuries of typological speculation, "many years before he was incarnated and born."[5] Similarly, in Joos van Gent's panel, time is twisted back upon itself, so that in this case, end and origin meet and touch, with Jesus depicted as a priest performing an institutional ritual not fully established until the thirteenth century when the Feast of Corpus Domini became an official part of the Church calendar. There is, Lavin observes, "an allusion to a narrative dining scene, the straw-covered flask on the floor in the left foreground" (p. 13), but it leans at the extreme margin of the painting's world, an isolated, humble trace of an unrepresented event. The altarpiece has no interest in imagining or dramatizing the supper described in the synoptic Gospels; it wishes to represent not History but Truth.

Joos van Gent's altarpiece is art in the service of faith, the faith of a community that built and maintained magnificent churches of the kind depicted on his panel; established cults to honor local saints; housed precious relics; sponsored Corpus Christi processions adorned with banners, garlands, and lights; created confraternities to carry the Eucharist to the sick and dying. And it is at the same time art in the service of doctrine. Its point is theological: the Roman Catholic Mass is not an institutional interpretation or ritualized recollection of the Last Supper; it *is* the Last Supper, constantly renewed through the Christlike offices of the priesthood. The painting's representational mode is doctrinal formalism; that is, it expresses in structural rather than narrative terms the ideological consensus of a dominant institution, a ruling class, or a hegemonic elite. Doctrinal formalism rarely eschews narrative altogether. Thus somewhere "behind" the figures at the rear of the painting are histories that can be reconstructed. These histories could conceivably extend into the distant past, to the figure of a Jew in Palestine who may or may not have sat at a Passover Seder and likened himself to the matzoth. For the original viewers of Joos van Gent's altarpiece, they would have certainly included not only the spectacular conversion of Uzun Hasan's emissary, but also, as Lavin observes, a wave of anti-Semitic agitation in Italy in the 1460s largely motivated by the increasing power and success of Jewish moneylenders, who posed, or were thought to pose, an economic threat to local merchants. The agitation was instigated or at the least greatly fanned by the Franciscans. The Minorite friars' impassioned preaching against Jewish usury and indeed against the very existence of Jews was a key element in their campaign for religious renewal. This renewal in turn was linked with the Monte di Pietà, an institutional strategy for combating the power of Jewish bankers. The no-interest loans offered by the Monte di Pietà were associated with the Confraternity of the Corpus Domini, which, let us recall, commissioned the altarpiece.[6] In the wake of Franciscan sermons, Jews were in extreme danger; many were beaten and killed by mobs, while others were protected by papal officials and civic leaders anxious to avoid popular riots and disorder.[7]

But Joos van Gent does not directly narrate any of these dramatic events. Rather, insofar as it figures in the painting at all, the history at which we have briefly glanced is very indirectly evoked by placing the ambassador Isaac, if that indeed is whom the bearded figure depicts, near the symbols of the old Jewish sacrifice and by setting him against the figure of Judas, wrapped in a prayer shawl and clutching his bag of silver at the left. The figures may thus be responding indirectly to contemporary debates about the fate of the Jews by suggesting that at least some Jews may be saved through conversion, but the response, if it is one, does not assume the form of a story. Narrative presses closer to representation in the painting's principal subject, Jesus feeding his disciples. The scene alludes to the Gospel story:

> And as they were eating, Jesus took bread, and blessed it, and brake it, and gave it to the disciples, and said, "Take, eat; this is my body." And he took the cup, and gave thanks, and gave it to them, saying, "Drink ye all of it; For this is my blood of the new testament, which is shed for many for the remission of sins." (Matthew 26: 26–8)[8]

But, as we have remarked, the placement of this scene in a church and the representation of the supper as a Mass moves the image away from narrative and toward theology. The temporal unfolding of an action, with a beginning, middle, and end, is absorbed into the representation of a timeless ritual that makes manifest what Paul in the Epistle to the Hebrews formulated as "the Eternal Priesthood of Christ."[9]

Doctrinal formalism then reduces the presence and weight of the stories to which it alludes, as if it had something to lose by history, as if any determinate location and time would invalidate its claim to eternal efficacy, as if any record of struggle and process and change would necessarily threaten its universal validity. The allusions, however, offer a standing invitation to the viewer to recover and interpret those narratives that are not directly represented but are half hidden in the "background," and for centuries connoisseurs, art historians, and literary critics encountering doctrinal forms have accepted this invitation. They have turned the elements of synchronic structure back into diachronic history, translating representations of eternal truth into a tangle of likely stories: the humble flask can be made to conjure up the supper recounted in the Gospel; there is "every possibility" that the turbaned, bearded figure is Sixtus né Isaac, who might well have visited Urbino on his way from Rome to Venice ("roughly after September 12, 1472 and before January 28, 1473"[10]); Federico da Montefeltro touches the convert's arm in order to give him personal encouragement to persevere in his new faith; the courtier to Federico's left who seems to be counting on his fingers is enumerating arguments for Christianity's superiority to Judaism; the bread and the salt on the table probably refer to the Jewish sacrificial meal; and so forth.[11]

We assume, perhaps incorrectly, that contemporaries read such ceremonial symbols effortlessly – what is laborious research for us, the argument goes, was life experience for them – but even they would have viewed certain figures, such as the man with the turban and beard, through a veil of rumor, speculation, and uncertainty. (There is no probability of an actual portrait likeness, since Joos van Gent's time in Urbino did not correspond to the time of the ambassador Isaac's presumed visit, and the figure he depicts is borrowed, as Lavin shows, from a painting by Dirk Bouts.) Nor was sacred history a secure and uncontested possession. After all, the Gospel accounts of the Last Supper are themselves various, and the more knowledgeable the viewers, the more mindful they would have been of the long history of doctrinal dispute over their meaning. That dispute, centering on the interpretation of Jesus' words "This is my body," is not directly figured in the panel, but it lurks behind any representation of the Eucharist, all the more one that includes the figure of a Jewish convert. If Joos van Gent's panel works to contain the potentially disruptive energies of history – *excluding* conflict, *relegating* contemporary events to its background, and *marginalizing* narrative – it cannot and does not eliminate history altogether. Indeed its very exclusions, relegations, and marginalizations constitute, as we have seen, a network of allusions that stimulate a rich variety of historical speculations.

Confronted by doctrinal formalism in objects and texts, cultural historians have eagerly tracked down the allusions, but they have seldom reflected on the fact that their own activity is both stimulated by the exclusions that structure the works they study and in tension with these exclusions. Interpretive practice should, we believe, keep this paradoxical relationship to the work in mind, acknowledging the strange blend of identification and aggression, "reading with" and "reading against," that motivates historical analysis. If Joos van Gent's painting relegates its contemporary figures (Federico da Montefeltro, Sixtus né Isaac, et al.) to the background, interpretation pulls them toward the front and center; if it makes those contemporaries witnesses to a sacred ritual in which they do not themselves participate, interpretation insists that they are in fact the crucial participants; if the altarpiece strives to represent doctrinal order by lifting recognizable individuals into a realm of timeless communion, where their historical particularity no longer counts and is, like the wafer's materiality, a mere appearance and accident, then interpretation sets itself against this striving and pulls them back toward the time-bound and material world. The interpreter behaves in this regard like Castiglione's Emilia Pia – to recall another great work from Renaissance Urbino – who listens with mingled delight and skepticism to Cardinal Bembo's ecstatic hymn to the transcendent power of divine love. "Take care, messer Pietro," she replies, tugging at the hem of his robe, "that with these thoughts your soul, too, does not forsake your body."[12]

This is not the place for a full-scale interpretation of Joos van Gent's painting, nor are we equipped to attempt one. But we can use our response as a model for the interpretive practice to which we aspire. Thus, in looking at the painting, we observe that it is the site of a struggle between doctrinal and historical impulses, a struggle in which our own interpretive choices will be implicated. We do not, therefore, take either doctrinal formalism or historical narrative on its own terms. We tend to pull away from the exposition of abstract doctrine, from the explication of beliefs or the analysis of institutional structures – though some attempt at exposition, explication, and institutional analysis is necessary – and attempt to recover repressed, subordinated, or forgotten narratives. We ask not only what stories were occluded, but also how they have been concealed from view in order to facilitate the elaboration of a closed system. But we also tend to pull away from straightforward retelling of the story and toward the recovery of occulted or implicit doctrine. Here the implication is that the story, however pleasurable or absorbing, is shoring up ideological propositions or confirming the legitimacy of institutional arrangements. What is the doctrinal point, for example, of including the image of Sixtus né Isaac among the observers of the *Communion of the Apostles* and what institutional need does his marginalized presence meet? By insisting on the claims or the ruses of doctrine, we attempt to break the spell of historical narration – its "once upon a time" siren song – even as we attempt to reconstruct a half-effaced history.

But our interpretation should acknowledge more than the tension between doctrine and story both in the painting and in our own account of it. We must also recognize that the tension in Joos van Gent's altarpiece involves the status of likenesses, of icons, themselves. That status is most clearly at issue in the figures of the young woman and child that may be glimpsed between the heads of Federico and the ambassador. In part, but only in part, because of some deterioration in the condition of the painting, the nature of these figures is unclear: are they people standing in a niche, or polychrome sculptures, or figures on a painted panel? Since the child is crowned and the woman, tenderly declining her head toward his, is depicted only to the waist, they give the initial appearance of the Virgin and child in a painting, an icon whose familiar unreality in this ecclesiastical setting would confirm by contrast the implicit assertion that the other figures – including Jesus and the apostles as well as the duke of Urbino and his entourage – are present, as it were, in the flesh. But if this is an icon, painting, or statue, there is no devotional apparatus, no altar, no frame, no formal setting-off of this image from its surroundings. The woman and child appear rather to be figures like the others, only half hidden in the background. Once again, art historians – responsive to allusion, inclined to pull background figures into the foreground, and determined to reintroduce history onto the scene of doctrine – have proposed that the child is Prince Guidobaldo, the cherished son given to Federico da Montefeltro by his wife Battista Sforza after eight daughters. Poor Battista had offered her life in exchange for divine assistance in producing a male heir; six months after his birth, she was dead, aged twenty-six. Since Battista died the year before the altarpiece was painted, the simply dressed woman holding the child has been identified in several studies as a nursemaid, but Lavin suggests plausibly enough that she is Battista Sforza herself, her modest dress reflecting the Franciscan robes in which at her request she was buried. She is present then not in the flesh but in the spirit, for painting has the power to represent what no longer exists or what never existed at all – and in the spirit mother and child can be reunited. The pair, so charged with hope and loss and sacrifice, can in turn be assimilated to the Virgin and child. The figures then are at once portrait and memorial, sacred icon and secular representation, consoling sign of presence and mournful acknowledgment of absence.

The complex issues that gather around these figures are related to the larger questions about the status of memorial representation and presence that inhere in the doctrine of the Eucharist. The *painting* of this particular doctrine is in tension with its doctrinal point – that one should learn to look with the eyes of faith past appearances to a reality invisible to the senses – because it is, after all, a painting, an image that appeals to the senses even as it tries to limit the authority of their

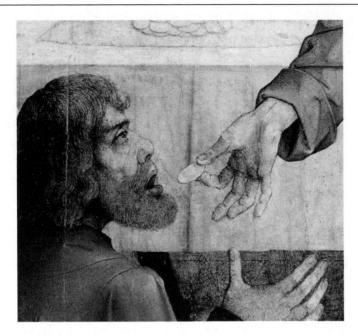

PLATE 2   The Host, Jesus' body, between the fingers of Jesus. Joos van Gent (*c.* 1460/80). *Communion of the Apostles* (detail). Galleria Nazionale delle Marche, Urbino, Italy. Photograph: SCALA, Florence.

testimony. Thus there is a fundamental difference between the painting's other figures – including the woman and child – and the Host that Jesus administers. Despite their stiffness, the figures are recognizable as likenesses, but the Host, far from looking like the body of Christ, which the doctrine affirms it *is*, does not even look like the bread of the Gospel story or, for that matter, the bread in the small loaves on the table. Rather, the painting's representation of the specially prepared and consecrated wheaten disc under whose accidents that body supposedly exists and is eaten is a small blank in the center of the composition. Indeed, though its elliptical shape signifies by the logic of perspective a foreshortened disc, this blank, this dab of white in the space between the thumb and index finger of the painted Savior, is by doctrinal logic less a representation than a space where visual representation is emphatically refusing to happen.

To be sure, Joos van Gent's painting is atypical in this regard; most doctrine is not necessarily or essentially at war with iconicity, and hence the visual representation of doctrine is not always so deeply paradoxical. Nevertheless, even representations that signify within systems of thought far more amenable to the idea of representation demonstrate the impossibility of a complete congruence between instantiation and idea. We must be alert to this incongruity, bringing to light the complex tension in traditional societies between doctrine and historical narrative and the still more widespread tension between representation and meaning. Disclosing and analyzing these tensions not only reveals ideological contradictions, but also traces the paths along which representational energies and historical motivations flow. The tension between doctrine and iconicity, tenor and vehicle, signified and signifier is not the consummation of new historicist analysis but its starting point.

In the *Communion of the Apostles*, the portion of the Urbino altarpiece we have discussed thus far, both narrative and image are tautly controlled by doctrine. Their energies, however, do not seem similarly constrained in the altarpiece's separate predella, the long rectangular panel situated beneath the main panel. Those things at the margins of doctrine in Joos van Gent's conception – the pleasures of story and vividness – have been accommodated directly beneath it. A predella often differs in style as well as scale from the panel beneath which it is placed, though this is an extreme case both because Joos van Gent's painting is huge, its figures just under life-size, and because the predella is by a different artist from a different culture, the Italian Paolo Uccello. We do not know why the altarpiece, begun by Uccello, was finished by Joos van Gent,[13] but it is at least possible that the features in the main panel on which we have been concentrating are responses – answers or solutions – to problems raised by the extraordinary but deeply disturbing predella. Far from attempting to arrest or constrain narrative energy, Uccello's predella tells a story in six episodes, proceeding from left to right and divided by painted columns. In the first, a woman in a shop stands at a counter and holds out a small white round object, vividly highlighted against a black background, to a shopkeeper. In the second, the shopkeeper, standing with his wife and two children, looks with astonishment at a shallow pan that is cooking over a fire in the fireplace toward the back of the room. The pan is overflowing with a red liquid that runs along the floor. Outside, a group of soldiers are beating at the door and trying to enter. The third scene shows a procession in which a figure in a papal tiara, with priests and citizens, is walking toward the altar of a church. In the fourth scene, the woman from the first episode is about to be hanged by soldiers. She and the soldiers look up and see an angel making a gesture above her head. In the fifth scene the shopkeeper, his wife, and children are tied to a single stake in what appears to be a cauldron and burned to death. Finally, in the sixth scene, the woman, now clad in a red robe and dead or near death, is lying on a litter. Two angels are at her head; two devils are pulling at her feet.

These scenes evidently recount one of the legends of miraculous Hosts, legends that circulated in substantial numbers from the thirteenth century onward. Typically, a desecration of the Host by an enemy of the faith is followed by spectacular, incontrovertible proof of the Real Presence of Christ under the accidents of bread and wine. The most famous of these eucharistic miracles was one that supposedly occurred in Paris in 1290, and it is to this that Uccello's panel seems to refer. The story, circulated in sermons, chronicles, miracle plays, and visual images, is of a Jew who purchases a consecrated Host in order at once to profane it and to expose the fraudulence of the doctrine – "Are not these Christians fools to believe in this Host?"[14] But when he stabs the wafer and then attempts to boil it, it bleeds and returns to the form of flesh, whereupon (depending on the version) the Jew either converts or is burned to death.

Obviously, the predella's story is relevant to the main panel: both are concerned with the mystery of the Eucharist, both allude to the doctrine of the Real

Presence – the actual body and blood of Christ in the ritual of the Mass – and both establish the meaning of the Christian symbol in relation to the figure of the Jew. But if Joos van Gent's panel is in the mode of doctrinal formalism, Uccello's predella is in the very different mode of legendary narrative. There is doctrine "behind" Uccello's represented actions, as there is story "behind" Joos van Gent's represented ritual, but the predella's concern is with events unfolding in time – with actions and their consequences – rather than with eternal structures and the formal rituals consecrated to the manifestations of these structures. The predella does not relate any of the histories, recondite or common, biblical or contemporary, alluded to and marginalized in the main panel; rather it tells a miraculous legend of the sort that mediated between everyday understanding and abstruse doctrine. The doctrine of the Eternal Priesthood of Christ is esoteric; as we have remarked, though representations of the Last Supper are common, the scene of Christ holding the wafer in which he himself is bodily present is relatively rare in Western art,[15] probably because it brings uncomfortably close to the surface certain recurrent objections to orthodox eucharistic theology. Those objections are more commonsensical than esoteric: their characteristic substance and tone are conveyed by the English Protestant John Frith, burned at the stake for heresy in 1533. Christ's body, Frith writes,

> was natural and not phantasticall, but had the qualyties of an other body in all thynges saue synne, nether was it more possible for that naturall body so beyng mortal and not gloryfied to be in dyuers places at once, then for myne. So that when we heare these wordes spoken, this is my body, and se that they were spoken before his body was gloryfied, knowyng also that a natural body vngloryfied can not be in many places at once, and that yf these wordes were vnderstanden as they sounde he shuld haue ben at ye least in .xii. or .xiii. places at once in his Disciples mouthes, and syttyng at the table with them, It causeth vs to loke better vpon it, and so to saerch out the pure vnderstandyng.[16]

Catholic theologians had subtle answers to these objections, of course, but they were answers whose sophisticated intellectual acrobatics tended to confirm the wisdom of avoiding the frequent depiction of a scene whose full doctrinal meaning could only have been the possession of the clerical elite and that could inadvertently raise doubts about the flesh-and-blood presence of Christ in the baked wafer.[17] The story in the predella, by contrast, concretized doctrine (this is what the Real Presence means; this is ocular proof of the mystery; this is the resolution of all doubt) and set people in motion. The teaching must have seemed effective: certain elements of the elite made a substantial effort to ensure the story's wide diffusion, particularly in the service of heightening piety and of inciting popular hatred, beating, and massacres of the Jews.

Distinct representational modes thus organize the major and minor panels of the altarpiece. The upper panel's mode is primarily doctrinal. It is principally interested not in telling a story but in expressing a set of abstract ideas and relations. It pulls away from the particular and the time-bound and toward the institutional and the structural. It is associated with high culture, with intellectual and administrative elites, and with the institutional apparatuses in which these

PLATE 3   Jewish shopkeeper purchases the consecrated Host. Paolo Uccello (1397–1475). *Profanation of the Host*. Palazzo Ducale, Urbino, Italy. Photograph: SCALA, Florence.

PLATE 4   The miracle of the bleeding Host. Paolo Uccello (1397–1475). *Profanation of the Host*. Palazzo Ducale, Urbino, Italy. Photograph: SCALA, Florence.

elites participate. The lower panel's mode is legendary narrative. Such narrative is by no means innocent of doctrine, but it can pass more readily – and in both directions – between high culture and low, elite and popular. It is concerned with events that take place in a particular sequence. Where the doctrinal image focuses on a single central figure around whom the others are grouped in a circle, the narrative is broken into discrete units, a succession of episodes conspicuously detached from one another and arranged in a set order. Meaning

PLATE 5 The Host is returned to the altar. Paolo Uccello (1397–1475). *Profanation of the Host.* Palazzo Ducale, Urbino, Italy. Photograph: SCALA, Florence.

does not radiate out from a sacred center but is established through a linear visual progress.

The doctrinal mode does not insist that the represented action took place as depicted; on the contrary, it collapses the future into the past, so that the Communion of the apostles can be celebrated in the cathedral that could not yet exist at the time of the historical Jesus. This seeing of the future in the past resembles what in grammar is called the future perfect tense – the future is conceived as having already happened – but it is still closer to what we might call the present perfect tense: when this happened long ago, the future was already present, and that future is now. Hence Joos van Gent can introduce Federico da Montefeltro and his contemporaries as witnesses to the sacred scene. The episodes in the narrative mode by contrast lay claim to the representation of actual events, events involving a particular set of agents at a given place and time (though the details – the names, the dates, and so forth – may be given with greater or lesser specificity). The legend lays emphasis on event rather than institution, on process rather than structure.

But the modal energies that characterize the separate works also circulate between them. As we have already noted, Joos van Gent's panel has traces of many stories. And there are signs of the institutional in Uccello's predella: in one of the episodes the papal procession moves toward an altar situated in a domed apse; in another, the body of the Christian woman is laid out in front of a similar structure. But these are more allusions than full representations: in both instances, only the apse is present; where the rest of the church should be, we see a landscape. Institutional containment, so dominant in the main panel, gives way to movement through space and (by way of the flowering of the trees in the successive glimpses of the landscape) time. What matters most are the temporally unfolding events, not

PLATE 6   Angel intervenes in hanging of guilty woman. Paolo Uccello (1397–1475). *Profanation of the Host.* Palazzo Ducale, Urbino, Italy. Photograph: SCALA, Florence.

the structures in which those events transpire. Indeed, as we will see, the narrative progress depends upon a literal tear or rupture in one of these structures.

As the idea of circulation implies, there is no fixed relation between doctrine and legend, no set order and hence no a priori determination of precedence or causality. Uccello's Urbino predella was commissioned and painted before Joos van Gent's main panel: in this case, then, the narrative sequence preceded the doctrinal representation, a representation that seems to have been designed to correspond with it. The mystical, timeless *Communion of the Apostles* sits on top of the story of Jewish profanation, just as some bleeding Host shrines of the Middle Ages were built on the sites where Jews had allegedly desecrated the Eucharist.[18] But the story of the profanation is itself built upon doctrine, unless, that is, one were actually inclined to *believe* that a Parisian Jew bought a Host in order to put it to the test – a perilous submission to narrative charm that would altogether collapse the distinction between history and legend. And even if one were so inclined, one would nevertheless be drawn to concede, if not that the doctrine *produced* the events, then that the events as depicted fulfilled and manifested a doctrinal design. The point here is not only that in some cases narrative precedes doctrine and in other cases doctrine precedes narrative, but also that any determination of precedence is necessarily local and limited.

Our discussion of Joos van Gent's painting deployed a set of opposed terms:

doctrinal formalism	historical narrative
synchrony	diachrony
universal truth	local contingency
structure	process
substantial identity	accidental likeness

PLATE 7   Execution of Jewish family. Paolo Uccello (1397–1475). *Profanation of the Host.* Palazzo Ducale, Urbino, Italy. Photograph: SCALA, Florence.

These oppositions are obviously closely connected to the relation between the main panel and the predella, a relation we have characterized as that between doctrinal formalism and legendary narrative. It is important to emphasize that history and legend are not the same, that they have distinct structures, functions, institutional affiliations, ways of establishing authenticity, and long-term trajectories.[19] But the narrative mode that they share – that links the historical figure of Sixtus né Isaac above and the legendary Jewish violator of the Host below – unsettles and destabilizes this distinction, as indeed the complex thematic circulation between main panel and predella destabilizes all of the binary oppositions. It is not that the distinctions are useless: on the contrary, it is impossible to get an analytical purchase without them. But they are always contingent, and if we treat them as stable givens, we risk missing the actual work of cultural objects. We know that the subject of Joos van Gent's panel is rare in Western art and that the story depicted in Uccello's predella is repeated in sermons, miracle plays, poems, stained-glass windows, woodcuts, and the like. Hence it is perfectly reasonable to characterize them in terms of elite and popular spheres of culture. But eucharistic piety is at the heart not only of abstruse theological doctrine but also of popular religion in the fifteenth century. It is misleading to treat the subject of the altarpiece, however rare, as divorced from a community whose solidarity was to a considerable extent built around the ritual of the Mass. And if there is ample evidence in Italy and elsewhere of popular anti-Semitism in the period, it nonetheless is misleading to suggest that anti-Semitism welled up from the people, as if it only found its origin and expression among the unlettered.[20] Anti-Semitism was repeatedly instigated and manipulated from above and could

PLATE 8   Angels and devils fight over body of woman. Paolo Uccello (1397–1475). *Profanation of the Host*. Palazzo Ducale, Urbino, Italy. Photograph: SCALA, Florence.

be used to make complex doctrinal points: we need look no further than the connection between the perfidious Jewish merchant in Uccello's predella and the figure of Judas lurking at the left of Joos van Gent's *Communion of the Apostles*.

The connection should not obscure an important difference in the conception of Jews in the main panel and in the predella. In Uccello's scenes, the fate of the soul of the Christian woman who sells the Host is ambiguous. Angels and devils seem to be struggling over her on her deathbed, and the outcome was evidently sufficiently unclear to drive an early viewer to attempt to intervene on her behalf: someone has carefully scratched the paint off the devils, as if in the hope of driving them away. But there is no ambiguity about the fate of the Jews. Though the desecration legends often ended in the conversion to Christianity of the wife and children of the wicked Jew who was executed, Uccello makes no such distinction: in his vision, not only the merchant but also his wife and children are burned at the stake. In the *Communion of the Apostles*, by contrast, Judas is set over against the figure of the converted Jew. We have in effect contrasting visions of Jewishness: in Uccello's narration it seems inseparable from the bodies of the Jews, so that they must all be destroyed; in Joos van Gent's doctrinal image, Jewishness can be discarded as an accident, and the substance – the soul – of the Jew redeemed. Though the latter was the Church's official policy, both positions were voiced in Christian communities of the fifteenth century and are in effect debating with one another in the Urbino altarpiece.[21]

The account we have given thus far establishes a dynamic interchange between the main panel and the predella, an interchange set in motion by the exclusions and allusions that each representational mode practices. This interchange, we suggest, allows the complete altarpiece to function as a critical relay point in circuits not only between formal categories, but also between social levels and even degrees of coercive and violent action. And yet the circuitry, we would now like to argue, does not function smoothly. Both paintings contain sites of resistance and disruption, sites that increase the dynamic flow between them but also undermine the complementarity on which their cooperation depends.

We have already looked at one point of trouble, the Host in Joos van Gent's panel, the circle of white that serves as a representational challenge to representation itself, the emblem of a doctrine that points beyond iconicity by commanding the believer to regard appearances as accidents. To view the painting from this doctrinal perspective is to derealize its other figures, to notice their illusionistic quality. Focusing on the anti-iconicity of the doctrine interferes with the suspension of disbelief on which paintings such as this rely. Challenged at the main panel's center, we might say, the suspended disbelief seems to travel, as did the narrative impulse generated at the panel's margins, to the predella. In the predella, which we should remember was painted first, iconicity and narrative seem equally indulged. We are given a story that not only supports eucharistic doctrine but also asks us to believe our eyes. At precisely the place, however, where the legendary and visual come together most emphatically, the predella also seems to expose its own iconicity to critical scrutiny, to strain the conventionality of its representation to the breaking point, and to provide an aporia like the Host in Joos van Gent's panel. In the predella, this place is a wound in the wall.

Uccello's second scene depicts the Jewish family in their house, boiling the Host in a frying pan over a brazier. We can see into the house because the fourth wall has been removed entirely, exposing the interior to our view. The interior does not occupy the entire panel; it is painted at an angle, enabling us to see the outside as well, by the front door, where the soldiers are hammering for entrance.[22] We can look into the secret recesses of the Jews' chamber – recesses elegantly intensified by the perspectival depiction of the tile floor – but, as in a theater, we cannot be seen and are not implicated in the acts we are watching. But how have the soldiers – who do not, after all, have the privileged vantage point afforded to us by the excision of the fourth wall – been alerted to the profanation of the Host? No window is depicted through which someone might have glimpsed the crime.[23] If Uccello had not bothered to provide an explanation, we might not have given the matter a thought. But evidently he felt that his representation called for a link between inside and outside, a clue that would alert the Christian community. The narrative link he depicts is at the same time an elegant and witty aesthetic device: the blood that overflows from the pan spreads out on the tile floor. According to the rules of perspective by which Uccello was so deeply fascinated, that floor is tilted up, in order to suggest distance, and it is as if the blood felt the tilt. For it gathers together into a narrow stream, runs down across the tiles, and seeps out of the house through a passage resembling a bruise or wound, the size of a mouse hole in a cartoon, in the front wall near the door.

The wound in the wall is at once an important structural element in the aesthetic representation and a tear in the fabric of that representation. Narratively it works as a way of explaining how the secret Jewish profanation was discovered by the surrounding community; aesthetically it works as a way of concentrating and focusing the threads of red paint, paint that stands for the blood that courses from the dab of white paint that stands for the wafer that for believers is the body of Christ. Abstractly, the little dab of white in this panel may be just as problematic as the represented Host in Joos van Gent's painting, but since we are being asked to see the red paint as blood, just as the Real Presence supposedly manifested itself miraculously to the eyes, believing in this legend is homologous (rather than antagonistic) to practicing the aesthetic suspension of disbelief. At first glance, the Real Presence in this instance seems to have been rendered unproblematically visible. On closer inspection, however, we notice that its visibility to the Christian community in the painting relies on the wound in the wall.

To understand why the question of visibility should reappear just where it seemed most likely to be mooted, in the panel depicting the miracle of the bleeding Host, we should look more closely at the structure of these miraculous narratives in the early Renaissance. They provided a vivid image of the ocular proof that tantalized Christianity in the wake of the elaboration of eucharistic orthodoxy. Orthodoxy obliged the faithful to believe that what they saw (and, at least once a year, tasted and swallowed) was not what it manifestly appeared to be; that their direct experience was at the utmost remove from the truth. The distance between sense experience and higher reality could be transcended by the faith that bound individual and community to God, but, judging from the widespread stories of miraculously bleeding Hosts, this transcendence left an intense residual desire for confirmation. Such confirmation was on rare occasions given, as if in reward for exceptional piety, to the blessed: hence, for example, Colette of Corbie received a vision of "a dish completely filled with carved-up flesh like that of a child."[24] But it came more frequently and disturbingly to those who showed, even inadvertently, some doubt: a story, related in an anti-Protestant tract by an English Jesuit of the late sixteenth century, tells of one such person, an English gentlewoman who traveled to Rome for the Jubilee Year. Upon her arrival, the woman went

> to Father Parsons, who was her Confessor: and he administring vnto her the blessed Sacrament (which in the forme of a little Wafer, hee put into her mouth) obserued shee was long chewing, and could not swallow the same: whereupon he asked her, whether shee knew what it was shee receiued? She answered, Yes, a Wafer. At which answer of hers, Father Parsons beeing much offended, he thrust his finger into her mouth, and thence drew out a piece of red flesh, which after was nailed vp against a post in a Vespery or priuate Chappell within our Lady-Church: and though this were done about some twenty yeeres since or more, yet doth that piece of flesh there remaine to bee seene, very fresh and red as euer it was.[25]

The proof of the Real Presence here comes not as a reward for perfect faith, but as a rebuke to imperfect faith, a polemical version of Jesus' words to "doubting Thomas": "Thomas, because thou hast seen me, thou hast believed: blessed are they that have not seen, and yet have believed" (John 20:29).

Theologians argued that the fact that one could not ordinarily see God's flesh and blood in the Host was a sign of God's grace, since it would be horrible to experience in the senses what one was actually eating. This is why it so often falls

PLATE 9   Detail of devils. Paolo Uccello (1397–1475). *Profanation of the Host* (detail). Palazzo Ducale, Urbino, Italy. Photograph: SCALA, Florence.

to unbelievers, heretics, and Jews, caught in the act of profanation, to encounter the true nature of the Eucharist. In Uccello's painting, when the rescued Host is brought back into the church and placed on the altar, it is no longer bleeding: it has returned mercifully to the form of bread. It is the Jewish merchant and his family who are the prime witnesses of the sacred blood, blood that Christian believers know is present but need not see or taste. For a Jew to attack the Host seems strange, since there would appear to be no reason to attack something you believe to be a mere piece of bread, particularly if the assault, conducted in a windowless, barred room, can serve no public polemical purpose. From a Christian point of view, to be sure, the Jew is not attacking a piece of bread but directly reenacting the Crucifixion: indeed this is a crime worse than the alleged Jewish murders of Christian children to make matzoth, for here the violence is directed at the very body of God.[26] But only a believer could know that the wafer is God's body; the unbeliever would have to think that he was dealing with common baked bread – until, that is, the blood began to flow.

Church officials were at least sporadically aware of the problems of verification associated with bleeding wafers, and particularly with any wafer that had been removed from the altar: How could it be proved that the wafer had been consecrated? What if the priest's finger happened to be bleeding when he touched the Host?[27] How could counterfeit wafers be distinguished from authentic ones? What was to prevent someone, eager to cause trouble, from putting a wafer on which he had smeared some blood on the doorstep of a Jew's house? Beyond such concerns, the icon of the holy blood – even in a case that the Catholic Church accepted, such as the "miracle" depicted by Uccello purports to be – raises three related problems. First, the Jewish unbeliever has to behave as if he were instead a doubter, determined to test the validity of the doctrine by seeking direct corporeal evidence of its truth or falsehood.[28] Second, since the Host

PLATE 10   The Wound in the Wall. Paolo Uccello (1397–1475). *Profanation of the Host* (detail).
Palazzo Ducale, Urbino, Italy. Photograph: SCALA, Florence.

bleeds in response to doubt, unbelief, or desecration, the viewer's pleasure in its
appearance indicates a barely submerged lack of faith, the stubborn persistence of
reliance on the senses, even when one is trying to acknowledge and comprehend
their inadequacy. And third, because the painting is an icon, a representation of
the miracle, it seems to reintroduce imagination and illusion precisely where they
are meant to be excluded. The miracle, after all, supposedly defeated representation in the name of reality, but representation comes back in the substitution of
paint for blood. The miracle itself was already disturbingly dependent on doubt,
and the icon increases the disturbance by confounding the conquest over doubt
with the mere suspension of disbelief. Faith, that elusive gift of God so ardently
prayed for, then moves into uncomfortable proximity with the aesthetic experience of "seeing" the pigment as blood, an easy, pleasurable make-believe.

Faced with these problems, the best Uccello's painting can do is to externalize
the doubt by implying that it is Jewish. It is the Jews who doubt that the
consecrated bread has literally become body, just as their ancestors doubted that
Jesus was the Messiah; and it is the Jews – imagining perhaps that the wafer is only a
version of the unleavened bread that they eat at Passover in commemoration of the
Exodus – who perversely put the Host to the test and discover that it bleeds.
Having burdened the Jews with the Christian community's doubt and need for
verification, the painting then allows believers the ocular gratification of the
represented blood and punishes the Jews for the desire, confounding them and
showing the fate of the doubter and his whole family. Thus the problem of doubt is
finessed; but the problem of representation remains.

Let us return to the wound or bruise in the wall, for it is both the crucial agent of
the terrible fate of the Jews and the emblem of the representational dilemma. The
passing of the blood through the wall, we have said, works as both a narrative and as
an aesthetic device. It is thus different from the panel's preeminent aesthetic device:

PLATE 11   Christ frees Adam and Eve from Limbo. Master of the Osservanza (1425–1450). *The Descent into Limbo* (*c.* 1440–1444). Courtesy of the Fogg Art Museum, Harvard University Art Museums, Gift of Paul J. Sachs, "A testimonial to my friend Edward W. Forbes." Photograph: Photographic Services © President and Fellows of Harvard College, Harvard University.

the removal of the wall that enables us to look into the locked and windowless house of the Jewish merchant and his family. The removal is strictly detached from the represented world of the painting; to allow it to contaminate that world would be to make a mockery of the soldiers beating at the door or of the Jewish merchant, who has withdrawn into the privacy of his house in order to conduct the secret profanation. The missing wall is a convention, just as the side of the cave is missing in a quattrocento Florentine panel now in the Fogg Art Museum, so that we can see into the darkness where Christ frees Adam and Eve from Limbo. In the case of the cave, the convention has been complicated – we might say muddied – by the artist's attempt to naturalize the opening by rusticating the edges: the effect is to make one wonder why on earth the poor prisoners did not simply walk out or why Christ had to break the door down to gain entry.

Uccello is too sophisticated to attempt anything comparable: the wall is neatly, one might say surgically, cut away, enabling us to see the image of the blood streaming across the floor. We observe an interior space marked "Jewish," the space of doubt, while we remain safely outside. The phantom wall acts, therefore, as an invisible shield against identification with the need for ocular proof; it is another device of disavowal. But it is also a reminder that the painting achieves its effects only because the viewer is willing to go along with certain representational conventions; it emphasizes the gap between aesthetic illusion and the Real Presence. A salutary admission of the distinction between paintings and miracles, representation and sacrament, the wall's transparency does not require

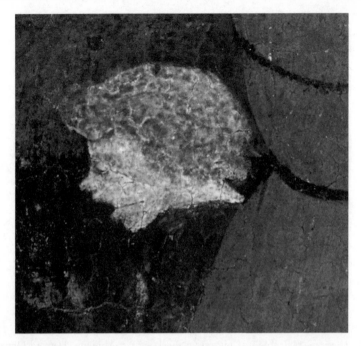

PLATE 12   Child screaming. Paolo Uccello (1397–1475). *Profanation of the Host* (detail). Palazzo Ducale, Urbino, Italy. Photograph: SCALA, Florence.

faith, only the suspension of disbelief. Its patent conventionality, that is, sorts out the ontological layers.

The surgical cut, however, is complicated, one might say infected, by the passage through which the blood seeps into the street. This passage is supposed to stand on a different plane of reality; it is, as it were, in the picture, a crucial element in the miracle itself. Some unexpected escape route for the blood is necessary for the discovery of the secret profanation – a wicked act in a windowless room, with the door bolted – as well as for the demonstration of the truth of transubstantiation. But what are we to make of the escape route? Or rather what are we to make of its relation to its world? Are we to think that the sacred blood possessed some mystical quality that enabled it to pass through the wall (as the Glorified Body of Christ was said to be able to do)? But what, in this case, are we to make of the impression of a stain or bruise in the wall – an impression that the Glorified Body would certainly not leave? Are we to think rather that its passage is strictly natural? But how is it possible to construct a coherent natural explanation for a stream of blood to pass through a wall of this represented thickness? Should we imagine, despite appearances, that there is a hole in the wall, through which the blood is passing?[29] But if so, how can we account for such a hole? Are we to think that Italian houses of the period had holes cut in the front walls for drainage – that is, that the hole is an architectural feature? Are we to imagine that it is there quite by accident – that is, that the husband might have said to his wife, "My dear, one of these days we've got to do something about that hole"? Are we to conjure up a providential story to account for it, to think, for example, that a divinely driven mouse made the hole unbeknownst to the inhabitants? Are we to believe that the sacred blood, like a corrosive, burned its way through the wall? And, of course, there is something absurd about any of these desperate explanatory measures, since the blood is flowing before our eyes from a tiny Host, a Host in which miraculously is found the crucified flesh from whose wounds the blood once flowed and flows even now. The wound in the wall – as if displaced from Jesus' own buffeted and pierced body – is there for one overwhelming reason: to gather the streaming blood into a satisfying narrow ribbon, which runs through it and thereby awakens the community to the crime within.

The uncertainty about the origin and logic of the wound in the wall is the inescapable consequence of the panel's attempt to conjoin aesthetic, narrative, and doctrinal functions in a single visible sign. Uccello's very brilliance as a painter, his ability to satisfy the craving to see what cannot be seen, thereby threatens to expose the conspiracy, as it were, behind the represented conspiracy, the crime hidden within the represented crime: the Jewish family has been framed, both literally and figuratively. In the desecration stories that circulated after 1290, whether in popular legends and sermons or in formal legal investigations held in the wake of an accusation or a murderous riot or a precipitous execution, there was always some way or other in which secret Jewish guilt was exposed. In one version it was one of the merchant's children who casually remarked to a Christian woman of his acquaintance that she did not have to seek her god in church since he was being tortured at this very moment by his father; in other versions the threatened Host itself emitted a strange light or noise; and in testimony taken from witnesses, it sometimes turned out that the Host – or, in any case, a small piece of bread rumored to be a consecrated Host – was found on the threshold outside the Jews' door.

The Jews are inevitably guilty in such stories because they do not believe and because at the same time they are made to act out, to embody, the doubt aroused among the Christian faithful by eucharistic doctrine. In Uccello the doubt projected onto them has to run through the wall of their enclosure in order to call up the soldiers who will burn them at the stake, killing not only the merchant but also his wife and children – for their crime is not strictly limited to the merchant's act but is bound up with the very existence of Jews. Here too Uccello's genius has the odd effect of at once intensifying and undermining the legend he paints. For in most versions there is a kind of Jewish residue, in the form of the children who are taken away from their guilty parents and converted to the true faith. In Uccello's predella, by contrast, the Christian community triumphs altogether over Jewish doubt, but the narrative vividness, the *enargeia*, that characterizes the scene of the flowing blood also manifests itself in the execution scene. Once again Uccello has removed an obstacle to our sight – here half of the metal cauldron or fire screen – and once again the effect is profoundly unsettling. What we see is not a doctrinal emblem of doubt but a family in flames. One of the children, his face in profile, is screaming.[30]

To proceed further with an analysis of the altarpiece, we would need to follow and, if possible, extend Marilyn Lavin's investigation of the status of Jews in fifteenth-century Urbino, along with the cultural politics of confraternities, the shifting theological and diplomatic currents in Italy, the social history and devotional uses of altarpieces, as well as their formal resources and constraints.[31] Following recent work on the distinction between the natural and the preter-natural and between both of these and the supernatural, we would want to explore the complex aesthetic and philosophical dimensions of wonder. We would hope to use recent scholarship – we think particularly of Caroline Walker Bynum's *Holy Feast and Holy Fast*, Miri Rubin's *Corpus Christi*, and R. Po-chia Hsia's *The Myth of Ritual Murder* – to bring into sharper focus the gender concerns at which we have only briefly glanced. Above all, we would want to return with redoubled attention to the formal design of the paintings,[32] attention not only to the internal structures of the individual works but also to the formal relations that would have been established in the original setting and that are now difficult to perceive. The two panels are currently displayed side by side on the bare whitewashed walls of the Ducal Palace; but if, as seems likely, they were actually set together in a single altarpiece within an ecclesiastical setting, then their full significance must have derived to a very considerable degree from the implications of this placement and from the ritual in which the altarpiece participated. We have already alluded several times to the possibility that Joos van Gent's panel is a response to Uccello's predella, but a thorough exploration of this response would require a slow, patient, detailed analysis of the complex echoes and tensions that would have been more completely manifest when the two pieces were placed in the aesthetic and institutional structure for which they were intended. That structure would have included the altar itself upon which the sacrifice of the Mass was performed and toward which the blood that flows out through the wound in the wall was tending. There would have been a complex movement then, at once formal, representational, and institutional, from the painted figure of Christ standing before an altar and holding the wafer between his fingers, to the predella narrative of the bleeding wafer restored to the altar, to the actual altar on which the holy wafers and the other elements and implements of the sacrifice would be placed, and thence to the priest who would stand at Mass and take up a consecrated Host between his fingers, exactly as the painted figure of Christ as priest was shown to be doing.

But for the moment we must be content simply to acknowledge the incom-pleteness of our discussion and to stop with a few closing observations. First, we have spoken of doubt as a Christian *projection* on the Jews, but of course Jews did (and do) deny the truth of eucharistic doctrine.[33] The reality of that disbelief hardly licenses persecution, but it does mean that the altarpiece participates in a historical encounter that includes but is not limited to the representation of Christian faith and Christian doubt. Christian doubt is projected upon Jewish disbelief, while at the same time Christian doctrine draws upon certain aspects of the sacrificial logic of Jewish faith. The boundary line between Jews and Chris-tians was crucial – it could be, and frequently was, a matter of life and death – but it was porous and unstable, subject to holes and wounds. Second, even on the evidence of the altarpiece alone, Christian attitudes toward Jews were ambiguous and complex. Analysis of an aesthetic representation must not be a way of containing or closing off this complexity but rather of intensifying it. The boundary line between the attitude toward Jews expressed in the main panel and the attitude expressed in the predella is crucial – again, it could, when transformed into actions, be a matter of life and death – but here too it is, as we have already seen, porous and unstable. Third, we have spoken of the legendary narratives of Host desecration as the expression of doubt, but the narratives, and the doctrinal claims that they represent, are also manifestly the expression of an intensified faith across the Christian community in the mystical truth of transubstantiation. The boundary line between faith and doubt is crucial – it was a matter of eternal life and death – but once again it is porous and unstable. Doubt is the consequence of the heightened claims of faith, and faith is tested and renewed on the dangerous shoals of doubt.

Fourth, and finally, we are deeply concerned with the tension between beliefs and their representations. The altarpiece at which we have been looking is an especially fraught case, since it makes its doctrinal point about the irrelevance of visible appearances to the eyes of faith through the vehicle of those very appearances and then further stigmatizes the craving for ocular proof as wicked unbelief. The doctrine of the Real Presence might be said to exceed all representational claims – the Host *is* the body and blood of Christ – while the painting relies on the representational efficacy of the icon, which ensures that we will embrace the make-believe and recognize, for example, the redness of blood in the redness of paint. The painting also, however, relies on several non-iconic representational conventions – such as the cutaway fourth wall – that require a different and still greater act of make-believe. Here the pleasure the altarpiece offers you depends not on a resemblance between what you see and what you are willing to imagine that you see, but rather on a violation of the normal perceptual world, a transfiguration of vision as if by magic, miracle, or (in our own cultural terms) technology.

We have focused on two places in the altarpiece that strain these representational conventions to the breaking point and confound the different modes of make-believe. The represented Host between Christ's fingers, an object whose centrality and minimalism seem to render its very iconicity problematic, pulls representation toward its opposite, toward the blank spot where what is visible is a mere insignificant accident. The blankness of the Host is the "point" of the doctrine. The second of these places, the wound in the wall, is the consequence of Uccello's attempt to negotiate not between Real Presence and representation, but between visual likeness and self-conscious conventionality. This attempt is at once a formal solution and the solution to a narrative problem, a forensic question: How did the Christian community discover the secret Jewish crime? But because the wound so thoroughly confounds any distinction between an illusionistic detail and a formal convenience, it also calls iconicity into question, putting pressure, as we have seen, on the partition between perfidious Jews and pious Christians who long to see the Host bleed. The Host reminds us that if we truly believe, we should not need paintings; the wound reminds us that paintings require us to acquiesce, for the sake of ocular satisfaction, in many things we do not necessarily believe.

If the altarpiece seems overloaded with riddles and with the peculiar paradoxes of eucharistic faith, it nevertheless only exaggerates a tendency in all representation, for, whether doctrinal or legendary, any representation is distinct from that which it purports to exemplify. The pleasure of representation is bound up with this distinction, with perceived differences that mark the gap, in Elaine Scarry's terms, between the made-up and the made-real. We contend that these differences are not what remove representations from ordinary reality, but rather what connect them to reality's collaborations, tensions, and murderous conflicts. Aporia are not places where forms refer only to themselves, but are rather the tears where energies, desires, and repressions flow out into the world.

NOTES

1 In a response to this paper (Center for Hermeneutical Studies, May 1995), Harry Berger Jr. notes that, perhaps in response to Uccello, Joos "restores the standard tipped-up Flemish ground plan that implies a high viewing point bird's-eye view, and that also resists the drive into deep space by bringing – bending – the higher, putatively more distant objects toward the picture plane, as if for better viewing." The effect, Berger suggests, is at once to allow the viewer extraordinary access and to maintain a certain distance: "opening, showing all, inviting the eye in to travel around only loosely constrained by perspective effects – but making it hard for you to imagine yourself walking in – or able to walk in and stand." Not all the figures in the painting, however, submit to the same scheme and hence are seen from above. As Berger notes, the witnesses, the patron and his group, are "foreshortened a little so as to imply a lower viewing point – i.e., you see them from below." This shift perhaps implies a slight invitation to the viewer to imagine himself or herself in this group, though not one of the apostles who are taking Communion directly from Christ.
2 John E. Booty, *John Jewel as Apologist of the Church of England* (London: SPCK, 1963), p. 152.
3 Marilyn Aronberg Lavin, "The Altar of Corpus Domini in Urbino: Paolo Uccello, Joos Van Gent, Piero della Francesa," *Art Bulletin* 49 (1967): 1–24.
4 For the relation in altarpieces between historical time and eternal truths of Christian doctrine, see Lotte Brand Philip, *The Ghent Altarpiece and the Art of Jan van Eyck* (Princeton: Princeton University Press, 1971), pp. 167–8. In an altarpiece, Philip observes, Christ had to be present both as sacrificing priest and as sacrifice (cf. the discussion of the representation of the lamb in the upper and lower panels in Gent, 62ff.). Philip (62n.) cites Aquinas: "Sacerdos gerit imaginem Christi, in cuius persona et virtute verba pronuntiat ad consecrandum.... Et ita quodammodo idem est sacerdos et hostia" (*Summa* III, 83, 1–3).
5 Thomas Cranmer, *A Defence of the True and Catholick Doctrine of the Sacrament* (London, 1550) in *The Work of Thomas Cranmer*, ed. G. E. Duffield (Philadelphia: Fortress Press, 1965), p. 145.
6 Anna Padoa Rizzo observes that the duchess (Battista Sforza) was herself involved in the creation at Urbino of a Monte di Pietà, which was in turn linked to the anti-semitic rhetoric of Uccello's predella and possibly of Joos van Gent's main panel. *Paolo Uccello* (Firenze: Cantini, 1991), pp. 111–17.
7 The itinerant friars encouraged the Holy Week *sassaiola*, the traditional stoning of Jewish houses at the close of the Easter procession. See Ariel Toaff, *Love, Work, and Death: Jewish Life in Medieval Umbria*, trans. Judith Landry (London: Vallentine Mitchell & Co., 1996), pp. 179–86. They also generally called for enforcement of the so-called "badge for Jews" – a circle of yellow cloth for men, to be attached to the

left-hand side of the garment, above the belt, and circular earrings for women. See Diane Owen Hughes, "Distinguishing Signs: Ear-Rings, Jews, and Franciscan Rhetoric in the Italian Renaissance City," *Past and Present* 112 (1986): 3–59. In the Uccello predella, discussed below, the Jewish man is not wearing the badge, but his wife's headscarf may have signaled Jewishness, since a yellow veil was introduced at approximately this time as a substitute for the distinctive earrings. See Jeremy Cohen, *The Friars and the Jews: The Evolution of Medieval Anti-Judaism* (Ithaca: Cornell University Press, 1982). For papal policy, see Shlomo Simonsohn, *The Apostolic See and the Jews*, 3 vols. (Toronto: Pontifical Institute of Mediaeval Studies, 1988–1990).

8　In the ewer and basin on the floor there is, it seems, a further narrative allusion, to the washing of the disciples' feet.

9　Lavin, "The Altar of Corpus Domini in Urbino," p. 13.

10　Lavin, "The Altar of Corpus Domini in Urbino," p. 16.

11　Part of the pleasure and interest of the invitation is that there can be competing or overlapping meanings: in England, according to Eamon Duffy, the High Mass began with "an elaborate procession round the church, at the commencement of which salt and water were solemnly exorcised, blessed, and mixed," while at its end a loaf of bread presented by one of the parishioners was blessed, cut up, and distributed to the congregation. Eamon Duffy, *The Stripping of the Altars: Traditional Religion in England, 1400–1580* (New Haven: Yale University Press, 1992), pp. 124–5. It is at least possible that these ceremonies had their equivalents in Italy and were reflected in the salt, water, and bread on the left-hand side of the table. Such meanings would not be incompatible with an allusion to the Jewish sacrificial meal, but would pull in a different direction, away from Isaac, as it were, and toward Sixtus.

12　Baldesar Castiglione, *The Book of the Courtier*, trans. Charles Singleton (New York: Doubleday, 1959), p. 357.

13　Anna Padoa Rizzo rejects Pope-Hennessy's hypothesis that Uccello lost the commission for the main panel after his work was criticized; rather, she suggests, he was recalled to Florence, necessitating that the painting of the main panel be done by Joos van Gent (and, she argues, by Piero della Francesca (pp. 111–17)). The influence, if not the direct involvement, of Piero is suggested by Mario Salmi, *Paolo Uccello, Andrea del Castagno, Domenico Veneziano*, trans. Jean Chuzeville (Paris: Weber, 1937), p. 38.

14　Lavin, "The Altar of Corpus Domini in Urbino," p. 3.

15　In *Outcasts: Signs of Otherness in Northern European Art of the Late Middle Ages*, 2 vols. (Berkeley: University of California Press, 1994), Ruth Melinkoff gives several images of the Last Supper that show Christ feeding the wafers to his disciples: a Passion Altar by Master Bertram (late fourteenth century), Hanover, Niedersächsisches Landesmuseum Landesgalerie; King's College Chapel; Jörg Ratgeb (c. 1500–1510), Rotterdam Museum, Boymans-van Beuningen.

16　John Frith, *A Christen Sentence*, appendix C in Thomas More, *Letter to Bugenhagen; Supplication of Souls; Letter Against Frith*, in *The Complete Works of St. Thomas More*, ed. Frank Manley et al. (New Haven: Yale University Press, 1990), 7:429.

17　For an example of the complexity of the doctrinal response to the objection that an incarnate body could not violate the laws of physics, see Thomas More's *Letter Against Frith*, in *The Complete Works*, 7:249ff.

18　See Charles Ziha, "Hosts, Processions and Pilgrimages in Fifteenth-Century Germany," *Past and Present* 118 (1988): 48ff. Cf. Peter Browe, *Die eucharistichen Wunder des Mittelalters* (Breslau, 1938), esp. p. 56 n. 53 and p. 157.

19   In a critique of this paper at the Center for Hermeneutical Studies, Deborah Shuger
     argues that this distinction is the whole point of Uccello's panel, which she
     associates with the humanist attack on medieval credulity.

20   For an account challenging the popular origins of anti-Semitism in the earlier
     Middle Ages, see R. I. Moore, *The Formation of a Persecuting Society: Power and
     Deviance in Western Europe, 950–1250* (Oxford: Basil Blackwell, 1987).

21   The positions could be in tension even in the rhetoric of an individual preacher.
     Hence, for example, Bernardino of Siena begins by speaking against usurers in
     general, not against Jews in particular, but as he warms to his subject, the condem-
     nation becomes more pointed and more extreme:

> Il denaro è il calore vitale di una città. Gli usurai sono sangui-sughe che si applicano
> con delizia a divorare un membro malato, dal quale succhiano il sangue con insaziabile
> ardore. Quando il sangue e il calore abbandonano la estremità del corpo per fluire al
> cuore, è il segno della prossima morte. Ma il pericolo è piu incalzante quando le
> ricchezze di una città sono nelle mani degli ebrei. Allora il calore non ha più il suo
> normale corso verso il cuore. Come nella peste, si dirige verso il membro malato del
> corpo; poiché ogni ebro, sopprattutto quanto è prestatore, e nemico capitale cristiano.

("Money is a city's vital heat. Usurers are leeches that apply themselves with delight
to devour a sick limb from which with insatiable ardor they suck the blood. When
blood and heat abandon the extremities of the body in order to flow toward the
heart, it is a sign that death is near. But the danger is greater when a city's riches are
in the hands of the Jews. For then the vital heat no longer has its normal course
toward the heart. As in cases of plague, it flows toward the sick limbs of the body.
Therefore every Jew, above all the Jewish moneylender, is a Christian's mortal
enemy.") Quoted in Robert Bonfil, *Gli ebrei in Italian nell'epoca del Rinascimento*
(Firenze: Sansoni, 1991), p. 27.

22   The soldiers wear contemporary costumes but have "S.P.Q.R." on their shields and
     standards. Lavin suggests that the insignia gives them an air of "antiquity" (the
     miracle had, after all, taken place more than a century before), while another
     interpreter proposes that it gives them an "Italian" rather than "French" identity
     (Pierre Francastel, in Lavin, "The Altar of Corpus Domini in Urbino," p. 7).

23   As Berger has pointed out to us, the light that floods into the room seems to come –
     can only come – from the opening made by removing the wall.

24   Caroline Walker Bynum, *Holy Feast and Holy Fast* (Berkeley: University of Cali-
     fornia Press, 1987), p. 67.

25   The story is attributed to "I. Markes Iesuite, in a book of his written of late, and
     intituled, The Examination of the new Religion, page 128" and is cited in John
     Gee, *The Foot out of the Snare: with a Detection of Svndry Late Practices and Impostures of
     the Priests and Iesuits in England* ... (London: Printed by H. L. for Robert Mil-
     bourne, 1624), pp. 28–9.

26   In *Les Intellectuels chrétiens et les juifs au Moyen Age* (Paris: Cerf, 1990), Gilbert Dahan
     observes that Host desecration is strictly parallel to charges of ritual murder and was
     regarded as a greater crime: "la répétition de la Passion se faisant alors non par
     l'intermédiaire d'un homme, c'est-à-dire l'image de Dieu, mais pour ainsi dire
     directement dans la chair même de Dieu, matérialisée sous les espèces de l'hostie"
     (p. 27). (In the context of our analysis, it is particularly worth noting the complex
     play here on representation or image and 'direct' reality – namely, the bread!)
     Dahan cites as prehistory the ruling at the Fourth Lateran Council by Innocent

III against the "abominable acts" committed by Jews with their Christian wet nurses: when the latter have had Communion, the Jews make them throw away their milk for three days:

> Henri de Suse nous explique qu'ainsi les juifs comprennent que le Corps du Christ s'est diffusé dans les organes des nourrices. Ils croient donc eux aussi en la trans-substanti-ation et cela à la fois explique leur comportement, quand ils se vengent sur les hosties consacrées, et souligne la gravité de leurs actes, puisque c'est véritablement Dieu qu'ils attaquent. (p. 28)

27   Protestants cited instances when such bleeding was not accidental: "Anno 36 of Henry the Eighth, a Priest did pronounce at Pauls Crosse, and there confessed in publick, that hee himselfe saying Masse, pricked his finger, and bebloudied the Corporas with the Altar-clothes, purposing to make the people beleeue, that the Host had bled miraculously." Gee, *The Foot out of the Snare*, p. 42.

28   For the relation between Jewish unbelief and Jewish doubt, see the problem addressed in a quodlibet by Henri de Gand: "Utrum Iudaeus pungens hostiam consecratam, qui videns sanguine emergente ex puncturis ipsam rubescere et viso miraculo conuertitur et baptizatur, debeat pro isto delicto puniri a iustitia publica." ("If a Jew stabs a consecrated host and, seeing that it reddens with blood flowing from its wounds, converts and is baptized in response to the miracle, should he be punished by public justice for his crime?") Henri's second argument in favor of punishment hinges on whether Jews could be expected to punish such a person: "Nisi Iudaeus iste super dicto facto punietur a public iustitia secundum legem Christianam, tunc maleficium illud maneret impunitum, quia Iudaei non punient illud secundum legem suam." Henri de Gand, *Quodl* XIV, q. 15, edn de Paris 1518, ff. 470v–472v, quoted in Dahan, *Les Intellectuels chrétiens*, p. 105.

29   In the most careful account of the painting, Lavin (p. 7) refers to the passage as a hole, though the term does not seem entirely accurate.

30   In *Pictures and Punishment: Art and Criminal Prosecution during the Florentine Renaissance* (Ithaca: Cornell University Press, 1985), Samuel Y. Edgerton Jr. remarks of this scene: "In spite of the painter's almost whimsical style, we detect in this and his other scenes of the story a peculiar sympathy for the unfortunate Jews, an attitude perhaps stirred in him by firsthand confrontation with the actual horror of the similar event in Florence" (p. 148). Not all observers detect this peculiar sympathy. Mary Pittaluga, for example, suggests that Uccello's exquisite use of color – his "pure, fantastic effervescence" – in these scenes effaces any anxiety that the scene might otherwise arouse (*Paolo Uccello* (Roma: Tumminelli, 1946), p. 19); and the claim that the violence is entirely aestheticized is seconded by Franco and Stefano Borsi: "Even in the scenes showing the hanging and burning at the stake, the composition's balance and the elegance of the knights and their standards create an atmosphere more akin to a tournament" (*Paolo Uccello*, trans. Elfreda Powell (New York: Harry Abrams, 1994), p. 260).

31   On the worsening situation of Jews in northern Italy in the late fifteenth century, see Attilio Milano, *Storia degli ebrei in Italia* (Torino: Einaudi, 1963), esp. pp. 197ff. On Jewish banking in Urbino, see Gino Luzzatto, *I Banchieri ebrei in Urbino nell'età ducale* (Padova: Arnaldo Forni, 1902). Particular attention should be paid to the repercussions for Jews of the charges of ritual murder made in the city of Trent in 1475 by Bernardino of Feltre. See R. Po-Chai Hsia, *Trent 1475: Stories of a Ritual Murder Trial* (New Haven: Yale University Press, 1992).

32 For an illuminating formal and doctrinal analysis of a eucharistic altarpiece, see Aloys Butzkamm, *Bild und Frömmigkeit im 15. Jahrhundert: Der Sakramentsaltar von Dieric Bouts in der St.-Peters-Kirche zu Löwen* (Paderborn: Bonifatius, 1990). Margaret D. Carroll has a suggestive analysis of the relation between a painting's formal design and anti-Semitic ideology in "Dürer's *Christ among the Doctors* Re-examined," in *Shop Talk: Studies in Honor of Seymour Slive* (Cambridge: Harvard University Press, 1995), pp. 49–54.

33 See, for example, Hasdai Crescas, *The Refutation of the Christian Principles* (c. 1398), trans. Daniel Lasker (Albany: State University of New York Press, 1992): "Jeremiah has already said: 'Can a man make gods for himself? No gods are they!' And they make him every day. There is no difference between making him by hand or by word, since their priests believe that they make God by word when they say, 'This is my body; this is my blood'" (p. 61). See also Dahan, *Les Intellectuel chrétiens;* and D. Berger, *The Jewish–Christian Debate in the High Middle Ages: A Critical Edition of the Nizzahon Vetus* (Philadelphia: Jewish Publication Society of America, 1979), p. 225.

5

MARVELOUS POSSESSIONS

Let us begin at the most famous of beginnings:

> As I know that you will be pleased at the great victory with which Our Lord has
> crowned my voyage, I write this to you, from which you will learn how in thirty-
> three days, I passed from the Canary Islands to the Indies with the fleet which the
> most illustrious king and queen, our sovereigns, gave to me. And there I found
> very many islands filled with people innumerable, and of them all I have taken
> possession for their highnesses, by proclamation made and with the royal standard
> unfurled, and no opposition was offered to me. To the first island which I found,
> I gave the name *San Salvador*, in remembrance of the Divine Majesty, Who has
> marvelously bestowed all this; the Indians call it 'Guanahani'. To the second, I gave
> the name *Isla de Santa María de Concepción*; to the third, *Fernandina*; to the fourth,
> *Isabella*; to the fifth, *Isla Juana*, and so to each one I gave a new name.[1]

Thus begins Columbus's celebrated account, in a letter to Luis de Santangel, of his
first voyage.[2] The moment, of course, has become fixed in the popular imagination: the great adventurer on the beach, unfurling the royal standard and taking
possession of the New World. Columbus's words are filled out by what we know
to have followed: other voyages, widening discoveries, the dawning realization
that classical geography was wrong and that a whole new hemisphere had been
discovered, the violent encounter of civilizations, the missionary enterprise, mass
enslavement and death, the immense project of colonization.

Apart from the determination to return, Columbus could not have known or
anticipated any of this subsequent history; what from this distance is striking is
how little he could grasp in 1492 where he was or what he was initiating. His
words then, like the words of the Articles of Agreement with which he set sail,
were in some important sense written as empty place-holders for uncharted lands
and unimaginable future events – *todo esto*, 'all this,' as he puts it, with an
expansive gesture that prudently avoids any specification of what 'all this'
amounts to. And yet Columbus's letter does seem to anticipate and to promote

This chapter was first published in *Marvelous Possessions: The Wonder of the New World* (1991,
pp. 52–85).

the mythic sense with which time has invested his account. We can sense his myth-making already in the flourish with which he proclaims 'la gran vitoria,' a phrase more appropriate in 1492 to the conquest of Granada than to landfall in the Caribbean,[3] and in the term used to describe God's bestowal of the discovered islands: 'marvelously' (*maravillosamente*). I shall argue that Columbus had a highly self-conscious interest in the marvelous.

Why did Columbus, who was carrying a passport and royal letters, think to take possession of anything, if he actually believed that he had reached the outlying regions of the Indies? It did not, after all, occur to Marco Polo in the late thirteenth century to claim for the Venetians any territorial rights in the East or to rename any of the countries; nor in the fourteenth century did Sir John Mandeville unfurl a banner on behalf of a European monarch. Indeed, as we have seen, in the climactic moment of Mandeville's account the knight and his companions piously refuse to pick up the gold and precious stones that litter the valley through which they pass. Columbus, who almost certainly had carefully read the travel accounts of both Marco Polo and Mandeville, behaved startlingly differently.

The difference may be traced of course to the fact that, unlike Marco Polo or Mandeville, Columbus was neither a merchant nor a pilgrim: he was on a state-sponsored mission from a nation caught up in the enterprise of the *Reconquista*. But the objective of this mission has been notoriously difficult to determine. Columbus's passport appears to suggest that he is to proceed to a known place – the Indies – on business concerning the orthodox faith.[4] The original of his *Diario* or log-book has disappeared, but the transcription by his contemporary Las Casas indicates that Columbus was charged to go to the city of Quinsay – that is, Hangzhou – 'to give Your Highnesses letters to the Grand Khan, and to ask for, and to come with, a reply.'[5] At the same time, the grant that Columbus received from Ferdinand and Isabella speaks of Columbus as 'going by our command, with certain vessels of ours and with our subjects, to discover and to gain certain islands and mainland in the Ocean Sea' (p. lxxii). This language – 'descobrir é ganar' – suggests something more than a diplomatic or commercial voyage, but neither the sailors nor the ships of the first expedition were appropriate for a serious military campaign, so that it is difficult to envisage what kind of 'gaining' the monarchs had in mind.[6] I have no solution to these famous enigmas, but I propose that we look carefully at the action Columbus reports and that we consider the extraordinary extent to which that action is *discursive*.

The claim of a 'great victory' and the unfurling of the royal standard suggest that we are about to hear an account of a battle, but what we get instead is an account of a series of speech acts: a proclamation (*pregón*) by which Columbus takes possession of the islands followed by the giving of new names. These speech acts – *he tomado posesión, puse nombre* – are so familiar to us that it is difficult to find anything in them worth remarking, but we would do well to look at them more closely.[7] Here, and throughout the early discourse of the New World, the reassuring signs of administrative order – bureaucratic formulas already well established in a very large number of earlier military, diplomatic, and juridical encounters in Europe and Africa – are deceptive; consciously or unconsciously, they draw us away from a sense of all that is unsettling, unique, and terrible in the first European contacts with the peoples of America.

It is important, I think, to resist the drift toward normalizing what was *not* normal. We can demonstrate that, in the face of the unknown, Europeans used their conventional intellectual and organizational structures, fashioned over centuries of mediated contact with other cultures, and that these structures greatly impeded a clear grasp of the radical otherness of the American lands and peoples. What else would we expect? But such demonstrations do not – or should not – efface the incommensurability, the astonishing singularity, of the contact initiated on October 12, 1492. Virtually all prior recorded encounters between Europeans and other cultures took place across boundaries that were to some degree, however small, porous; this means that all prior encounters had been to some degree, however small, anticipated. To be sure, there were many earlier occasions on which European voyagers experienced the shock of extreme cultural difference: 'And so on the third day after leaving Soldaia,' writes William of Rubruck in the thirteenth century, 'we came across the Tartars; when I came among them it seemed indeed to me as if I were stepping into some other world.'[8] But however strange the Tartars seemed to William, there had been a sporadic history of contact; William expected them to be there and knew roughly where to find them. Moreover, they were reached by a series of small stages that took William gradually away from his familiar world and toward the strange. Prior to Columbus there had been nothing comparable to the absolute break brought about by the exceptionally long ocean crossing, a break that effaced the process of acclimatization on the margins, the incremental signs of growing distance and difference that characterized earlier travel.[9] Alexander the Great managed to lead his army into India, but, as Arrian's biography makes clear, the advance consisted of innumerable smaller acts of reconnaissance, negotiation, and conflict. And this was the pattern for almost all episodes of expansion and warfare.

The European landfall in the Caribbean in 1492 was drastically different – the extreme length of the voyage, the invaders' total unfamiliarity with the land, and their absolute ignorance of its inhabitants' cultures, languages, socio-political organizations, and beliefs made it so. In consequence, all of the familiar procedures had, from the beginning, a quality of displacement. Detached from the world in which they had long functioned coherently (or at least routinely) and dropped into an entirely alien world, they have the odd air of quotations. Our initial interpretive move, I think, must be not to sweep away these quotations – the formularies and stereotypical gestures – but to realize how extremely strange they are or rather how strange they become in this unprecedented situation. Even if every detail is based on some precedent or other, each is destabilized, defamiliarized, uprooted. There are real bodies and real consequences, but the very conventions used to demarcate the real (in denoting sovereignty and legitimate possession) seem in the peculiar light of 1492 to be signs as much of the imaginary as of the real.

The display of the royal standard in the first moments after Columbus's landfall marks the formality of the occasion and officially designates the sovereign on whose behalf his speech acts are performed; what we are witnessing is a legal ritual observed by men whose culture takes both ceremony and juridical formalities extremely seriously. Columbus's journal entry for October 12 provides some of the details of the ritual:

> The Admiral called to the two captains and to the others who had jumped ashore and to Rodrigo Descobedo, the *escrivano* of the whole fleet, and to Rodrigo Sánchez de Segovia; and he said that they should be witnesses that, in the presence of all, he would take, as in fact he did take, possession of the said island for the king and for the queen his lords, making the declarations that were required, and which at more length are contained in the testimonials made there in writing.[10]

About twenty years later, in a royal instruction to Juan Díaz de Solís (a Portuguese navigator in the employ of the Crown of Castille), we get a more detailed account of the formal acts by which the crown's representatives took possession of 'new' lands:

> The manner that you must have in the taking of possession of the lands and parts which you shall have discovered is to be that, being in the land or part that you shall have discovered, you shall make before a notary public and the greatest possible number of witnesses, and the best known ones, an act of possession in our name, cutting trees and boughs, and digging or making, if there be an opportunity, some small building [*edificio*], which should be in a part where there is some marked hill or a large tree, and you shall say how many leagues it is from the sea, a little more or less, and in which part, and what signs it has, and you shall make a gallows there, and have somebody bring a complaint before you, and as our captain and judge you shall pronounce upon and determine it, so that, in all, you shall take the said possession; which is to be for that part where you shall take it, and for all its district [*partido*] and province or island, and you shall bring testimony thereof signed by the said notary in a manner to make faith.[11]

As the phrase 'if there be an opportunity' suggests, this is less a description of actual Spanish practice than an ideal type, a compact anthology of legitimating gestures: actual presence in the land (mere sighting from shipboard does not suffice), the mechanism of legal recording (requiring a notary and witnesses), the physical alteration or marking of the land, the construction of an edifice on a distinctive site that is mapped (and hence can be verified and reoccupied), the formal exercise of justice. From other documents in the period one can expand the list of common symbolic acts: placing stones, cutting grass, raising mounds or pillars, erecting crosses, even drinking water. Captains would in effect select from the repertory and, within its generic limits, improvise a formal ceremony. Cortés, we are told, 'moved walking on the said land from one part to another, and throwing sand from one part to another, and with his sword he struck certain trees that were there, and he commanded to the people who were there that they should have him for governor of His Majesty of those said lands, and did other acts of possession.'[12] Pedro de Guzmán 'delegated his authority to a seaman who swam ashore and there erected a cross, cut down boughs of trees, and took possession of the island, his acts being witnessed by two other seamen who had swum ashore with him and whose testimony formed the basis of the formal notarial act that was subsequently drawn up on board the ship.'[13] Columbus's version is more simple and abstract; he makes no mention of cutting boughs or throwing sand, let alone constructing a house or gallows. There are no attempts in the initial landfall to inscribe the Spanish presence on the land, to leave even an ephemeral mark such as a gash in a tree or a cleared patch of grass.[14] His actions are performed entirely *for a world elsewhere.*

For Columbus taking possession is principally the performance of a set of linguistic acts: declaring, witnessing, recording. The acts are public and official: the admiral speaks as a representative of the king and queen, and his speech must be heard and understood by competent, named witnesses, witnesses who may subsequently be called upon to testify to the fact that the unfurling of the banner and the 'declarations that are required' took place as alleged. At issue is not only the crown's claim to sovereignty but Columbus's own status; after months of difficult negotiation, he had obtained, in the Capitulations of April 17, 1492, appointment as Admiral, Viceroy, and Governor-General over all islands and mainland 'which by his labor and industry shall be discovered or acquired.'[15] He was also granted one-tenth of all the treasure and merchandise produced or obtained in these domains, free of all taxes. In a further, extraordinary concession, the crown agreed that Columbus's title and prerogatives would be enjoyed by his heirs and successors 'perpetually.' On October 12 then Columbus is not only the medium through which the crown could claim possession; he also enacts the ritual of possession on his own behalf and on behalf of his descendants.

And because Columbus's culture does not entirely trust verbal testimony, because its judicial procedures require written proofs, he makes certain to perform his speech acts in the presence of the fleet's recorder (for a fleet which had no priest had a recorder), hence ensuring that everything would be written down and consequently have a greater authority. The papers are carefully sealed, preserved, carried back across thousands of leagues of ocean to officials who in turn countersign and process them according to the procedural rules; the notarized documents are a token of the truth of the encounter and hence of the legality of the claim. Or rather they help to produce 'truth' and 'legality,' ensuring that the words Columbus speaks do not disappear as soon as their sounds fade, ensuring that the memory of the encounter is fixed, ensuring that there are not competing versions of what happened on the beach on October 12th. A priest may be said to facilitate a transaction with eternity, but an *escrivano* facilitates a transaction with a more immediately useful form of temporality, the institutional form secured by writing.

A distinction between peoples who have writing and peoples who do not will, as we have seen, become crucial in the discourse of the New World, but in the initial moments with which we are concerned Columbus does not know enough about those he has encountered to make such a distinction. He evidently does not feel the need to know anything about them at this moment, and we should note that the instruction to De Solís similarly does not include any provision for recognition of the cultural level, rights, or even the existence of the natives. Columbus's journal mentions that naked people were sighted on shore before the Spanish landed, but it is not altogether clear that the ritual of possession took place within earshot of these people who subsequently approached in large numbers.[16] Ceremonies take the place of cultural contacts; rituals of possession stand in for negotiated contracts. Columbus acts entirely within what Michel de Certeau calls 'the scriptural operation'[17] of his own culture, an operation that leads him not simply to pronounce certain words or alternatively to write them down but rather to perform them orally in the presence of the fleet's named and officially sanctioned recorder. Writing here fixes a set of public linguistic acts, gives them official standing, makes them 'historical' events. But what are these linguistic acts? For whom and by what right are they being performed? Why are they assumed to be efficacious?

In part the answer may lie in the odd phrase in his letter to Santangel, 'y no me fué contradicho' – not, as the English translation renders it, 'and no opposition was offered to me,' but rather 'and I was not contradicted.' This presumably refers not to the Spanish – who were called upon to bear witness and who would scarcely object[18] – but to the natives. But what can such a phrase mean? It is possible, I suppose, to imagine it as either a cynical sneer or a skeptical joke. In the former case, Columbus would be laughing at the impossibility of the natives contradicting something they are deliberately kept from understanding or, alternatively, at their impotence to contradict a seizure of their lands even if they were to understand the proclamation perfectly. In the latter case, Columbus would be laughing at the natives' hopeless ignorance: 'if the horse had anything to say, he would speak up.' But rarely if ever in his writings does Columbus seem either cynical or skeptical, least of all here, when he is recounting the crucial event of the entire voyage. We must assume that he is writing in earnest and that he takes seriously the 'fact' that he was not contradicted.

The absence of 'contradiction' had a specific force: such a fact would be important in establishing for the Spanish crown a legal claim to the newly discovered lands by the 'voluntary choice' of the original inhabitants.[19] That is, if those inhabitants actually wished to transfer title to their lands and possessions to the Spanish, they should be allowed to do so. The legal basis for such a transaction is found in Roman law where, according to Justinian's *Institutes*, 'there is nothing so natural as that the intent of the owner to transfer his property to another should have effect given to it.'[20] In the *Digest* of Justinian Ulpian writes that 'We say that a person possesses by stealth who has entered into possession without the knowledge of him who, he suspects, would oppose his taking [*quem sibi controuersiam facturum suspicabatur*]. . . . No one acquires possession by stealth who takes possession with the knowledge or consent [*sciente aut uolente*] of the thing's owner.'[21] And in his important mid-thirteenth-century gloss on this passage, Accursius adds the phrase 'et non contradicente.'[22] From this phrase would seem to derive Columbus's declaration 'and I was not contradicted,' or in the Latin translation of his letter, 'contradicente nemine possessionem accepi.'[23]

But how should such a principle be thought to apply in this case? The problem is not simply opposing interests – the natives' desire to retain possession of their land against the Spanish desire to appropriate it – but incommensurable positions.[24] The Arawak are not simply denied the opportunity to dispute the Spanish claim; they are not in the same universe of discourse. Even if one discounts the incompatibility of a bureaucratic system based on legal title and a way of life that does not conceive of the land as alienable 'real estate,' the abyss between the two parties remains so overwhelming that Columbus's claim that he was not contradicted seems absurd.[25] Why should words spoken in a language the native inhabitants had obviously never before heard be thought to constitute a valid speech act, transferring their lands to those whose utterly incomprehensible visual signs – a cross, two crowns, the letters F and Y – were printed on the Spanish banners? Why should the natives be thought capable, under the circumstances, of assenting or offering a contradiction?[26]

The answer, I think, may lie in the extreme formalism of Columbus's linguistic acts. That is, Columbus is observing a form – the journal, let us recall, spoke of making the 'required declarations' – and that form evidently calls for the possibility of a contradiction, a counter-declaration to the one by which possession is claimed. It is this formal occasion that must be observed rather than the contingency for which the formal occasion must originally have been conceived. Fulfilling the forms is enough: what we would be tempted to dismiss as *mere* form is for Columbus and for the Spanish whom he serves the heart of the matter. Hence Columbus does not write, 'the natives did not contradict me,' but rather, 'I was not contradicted.' He is not concerned with a particular subjective consciousness responding to the proclamation and hence with consent as an inner act of volition but with the formal absence of an objection to his words. *Why* there was no objection is of no consequence; all that matters is that there was none. The formalism of Columbus's proclamation derives not only from the fact that it represents the scrupulous observance of a preconceived form (hence is not spontaneous or aleatory) but also from its complete indifference to the consciousness of the other. The words are a closed system, closed in such a way as to silence those whose objection might challenge or negate the proclamation which formally, but only formally, envisages the possibility of contradiction.

According to medieval concepts of natural law, uninhabited territories become the possession of the first to discover them.[27] We might say that Columbus's formalism tries to make the new lands uninhabited – *terrae nullius* – by emptying out the category of the other. The other exists only as an empty sign, a cipher. Hence there can be no contradiction to the proclamation from anyone on the islands themselves, because only linguistic competence, the ability to understand and to speak, would enable one to fill in the sign. There is, of course, a whole multinational culture – the Europe from which Columbus has come – that has this competence and could both understand and dispute the claimed possession, but then this culture is not in the right place at the right time. When the moment arrived to contradict the proclamation, those who could contradict it were absent, and all subsequent claims will be forever belated and thus invalid. When, almost immediately after his return, Columbus's letter is published in several languages all over Europe, in effect it promulgates the Spanish claim and affirms that the moment for contradiction has irrevocably passed. The ritual of possession, though it is apparently directed toward the natives, has its full meaning then in relation to other European powers when they come to hear of the discovery. It is as if from the instant of landfall Columbus imagines that everything he sees is already the possession of one of the monarchies he has offered to serve – Portuguese, English, Spanish – and he proceeds to establish the correct claim by the proper formal speech act. I said at the outset that Columbus's words – 'And there I found very many islands filled with people innumerable, and of them all I have taken possession for their highnesses' – were empty place-holders for the unknown and unimaginable. We could call this quality of the words their *open formalism*, since it is precisely their formal vacancy (a set of blanks that have not yet been filled in) that makes possible the imperial indeterminacy of the claim to possession. But now we find that this openness is itself the effect of an underlying *closed formalism*, since the ritual of possession itself precludes the intervention (or even the understanding) of those who, the ceremony implicitly acknowledges, are most likely to object. Formalism then has the virtue of at once inviting and precluding contradiction both in the present and in the future: 'Speak now or forever hold your peace.'[28]

The formalism I have described is generally important in the functioning of legal and religious rituals, but it is by no means limited to these discourses. The letter to Santangel, after all, is not a legal document but a narrative.[29] Narrative is a comfortable home for the discursive strategy I have been describing because the pressure of linked events and the assumed coherence of the tale help to pull the reader past the awkwardness of incommensurable positions and silenced voices. It is one of the principal powers of narrative to gesture toward what is not in fact expressed, to create the illusion of presences that are in reality absent. For this reason, the formal acknowledgment of beings who are at the same time rendered silent is less discordant in Columbus's narrative, less obviously anomalous, than it is in juridical or theological discourse where it soon provoked eloquent and sustained protest.

If we recognize that formalism in the letter to Santangel functions as the discursive agent of Columbus's power, I think we should resist the notion that formalism has a necessary and inherent politics, and that this politics is colonialist. For in the next generation a comparable formalism led Francisco de Vitoria (*c.* 1492–1546) to argue from the tenets of natural law that the indigenous peoples had not had their rights respected, and to challenge the basis for the whole Spanish claim to the Indies. Thus, for example, Vitoria quickly dispatches the claim to sovereignty through the right of discovery. There is a title, he writes in *De indiis*,

which can be set up, namely, by right of discovery; and no other title was originally set up, and it was in virtue of this title alone that Columbus the Genoan first set sail. And this seems to be an adequate title because those regions which are deserted become, by the law of nations and the natural law, the property of the first occupant [*Inst.*, 2. 1. 12]. Therefore, as the Spaniards were the first to discover and occupy the provinces in question, they are in lawful possession thereof, just as if they had discovered some lonely and thitherto uninhabited region.

Not much, however, need be said about this . . . title of ours, because, as proved above, the barbarians were true owners, both from the public and from the private standpoint. Now the rule of the law of nations is that what belongs to nobody is granted to the first occupant, as is expressly laid down in the aforementioned

passage of the *Institutes*. And so, as the object in question was not without an
owner, it does not fall under the title which we are discussing. . . . In and by itself
[this title] gives no support to a seizure of the aborigines any more than if it had
been they who had discovered us.[30]

It could be demonstrated then, on purely formal grounds, that Columbus's
ritual of possession was not valid.[31] Conversely, a theoretical position quite
opposed to formalism could be used to support the Spanish claim. Thus, from
the perspective of an anti-formalist historicism, Gonzalo Fernandez de Oviedo,
the official chronicler for Charles V, in effect discounts the paramount importance of Columbus's formal acts. To be sure, Oviedo celebrates the voyage for its
visionary daring, its unprecedented use of navigational instruments, its geopol-
itical significance, but then he carefully collects stories designed to show that
Columbus learned his route from a dying pilot, that others had been there before,
that the alleged discovery is in reality a rediscovery. Above all, Oviedo proves to
his own satisfaction at least that the Indies are identical to the Hesperides. And on
the principle that 'provinces and kingdoms in olden days took the name of the
princes or lords who founded, conquered, settled or fell heir to them,' he
concludes that the Hesperides were named for Hesperus, twelfth king of Spain
in descent from Tubal Cain, and hence that 'it has now been 3193 years that
Spain and Hesperus, her king, have held dominion over these islands.' 'So, with
such very ancient right,' he declares, 'God returned this domain to Spain after so
many centuries.'[32]

Oviedo's argument was not a quaint expression of historical curiosity; it was a
sophisticated intervention in the long legal battle, the *pleitos de Colón*, between the
crown and Columbus's heirs over the latter's claim to hereditary rights in the
New World. Those rights had been granted for any lands that Columbus had
'discovered or gained;' if there was no authentic discovery but only a restoration
of rights, then the position of the heirs would be substantially weakened. A
further function of Oviedo's historicizing claim was to weaken the link between
Spanish sovereignty in the New World and the 'donation' of the Indies to Spain
by Pope Alexander VI in 1493. Papal bulls granted to Ferdinand and Isabella
dominion over all the lands inhabited by non-Christians that they might discover
in the Atlantic. But, as Anthony Pagden notes, this donation 'rested on the two
claims which Spanish jurists and theologians found hardest to accept: the claims
that the papacy possessed temporal as well as spiritual authority and that it could
exercise this authority over pagans as well as Christians.'[33] Moreover, when the
Catholic Church began to play a more independent role in Spain's American
possessions and to dispute certain of its policies, especially its treatment of the
Indians, the crown sought to create some distance between the papal donation
and its own 'right of possession,' now revealed to be of great antiquity. Hence a
Spanish jurist of the late seventeenth century, Diego Andrés Rocha, maintains
that from a theological perspective Spain's claim to the New World derives from
God's providential design to propagate the true faith through the agency of the
Spanish, but that from a juridical perspective it derives from the *derecho de
reversion*, the right of restitution, whereby lands are returned to their legitimate

possessors.[34] We should add that comparable 'historical' arguments – claims to prior migrations and possession by ancient rulers – were made for other European peoples, including the Portuguese, the Frisians, and the Welsh.[35] But obviously the further we get from actual power, the more idle (in a sense, the more 'merely formal') these claims become: even if all of Europe had freely granted that there was a strong resemblance between Nahuatl, the Aztec language, and Welsh, the Spanish crown was not about to cede its territorial claims in Mexico.

Should we not say then that the words do not matter, that the discursive tactics are interchangeable, that language is a mere screen for the brutal reality of power? There is a flood of words about the New World in the generations after Columbus, there are serious debates in Salamanca and elsewhere about the legitimacy of the Spanish rule, there are denunciations of atrocities and passionate defenses of the necessity of military sternness – but what difference does any of it make? Isn't the whole miserable story, the story of an absolute denial of consent, already written in the first Spanish sneeze, with its millions of invisible bullets? Isn't the fate of the natives sealed in the first innocently drawn blood: 'I showed them swords and they took them by the edge and through ignorance cut themselves' (*Diario*, p. 67). This 'ignorance' – the first glimpse of a decisive imbalance in military technology, carefully noted at the initial encounter – would, in conjunction with vulnerability to European disease, doom the natives of the Caribbean and fatally weaken the great Indian empires that the Spaniards were shortly to encounter. One should perhaps add another brute physical fact: the horrible misfortune that the earth of the New World harbored gold and that many of the native peoples worked this gold into ornaments and hence carried it on their bodies for the Spanish to see. No doubt the weapons and microbes would have reached the New World peoples anyway, but without the gold the destructive forces would have come more slowly, and there might have been time for a defense.

From this vantage-point, words seem like mere covers for Spanish actions and the physical consequences of those actions. The webs of discourse should be stripped away and discarded in order to face unflinchingly the terrible meaning of 1492 and its aftermath: swords and bullets pierce naked flesh and microbes kill bodies that lack sufficient immunities. I am a teacher of literature, and so by training and impulse hostile to such an argument, but I find it very difficult to dismiss. Words in the New World seem always to be trailing after events that pursue a terrible logic quite other than the fragile meanings that they construct.

But if we are thus forced to abandon the dream of linguistic omnipotence, the fantasy that to understand the discourse is to understand the event, we are not at the same time compelled or even permitted to discard words altogether. For if microbes lie altogether beyond the grasp of Renaissance discourse, the other forces that we have cited as brute facts should under no circumstances be naturalized. The possession of weapons and the will to use them on defenseless people are cultural matters that are intimately bound up with discourse: with the stories that a culture tells itself, its conceptions of personal boundary and liability, its whole collective system of rules. And if gold is a natural phenomenon, the all-consuming craving for gold most assuredly is not.

The *unnaturalness* of the desire for gold is one of the great themes of the fifteenth and sixteenth centuries, a theme tirelessly rehearsed by poets, playwrights, and moralists and frequently illustrated by tales of European behavior in the New World. One of the most famous images of the Spanish in America depicts a group of Indians punishing a *conquistador* for his insatiable thirst for gold by pouring the molten metal down his throat.[36] In part such images, which drew upon ancient polemics against greed, reflected sectarian hostilities – here Protestant against Catholic – but in part they reflected a more ecumenical uneasiness in the face of the growth of a money economy and an uncertainty about the status of gold.

Moreover, if certain crucial aspects of the European encounter with the New World were beyond words (and beyond the comprehension of any of the participants), the Europeans themselves struggled to bring as much of their experience as possible under the control of discourse. How could they – or, for that matter, how could we – do otherwise?[37] And it is not only as a futile attempt to comprehend the unimaginable that this discourse may interest us but as both an instrument of empire and an expression, however constrained and half-hearted, of resistance.

Hence, to return to Columbus's initial proclamation, if the declaration that he was not contradicted is absurd, it is also a sign – one of the few signs that we have from this first voyage – of an ethical reservation, a sense that the wishes of the native inhabitants should be respected. The reservation is not direct, it may not have been conscious, and it was certainly not effective, but it nevertheless exists, so deeply entrenched in the language of the judicial procedure that it could not be simply forgotten or eliminated. The procedure was directed, I have observed, to other Europeans, in order to record and legitimate the Spanish claim, but legitimation necessarily included an acknowledgment of the existence of the natives and a recognition of values other than superior force. And though it is important to recognize the practical emptiness of this acknowledgment and to understand how it was emptied out, there seems to me nothing to be gained from a contemptuous dismissal of the discourse in which the acknowledgment is embedded. Where else do we get our own ragged sense that there is something other than force, our own craving for justice? In a dark time (or for that matter an expansive time filled with a sense of infinite possibility and an indifference to the human cost), the awareness of a 'contradiction' is carried precisely in the small textual resistances – a kind of imagined possibility, a dream of equity – that Columbus had to contrive to overcome.

The overcoming in this case is made possible by formalism. If there is no theoretical necessity to his formalism, no innate politics, and no determining power, there are none the less strategic reasons for its presence as a shaping force in his discourse. It enables him, as we have seen, to stage a legal ritual that depends upon the formal possibility of contradiction without actually permitting such contradiction; that is, it enables him to empty out the existence of the natives, while at the same time officially acknowledging that they exist. But does this paradox not simply empty out the legal ritual itself? Does it not make a mockery of the basis on which Columbus is grounding the Spanish claim to the

Indies? Columbus's founding speech act in the New World is spectacularly 'infelicitous' in virtually every one of the senses detailed by Austin in *How To Do Things With Words*: it is a misfire, a misinvocation, a misapplication, and a misexecution.[38] And it is difficult to believe that Columbus is unaware of these infelicities, for he knows very well that these are *not* uninhabited territories; indeed he notes that they have an immense population – *gente sin número*. It might have been possible to argue that these numberless people were so barbarous that they had no rights – the argument was made repeatedly in the sixteenth century and beyond – but Columbus does not do so and would probably have resisted the suggestion, since he wishes to believe that he has arrived in the 'Indies' and hence he must assume that he is in the outlying regions of a great empire, ultimately under the control of the Grand Khan.[39] And he recognizes almost at once that even here, on these small islands with their naked inhabitants living in tiny hamlets and appearing to share everything, there is a political and social order of some kind.

Indeed in the log-book Columbus describes communities characterized not by savage confusion but by an admirable orderliness. He admires the 'wonderful dignity' of the native 'king' whose people 'all obey him so that it is a marvel.' 'All of these lords,' he goes on to note, 'are of few words and of very attractive customs; and their commands are for the most part carried out by hand signs so soon understood that it is a marvel' (*Diario*, p. 275). Columbus makes no mention of this indigenous social order in the opening sentences of the letter to Santangel – evidently he did not consider it relevant to the ceremony of possession – but he subsequently refers to their 'chief or king' who is given as many as twenty wives, while common men have only one.[40]

The recognition of a hierarchical society returns us to the question, how is it possible to 'take possession' of such a place in the presence of those who inhabit it? For Francisco de Vitoria, such a recognition should invalidate the Spanish claim; the Indians manifestly are rational human agents, 'because there is a certain method in their affairs, for they have polities which are orderly and arranged and they have definite marriage and magistrates, overlords, laws, and workshops, and a system of exchange, all of which call for the use of reason.'[41] The territory of people who live in such polities cannot justly be appropriated, even if the people are pagans and hence in a state of mortal sin. The juridical problem does not arise if the lands are uninhabited – for under the law of nations and natural law, deserted regions become the property of the first occupant – nor does it arise, at least in the same terms, if one is conquering a recognized enemy. In his account of the third voyage (1498–1500), Columbus, responding to attacks upon his conduct, attempts to recast his role. 'At home,' he writes to Doña Juana, governess to the Infante D. Juan, 'they judge me as a governor sent to Sicily or to a city or two under settled government, and where the laws can be fully maintained, without fear of all being lost.' Such a perspective on the situation, he argues, is wholly inappropriate:

I ought to be judged as a captain who went from Spain to the Indies to conquer a people, warlike and numerous, and with customs and beliefs very different from ours, a people, living in highlands and mountains, having no settled dwellings, and apart from us; and where, by the will of God, I have brought under the dominion of the king and queen, our sovereigns, another world, whereby Spain, which was called poor, is now most rich.[42]

The first letter is careful to indicate that the formal rites of legality had been observed; this letter by contrast insists that such observation would be wholly inappropriate, a kind of theoretical fastidiousness that ends by losing everything. By 1498 both Columbus's personal circumstances and the institutional context in which he was operating had changed profoundly. In 1493 Pope Alexander VI had issued the bull *Inter caetera*, donating the newly discovered lands, out of 'mere liberality, certain science, and apostolic authority,' to the sovereigns of Spain and Portugal.[43] The Indians in Columbus's account can now be assigned the marks of outlaws or rebels; they are people who live on the margins – 'sierras y montes, syn pueblo asentado, ni nosotros.' This marginal existence, the lives of those who are 'not us,' marks their distance from civility. The 'infinity of small hamlets' mentioned in the first letter have disappeared, and the Indians have been assimilated to a conception of nomadic barbarism as old as ancient Greece. They are the people who live outside of all just order, apart from settled human community and hence from the very condition of the virtuous life. 'He who is unable to live in society, or who has no need because he is sufficient for himself,' Aristotle wrote, 'must be either a beast or a god.'[44] The Indians were clearly not gods and hence could in this light be regarded as beasts.

Their unsettled life, in Columbus's self-justifying account, not only reveals their bestial nature but also marks the difficulty of pacifying or containing them. For European authority in the early modern period was the authority of the plain, of walled towns that could if necessary be besieged and starved into submission; the central authorities feared and hated the mountains. And, of course, for Columbus the natives of the New World are not merely like the untamed dwellers of the European wastelands; from the first days he suspects something worse, and the suspicion hardens into a certainty that many of the islands are inhabited by cannibals.[45]

But in 1492 Columbus goes out of his way to present a very different picture of all of the natives whom he actually encounters. These natives do not, to be sure, live in towns or villages, but they inhabit small hamlets (*pequeñas poblaciones*), and they are utterly harmless: 'They have no iron or steel or weapons, nor are they fitted to use them, not because they are not well-built men and of handsome stature, but because they are very marvellously timorous [*muy temerosos á maravilla*]' (i. 6). What makes their timorousness marvelous? They flee at the approach of the Spaniards, Columbus explains, 'even a father not waiting for his son' (i. 8). The example assumes a norm of natural courage, the courage that instinctively arises in all men to defend their offspring, or, more precisely, their male offspring. And this creatural instinct is inexplicably absent in the timorous natives, inexplicably not only in relation to a father's natural care for his son but in relation to the entirely friendly and generous deportment of the Spanish.

It is odd: Columbus has just unilaterally taken possession of everything he sees on behalf of the king and queen of Spain; he declares moreover that 'as soon as I arrived in the Indies, in the first island which I found, I took by force some of them, in order that they might learn and give me information' (i. 10).[46] Yet this armed invader who seizes lands and people regards his own intentions as impeccably generous: 'at every point where I have been and have been able to have speech, I have given to them of all that I had, such as cloth and many other things, without receiving anything for it' (i. 8). It is characteristic of Columbus's discourse that it yokes together actions, attitudes, or perceptions that would seem ethically incompatible, here seizing everything on the one hand and giving everything on the other. The two are clearly related in some way, but they do not directly impinge on one another, just as there is an unexpressed, unacknowledged relation between the fact that the natives do not understand his language and the fact that no one contradicts his proclamation. It would, I suppose, be possible to term this hypocrisy, but the term suggests a staging of moral attitudes that are not actually felt in the deep recesses of the heart, a theatrical self-consciousness, that seems to me quite alien to Columbus's ardent faith. I think rather that we are encountering an important aspect of Columbus's discursive economy, a characteristic rhetorical feature of what we may call his Christian imperialism.

This discursive economy brings opposites into the closest conjunction with one another and yet leaves the heart of their relation a mystery. Columbus takes absolute possession on behalf of the Spanish crown in order to make an absolute gift; he seeks earthly gain in order to serve a divine purpose; the Indians must lose everything in order to receive everything; the innocent natives will give away their gold for trash, but they will receive a treasure far more precious than gold; the wicked natives (the 'cannibals') will be enslaved in order to be freed from their own bestiality. Empowering these paradoxes is an ancient Christian rhetoric that has its most famous Renaissance English expression in the Holy Sonnets of John Donne:

> That I may rise, and stand, o'erthrow mee, and bend
>   Your force, to break, blowe, burn, and make me new ...
>   Take me to you, imprison me, for I
>   Except you'enthrall mee, never shall be free,
>   Nor ever chast, except you ravish me.

Columbus's version of this rhetoric is at once less histrionic and more paradoxical, since it is cast neither in a prayer nor in a poem but in a report establishing secular authority over newly discovered lands and peoples: imperialism is by no means the opposite of Christianity but neither is it simply identical with it. For like the legal formalism at which we have glanced, Christian faith could empower radically opposed positions: if in the name of Christianity, Queen Isabella could decree the use of force against the Indians 'whenever conversion to the holy Catholic Faith and allegiance to the Crown were not immediately forthcoming,'[47] so too in the name of Christianity, Bartolomé de Las Casas could bitterly condemn the entire Spanish enterprise.

From the first moments, the encounter with the New World mobilizes in Columbus cravings for power and status and wealth, cravings that sit in an uneasy relation to his Franciscan religiosity, his appetite to convert and save, his apocalyptic dreams. It would be a mistake to think of these simply as opposed desires – a spiritual side of Columbus at war with his carnal side – for the whole achievement of the discourse of Christian imperialism is to represent desires as *convertible* and in a constant process of exchange. Were these desires actually identical, Columbus would have no need to articulate all of the ways in which they are cross-coupled; were they actually opposed, he would not be able to exchange one for the other. The possibility of such an exchange, rooted perhaps in his experience of Italian merchant life, haunts his writing:

> Genoese, Venetians, and all who have pearls, precious stones, and other things of value, all carry them to the end of the world in order to exchange them, to turn [*convertir*] them into gold. Gold is most excellent. Gold constitutes treasure, and he who possesses it may do what he will in the world, and may so attain as to bring souls to Paradise. (ii. 102–4)

In this rhapsodic moment, from his account of the fourth voyage, the conversion of commodities into gold slides liquidly into the conversion and hence salvation of souls. If it seems strange, we might recall that in the Spanish of the Middle Ages and Renaissance, the Crusade to the Holy Land was called not the *cruzada* – that word referred to the special papal concessions granted to the Spanish crown to fight against the infidel within its own territory – but rather the *empresa* or *negocio*, terms in which the mercantile and the religious are intertwined.[48]

The rhetorical task of Christian imperialism then is to bring together commodity conversion and spiritual conversion.[49] Most often these are simply juxtaposed by Columbus, as if the energies of the one would naturally spill over into the other but, on occasion, their interchange is articulated more directly: 'You shall say to their highnesses,' writes Columbus to his agent Antonio de Torres in 1494,

> that the welfare of the souls of the said cannibals [the natives whom the Spanish have enslaved and shipped back to Spain], and also of those here, has induced the idea that the more that may be sent over, the better it will be, and in this their highnesses may be served in the following way. That, having seen how necessary cattle and beasts of burden are here, for the support of the people who have to be here, and indeed for all these islands, their highnesses might give licence and a permit for a sufficient number of caravels to come here every year and to carry the said cattle and other supplies and things for the colonization of the country and the development of the land, and this at reasonable prices at the cost of those who transport them. Payment for these things could be made to them in slaves, from among these cannibals, a people very savage and suitable for the purpose, and well made and of very good intelligence. We believe that they, having abandoned that inhumanity, will be better than any other slaves, and their inhumanity they will immediately lose when they are out of their own land. (i. 90–2)

Beasts of burden will be exchanged for beasts of burden: so many Indians for so many cattle. Columbus cannot be content, however, with a purely mercantile transaction, nor is this his overriding interest. He cannot allow himself, for reasons both tactical and more deeply spiritual, to say simply, 'We need cattle; we have slaves; let us trade one for the other.' The exchange must be presented as undertaken in the interests of the enslaved. We might call this enslavement with a human face, or rather, liberating enslavement. For the exchange Columbus envisions would put into practice the religious rhetoric that we glimpsed in Donne: at its core is not an economic transaction but a dream of marvelous transformation. Those Indians identified as cannibals will be hunted down, seized, torn from their lands and their culture, loaded onto ships still stinking of the animals for whom they are being exchanged, and sent into slavery. But the economic transaction as Columbus conceives it will be undertaken for the welfare of the souls of the enslaved: the Indians are exchanged for beasts in order to convert them into humans. This transformation will not enfranchise them; it will only make them into excellent slaves.[50] But they will have gained their spiritual freedom. At the heart of the transaction is not wealth or convenience, though these are welcome, but a metamorphosis from inhumanity into humanity. The Crown, we might note, evidently had doubts, on legal and religious grounds, about the legitimacy of the proposed exchange: Isabella intervened and stopped the sale of the slaves.[51]

The occult relation between apparent opposites in the Christian discourse of John Donne draws the reader toward contemplation of the mysterious nature of the Incarnation; the occult relation between apparent opposites in the Christian imperialist discourse of Columbus draws the reader toward contemplation of the 'marvelous' nature of the New World and its inhabitants. The wonder aroused by the cannibals is twofold; it lies in the uncanny conjunction of native intelligence and inhumanity, and again in the uncanny power of enslavement to humanize. But, as we have already observed, it is not only the warlike cannibals who awaken wonder. In the letter of 1500 Columbus wishes his readers to think of the Indians as warlike; in the letter of 1492 he wishes that they be thought timid, indeed marvelously timid.[52] The term 'marvelous,' which we have already seen Columbus use in the first sentence of the first letter, obviously appeals to readerly expectations about the genre of travel literature. But timidity in this context is a peculiar marvel, and Columbus intensifies its peculiarity by stressing that the natives are 'well-built men and of handsome stature.' We are not dealing here with a strange race of creatures that do not bear arms because they literally do not have arms, or legs, or heads on their shoulders. Columbus's readers would be well-prepared for the monstrous. What they might not expect to find is the marvelous in human timidity. In urging them to do so, and by thus relocating the marvelous from the grotesque to the ordinary, Columbus induces his readers to join him in what we may call an act of ideological forgetting. If one clearly remembered the actions Columbus has just described – the sudden arrival of armed and armored strangers, kidnapping, and expropriation of lands – it would be more difficult to find the natives' panic fear all that marvelous.

Columbus does not use the discourse of the marvelous in order to create a momentary amnesia about his actions; he induces a momentary amnesia about his actions in order to create the discourse of the marvelous. Indeed the production of a sense of the marvelous in the New World is at the very center of virtually all of Columbus's writings about his discoveries, though the meaning of that sense shifts over the years.[53] His constant insistence on the marvelous is generally treated as if it were a simple record of what he and his companions felt, as if Columbus's discourse were perfectly transparent and his feelings those 'naturally' evoked by his experiences. (Alternatively, it is possible to argue – incorrectly, I think – that Columbus had such an impoverished vocabulary that he could think of no other word to describe his experiences.)[54] But we may take Columbus himself in testimony to the special significance of the experience of wonder. In his official report to Ferdinand and Isabella on the third voyage, Columbus writes that in response to 'the defaming and disparagement of the undertaking that had been begun' in the New World, because he 'had not immediately sent caravels laden with gold,' he 'decided to come to Your Highnesses, and to cause you to wonder at everything, and to show you the reason that I had for all [*y maravillarme de todo, y mostrarles la razón que en todo avía*]' (ii. 4–6).[55] There is by the third voyage a specific political and rhetorical reason for the performance and production of wonder: the marvelous is precisely the sense that will confirm the power and validity of Columbus's claims against those cavilling skeptics who want more tangible signs of gain. Not to manifest and arouse wonder is to succumb to the attacks against him. The marvelous stands for the missing caravels laden with gold; it is – like the ritual of possession itself – a word pregnant with what is imagined, desired, promised.

The production of wonder then is not only an expression of the effect that the voyage had upon Columbus but a calculated rhetorical strategy, the evocation of an aesthetic response in the service of a legitimation process. It is possible that the *explicit* calculation marks the frustration of Columbus's early hopes and the darkening of his situation, and that his constant expressions of wonder in the earlier voyages are a more spontaneous response to the innocence, beauty, and freshness of the Caribbean islands and their peoples. But we should recall that Columbus's first use of the marvelous refers not to the land itself but to its possession – Columbus gives thanks to the 'Divine Majesty, Who has marvelously bestowed all this.' If the use of wonder as a rhetorical strategy becomes explicit in the third voyage, when an increasingly embattled Columbus is forced to articulate his purposes, its place in the legitimation process is already at work, as we have seen, in the first voyage.

Wonder, however, does not inherently legitimate a claim to possession. Indeed, as we have seen in *Mandeville's Travels*, in the Middle Ages the experience of marvels seems to lead precisely to a sense of dispossession, a disclaimer of dogmatic certainty, a self-estrangement in the face of the strangeness, diversity, and opacity of the world. The medieval sense of the marvelous, Jacques Le Goff has suggested, expressed perceptions of nature potentially or actually inimical to the transcendental being and providential authority of the Christian God and His servant the Church.[56] It stood then for all that could not be securely held, all that resisted appropriation. Why should Columbus, whose interests are diametrically opposed to dispossession and self-estrangement, continually invoke wonder? In part, he may do so because the marvelous is closely linked in classical and Christian rhetoric to heroic enterprise. The voyages of Odysseus in particular were for centuries the occasion for aesthetic and philosophical speculations on the relation between heroism and the arousal of wonder through a representation of marvels. In part, he may do so to associate his discoveries with a specifically 'Christian marvelous' that, in opposition to all that is irregular and heterodox in the experience of wonder, identifies spiritual authenticity with the proper evocation of marvels.[57] And, most simply and directly, Columbus may strive to arouse wonder because marvels are inseparably bound up in rhetorical and pictorial tradition with voyages to the Indies. To affirm the 'marvelous' nature of the discoveries is, even without the lucrative shipments yet on board, to make good on the claim to have reached the fabled realms of gold and spices. This is the significance, I think, of Columbus's mention in the first letter of a province in Cuba that the Indians call 'Avan' where 'the people are born with tails';[58] such prodigies were a virtual requirement for travelers to the Indies. That he singles out Cuba in particular as the probable site of the authenticating wonders of the East is probably a reflection of the hope Columbus recorded in the log-book that this island – toward which the natives seemed to be directing him – was Japan, or 'Cipango' as Marco Polo called it. 'And I believe so,' Columbus writes with a blind conviction born of wish-fulfillment, 'because I believe that it is so according to the signs that all the Indians of these islands and those that I have with me make (because I do not understand them through speech) [and] that it is the island of Cipango of which marvelous things [*cosas maravillosas*] are told' (*Diario*, p. 113).

Yet the observations that he records to create the effect of the marvelous are for the most part strikingly unlike the marvels conventionally recorded in travelers' tales. Once, off the coast of Haiti, Columbus sighted 'three mermaids [*serenas*] who came quite high out of the water,' but his log-book description of these prodigies – in all likelihood, Caribbean manatees or sea-cows – tellingly suggests a resistance to the traditional iconography: they 'were not as pretty as they are depicted, for somehow in the face they look like men' (*Diario*, p. 321).[59] In his log-book entry for November 4, 1492, Columbus notes apparent native confirmation of marvels about which he must have been inquiring: 'far from there,' the natives supposedly inform him, 'there were one-eyed men, and others, with snouts of dogs, who ate men, and that as soon as one was taken they cut his throat and drank his blood and cut off his genitals' (*Diario*, p. 133). (The display of signs that Columbus must have made to elicit this information may help to explain why the natives, as he notes in the same entry, were 'very timid.') But by the time he writes the first letter, he seems far more skeptical: 'In these islands I have so far found no human monstrosities, as many expected, but on the contrary the whole population is very well-formed' (i. 14). He appears to be distinguishing then between monstrosities and marvels: the former are vivid, physical violations of universal norms, the latter are physical impressions that arouse wonder. Columbus is not willing to rule out the possibility of the monstrous, but he is scrupulous in limiting his claims to have personally witnessed monstrosities; the marvelous, by contrast, he notes at first-hand again and again.

The marvelous functions for Columbus as the agent of conversion: a fluid mediator between outside and inside, spiritual and carnal, the realm of objects and the subjective impressions made by those objects, the recalcitrant otherness of a new world and the emotional effect aroused by that otherness. More precisely it registers the presence of Columbus's fears and desires in the very objects he perceives and conversely the presence in his discourse of a world of objects that exceed his understanding of the probable and the familiar. Hence, for example, he writes that he 'saw many trees very different from ours, and among them many which had branches of many kinds, and all on one trunk. And one little branch is of one kind, and another of another, and so different that it is the greatest wonder in the world [*la mayor maravilla del mundo*]' (*Diario*, p. 89). 'Here the fish are so different from ours,' he notes in the same log-book entry for October 16, 'that it is a marvel. There are some shaped like dories, of the finest colors in the world: blues, yellows, reds, and of all colors; and others colored in a thousand ways. And the colors are so fine that there is no man who would not marvel and take great delight in seeing them' (*Diario*, pp. 89–91). As such passages suggest, it is not simply the recognition of the unusual that constitutes a marvel but a certain excess, a hyperbolic intensity, a sense of awed delight.[60]

The marvelous for Columbus usually involves then a surpassing of the measure but not in the direction of the monstrous or grotesque; rather, a heightening of impressions until they reach a kind of perfection. Española, he writes in the first letter, is 'very fertile to a limitless degree'; its harbors are 'beyond comparison with others which I know in Christendom,' it has many good and large rivers 'which is marvellous' (*que es maravilla*); and its mountains are 'beyond comparison with the island of Teneriffe' (i. 4).[61] These mountains, however, are not forbidding; 'all are most beautiful, of a thousand shapes, and all are accessible and filled with trees of a thousand kinds and tall, and they seem to touch the sky' (i. 4–6). The trees, Columbus is told, never lose their foliage, and he believes what is told, 'for I saw them as green and as lovely as they are in Spain in May. . . . And the nightingale was singing and other birds of a thousand kinds in the month of November' (i. 6). Large numbers, particularly 'a thousand,' are repeated as conventional talismans of wonder, though even much smaller figures will do: 'There are six or eight kinds of palm, which are a wonder to behold [*que es admiración verlas*] on account of their beautiful variety,' and there are 'marvellous pine groves [*pinares á maravilla*].' The marvellous, as can be seen here, has little or nothing to do with the grotesque or outlandish. It denotes, to be sure, some departure, displacement, or surpassing of the normal or the probable, but in the direction of delicious variety and loveliness.

This loveliness extends in the first letter to the natives. When they overcame their 'marvelous timorousness,' the natives 'all brought something to eat and drink, which they gave with extraordinary affection [*con un amor maravilloso*]' (i. 10). The log-book entries are even more explicit: 'they brought us all that they had in the world and knew that the Admiral wanted; and all so bigheartedly [*con vn Coraçon tan largo*] and so happily that it was a wonder [*maravilla*]' (*Diario*, p. 255).[62] Columbus's response to this marvelous generosity is revealing:

> The Admiral gave them glass beads and brass rings and bells: not because they asked for something, but because it seemed to him that it was right; and above all, says the Admiral, because he already considers them as Christians and as more the subjects of the sovereigns of Castile than the Castilians. And he says that nothing is lacking except to know the language and to give them orders, because everything they are ordered to do they will do without any opposition [*sin contradiçion algua*]. (*Diario*, p. 259)

The spirit of the gift-giving, as Columbus understands it, is not reciprocal: the Indians give out of an unconstrained openness of heart that is a marvel; the Spanish in return give out of a sense of what is right, a sense of obligation bound up with the conviction that the Indians have *already* become the Christian subjects of the sovereigns of Castile.[63] They are easily imagined as subjects because they are so easily imagined as already subjected, inhabitants of lands appropriated without contradiction (*y no me fué contradicho*) on the day of the initial encounter. 'They should,' Columbus writes in the log-book entry for that day, 'be good and intelligent servants' (*Diario*, pp. 67–9).

Columbus does not imagine that the Indians could have anything like a comparable thought about the Spanish. Their extraordinary affection, Columbus implies, is powered by their conviction that he, with his ships and men, have come from heaven;[64] that is, for the Indians who had never before seen large ships or clothed men the Spanish too are a marvel. But this recognition of a reverse wonderment does not qualify Columbus's own perceptions or render the marvelous a mere sign of unfamiliarity or *naïveté*. The natives do not make their mistake because they are stupid; they possess, he says, a very acute intelligence, 'so that it is amazing [*es maravilla*] how good an account they give of everything' (i. 10).[65] All of his delighted impressions cohere for Columbus in a single overwhelming perception: 'la Española es maravilla' (i. 7).[66]

In such a phrase the marvelous has been detached altogether from the enumeration of bizarre particulars and has been broadened in scope to characterize an entire place, a place of surprising and intense beauty. To look (*mirar*) at such a place is to wonder (*maravillar*). This characterization associates the discoveries with a long tradition of poems evoking the *locus amoenus*, the landscape of delight. Again and again Columbus's log-book records the intense pleasure of looking:

> [October 14:] And later [I noticed], near the said islet, groves of trees, the most beautiful that I saw and with their leaves as green as those of Castile in the months of April and May. (*Diario*, pp. 75–7)
> [October 17:] In this time I also walked among those trees, which were more beautiful to see than any other thing that has ever been seen, seeing as much verdure and in such degree as in the month of May in Adalusia. (*Diario*, p. 93)
> [October 19:] [T]he island [is] the most beautiful thing that I have seen. For if the others are very beautiful this one is more so. It is an island of many very green and very large trees. . . . I do not know where to go first; nor do my eyes grow tired of seeing such beautiful verdure and so different from ours. (*Diario*, pp. 99–101)

[October 21:] [If the other islands] already seen are very beautiful and green and fertile, this one is much more so and with large and very green groves of trees. Here there are some big lakes and over and around them the groves are marvelous. And here and in all of the island the groves are all green and the verdure like that in April in Andalusia. And the singing of the small birds [is so marvelous] that it seems that a man would never want to leave this place. And [there are] flocks of parrots that obscure the sun; and birds of so many kinds and sizes, and so different from ours, that it is a marvel. (*Diario*, p. 105)

'It seems that a man would never want to leave this place.' If the dream of marvelous possession in such passages is tinged with an undertone of loss, it is not only because Columbus feels the urgent compulsion to pass on to other islands – 'I am not taking pains to see much in detail because I could not do it in 50 years and because I want to see and explore as much as I can so I can return to Your Highnesses in April' (*Diario*, p. 103) – but also because in Christian poetry the *locus amoenus* at its most intense is always touched with remembrance of paradise lost. In the years that follow, the location of the Earthly Paradise interests Columbus with increasing intensity and becomes intertwined with other dreams: the discourse of enraptured looking is shaped by a longing at once erotic and infantile, by the gaze, marveling and forever unsatisfied, of love poetry.

The world is not perfectly round, he writes in a letter sent from Hispaniola in 1498, during his third voyage, but rather has the shape of a pear or of a ball on which is placed 'something like a woman's nipple' (ii. 30). The nipple of the world is the newly discovered land and all signs point to the location at its center of the Earthly Paradise.[67] And if these signs – above all the great streams of fresh water that emanate from the land – do not point to Eden, if the water does not come from paradise, it seems, Columbus writes, 'to be a still greater marvel (*pareçe aun mayor maravilla*), for I do not believe that there is known in the world a river so great and so deep' (ii. 38). The notion of a marvel greater than paradise is startling, but it arises from the only other hypothesis Columbus can posit for his observations: 'And I say that if it be not from the earthly paradise that this river comes, it originates from a vast land, lying to the south, of which hitherto no knowledge has been obtained' (ii. 42). Faced with such a staggering thought – the idea, in effect, of South America – Columbus retreats to the safer ground of the land of Eden: 'But I am much more convinced in my own mind that there where I have said is the earthly paradise.'

An actual recovery of the earthly paradise would partake of the miraculous, but Columbus stops short of such a claim, as he does throughout most of his writings.[68] In effect, the marvelous takes the place of the miraculous, absorbing some of its force but avoiding the theological and evidentiary problems inherent in directly asserting a miracle. Instead of a theological claim, the term *maravilla* as Columbus uses it makes a different kind of claim, one that combines religious and erotic longings in a vision of surpassing beauty. That marvelous vision had since late antiquity played a crucial role in European aesthetics, a role that intensified in the Middle Ages and was exhaustively theorized in the generations after Columbus. 'No one can be called a poet,' writes the influential Italian critic

Minturno in the 1550s, 'who does not excel in the power of arousing wonder.'[69] For Aristotelians wonder is associated with pleasure as the end of poetry; in the *Poetics* Aristotle examines the strategies by which tragedians and epic poets employ the marvelous to arouse pleasurable wonder. For the Platonists too wonder is an essential element in art, for it is one of the principal effects of beauty. In the words of Plotinus, 'This is the effect that Beauty must ever induce, wonderment and a pleasant astonishment, longing and love and a dread that is pleasurable.'[70] In the sixteenth century, the Neoplatonist Francesco Patrizi defines the poet as a 'maker of the marvelous,' and the marvelous is found, as he puts it, when men 'are astounded, ravished in ecstasy.' Patrizi goes so far as to posit marveling as a special faculty of the mind, a faculty which in effect mediates between the capacity to think and the capacity to feel.[71]

The aesthetic theory of the marvelous sidesteps the miraculous but does not altogether resolve questions of credibility. Indeed for the Aristotelian Francesco Robortelli, the marvelous and the credible are in conflict, a conflict that may be masked by a variety of poetic devices but cannot be altogether eliminated.[72] But other poets and theorists saw the two as working in conjunction to produce pleasure. Lodovico Castelvetro wrote that the poet 'must above all seek credibility or verisimilitude in combination with the marvelous: credibility so that the unimaginative audience will believe, the marvelous so that it will find pleasure in the uncommon and the extraordinary';[73] 'we find some true things more marvelous than the false,' argued Jacopo Mazzoni, 'not merely in natural things . . . but also in human history';[74] and Tasso elaborated a theory of the Christian marvelous in which verisimilitude is conferred by faith: 'One and the same action may therefore be both marvelous and verisimilar: marvelous if one consider it in itself and hemmed in by natural limitations, verisimilar if one consider it separated from such limitations with respect to its cause, which is a supernatural force capable of and accustomed to producing such marvels.'[75]

In Renaissance aesthetic theory wonder is associated with the overcoming of great difficulties and with a strange blend of chance and human intention (Castelvetro); or with the spectacle of the unexpected and the extraordinary (Robortelli); or with passions, reversals, and discoveries (Vettori); or with the reconciliation of unity and variety (Tasso); or with novel and surprising twists of narrative (Denores, Talentoni), or with the effects of awe and wonder associated with religious feelings and hence with sublimity and high gravity (Patrizi).[76] Virtually all of these aesthetic categories are implicit in Columbus's insistent use of the marvelous, not, of course, because he is deliberately alluding to them – they are, for the most part, fully articulated only after his time – but because they emerged from the same cultural matrix that shaped his language and perceptions.

We are now perhaps in a position to understand why the term is so important to him and how it bears on the formal legal ritual by which he claims Spanish possession of the Indies.[77] That ritual had at its center, as we have seen, a defect, an absurdity, a tragicomic invocation of the possibility of a refusal that could not in fact conceivably occur: *y no me fué contradicho*. The legal declaration could take place in the spirit of a radical formalism, but that formalism leaves in its wake an emotional and intellectual vacancy, a hole, that threatens to draw the reader of Columbus's discourse toward laughter or tears and toward a questioning of the legitimacy of the Spanish claim.[78] Columbus tries to draw the reader toward wonder, a sense of the marvelous that in effect fills up the emptiness at the center of the maimed rite of possession. Immediately after describing that rite, let us recall, Columbus declares that 'To the first island which I found, I gave the name *San Salvador*, in remembrance of the Divine Majesty, Who has marvelously bestowed all this.' The marvel of the divine gift here is at once a legitimation and a transcendence of the legal act. Roman law procedures dictate the principal gesture of appropriation, but they are supplemented by an incommensurable and marvelous assurance, the assurance in effect of the Biblical promise:

> If you diligently keep all these commandments that I now charge you to observe, by loving the Lord your God, by conforming to his ways and by holding fast to him, the Lord will drive out all these nations before you and you shall occupy the territory of nations greater and more powerful than you. Every place where you set the soles of your feet shall be yours. (Deut. 11: 22–4)

By itself a sense of the marvelous cannot confer title; on the contrary, it is associated with longing, and you long precisely for what you do not have. Columbus's whole life is marked by a craving for something that continually eluded him, for the kingdom or the paradise or the Jerusalem that he could not reach, and his expressions of the marvelous, insofar as they articulate this craving, continue the medieval sense that wonder and secure temporal possession are mutually exclusive. But something happens to the discourse of the marvelous when it is linked to the discourse of the law: the inadequacy of the legal ritual to confer title and the incapacity of the marvelous to confer possession cancel each other out, and both the claim and the emotion are intensified by the conjunction. Neither discourse is freestanding and autonomous; on the contrary, each – like individual words themselves – takes its meaning from its conjunction with other motifs, tropes, and speech acts, and from the situation in which it is inserted. And there is a further motive for the conjunction: under the actual circumstances of the first encounter, there was no discourse adequate to the occasion. In the unprecedented, volatile state of emergence and emergency in which Columbus finds himself, anything he says or does will be defective. His response is to conjoin the most resonant legal ritual he can summon up with the most resonant emotion.

In a remarkable passage to which I have already alluded, Aquinas's teacher, Albertus Magnus, attempts in his *Commentary on the Metaphysics of Aristotle* to provide a convincing account of the internal dynamics of wonder:

> wonder is defined as a constriction and suspension of the heart caused by amazement at the sensible appearance of something so portentous, great, and unusual, that the heart suffers a systole. Hence wonder is something like fear in its effect on the heart. This effect of wonder, then, this constriction and systole of the heart, springs from an unfulfilled but felt desire to know the cause of that which appears portentous and unusual: so it was in the beginning when men, up to that time unskilled, began to

philosophize.... Now the man who is puzzled and wonders apparently does not know. Hence wonder is the movement of the man who does not know on his way to finding out, to get at the bottom of that at which he wonders and to determine its cause.... Such is the origin of philosophy.[79]

Wonder here is not a steady state; it is inherently unstable, a shifter, not only the sign but the principal instigator of movement. For Albertus Magnus the movement driven by the marvelous is from the blankness of ignorance to the fullness of philosophical understanding.[80] Obviously, wonder does not lead Columbus toward philosophy, but it does, in response to God's portentous and unusual gift, lead him toward an act that is closely linked in the Middle Ages and Renaissance to philosophy: the act of naming. That naming, to be sure, has much to do with the manifestation of power through eponymous titles – hence Fernandina, Isabella, and Isla Juana (for Prince Juan, islands traditionally having feminine endings). Moreover, the legal act of possession customarily involved naming, since crown lawyers 'believed that no one could well lay claim to a nameless city, and that a province without a name was hardly a province at all.'[81] But more than legal formality is involved here. The first two names – San Salvador and Isla de Santa María de Concepcíon – suggest once again that the assertion of possession is bound up for Christian imperialism with the giving of a precious gift. And the giving of the gift is in turn bound up with superior knowledge, the knowledge of the truth.

When in Genesis 2: 19 Adam names the animals, medieval commentators understood this to be an act of marvelous *understanding*. Martin Luther is following a long exegetical tradition when he glosses the verse as follows:

> Here again we are reminded of the superior knowledge and wisdom of Adam, who was created in innocence and righteousness. Without any new enlightenment, solely because of the excellence of his nature, he views all the animals and thus arrives at such a knowledge of their nature that he can give each one a suitable name that harmonizes with its nature.[82]

Such understanding, Luther continues, is linked with power:

> From this enlightenment there also followed, of course, the rule over all the animals, something which is also pointed out here, since they were named in accordance with Adam's will. Therefore by one single word he was able to compel lions, bears, boars, tigers, and whatever else there is among the most outstanding animals to carry out whatever suited their nature. (pp. 119–20)

As Francis Bacon puts it, when man 'shall be able to call the creatures by their true names he shall again command them.'[83]

Columbus may have thought that he was near to Paradise, but he also knew that he was the inheritor of Adam's sin through which, as Luther remarks, we lost Paradise as well as this power to bestow primal names and to compel through naming. In his letter, moreover, Columbus makes it clear that he is encountering not a world that has never before been named but rather a world of alien names:

'the Indians call it 'Guanahaní'' His act then is a cancellation of an existing name.[84] But why should Columbus, unlike Marco Polo or Mandeville, think to rename the lands he has encountered? Why should he confer on each island 'una nombre nuevo?' In order, he says, to commemorate the Savior's marvelous gift. The founding action of Christian imperialism is a christening.[85] Such a christening entails the cancellation of the native name − the erasure of the alien, perhaps demonic, identity − and hence a kind of making new; it is at once an exorcism, an appropriation, and a gift. Christening then is the culminating instance of the marvelous speech act: in the wonder of the proper name, the movement from ignorance to knowledge, the taking of possession, the conferral of identity are fused in a moment of pure linguistic formalism.

In the first encounter, Columbus had seized several of the natives to use them as informants and interpreters. Six of these survived the voyage back to Spain and in a remarkable ceremony, with Ferdinand, Isabella, and the Infante acting as godparents, were baptized.[86] The cleverest of the natives, the one most serviceable to the Spanish, was given Columbus's own surname and the Christian name of his first-born child: he was christened Don Diego Colón. The magic of renaming extended to Columbus himself: after the Discovery, in place of Cristóbal, he began to sign his letters Christoferens, the Christ-bearer.[87] And according to the cosmographer Sebastian Münster, the king of Spain said that Columbus should be called not *Almirante*, the admiral, but *Admirans*, the one who wonders.[88] This playful christening conveys in tiny compass the trajectory we have been following: from legal ritual through the experience of the marvelous to the mystical understanding and appropriative power of naming. The claim of possession is grounded in the power of wonder.

As Columbus's vision darkened over the years, he seems to have invested more and more of his hopes for possession in the marvelous power of the name. Looking back on his years of fruitless searching for royal support, he declares that he never gave up hope, because God 'spake so clearly of these lands by the mouth of Isaiah, in many places of his Book, affirming that from Spain His holy name should be proclaimed to them' (ii. 4). Columbus's first act of naming then − San Salvador for Guanahaní − is the fulfillment of a Biblical prophecy.[89] Making new is paradoxically the realization of the old. If the act of naming makes the world conform to the word, Columbus believes at the same time that the word is conforming at last to the world.[90] In the words of Scripture, 'As his name is, so is he' (1 Samuel 25: 25).

On his last voyage to the New World, in despair, surrounded by hostile natives, 'utterly alone, in a high fever and in a state of great exhaustion,' Columbus falls alseep and hears a 'compassionate voice' that speaks to him about his own name:

> O fool and slow to believe and to serve thy God, the God of all! What more did He for Moses or for His servant David? Since thou wast born, ever has He had thee in His most watchful care. When He saw thee of an age with which He was content, He caused thy name to sound marvellously in the land [*maravillosamente hizo sonar tu nombre en la tierra*].

Now it is not the divine name but Columbus's own that is the heart of the wonder. And now, in Columbus's mind and in his text, the conjunction of the land, the marvelous, and the name produces an absolute possession, not for the king and queen of Spain but for himself alone. 'The Indies, which are so rich a part of the world,' the mysterious voice continues,

> He gave thee for thine own; thou hast divided them as it pleased thee, and He enabled thee to do this. Of the barriers of the Ocean sea, which were closed with such mighty chains, He gave thee the keys; and thou wast obeyed in many lands and among Christians thou hast gained an honourable fame. What did He more for the people of Israel when He brought them out of Egypt? Or for David, whom from a shepherd He made to be king in Judaea?[91]

For a moment at least – a moment at once of perfect wonder and of possessive madness – Columbus has become king of the Promised Land.

NOTES

1   *Select Documents Illustrating the Four Voyages of Columbus*, trans. and ed. Cecil Jane, 2 vols. (London: Hakluyt Society, 1930), i. 2.

> Señor, porque sé que avréis plazer de la gran vitoria que Nuestro Señor me ha dado en mi viaje, vos escrivo esta, por la qual sabréys como en .xxxiii. días pasé de las islas de Canaria á las Indias con la armada que los ilustrísimos rey é reyna nuestros señores me dieron, donde yo fallé muy muchas islas pobladas con gente sin número; y d'ellas todas he tomado posesión por Sus Altezas con pregón y vandera real estendida, y no me fué contradicho. á la primera que yo fallé puse nombre "San Salvador", á comemoración de Su Alta Magestad, el qual maravillosamente todo esto ha dado; los Indios la llaman "Guanahaní"; á la segunda puse nombre "la isla de Santa María de Concepción"; á la tercera "Fernandina"; á la quarta "la Ysabela"; á la quinta "la isla Juana", é así á cada una nombre nuevo.

Quotations from Columbus's letters, unless otherwise noted, will be from this edn.

2   Santangel, the *escribano de ración*, had helped Columbus find the money to finance his voyage. Santangel was a member of a family of *conversos*. A copy of the letter was also sent to Gabriel Sanchez, the treasurer of Aragon and also from a family of *conversos*.

3   Over whom does Columbus imagine that he has achieved a victory: over the Indians? over the destructive power of the sea? over his detractors in Europe? over the classical geographers and indeed the whole classical world? At the close of the letter, Columbus returns to the language of victory. He speaks of 'the eternal God, our Lord, Who gives to all those who walk in His way triumph [*victoria*] over things which appear to be impossible,' and he urges all of Christendom to share this sense of triumph:

> So that, since Our Redeemer has given this victory to our most illustrious king and queen, and to their renowned kingdoms, in so great a matter, for this all Christendom ought to feel delight and make great feast and give solemn thanks to the Holy Trinity with many solemn prayers for the great exaltation which they shall have, in the turning of so many peoples to our holy faith, and afterwards for temporal benefits, for not only Spain but all Christians will have hence refreshment and gain. (Jane, i. 18)

Theodore J. Cachey, Jr. points out that the Latin translation of Columbus's letter, by Leandro de Cosco (a chancellor in the Roman Curia, an Aragonese at the court of Alexander VI), omits Columbus's martial rhetoric. Instead of 'la gran victoria,' the Latin renders the sentence, 'Since I know that it will please you that I have carried to completion the duty which I assumed...' ('The Earliest Literary Response of Renaissance Italy to the New World Encounter, in *Columbus*, ed. Anne Paolucci and Henry Paolucci (New York: Griffin House for the Council on National Literatures, 1989), p. 28). Cachey calls attention to the recurrence of the verbal motif of the *victoria* at the close of the letter (so that the motif, in effect, frames the narrative): 'since, thus Our Redeemer has given this victory to our most illustrious King and Queen....' 'The martially connotated language of Columbus's *exordium*,' Cachey writes, 'is based upon the link in Columbus's mind (established explicitly in the dedicatory letter to the *Diario*) between his Discovery and the 'victoria' at Granada, the final act of the Reconquest' (p. 28).

4 'Mittimus in presenciarum nobilem virum Christoforum Colon cum tribus caravelis armatis per maria oceania ad partes Indie pro aliquibus causis et negotiis seruicium Dei ac fidem ortodoxe concernentibus' (Jane, p. lxx).

5 *The 'Diario' of Christopher Columbus's First Voyage to America, 1492–1493*, transcribed and trans. by Oliver Dunn and James E. Kelley, Jr. (Norman: University of Oklahoma Press, 1989), p. 109.

6 An often-repeated modern theory is that no one had really thought ahead of time about the difficulties. 'Surely, the reader will ask, you do not suppose that Ferdinand and Isabella (and Henry VII) were so simple as to suppose that three small vessels (or one still smaller) with ninety (or eighteen) men could sail into a harbor of Japan or China and simply take over? The answer is, yes, they were as simple as that' (Samuel Eliot Morison, *Admiral of the Ocean Sea: A Life of Christopher Columbus* (Boston: Little, Brown, 1942), pp. 106–7). This view is supported by the recent study of Spanish practices before 1492: In the Spanish invasion of Majorca, we are told, 'A pattern was established which remained influential throughout the history of the expansion of the Crown of Aragon – indeed, in some respects, throughout the history of western Mediterranean expansion generally. The problems were not considered in advance' (Felipe Fernández-Armesto, *Before Columbus: Exploration and Colonization from the Mediterranean to the Atlantic, 1229–1492* (Philadelphia: University of Pennsylvania Press, 1987), p. 18). I might add that in his letter to Santangel, Columbus supplements the language of legal possession with the language of occupation.

7 In an important unpublished paper, Patricia Seed suggests that the Spanish term *tomar posesión* (and the Portuguese *tomar posse*) did not have the same meaning as the English 'to take possession.' 'Possession' in Elizabethan royal patents such as that granted to Sir Humphrey Gilbert and Sir Walter Ralegh means to 'have, hold, occupy and enjoy,' and to wield over the territory so held 'full power to dispose thereof...according to the lawes of England.' In Spanish usage, Seed argues, the phrase 'tomar posesión' referred to the repertory of symbolic actions and formulaic pronouncements. The difference is reflected in Elizabeth's response to Spanish complaints against Francis Drake. According to William Camden, the queen denied that the Spanish had established 'possession': Spaniards, she said, 'had touched here and there upon the Coasts, built Cottages, and given Names to a River or Cape which does not entitle them to ownership;... Prescription without possession is worth little [*cum praescriptio sine possessione haud valeat*]' (William Camden, *Rerum Anglicarvm et hibernicarvm Annales regnante Elisabetha* (London: Ludwig Batavorvm,

1639), p. 328). The actions that Elizabeth characterizes as mere 'prescription' are precisely what the Spanish seem to have meant by 'taking possession.'

8 Christopher Dawson (ed.), *The Mongol Mission: Narratives and Letters of the Franciscan Missionaries in Mongolia and China in the Thirteenth and Fourteenth Centuries* (London: Sheed & Ward, 1955), p. 93.

9 The Sahara is in some way a similar obstacle, but there had been, of course, many contacts over the centuries, esp. along the coasts of Africa.

10 *Diario*, 63–5. Morison translates *escrivano* as 'secretary'; other translations render it 'ship's clerk,' 'recorder,' and 'purser.' The *escrivano* was also an 'officer of the court'; as such, his testimony was equal to that of three other witnesses (see Stanley S. Jados, *Consulate of the Sea and Related Documents* (Tuscaloosa: University of Alabama Press, 1975), art. 330).

11 Quoted in Arthur S. Keller, Oliver J. Lissitzyn, Frederick J. Mann, *Creation of Rights of Sovereignty through Symbolic Acts, 1400–1800* (New York: Columbia University Press, 1938), pp. 39–40. For the Spanish text, see 'Instrución que dió el Rey á Juan Diaz de Solís para el viage expresado,' 24 de Nov., 1514, in Don Martin Fernandez de Navarrete (ed.), *Colección de los viages y descubrimientos que hicieron por mar los Españoles*, 5 vols. (Buenos Aires: Editorial Guarania, 1945; orig. pub. 1825), iii. 149–50.

12 Keller *et al.* p. 41.

13 Ibid. p. 35.

14 On Hispaniola, on December 12, Columbus had his men raise 'a large cross at the western side of the entrance to the harbor on a conspicuous height, as a sign, he says, that Your Highnesses claim the land as your own, and chiefly as a sign of Jesus Christ Our Lord and in honor of Christianity' (*Diario*, p. 219).

15 *Journals and Other Documents on the Life and Voyages of Christopher Columbus*, trans. and ed. Samuel Eliot Morison (New York: Heritage Press, 1963), p. 27.

16 After describing the ritual, the log-book entry goes on to say, 'Soon many people of the island gathered there' (*Diario*, p. 65). Given the Arawaks' timidity, it is possible that they kept their distance at this point.

17 Michel de Certeau, *The Writing of History*, trans. Tom Conley (New York: Columbia University Press, 1988), p. 212.

18 It is remotely conceivable that the phrase was intended to include the Spanish as well as the natives, since it was certainly possible for Columbus to imagine a Spaniard who would dispute his authority. But the principal reference must be to the inhabitants of the land whose possession is being claimed.

19 For a useful collection of legal texts bearing on the possession of Indian lands in North America, see Charles M. Haar and Lance Liebman, *Property and Law* (Boston: Little, Brown, 1977).

20 *Institutes* 11. i. 40. This passage is cited by Francisco de Vitoria in his brilliant review of the Spanish (and, more generally, the European) claims to the Indies. See James Brown Scott, *The Spanish Origin of International Law: Francisco de Vitoria and His Law of Nations* (Oxford: Clarendon Press, 1934), p. xxxiii.

21 *Digest* 41. 2. 6.

22 Accursius, *Glossa ordinaria*, on *Digest* 41. 2. 6. I am indebted for this reference to Laurent Mayali.

23 *The Letter of Columbus on the Discovery of America* (New York: Lenox Library, 1892), p. 19.

24 This is an instance of the situation Jean-François Lyotard has called the 'differend': 'the case where the plaintiff is divested of the means to argue and becomes for that reason a victim' (*The Differend: Phrases in Dispute*, trans. Georges Van Den Abbeele (Minneapolis: University of Minnesota Press, 1988), p. 9). A differend – rather than simply a difference – between two parties takes place, Lyotard explains, 'when the 'regulation' of the conflict that opposes them is done in the idiom of one of the parties while the wrong suffered by the other is not signified in that idiom' (p. 9). Columbus and the Arawak are an extreme version of such a case. But it would not necessarily have been better had Columbus recognized the incommensurability of Spanish and native cultural constructions of reality. For such a recognition was in the early sixteenth century precisely the argument of those who sought to deny the natives any right to have rights. Thus, as Anthony Pagden points out, the jurist Palacios Rubios had argued in 1513 that a society that did not possess property relations (and hence did not live within a legitimate civil community) could not for that reason claim on behalf of any of its individuals *dominium rerum* when confronted by invaders attempting to seize their lands. In other words, a full recognition of the profound disparity between the indigenous culture and that of the invaders would not necessarily lead to what we regard as equity: on the contrary, it could lead to a justification for seizure. See, similarly, the argument made in 1550 by Juan Ginés de Sepúlveda that 'since no Indian society had had a monetary economy, no Indian could be said to have exercised any rights over any precious metal. These were, therefore, still a common part of Adam's patrimony, to which the Spaniards had a high moral claim by having traded metals which had been useless in the ancient Indian world for such useful things as iron, European agricultural techniques, horses, donkeys, goats, pigs, sheep, and so on' (Anthony Pagden, 'Dispossessing the Barbarian: the Language of Spanish Thomism and the Debate over the Property Rights of the American Indians,' in *The Languages of Political Theory in Early-Modern Europe*, ed. Anthony Pagden (Cambridge: Cambridge University Press, 1987), pp. 81, 92).

25 For an illuminating discussion of the problem of cultural incompatibility, see Don F. McKenzie, 'The Sociology of a Text: Oral Culture, Literacy and Print in Early New England,' *The Social History of Language*, ed. Peter Burke and Roy Porter (Cambridge: Cambridge University Press, 1987), pp. 161–96.

26 Vitoria's refutation of the claim in the 1530s is worth quoting:

> This title, too, is insufficient. This appears, in the first place, because fear and ignorance, which vitiate every choice, ought to be absent. But they were markedly operative in the cases of choice and acceptance under consideration, for the Indians did not know what they were doing; nay, they may not have understood what the Spaniards were seeking. Further, we find the Spaniards seeking it in armed array from an unwarlike and timid crowd. Further, inasmuch as the aborigines, as said above, had real lords and princes, the populace could not procure new lords without other reasonable cause, this being to the hurt of their former lords. Further, on the other hand, these lords themselves could not appoint a new prince without the assent of the populace. Seeing, then, that in such cases of choice and acceptance as these there are not present all the requisite elements of a valid choice, the title under review is utterly inadequate and unlawful for seizing and retaining the provinces in question. (pp. xxxiii–xxxiv)

27 See Richard Epstein, 'Possession as the Root of Title,' in *Georgia Law Review* 13 (1979): 1221–43; Carol M. Rose, 'Possession as the Origin of Property,' *University of Chicago Law Review* 51 (1985): 73 ff.

28   Closed formalism is in fact one step beyond the marriage ritual whose formulaic
      phrases after all are actually spoken in the presence of those who could, if they
      wished, 'speak now.' Columbus's required declarations are presumably made in the
      present tense, but their actual orientation is the future perfect: they are directed to
      those who will have heard that they were already made. The future perfect tense is a
      highly serviceable, if often unacknowledged, device in legal ritual.

29   'Narrative,' writes Lyotard, 'is perhaps the genre of discourse within which the
      heterogeneity of phrase regimens, and even the heterogeneity of genres of dis-
      course, have the easiest time passing unnoticed.... The narrative function is
      redeeming in itself. It acts as if the occurrence, with its potentiality of differends,
      could come to completion, or as if there were a last word' (*The Differend*, p. 151).

30   Francisco de Vitoria, in *The Spanish Origin of International Law*, ed. Scott,
      pp. xxiv–xxv.

31   See Anthony Pagden, *The Fall of Natural Man: The American Indian and the Origins of
      Comparative Ethnology* (Cambridge: Cambridge University Press, 1982). Pagden's
      remarkable book makes it clear that the most sustained and intellectually coherent
      challenge to the Spanish claim to possession was mounted on formal principles by
      Spanish jurists and theologians.

32   Gonzalo Fernandez de Oviedo y Valdes, *General and Natural History of the Indies*,
      trans. Earl Raymond Hewitt and Theodor Terrones, 2 vols. (Madrid: Royal
      Academy of History, 1851), i. 36–40 [I. 1. 1. iii].

33   Pagden, *The Fall of Natural Man*, p. 30.

34   Giuliano Gliozzi, *Adamo e il nuovo mondo. La nascita dell'antropologia come ideologia
      coloniale: dalle genealogie bibliche alle teorie razziali* (1500–1700) (Florence: La nuova
      Italia editrice, 1976), p. 47. 'O the profound wisdom and knowledge of the Most
      High,' writes Rocha, 'that after so many centuries ordained that these islands would
      be returned by Columbus to the Spanish crown.'

35   See ibid. pp. 15–48. The evidence for the Welsh claim includes Montezuma's
      testimony that he and his people are descended from foreigners, along with what
      seemed to a Welsh observer the obvious linguistic parallels. (Cf. *New American
      World, A Documentary History of North America to 1612*, ed. David Beers Quinn,
      5 vols. (New York: Arno Press and Hector Bye, 1979), i. 66–8).

36   Montezuma is said to have asked Cortés why the strangers had such a hunger for
      gold, and Cortés is said to have replied that Spaniards had a disease about the heart,
      for which the only cure was gold.

37   The drive to bring experience under discursive control is inseparable from the task of
      ethical justification and legitimation. The disastrous epidemic diseases that afflicted
      the Indians may ultimately have proved a more decisive historical factor than the
      Spanish atrocities, but the ethically compelling concern is an inner account of what
      guides actions, that is, an account of intentions. I should add that sixteenth-century
      observers attempted to moralize the epidemic diseases in a variety of ways: as God's
      punishment of pagan unbelief, for example, or as the horrible consequence of Spanish
      cruelty. These moralizations may be understood as attempts to understand and hence
      imaginatively control the natural. Post-Enlightenment strategies for achieving such
      control have centered on science rather than religious polemic and have character-
      istically involved searching for cures (or at least medical causes) on the one hand and
      searching for means to inflict disease (through biological agents) on the other.

38   J. L. Austin, *How to Do Things with Words*, ed. J. O. Urmson and Marina Sbisà
      (Cambridge, Mass.: Harvard University Press, 1975). See also the remarks of John

Searle about the conditions that must be met for a declaration, proclamation or any speech act that involves a 'double direction of fit' (the world to the word and the word to the world) to be valid (John Searle and Daniel Vanderverken, *Foundations of Illocutionary Logic* (Cambridge: Cambridge University Press, 1985), p. 52 ff.)

39   It is not entirely clear whom the Spanish imagined the Grand Khan to be or how they conceived of his rule, but it is clear that they imagined that there was some kind of empire with a centralized authority structure.

40   *Select Documents*, ed. Jane, i. 14 (*su mayoral ó rey*). Men, Columbus writes, appear generally to be content with one woman, but the chief is given as many as twenty wives. And these wives, he implies, have economic value: 'It appears to me that the women work more than the men.' Columbus is uncertain, however, if this social arrangement entails a notion of private property: 'I have not been able to learn if they hold private property [*bienes propios*]; what seemed to me to appear was that, in that which one had, all took a share, especially of eatable things' (i. 14).

41   Quoted in Etienne Grisel, 'The Beginnings of International Law and General Public Law Doctrine: Francisco de Vitoria's *De Indiis prior*,' in *First Images of America: The Impact of the New World on the Old*, ed. Fredi Chiappelli, 2 vols. (Berkeley: University of California Press, 1976), 1. 309. See also Pagden, for a wonderfully detailed and intelligent discussion of the categories at issue here.

42   *Select Documents*, ed. Jane, ii. 66.

43   For the texts of the two drafts of this famous papal bull, see *Bullarum diplomatum et privilegiorum sanctorum romanorum pontificum* (Rome: Franco and Henrico Dalmazzo, 1858).

44   *Politics*, 1253a, pp. 28–9.

45   In the letter to Santangel, Columbus mentions an island he calls 'Quaris,' which is inhabited 'by a people who are regarded in all the islands as very fierce and who eat human flesh' (i. 14). On Columbus's perceptions of cannibalism, see the remarkable book by Peter Hulme, *Colonial Encounters: Europe and the Native Caribbean, 1492–1797* (London: Methuen, 1986); Michael Palencia-Roth, 'Cannibalism and the New Man of Latin America in the 15th-and 16th-century European Imagination,' in *Comparative Civilizations Review* 12 (1985): 1–27.

46   Earlier in the letter he casually mentions that he 'understood sufficiently from other Indians, *whom I had already taken*, that this land was nothing but an island' (i. 4) (emphasis added). And in his journal entry for October 12, 1492, he writes, 'Our Lord pleasing, at the time of my departure I will take six of them from here to Your Highnesses that they may learn to speak' (*Diario*, 69). For a discussion of the policy of kidnapping, see chapter 4.

47   See Bartolomé de Las Casas, *History of the Indies*, trans. Andrée M. Collard (New York: Harper & Row, 1971), p. 127.

48   See Alain Milhou, *Colón y su mentalidad mesianica*, p. 289: 'El 'negocio' o la 'negociación' de las Indias tiene, como la palabra 'empresa,' unas connotactiones dobles: una mercantil, la del mundo de los 'negocios' en que se crió Colón, pero también otra religiosa, la del *negotium crucis* de los cruzados as cual equiparaba su 'negocio' ultramarino . . . .'

49   For the paradoxicality of Christian imperialism, see the letter on the 3rd voyage:

> I came with the mission to your royal presence, as being the most exalted of Christian princes and so ardently devoted to the Faith and to its increase. . . . On this matter I spent six or seven years of deep anxiety, expounding, as well as I could, how great service might in this be rendered to the Lord, by proclaiming abroad His holy name

and His faith to so many peoples, which was all a thing of so great excellence and for
the fair fame of great princes and for a notable memorial for them. It was needful also to
speak of the temporal gain therein. . . . (ii. 1)

It is possible, of course, to see such passages as evidence not of paradox but of
unresolved tension, comparable to the class tension explored with great intelligence
by David Quint in 'The Boat of Romance and Renaissance Epic' (*Romance: Generic
Transformation from Chrétien de Troyes to Cervantes*, ed. Kevin and Marina Brownlee
(Hanover, NH: University Press of New England, 1985), pp. 178–202). Quint
argues that the central contradiction was between an aristocratic account of the
voyages of discovery and a 'bourgeois' account; the former allied itself with epic,
the latter with romance. Columbus seems to me to combine both with a reckless
disregard for literary decorum.

50   Claude Lévi-Strauss quotes (or paraphrases) the finding of the commission of the
      monks of the Order of St. Jerome in 1517: the Indian 'is better off as a slave, among
      men, than as an animal on his own' (*Tristes Tropiques*, trans. John Russell (New
      York: Atheneum, 1961; orig. pub. 1955), p. 80).

51   'Because we wish to be informed by civil lawyers, canonists and theologians
      whether we may, with a good conscience, sell these Indians or not' (Pagden, *Fall of
      Natural Man*, p. 31). Pagden notes that one year later the queen 'ordered all the
      Indian slaves in Seville to be taken from their masters and sent back to their former
      homes.'

52   In his log-book entry for October 12, Columbus also emphasizes that the Indians
      were friendly, so friendly in fact 'that it was a marvel' [*quedarō tanto nro(s?) q̄ era
      maravilla*] (*Diario*, pp. 64–5).

53   There are obviously some parallels between the role of the marvelous in the early
      literature of discovery and the stylistic feature of contemporary Latin American
      writing, known as the 'real maravilloso.' See J. Edgardo Rivera Martínez, 'La
      literatura geografica del siglo xvi en Francia como antecedente de lo real maravil-
      loso,' in *Revista de Critica Litteraria Latinoamericana* 5/9 (1979): 7–19. But my aim is
      to insist on the very specific purposes served by the marvelous in late fifteenth- and
      early sixteenth-century writing.

54   Columbus appears to have been fluent in Castilian (all of his surviving writings,
      including letters he wrote to Italian correspondents, are in Castilian), and he had
      what by our standards would be reasonably impressive linguistic gifts. See Pauline
      Watts, 'Prophecy and Discovery': 'Columbus did not have the advanced, special-
      ized education of a professional academic. But he did read and annotate works
      composed in Latin (for example, d'Ailly's *Imago mundi* and Pius II's *Historia*),
      Castilian (Alfonso de Palencia's translation of Plutarch's *Lives*), and Italian (Cristo-
      foro Landino's translation of Pliny's *Naturalis historia*),' p. 75. See likewise V. I.
      Milani, *The Written Language of Christopher Columbus* (Buffalo: State University of
      New York at Buffalo (for *Forum Italicum*), 1973) and Paolo Emilia Taviani, *Chris-
      topher Columbus: The Grand Design*, trans. Taviani and William Weaver (London:
      Orbis, 1985). It is very unlikely that Columbus could not, if he had wished, have
      found a synonym for 'marvelous.'

55   Jane's rendering of 'maravillarme' as 'to cause you to wonder' may be misleading.
      The phrase appears to mean 'to show or perform my wonder.'

56   Jacques Le Goff, *L'Imaginaire médiéval* (Paris: Gallimard, 1985), pp. 17–39.

57   See esp. Baxter Hathaway, *Marvels and Commonplaces: Renaissance Literary Criticism*
      (New York: Random House, 1968), pp. 133–51. See also Hathaway's *The Age of*

Criticism: The Late Renaissance in Italy (Ithaca, NY: Cornell University Press, 1962). Le Goff, however, denies the ultimate compatibility of Christianity and the marvelous: 'Si je simplifiais ma réflexion sur le merveilleux dans l'Occident médiéval jusqu' à la caricature, je dirais qu'en définitive il n'y a pas de merveilleux chrétien et que le christianisme, en tout case le christianisme médiéval, est allergique au merveilleux' (*L'Imaginaire médiéval*, p. 37).

58 i. 12; cf. the skeptical remark by Andrés Bernáldez, who believes that these stories are told by some Indians in mockery of others who wear clothing (i. 128).

59 Samuel Eliot Morison's translation of this passage (*Admiral of the Ocean Sea: A Life of Christopher Columbus* (Boston: Little, Brown, 1942), pp. 309–10) is rather more flattering to men: the mermaids 'were not as beautiful as they are painted, although to some extent they have a human appearance in the face.'

60 In the *Diario*, Columbus repeatedly uses the term 'maravilla' and its variants to characterize the natural features of the world he has discovered: the trees and fish (Oct. 16), the groves and the birdsong, and the diversity, size, and difference of the birds (Oct. 21), the sheer number of islands (Nov. 14), the harbors (Nov. 26), the fields and the general beauty of the lands and the trees (Nov. 27), the beauty of a harbor (Dec. 6), the beauty of a river (Dec. 7), the valleys, rivers, and good water (Dec. 16), the green mountains (Dec. 21), the green and cultivated mountains (Jan. 9).

61 In fact the highest peak on Teneriffe is considerably higher than the highest peak on Hispaniola.

62 Columbus (or, alternatively, Las Casas) evidently regards the point as worth repeating. In the same entry, he writes, 'all or most of the Indians began to run to the town, which must have been near, to bring him more food and parrots and other things of those that they had, with such open hearts that it was a marvel' (*Diario*, p. 259).

63 There is at least a latent polemical irony in this passage that makes one suspect that Las Casas is exercising a more active, shaping presence in the transcription than he admits, but in the absence of the original text there is no way of confirming the suspicion.

64 Several log-book entries record this Indian belief and thereby seem to indicate that Columbus had some curiosity about the native view of the encounter. On Oct. 21, Columbus notes that 'it is true that any little thing given to them, as well as our coming, they considered great marvels; and they believed that we had come from the heavens' (*Diario*, p. 109). Columbus does not quite put the two observations together and reflect that they might well treasure even almost worthless articles – bits of broken crockery, cheap cloth, rusted nails – if they believe that the givers come from the heavens. Why doesn't he put them together? Perhaps because it would have led to the ironic self-recognition so characteristic of Mandeville – just as we collect the relics (bits of wood supposedly from the cross, nails, shrivelled pieces of skin, and so forth) associated with those we regard as sanctified, so do these people collect relics from us.

On Nov. 5, Columbus notes similarly, 'The Indians touched them and kissed their hands and feet, marveling [*maravillandose*] and believing that the Spaniards came from the heavens, and so they gave them to understand' (*Diario*, p. 137). The last phrase, in Las Casas's transcription, is ambiguous, but it would seem to mean that the Spanish gave the Indians to understand that they, the Spanish, came from the heavens; if so, we are dealing not with a naïve misapprehension on the part of the natives but with an improvisatory lie.

In an important article on Cabeza de Vaca's *Naufragios* (in *Representations* 33 (1991): 163–99), Rolena Adorno suggests that the misapprehension was Spanish rather than Indian. She observes that the 'interpreters of Columbus's text, from Las Casas to Don Hernando Colón and Hernán Perez de Oliva, all claim that the natives meant that the Spaniards came down from heaven.' But she notes that in a phrase dropped from later editions Cabeza de Vaca offers a more plausible gloss; he writes that 'Among all these peoples, it was held for very certain that we came from the sky, because about all the things that they do not understand nor have information regarding their origins, they say that such phenomena come from the sky' (183).

65   Columbus does not seem greatly interested in disabusing the natives of their mistaken beliefs about the Spanish, though he does tell them that he comes from another kingdom and not from heaven. When, on the second voyage, he explains to an Indian cacique that he serves the rulers of that kingdom, the cacique is surprised: 'And the Indian, greatly marvelling [*muy maravillado*], replied to the interpreter, saying: 'How? Has this admiral another lord, and does he yield obedience?' And the Indian interpreter said: 'To the king and to the queen of Castile, who are the greatest sovereigns in the world.' And forthwith he recounted to the cacique and to the old man and to all the other Indians the things which he had seen in Castile and the marvels of Spain, and told them of the great cities and fortresses and churches, and of the people and horses and animals, and of the great nobility and wealth of the sovereigns and great lords, and of the kinds of food, and of the festivals and tournaments which he had seen, and of bull-fighting, and of that which he had learned of the wars' (i. 154). It is possible that Columbus regarded the arousal of wonder in the Indians as a potential source of power. Other writers in the period anticipate that such an arousal would lead to domination: see, for example, Hieronymus Müntzer's letter to D. Joao II (1493): 'O what glory you would gain, if you made the habitable Orient known to the Occident, and what profits would its commerce give you, for you would make those islands of the Orient tributaries, and their kings amazed [*sus reyes maravillados*] would quietly submit to your sovereignty!' (in Morison, *Admiral of the Ocean Sea*, p. 77).

66   We can also cite Andrés Bernáldez, with whom Columbus stayed on his return from the second voyage, and to whom he supplied information about the discoveries. Bernáldez notes that the Spanish saw 'more than a million and a half cormorants' all together in the sky and were amazed (*obieron por maravilla*) (i. 148). See, likewise, the 'marvelous' pastoral scene by the fountain (i. 132).

67   On Columbus and the location of Paradise, see Alain Milhou, *Colón y su mentalidad mesianica*, p. 407 ff.

68   Vitoria considers the possibility of a Spanish title to the Indies based upon a 'special grant from God.' He concludes that 'it would be hazardous to give credence to one who asserts a prophecy against the common law and against the rules of Scripture, unless his doctrine were confirmed by miracles.' Columbus, of course, explicitly claims that the discovery of the Indies had been prophesied by Isaiah and others, but he seems wary of claiming miraculous confirmation. Vitoria does not believe anyone has made the latter claim: 'Now, no such [miracles] are adduced by prophets of this type' (p. xxxiv). See Etienne Grisel, 'The Beginnings of International Law,' in *First Images of America*, i. 312.

   Las Casas does, however, quote Columbus as saying, upon the discovery of Trinidad, that God's 'exalted power guides me, and in such manner that He receives much service and your highnesses much pleasure, since it is certain that the discovery of this land in this place was as great a miracle as the discovery of land on the first voyage' (Jane ii. 13 n.). In Spanish writing of the period, however, 'maravilla' could on occasion function as the equivalent of miracle. See, for example, the anti-Semitic passage by the Franciscan Juan de Pineda: 'Llegado a Jerusalén, restaurará el templo de Salomón, en el cual . . . se sentará blasfemando de la divinidad del Redentor; y con esto se le darán los judios sus parientes muy obedientes, y habiendo él destruido los lugares sanctos, donde nuestro Redentor hizo sus maravillas, enviará sus mensajeros por el mundo . . . ' (quoted in Milhou, p. 446).

69 Quoted in J. V. Cunningham, *Woe or Wonder: The Emotional Effect of Shakespearean Tragedy* (Denver: Denver University Press, 1951), p. 82.

70 *Enneades*, 1. 6. 4, quoted in Cunningham, p. 67.

71 Hathaway, pp. 66–9. Hathaway's account of Patrizi is taken largely from Bernard Weinberg, *A History of Literary Criticism in the Italian Renaissance*, 2 vols. (Chicago: University of Chicago Press, 1961). See Francesco Patrizi, *Della poetica*, ed. Danilo Aguzzi Barbagli (Florence, Istituto nazionale di studi sul Rinascimento, 1969–71), vol. ii. For Patrizi, the poet is not only a 'facitore del mirabile' but also a 'mirabile facitore' (Weinberg, ii. 773).

72 For Robortelli, Weinberg writes, 'in the last analysis, the poet is virtually permitted to discard all concern for credibility in order to exploit all the available means of achieving the marvelous and the pleasure connected with it' (Weinberg, i. 397–8).

73 *Poetica d'Aristotele vulgarizzata et sposta* (1570), quoted in Weinberg, i. 69. Castelvetro's theory, like that of many of his contemporaries, is centrally concerned with the problem of obtaining the credence of the audience – this rhetorical motive is what makes their analysis so interesting in the context of the New World discourse, concerned as it was with a comparable problem and willing to alter the truth to achieve its effect: 'In all such considerations of historical truth or natural probability or necessity and verisimilitude, the primary aim is not the imitation of nature for the sake of making the poem resemble nature but rather the resemblance to nature for the sake of obtaining the credence of the audience' (ibid., i. 58).

74 *Discorso in difesa della 'Commedia' del divino poeta Dante* (1572), in Allan H. Gilbert, *Literary Criticism: Plato to Dryden* (Detroit: Wayne State University Press, 1962), p. 371. Cf. Lorenzo Giacomini: tragedy 'pleases through the marvelous, demonstrating that a thing not believed can readily come to pass' (*Sopra la purgazione della tragedia* [1586]), in Weinberg, i. 628.

75 *Discorsi del poema heroico* (c.1575–80), in Weinberg, i. 341. Tasso, Weinberg writes, 'thinks of the marvelous as consisting of those events which do not enter into natural probability. How, then, can they be credible and acceptable in the poem? The answer is in the beliefs, even the faith, of the audience. For Christians believe the miracles of the Bible, know them to be true even though they are improbable. This is the only kind of credibility which the poet seeks' (i. 630). One might note, for a pagan precedent, Aristotle's remark that 'there is a probability of things happening also against probability' (*Poetics* 25. 1461^{b}15).

76 All of these positions may be found in Hathaway, *passim*.

77 It is important to recognize that this use of the term 'marvelous' is not Columbus's individual signature; it is the mark of a shared emotional effect and a common rhetoric. Hence, for example, Dr Chanca who accompanied Columbus on the second voyage notes that the natives 'have many tools, such as hatchets and axes, made of stone, so handsome and so fashioned, that it is marvelous how they are able to make them without iron' (i. 68). Even when Chanca expresses distaste for the

natives, he does so in the idiom of the marvelous. 'These people,' he writes, 'are so degraded (*tan bestial*) that they have not intelligence enough to seek out a suitable place in which to live. As for those who live on the shore, it is marvelous how barbarously they build [*es maravilla cuan bestialmente edifcan*]' (i. 52). It is striking, however, how infrequently Columbus uses the language of the marvelous to express, as Chanca does here, his disapproval or disdain.

78 In the years that followed, both were in fact called forth: the tears of Las Casas, on the one hand; the laughter of those stories of Indians declaring that the Pope was drunk or mad to think that he could give away what was not his.

79 Albertus Magnus, trans. in J. V. Cunningham, *Woe and Wonder* (Denver: Denver University Press, 1951), pp. 79–80. I am greatly indebted to Cunningham's account of wonder. The intensity of the experience Albertus Magnus is attempting to define seems to me somewhat greater in the original:

> Nam omnes homines qui nunc in nostro tempore et primum ante nostra tempora philosophati sunt, non sunt moti ad philosophandum nisi admirative. Admirationem autem vocamus agoniam et suspensionem cordis in stuporem prodigii magni in sensum apparentis, ita quod cor systolem patitur. Proper quod etiam admiratio aliquid simile habet timori in motus cordis, qui est ex suspensione. Hujus igitur motus admirationis in agonia et systole cordis est ex suspensione desiderii ad cognoscendam causam entis quod apparet prodigii: et ideo a principio cum adhuc rudes philosophari inceperunt, mirantes erant quaedam dubitabilium quae paratiora erant ad solvendum, sicut Pythagorici de numerorum passionibus, est de pari et impari, et perfecto et abundanti et diminuto numero. . . . Qui autem dubitant et admiratus, ignorans videtur: est enim admiratio motus ignorantis procedentis ad inquirendum, ut sciat causam ejus de quo miratus: cujus signum est, quia ipse Philomithes secundum hunc modum Philosophus est: quia fabula sua construitur ab ipso ex mirandis. (vi. 30)

(In Albertus Magnus, *Opera Omnia*, ed. Augustus Borgnet, 20 vols. [Paris: Ludovicus Vives, 1890] vi. 30 [I Metaphysicorum, tract. II, caput vi].)

80 In a response to the version of this chapter that I delivered at the University of Chicago, Professor Arnold Davidson suggested that it is important not to confound the theology of the marvelous in Albertus Magnus with the aesthetics of the marvelous that I have earlier discussed. For the poet, the arousal of wonder is one of the ends of art; for Albertus wonder is used up and vanishes when the mind actually comes to understand those phenomena by which it has been seized. The distinction seems to me significant, but I have argued here that it is deconstructed by the actual historical circumstances in which Columbus found himself. We may, in effect, take the vanishing of wonder to be a model for the way in which legal title absorbs the potentially disruptive power of the marvelous, a power that in these extraordinary circumstances legal formality none the less needs in order to make up for the deficiency at its center.

81 George R. Stewart, *Names on the Land: A Historical Account of Place-Naming in the United States*, rev. edn. (Boston: Houghton Mifflin, 1958), p. 12. Stewart cites the 'Instrucción dada por el Rey à Pedrarias Dávila': 'Arrived there by good providence, first of all you must give a name to the country as a whole, and to the cities, towns, and places.'

82 *Luther's Works*, vol. i: 'Lectures on Genesis,' chaps. 1–5, ed. Jaroslav Pelikan (St Louis: Concordia Publishing House, 1958), p. 119.

83   Francis Bacon, in *A Selection of His Works*, ed. Sidney Warhaft (New York: Odyssey, 1965), p. 21.

84   It is then a renaming such as the renaming of Jacob after his struggle with the mysterious man. 'He said to Jacob, 'What is your name?' and he answered, 'Jacob.' The man said, 'Your name shall no longer be Jacob, but Israel, because you strove with God and with men, and prevailed'' (Gen. 32: 27–9). Such a context would place Columbus in the position of the messenger of God.

85   See Rudolf Schnackenburg, *Baptism in the Thought of St. Paul*, trans. G. R. Beasley-Murray (New York: Herder & Herder, 1964), p. 20: 'The naming of a person had the meaning of attaching the baptized to this person so that the baptized belonged to him. This is confirmed by exegesis; for the consequence and effect of baptism 'in the name' of Christ may be gathered from a consideration of Paul's assertion, 'you belong to Christ.'' (I owe this reference to Michael Ragussis.)

86   Morison, *Admiral*, p. 360.

87   See Paolo Emilio Taviani, *Christopher Columbus* (Paris, pp. 1980), 38–40. Columbus's son Ferdinand wrote about the 'mystery' of his father's name and linked that mystery to the original baptism:

> If we consider the common surname of his forebears, we may say that he was truly Columbus or Dove, because he carried the grace of the Holy Ghost to that New World which he discovered, showing those people who knew Him not Who was God's beloved son, as the Holy Ghost did in the figure of a dove when St. John baptized Christ; and because over the waters of the ocean, like the dove of Noah's ark, he bore the olive branch and oil of baptism, to signify that those people who had been shut up in the ark of darkness and confusion were to enjoy peace and union with the Church. (quoted in Pauline Moffitt Watts, 'Prophecy and Discovery', p. 101)

88   *First Images*, ii. 619.

89   See Columbus's *Libro de las profecías*, in *Raccolta di documenti e studi pubblicati dalla R. Commissione Colombiana pel quarto centenario dalla scoperta dell'America* (Rome: Ministero Sella pubblica istruzione, 1894), pt. I, vol. ii, *Scritti di Cristoforo Colombo*, ed. C. de Lollis, pp. 76–160. In the unfinished letter to the Catholic monarchs with which he intended to introduce the *Book of Prophecies*, Columbus says that his decision to sail westward was inspired by the Holy Ghost:

> Animated by a heavenly fire, I came to your highnesses: all who heard of my enterprise mocked at it; all the sciences I had acquired profited me nothing; seven years did I pass in your royal court, disputing the case with persons of great authority and learned in all the arts, and in the end they decided that all was vain. In your highnesses alone remained faith and constancy. Who will doubt that this light was from the Holy Scriptures, illuminating you as well as myself with rays of marvelous brightness? [*con rrayos de claridad maravillosos*]

(Trans. in John Leddy Phelan, *The Millennial Kingdom of the Franciscans in the New World*, 2nd rev. edn (Berkeley: University of California Press, 1970), p. 20. For the original see *Raccolta di documenti*, pp. 79–80).

On Columbus and prophecy, see Pauline Moffitt Watts, 'Prophecy and Discovery,' pp. 73–102; Marjorie Reeves, *Joachim of Fiore and the Prophetic Future* (London: SPCK, 1976), pp. 128–9. On his deathbed, Columbus took the habit of a Franciscan.

90   For the notion of the land 'conforming' to the name, see Columbus's relation of his
     third voyage: 'I called this place there *Jardines*, for it corresponded to that name
     [*porque así conforman por el nombre*]' (Jane ii. 24). See, similarly, the naming of
     Trinidad (ii. 12). There is, of course, in such naming an element both of magical
     hope and of tactical cunning. For a candid glimpse of the latter, see Lopez Vaz
     (1586), in Purchas xii. 292: 'The discoverer of these islands named them the Isles of
     Solomon, to the end that the Spaniards supposing them to be those Isles from
     whence Solomon fetched Gold to adorne the Temple at Jerusalem, might be the
     more desirous to goe and inhabit the same.'

91   ii. 90–2. The reference to the keys is paraphrased from Seneca's *Medea*. On
     Columbus and the figure of David there is a substantial literature, including a
     long-standing debate about the status of Judaism in Columbus's thought. See
     Alain Milhou, *Colón y su mentalidad mesianica*, esp. pp. 230–51; Juan Gil, *Colón y
     la Casa Santa*, 'Historiografia y Bibliografía Americanistas,' E.E.H.A., 21 (1977):
     125–35.

Part III

SHAKESPEARE STUDIES

6

INVISIBLE BULLETS

In his notorious police report of 1593 on Christopher Marlowe, the Elizabethan spy Richard Baines informed his superiors that Marlowe had declared, among other monstrous opinions, that "Moses was but a Juggler, and that one Heriots being Sir W Raleighs man Can do more than he."[1] The "Heriots" cast for a moment in this lurid light is Thomas Harriot, the most profound Elizabethan mathematician, an expert in cartography, optics, and navigational science, an adherent of atomism, the first Englishman to make a telescope and turn it on the heavens, the author of the first original book about the first English colony in America, and the possessor throughout his career of a dangerous reputation for atheism.[2] In all of his extant writings, private correspondence as well as public discourse, Harriot professes the most reassuringly orthodox religious faith, but the suspicion persisted. When he died of cancer in 1621, one of his contemporaries, persuaded that Harriot had challenged the doctrinal account of creation *ex nihilo*, remarked gleefully that "a *nihilum* killed him at last: for in the top of his nose came a little red speck (exceeding small), which grew bigger and bigger, and at last killed him."[3]

Charges of atheism leveled at Harriot or anyone else in this period are difficult to assess, for such accusations were smear tactics, used with reckless abandon against anyone whom the accuser happened to dislike. At a dinner party one summer evening in 1593, Sir Walter Ralegh teased an irascible country parson named Ralph Ironside and found himself the subject of a state investigation; at the other end of the social scale, in the same Dorsetshire parish, a drunken servant named Oliver complained that in the Sunday sermon the preacher had praised Moses excessively but had neglected to mention his fifty-two concubines, and Oliver too found himself under official scrutiny.[4] Few, if any, of these investigations turned up what we would call atheists, even muddled or shallow ones; the stance that seemed to come naturally to me as a green college freshman in mid-twentieth-century America seems to have been almost unthinkable to the most daring philosophical minds of late sixteenth-century England.

This version of this chapter was first published in *Shakespearean Negotiations* (1988, pp. 21–65).

The historical evidence is unreliable; even in the absence of social pressure, people lie readily about their most intimate beliefs. How much more must they have lied in an atmosphere of unembarrassed repression. Still, there is probably more than politic concealment involved here. After all, treason was punished as harshly as atheism, yet while the period abounds in documented instances of treason in word and deed, there are virtually no professed atheists.[5] If ever there were a place to confirm that in a given social construction of reality certain interpretations of experience are sanctioned and others excluded, it is here, in the boundaries that contained sixteenth-century skepticism. Like Machiavelli and Montaigne, Thomas Harriot professed belief in God, and there is no justification in any of these cases for dismissing the profession of faith as mere hypocrisy.

I am arguing not that atheism was literally unthinkable in the late sixteenth century but rather that it was almost always thinkable only as the thought of another. This is one of its attractions as a smear; atheism is a characteristic mark of otherness — hence the ease with which Catholics can call Protestant martyrs atheists and Protestants routinely make similar charges against the pope.[6] The pervasiveness and frequency of these charges, then, does not signal the existence of a secret society of freethinkers, a School of Night, but rather registers the operation of a religious authority, whether Catholic or Protestant, that confirms its power by disclosing the threat of atheism. The authority is secular as well as religious, since atheism is frequently adduced as a motive for heinous crimes, as if all men and women would inevitably conclude that if God does not exist, everything is permitted. At Ralegh's 1603 treason trial, for example, Justice Popham solemnly warned the accused not to let "Harriot, nor any such Doctor, persuade you there is no eternity in Heaven, lest you find an eternity of hell-torments."[7] Nothing in Harriot's writings suggests that he held the position attributed to him here, but the charge does not depend upon evidence: Harriot is invoked as the archetypal corrupter, Achitophel seducing the glittering Absalom. If the atheist did not exist, he would have to be invented.

Yet atheism is not the only mode of subversive religious doubt, and we cannot discount the persistent rumors of Harriot's heterodoxy by pointing to either his conventional professions of faith or the conventionality of the attacks upon him. Indeed I want to suggest that if we look closely at *A Brief and True Report of the New Found Land of Virginia* (1588), the only work Harriot published in his lifetime and hence the work in which he was presumably the most cautious, we can find traces of material that could lead to the remark attributed to Marlowe, that "Moses was but a Juggler, and that one Heriots being Sir W Raleighs man Can do more than he." And I want to suggest further that understanding the relation between orthodoxy and subversion in Harriot's text will enable us to construct an interpretive model that may be used to understand the far more complex problem posed by Shakespeare's history plays.

Those plays have been described with impeccable intelligence as deeply conservative and with equally impeccable intelligence as deeply radical. Shakespeare, in Northrop Frye's words, is "a born courtier," the dramatist who organizes his representation of English history around the hegemonic mysticism of the Tudor myth; Shakespeare is also a relentless demystifier, an interrogator of ideology, "the only dramatist," as Franco Moretti puts it, "who rises to the level of Machiavelli in elaborating all the consequences of the separation of political praxis from moral evaluation."[8] The conflict glimpsed here could be investigated, on a performance-by-performance basis, in a history of reception, but that history is shaped, I would argue, by circumstances of production as well as consumption. The ideological strategies that fashion Shakespeare's history plays help in turn to fashion the conflicting readings of the plays' politics. And these strategies are no more Shakespeare's invention than the historical narratives on which he based his plots. As we shall see from Harriot's *Brief and True Report*, in the discourse of authority a powerful logic governs the relation between orthodoxy and subversion.

I should first explain that the apparently feeble wisecrack about Moses and Harriot finds its way into a police file on Marlowe because it seems to bear out one of the Machiavellian arguments about religion that most excited the wrath of sixteenth-century authorities: Old Testament religion, the argument goes, and by extension the whole Judeo–Christian tradition, originated in a series of clever tricks, fraudulent illusions perpetrated by Moses, who had been trained in Egyptian magic, upon the "rude and gross" (and hence credulous) Hebrews.[9] This argument is not actually to be found in Machiavelli, nor does it originate in the sixteenth century; it is already fully formulated in early pagan polemics against Christianity. But it seems to acquire a special force and currency in the Renaissance as an aspect of a heightened consciousness, fueled by the period's prolonged crises of doctrine and church governance, of the social function of religious belief.

Here Machiavelli's writings are important. *The Prince* observes in its bland way that if Moses' particular actions and methods are examined closely, they appear to differ little from those employed by the great pagan princes; the *Discourses* treats religion as if its primary function were not salvation but the achievement of civic discipline, as if its primary justification were not truth but expediency.[10] Thus Romulus's successor Numa Pompilius, "finding a very savage people, and wishing to reduce them to civil obedience by the arts of peace, had recourse to religion as the most necessary and assured support of any civil society" (*Discourses*, p. 146). For although "Romulus could organize the Senate and establish other civil and military institutions without the aid of divine authority, yet it was very necessary for Numa, who feigned that he held converse with a nymph, who dictated to him all that he wished tio persuade the people to." In truth, continues Machiavelli, "there never was any remarkable lawgiver amongst any people who did not resort to divine authority, as otherwise his laws would not have been accepted by the people" (p. 147).

From here is was only a short step, in the minds of Renaissance authorities, to the monstrous opinions attributed to the likes of Marlowe and Harriot. Kyd, under torture, testified that Marlowe had affirmed that "things esteemed to be done by divine power might have as well been done by observation of men," and the Jesuit Robert Parsons claimed that in Ralegh's "school of Atheism," "both Moses and our Savior, the old and the New Testament, are jested at."[11] On the eve of Ralegh's treason trial, some "hellish verses" were lifted from an anonymous tragedy written ten years earlier and circulated as Ralegh's own confession of atheism. At first the earth was held in common, the verses declare, but this golden age gave way to war, kingship, and property:

> Then some sage man, above the vulgar wise,
> Knowing that laws could not in quiet dwell,
> Unless they were observed, did first devise
> The names of Gods, religion, heaven, and hell
> ... Only bug-bears to keep the world in fear.[12]

The attribution of these lines to Ralegh is instructive: the fictional text returns to circulation as the missing confessional language of real life. That fiction is unlikely to represent an observable attitude in the "real" world, though we can never altogether exclude that possibility; rather it stages a cultural conceit, the recurrent fantasy of the archcriminal as atheist. Ralegh already had a reputation as both a poet and a freethinker; perhaps one of his numerous enemies actually plotted to heighten the violent popular hostility toward him by floating under his name a forgotten piece of stage villainy.[13] But quite apart from a possible conspiracy, the circulation fulfills a strong cultural expectation. When a hated favorite like Ralegh was accused of treason, what was looked for was not evidence but a performance, a theatrical revelation of motive and an enactment of despair. If the motives for treason revealed in this performance could be various – ambition, jealousy, greed, spite, and so forth – what permitted the release iof these motives into action would always be the same: atheism. No one who actually loved and feared God would allow himself to rebel against an anointed ruler, and atheism, conversely, would lead inevitably to treason. Since atheism was virtually always, as I have argued, the thought of the other, it would be difficult to find a first-person confession – except, of course, in fiction and above all in theater. The soliloquy is lifted from its theatrical context and transformed into "verses" that the three surviving manuscripts declare were "devised by that Atheist and Traitor Ralegh as it is said." The last phrase may signal skepticism about the attribution, but such reservations do not count for much: the "hellish verses" are what men like Marlowe, Harriot, or Ralegh would have to think in their hearts.

Harriot does not voice any speculations remotely resembling the hypotheses that a punitive religion was invented to keep men in awe and that belief originated in a fraudulent imposition by cunning "jugglers" on the ignorant, but his recurrent association with the forbidden thoughts of the demonized other may be linked to something beyond malicious slander. If we look attentively at his account of the first Virginia colony, we find a mind that seems interested in the same set of problems, a mind, indeed, that seems to be virtually testing the Machiavellian hypotheses. Sent by Ralegh to keep a record of the colony and to compile a description of the resources and inhabitants of the area, Harriot took care to learn the North Carolina Algonquian dialect and to achieve what he calls a "special familiarity with some of the priests."[14] The Virginian Indians believe, Harriot writes, in the immortality of the soul and in otherworldly punishments and rewards for behavior in this world: "What subtlety soever be in the *Wiroances* and Priests, this opinion worketh so much in many of the common and simple sort of people that it maketh them have great respect to the

Governors, and also great care what they do, to avoid torment after death and to enjoy bliss" (p. 374).[15] The split between the priests and people implied here is glimpsed as well in the description of the votive images: "They think that all the gods are of human shape, and therefore they represent them by images in the forms of men, which they call Kewasowak. . . . The common sort think them to be also gods" (p. 373). And the social function of popular belief is underscored in Harriot's note to an illustration showing the priests carefully tending the embalmed bodies of the former chiefs: "These poor souls are thus instructed by nature to reverence their princes even after their death" (De Bry, p. 72).

We have then, as in Machiavelli, a sense of religion as a set of beliefs manipulated by the subtlety of priests to help instill obedience and respect for authority. The terms of Harriot's analysis – "the common and simple sort of people," "the Governors," and so forth – are obviously drawn from the language of comparable social analyses of England; as Karen Kupperman has most recently demonstrated, sixteenth- and seventeenth-century Englishmen characteristically describe the Indians in terms that closely replicate their own self-conception, above all in matters of *status*.[16] The great mass of Indians are seen as a version of "the common sort" at home, just as Harriot translates the Algonquian *weroan* as "great Lord" and speaks of "the chief Ladies," "virgins of good parentage," "a young gentlewoman," and so forth. There is an easy, indeed almost irresistible, analogy in the period between accounts of Indian and European social structure, so that Harriot's description of the inward mechanisms of Algonquian society implies a description of comparable mechanisms in his own culture.[17]

To this we may add a still more telling observation not of the internal function of native religion but of the impact of European culture on the Indians: "Most things they saw with us," Harriot writes,

> as mathematical instruments, sea compasses, the virtue of the loadstone in drawing iron, a perspective glass whereby was showed many strange sights, burning glasses, wildfire works, guns, books, writing and reading, spring clocks that seem to go of themselves, and many other things that we had, were so strange unto them, and so far exceeded their capacities to comprehend the reason and means how they should be made and done, that they thought they were rather the works of gods than of men, or at the leastwise they had been given and taught us of the gods. (pp. 375–6)

This delusion, born of what Harriot supposes to be the vast technological superiority iof the European, caused the savages to doubt that they possessed the truth of God and religion and to suspect that such truth "was rather to be had from us, whom God so specially loved than from a people that were so simple, as they found themseles to be in comparison of us" (p. 376).

Here, I suggest, is the very core of the Machiavellian anthropology that posited the origin of religion in an imposition of socially coercive doctrines by an educated and sophisticated lawgiver on a simple people. And in Harriot's list of the marvels – from wildfire to reading – with which he undermined the Indians' confidence in their native understanding of the universe, we have the core of the claim attributed to Marlowe: that Moses was but a juggler and that Ralegh's man Harriot could do more than he. The testing of this hypothesis in the encounter of the Old World and the New was appropriate, we may add, for though vulgar Machiavellianism implied that all religion was a sophisticated confidence trick, Machiavelli himself saw that trick as possible only at a radical point of origin: "If any one wanted to establish a republic at the present time," he writes, "he would find it much easier with the simple mountaineers, who are almost without any civilization, than with such as are accustomed to live in cities, where civilization is already corrupt; as a sculptor finds it easier to make a fine statue out of a crude block of marble than out of a statue badly begun by another."[18] It was only with a people, as Harriot says, "so simple, as they found themselves to be in comparison of us," that the imposition of a coercive set of religious beliefs could be attempted.

In Harriot, then, we have one of the earliest instances of a significant phenomenon: the testing upon the bodies and minds of non-Europeans or, more generally, the noncivilized, of a hypothesis about the origin and nature of European culture and belief. In encountering the Algonquian Indians, Harriot not only thought he was encountering a simplified version of his own culture but also evidently believed that he was encountering his own civilization's past.[19] This past could best be investigated in the privileged anthropological moment of the initial encounter, for the comparable situations in Europe itself tended to be already contaminated by prior contact. Only in the forest, with a people ignorant of Christianity and startled by its bearers' technological potency, could one hope to reproduce accurately, with live subjects, the relation imagined between Numa and the primitive Romans, Moses and the Hebrews. The actual testing could happen only once, for it entails not detached observation but radical change, the change Harriot begins to observe in the priests who "were not so sure grounded, nor gave such credit to their traditions and stories, but through conversing with us they were brought into great doubts of their own" (p. 375).[20] I should emphasize that I am speaking here of events as reported by Harriot. The history of subsequent English–Algonquian relations casts doubt on the depth, extent, and irreversibility of the supposed Indian crisis of belief. In the *Brief and True Report*, however, the tribe's stories begin to *collapse* in the minds of their traditional guardians, and the coercive power of the European beliefs begins to show itself almost at once in the Indians' behavior:

> On a time also when their corn began to wither by reason of a drought which happened extraordinarily, fearing that it had come to pass by reason that in some thing they had displeased us, many would come to us and desire us to pray to our God of England, that he would preserve their corn, promising that when it was ripe we also should be partakers of their fruit. (p. 377)

If we remember that the English, like virtually all sixteenth-century Europeans in the New World, resisted or were incapable of provisioning themselves and in consequence depended upon the Indians for food, we may grasp the central importance for the colonists of this dawning Indian fear of the Christian God.

As early as 1504, during Columbus's fourth voyage, the natives, distressed that the Spanish seemed inclined to settle in for a long visit, refused to continue to supply food. Knowing from his almanac that a total eclipse of the moon was imminent,

Columbus warned the Indians that God would show them a sign of his displeasure; after the eclipse, the terrified Indians resumed the supply. But an eclipse would not always be so conveniently at hand. John Sparke, who sailed with Sir John Hawkins in 1564–65, noted that the French colonists in Florida "would not take the pains so much as to fish in the river before their doors, but would have all things put in their mouths."[21] When the Indians wearied of this arrangement, the French turned to extortion and robbery, and before long there were bloody wars. A similar situation seems to have arisen in the Virginia colony: despite land rich in game and ample fishing grounds, the English nearly starved to death when the exasperated Algonquians refused to build fishing weirs and plant corn.[22]

It is difficult to understand why men so aggressive and energetic in other regards should have been so passive in the crucial matter of feeding themselves. No doubt there were serious logistic problems in transporting food and equally serious difficulties adapting European farming methods and materials to the different climate and soil of the New World, yet these explanations seem insufficient, as they did even to the early explorers themselves. John Sparke wrote that "notwithstanding the great want that the Frenchmen had, the ground doth yield victuals sufficient, if they would have taken pains to get the same; but they being soldiers, desired to live by the sweat of other mens brows" (Hakluyt 10:56). This remark bears close attention: it points not to laziness or negligence but to an occupational identity, a determination to be nourished by the labor of others weaker, more vulnerable, than oneself. This self-conception was not, we might add, exclusively military: the hallmark of power and wealth in the sixteenth century was to be waited on by others. "To live by the sweat of other men's brows" was the enviable lot of the gentleman; indeed in England it virtually defined a gentleman. The New World held out the prospect of such status for all but the poorest cabin boy.[23]

But the prospect could not be realized through violence alone, even if the Europeans had possessed a monopoly of it, because the relentless exercise of violence could actually reduce the food supply. As Machiavelli understood, physical compulsion is essential but never sufficient; the survival of the rulers depends upon a supplement of coercive belief. The Indians must be persuaded that the Christian God is all-powerful and committed to the survival of his chosen people, that he will wither the corn and destroy the lives of savages who displease him by disobeying or plotting against the English. Here is a strange paradox: Harriot tests and seems to confirm the most radically subversive hypothesis in his culture about the origin and function of religion by imposing his religion – with its intense claims to transcendence, unique truth, inescapable coercive force – on others. Not only the official purpose but the survival of the English colony depends upon this imposition. This crucial circumstance licensed the testing in the first place; only as an agent of the English colony, dependent upon its purposes and committed to its survival, is Harriot in a position to disclose the power of human achievements – reading, writing, perspective glasses, gunpowder, and the like – to appear to the ignorant as divine and hence to promote belief and compel obedience.

Thus the subversiveness that is genuine and radical – sufficiently disturbing so that to be suspected of it could lead to imprisonment and torture – is at the same time contained by the power it would appear to threaten. Indeed the subversiveness is the very product of that power and furthers its ends. One may go still further and suggest that the power Harriot both serves and embodies not only produces its own subversion but is actively built upon it: the project of evangelical colonialism is not set over against the skeptical critique of religious coercion but battens on the very confirmation of that critique. In the Virginia colony, the radical undermining of Christian order is not the negative limit but the positive condition for the establishment of that order. And this paradox extends to the production of Harriot's text: *A Brief and True Report*, with its latent heterodoxy, is not a reflection upon the Virginia colony or even a simple record of it – it is not, in other words, a privileged withdrawal into a critical zone set apart from power – but a continuation of the colonial enterprise.

By October 1586, rumors were spreading in England that Virginia offered little prospect of profit, that the colony had been close to starvation, and that the Indians had turned hostile. Harriot accordingly begins his report with a descriptive catalog in which the natural goods of the land are turned into social goods, that is, into "merchantable commodities": "Cedar, a very sweet wood and fine timber; whereof if nests of chests be there made, or timber thereof fitted for sweet and fine bedsteads, tables, desks, lutes, virginals, and many things else, . . . [it] will yield profit" (pp. 329–30).[24] The inventory of these commodities is followed by an inventory of edible plants and animals, to prove to readers that the colony need not starve, and then by the account of the Indians, to prove that the colony could impose its will on them. The key to this imposition, as we have seen, is the coercive power of religious belief, and the source of the power is the impression made by advanced technology upon a "backward" people.

Hence Harriot's text is committed to record what I have called his confirmation of the Machiavellian hypothesis, and hence too the potential subversiveness of this confirmation is invisible not only to those on whom the religion is supposedly imposed but also to most readers and quite possibly to Harriot himself. It may be that Harriot was demonically conscious of what he was doing – that he found himself situated exactly where he could test one of his culture's darkest fears about its own origins, that he used the Algonquians to do so, and that he wrote a report on his own findings, a coded report, since as he wrote to Kepler years later, "our situation is such that I still may not philosophize freely."[25] But this is not the only Harriot we can conjure up. A scientist of the late sixteenth century, we might suppose, would have regarded the natives' opinion that English technology was god-given – indeed divine – with something like corroboratory complacency. It would, as a colleague from whom I borrow this conjecture remarked, "be just like an establishment intellectual, or simply a well-placed Elizabethan bourgeois, to accept that his superior 'powers' – moral, technological, cultural – were indeed signs of divine favor and that therefore the superstitious natives were quite right in their perception of the need to submit to their benevolent conquerors."[26]

Now Harriot does not in fact express such a view of the ultimate origin of his trunk of marvels – and I doubt that he held the view in this form – but it is significant that in the next generation Bacon, perhaps recalling Harriot's text or others like it, claims in *The New Organon* that scientific discoveries "are as it were new creations, and imitations of God's works" that may be justly regarded *as if* they were manifestations not of human skill but of divine power:

> Let a man only consider what a difference there is between the life of men in the most civilized province of Europe, and in the wildest and most barbarous districts of New India; he will feel it to be great enough to justify the saying that 'man is a god to man,' not only in regard to aid and benefit, but also by a comparison of condition. And this difference comes not from soil, not from climate, not from race, but from the arts.[27]

From this perspective the Algonquian misconception of the origin and nature of English technology would be evidence not of the power of Christianity to impose itself fraudulently on a backward people but of the dazzling power of science and of the naive literalism of the ignorant, who can conceive of this power only as the achievement of actual gods.[28]

Thus, for all his subtlety and his sensitivity to heterodoxy, Harriot might not have grasped fully the disturbing implications of his own text. The plausibility of a picture of Harriot culturally insulated from the subversive energies of his own activity would seem to be enhanced elsewhere in *A Brief and True Report* by his account of his missionary efforts:

> Many times and in every town where I came, according as I was able, I made declaration of the contents of the Bible; that therein was set forth the true and only God, and his mighty works, that therein was contained the true doctrine of salvation through Christ, with many particularities of Miracles and chief points of religion, as I was able then to utter, and thought fit for the time. And although I told them the book materially and of itself was not of any such virtue, as I thought they did conceive, but only the doctrine therein contained; yet would many be glad to touch it, to embrace it, to kiss it, to hold it to their breasts and heads, and stroke over all their body with it; to show their hungry desire of that knowledge which was spoken of. (pp. 376–7)

Here the heathens' confusion of material object and religious doctrine does not seem to cast doubts upon the truth of the Holy Book; rather it signals precisely the naive literalism of the Algonquians and hence their susceptibility to idolatry. They are viewed with a touch of amusement, as Spenser in the *Faerie Queene* views the "salvage nation" who seek to worship Una herself rather than the truth for which she stands:

> During which time her gentle wit she plyes,
> To teach them truth, which worshipt her in vaine,
> And made her th'Image of Idolatryes;
> But when their bootlesse zeale she did restraine
> From her own worship, they her Asse would worship fayn.
>   (1.6.19)[29]

Harriot, for his part, is willing to temper the view of the savage as idolater by reading the Algonquian fetishism of the book as a promising sign, an allegory of "their hungry desire of that knowledge which was spoken of." Such a reading, we might add, conveniently supports the claim that the English would easily dominate and civilize the Indians and hence advances the general purpose of *A Brief and True Report*.

The apparent religious certainty, cultural confidence, and national self-interest here by no means rule out the possibility of what I have called demonic consciousness – we can always postulate that Harriot found ever more subtle ways of simultaneously recording and disguising his dangerous speculations – but the essential point is that we need no such biographical romance to account for the apparent testing and confirmation of the Machiavellian hypothesis: the colonial power produced the subversiveness in its own interest, as I have argued, and *A Brief and True Report*, appropriately, was published by the great Elizabethan exponent of missionary colonialism, the Reverend Richard Hakluyt.

The thought that Christianity served to shore up the authority of the colonists would not have struck Hakluyt or the great majority of his readers as subversive. On the contrary, the role of religion in preserving the social order was a commonplace that all parties vied with each other in proclaiming. The suggestion that religions should be ranked according to their demonstrated ability to control their adherents would have been unacceptable, however, and the suggestion that reinforcing civil discipline must be the real origin and ultimate purpose of Christianity would have been still worse. These were possible explanations of the religion of another – skeptical arguments about ideological causality always work against beliefs one does not hold – but as we might expect from the earlier discussion of atheism, the application of this explanation to Christianity itself could be aired, and sternly refuted, only as the thought of another. Indeed a strictly functionalist explanation even of false religions was rejected by Christian theologians of the period. "It is utterly vain," writes Calvin, "for some men to say that religion was invented by the subtlety and craft of a few to hold the simple folk in thrall by this device and that those very persons who originated the worship of God for others did not in the least believe that any God existed." He goes on to concede

> that in order to hold men's minds in greater subjection, clever men have devised very many things in religion by which to inspire the common folk with reverence and strike them with terror. But they would never have achieved this if men's minds had not already been imbued with a firm conviction about God, from which the inclination toward religion springs as from a seed.[30]

Similarly, Hooker argues, "lest any man should here conceive, that it greatly skilleth not of what sort our religion be, inasmuch as heathens, Turks, and infidels, impute to religion a great part of the same effects which ourselves ascribe thereunto," that the good moral effects of false religions result from their having religious – that is, Christian – truths "entwined" in them.[31]

This argument, which derives from the early chapters of the Epistle to the Romans, is so integral to what John Coolidge has called the Pauline Renaissance in England that Harriot's account of the Algonquians would have seemed, even for readers who sensed something odd about it, closer to confirmation than to subversion of religious orthodoxy. Yet it is misleading, I think, to conclude without qualification that the radical doubt implicit in Harriot's account is *entirely* contained. After all, Harriot was hounded through his whole life by charges of atheism, and, more tellingly, the remark attributed to Marlowe suggests that a contemporary could draw the most dangerous conclusions from the Virginia report. Both of these signs of slippage are compromised by their links to the society's well-developed repressive apparatus: rumors, accusations, police reports. But if we should be wary of naively accepting a version of reality proffered by the secret police, we cannot at the same time dismiss that version altogether. There is a perversely attractive, if bleak, clarity in such a dismissal – in deciding that subversive doubt was totally produced and totally contained by the ruling elite – but the actual evidence is tenebrous. We simply do not know what was thought in silence, what was written and then carefully burned, what was whispered by Harriot to Ralegh. Moreover, the "Atlantic Republican tradition," as Pocock has argued, does grow out of the "Machiavellian moment" of the sixteenth century, and that tradition, with its transformation of subjects into citizens, its subordination of transcendent values to capital values, does ultimately undermine, in the interests of a new power, the religious and secular authorities that had licensed the American enterprise in the first place.[32] In Harriot's text the relation between orthodoxy and subversion seems, at the same interpretive moment, to be both perfectly stable and dangerously volatile.

We can deepen our understanding of this apparent paradox if we consider a second mode of subversion and its containment in Harriot's account. Alongside the *testing* of a subversive interpretation of the dominant culture, we find the *recording* of alien voices or, more precisely, of alien interpretations. The occasion for this recording is another consequence of the English presence in the New World, not in this case the threatened extinction of the tribal religion but the threatened extinction of the tribe: "There was no town where we had any subtle device practiced against us," Harriot writes,

> but that within a few days after our departure from every such town, the people began to die very fast, and many in short space; in some towns about twenty, in some forty, in some sixty and in one six score, which in truth was very many in respect of their numbers. The disease was so strange, that they neither knew what it was, nor how to cure it; the like by report of the oldest man in the country never happened before, time out of mind. (p. 378)[33]

Harriot is writing, of course, about the effects of measles, smallpox, or perhaps simply influenza on people with no resistance to them, but a conception of the biological basis of epidemic disease lies far, far in the future. For the English the deaths must be a moral phenomenon – this notion for them is as irresistible as the notion of germs for ourselves – and hence the "facts" as they are observed are already moralized: the deaths occurred only "where they used some practice against us," that is, where the Indians conspired secretly against the English. And with the wonderful self-validating circularity that characterizes virtually all powerful constructions of reality, the evidence for these secret conspiracies is precisely the deaths of the Indians.[34]

It is not surprising that Harriot seems to endorse the idea that God protects his chosen people by killing off untrustworthy Indians; what is surprising is to find him interested in the Indians' own anxious speculations about the unintended biological warfare that was destroying them. Drawing upon his special familiarity with the priests, he records a remarkable series of conjectures, almost all of which assume – correctly, as we now know – a link between the Indians' misfortune and the presence of the strangers. "Some people," observing that the English remained healthy while the Indians died, "could not tell," Harriot writes, "whether to think us gods or men;" others, seeing that the members of the first colony were all male, concluded that they were not born of women and therefore must be spirits of the dead returned to mortal form. Some medicine men learned in astrology blamed the disease on a recent eclipse of the sun and on a comet – a theory Harriot considers seriously and rejects – while others shared the prevailing English view and said "that it was the special work of God" on behalf of the colonists. And some who seem in historical hindsight eerily prescient prophesied "that there were more of [the English] generation yet to come, to kill theirs and take their places." The supporters of this theory even worked out a conception of the disease that in some features resembles our own: "Those that were immediately to come after us [the first English colonists], they imagined to be in the air, yet invisible and without bodies, and that they by our entreaty and for the love of us did make the people to die . . . by shooting invisible bullets into them" (p. 380).

For a moment, as Harriot records these competing theories, it may seem to us as if there were no absolute assurance of God's national interest, as if the drive to displace and absorb the other had given way to conversation among equals, as if all meanings were provisional, as if the signification of events stood apart from power. Our impression is intensified because we know that the theory that would ultimately triumph over the moral conception of epidemic disease was already present, at least metaphorically, in the conversation.[35] In the very moment that the moral conception is busily authorizing itself, it registers the possibility (indeed from our vantage point, the inevitability) of its own destruction.

But why, we must ask ourselves, should power record other voices, permit subversive inquiries, register at its very center the transgressions that will ultimately violate it? The answer may be in part that power, even in a colonial situation, is not monolithic and hence may encounter and record in one of its functions materials that can threaten another of its functions; in part that power thrives on vigilance, and human beings are vigilant if they sense a threat; in part that power defines itself in relation to such threats or simply to that which is not identical with it. Harriot's text suggests an intensification of these observations: English power in the first Virginia colony *depends* upon the registering and even the production of potentially unsettling perspectives. "These their opinions I have set down the more at large," Harriot tells the "Adventurers, Favorers, and Wellwishers" of the colony to whom his report is addressed, "that it may appear unto you that there is good hope that they may be brought through discreet dealing and government to the embracing of the truth, and consequently to honor, obey, fear, and love us" (p. 381). The recording of alien voices, their preservation in Harriot's text, is part of the process whereby Indian culture is constituted as a culture and thus brought into the light for study, discipline, correction, transformation. The momentary sense of instability or plenitude – the existence of other voices – is produced by the monological power that ultimately denies the possibility of plenitude, just as the subversive hypothesis about European religion is tested and confirmed only by the imposition of that religion.

We may add that the power of which we are speaking is in effect an allocation method – a way of distributing to some and denying to others critical resources (here primarily corn and game) that prolong life. In a remarkable study of the "tragic choices" societies make in allocating scarce resources (for example, kidney machines) or in determining high risks (for example, the military draft), Guido Calabresi and Philip Bobbitt observe that by complex mixtures of approaches, societies attempt to avert "tragic results, that is, results which imply the rejection of values which are proclaimed to be fundamental." Although these approaches may succeed for a time, it will eventually become apparent that some sacrifice of fundamental values has taken place, whereupon "fresh mixtures of methods will be tried, structured . . . by the shortcomings of the approaches they replace." These too will in time give way to others in a "strategy of successive moves," an "intricate game" that reflects the simultaneous perception of an inherent flaw and the determination to "forget" that perception in an illusory resolution.[36] Hence the simple operation of any systematic order, any allocation method, inevitably risks exposing its own limitations, even (or perhaps especially) as it asserts its underlying moral principle.

This exposure is most intense at moments when a comfortably established ideology confronts unusual circumstances, when the moral value of a particular form of power is not merely assumed but explained. We may glimpse such a moment in Harriot's account of a visit from the colonists' principal Indian ally, the chief Wingina. Wingina, persuaded that the disease ravaging his people was indeed the work of the Christian God, had come to request that the English ask their God to direct his lethal magic against an enemy tribe. The colonists tried to explain that such a prayer would be "ungodly," that their God was indeed responsible for the disease but that in this as in all things, he would act only "according to his good pleasure as he had ordained" (p. 379). Indeed, if men asked God to make an epidemic, he probably would not do it; the English could expect such providential help only if they made sincere "petition for the contrary," that is, for harmony and good fellowship in the service of truth and righteousness.

The problem with these assertions is not that they are self-consciously wicked (in the manner of Richard III or Iago) but that they are dismayingly moral and logically coherent; or rather, what is unsettling is one's experience of them, the nasty sense that they are at once irrefutable ethical propositions and pious humbug with which the English conceal from themselves the rapacity and aggression, or simply the horrible responsibility, implicit in their very presence. The explanatory moment manifests the self-validating, totalizing character of Renaissance political theology – its ability to account for almost every occurrence, even (or above all) apparently perverse or contrary occurrences – and at the same time confirms for us the drastic disillusionment that extends from Machiavelli to its definitive expression in Hume and Voltaire. In his own way, Wingina himself clearly thought his lesson in Christian ethics was polite nonsense. When the disease spread to his enemies, as it did shortly thereafter, he returned to the English to thank them – I presume with the Algonquian equivalent of a sly wink – for their friendly help, for "although we satisfied them not in promise, yet in deeds and effect we had fulfilled their desires" (p. 379). For Harriot, this "marvellous accident," as he calls it, is another sign of the colony's great expectations.

Once again a disturbing vista – a skeptical critique of the function of Christian morality in the New World – is glimpsed only to be immediately closed off. Indeed we may feel at this point that subversion scarcely exists and may legitimately ask ourselves how our perception of the subversive and orthodox is generated. The answer, I think, is that the term *subversive* for us designates those elements in Renaissance culture that contemporary audiences tried to contain or, when containment seemed impossible, to destroy and that now conform to our own sense of truth and reality. That is, we find "subversive" in the past precisely those things that are *not* subversive to ourselves, that pose no threat to the order by which we live and allocate resources: in Harriot's *Brief and True Report*, the function of illusion in the establishment of religion, the displacement of a providential conception of disease by one focused on "invisible bullets," the exposure of the psychological and material interests served by a certain conception of divine power. Conversely, we identify as principles of order and authority in Renaissance texts what we would, if we took them seriously, find subversive for ourselves: religious and political absolutism, aristocracy of birth, demonology, humoral psychology, and the like. That we do not find such notions subversive, that we complacently identify them as principles of aesthetic or political order, replicates the process of containment that licensed the elements we call subversive in Renaissance texts: that is, our own values are sufficiently strong for us to contain alien forces almost effortlessly. What we find in Harriot's *Brief and True Report* can best be described by adapting a remark about the possibility of hope that Kafka once made to Max Brod: There is subversion, no end of subversion, only not for us.

II

Shakespeare's plays are centrally, repeatedly concerned with the production and containment of subversion and disorder, and the three practices that I have identified in Harriot's text – testing, recording, and explaining – all have their recurrent theatrical equivalents, above all in the plays that meditate on the consolidation of state power.

These equivalents are not unique to Shakespeare; they are the signs of a broad institutional appropriation that is one of the root sources of the theater's vitality. Elizabethan playing companies contrived to absorb, refashion, and exploit some of the fundamental energies of a political authority that was itself already committed to histrionic display and hence was ripe for appropriation. But if he was not alone, Shakespeare nonetheless contrived to absorb more of these energies into his plays than any of his fellow playwrights. He succeeded in doing so because he seems to have understood very early in his career that power consisted not only in dazzling display – the pageants, processions, entries, and progresses of Elizabethan statecraft – but also in a systematic structure of relations, those linked strategies I have tried to isolate and identify in colonial discourse at the margins of Tudor society. Shakespeare evidently grasped such strategies not by brooding on the impact of English culture on far-off Virginia but by looking intently at the world immediately around him, by contemplating the queen and her powerful friends and enemies, and by reading imaginatively the great English chroniclers. And the crucial point is less that he *represented* the paradoxical practices of an authority deeply complicit in undermining its own legitimacy than that he *appropriated* for the theater the compelling energies at once released and organized by these practices.

The representation of a self-undermining authority is the principal concern of *Richard II*, which marks a brilliant advance over the comparable representation in the *Henry VI* trilogy, but the full appropriation for the stage of that authority and its power is not achieved until *1 Henry IV*. We may argue, of course, that in this play there is little or no "self-undermining" at all: emergent authority in *1 Henry IV* – that is, the authority that begins to solidify around the figure of Hal – is strikingly different from the enfeebled command of Henry VI or the fatally self-wounded royal name of Richard II. "Who does not all along see," wrote Upton in the mid-eighteenth century, "that when prince Henry comes to be king he will assume a character suitable to his dignity?" My point is not to dispute this interpretation of the prince as, in Maynard Mack's words, "an ideal image of the potentialities of the English character,"[37] but to observe that such an ideal image involves as its positive condition the constant production of its own radical subversion and the powerful containment of that subversion.

We are continually reminded that Hal is a "juggler," a conniving hypocrite, and that the power he both serves and comes to embody is glorified usurpation and theft.[38] Moreover, the disenchantment makes itself felt in the very moments when Hal's moral authority is affirmed. Thus, for example, the scheme of Hal's redemption is carefully laid out in his soliloquy at the close of the first tavern scene, but as in the act of *explaining* that we have examined in Harriot, Hal's justification of himself threatens to fall away at every moment into its antithesis. "By how much better than my word I am," Hal declares, "By so much shall I falsify men's hopes" (1.2.210–11). To falsify men's hopes is to exceed their expectations, and it is also to disappoint their expectations, to deceive men, to turn hopes into fictions, to betray.

At issue are not only the contradictory desires and expectations centered on Hal in the play – the competing hopes of his royal father and his tavern friends – but our own hopes, the fantasies continually aroused by the play of innate grace, limitless playfulness, absolute friendship, generosity, and trust. Those fantasies are symbolized by certain echoing, talismanic phrases ("when thou art king," "shall we be merry?" "a thousand pound"), and they are bound up with the overall vividness, intensity, and richness of the theatrical practice itself. Yeats's phrase for the quintessential Shakespearean effect, "the emotion of multitude," seems particularly applicable to *1 Henry IV* with its multiplicity of brilliant characters, its intensely differentiated settings, its dazzling verbal wit, its mingling of high comedy, farce, epic heroism, and tragedy. The play awakens a dream of superabundance, which is given its irresistible embodiment in Falstaff.

But that dream is precisely what Hal betrays or rather, to use his own more accurate term, "falsifies." He does so in this play not by a decisive act of rejection, as at the close of *2 Henry IV*, but by a more subtle and continuous draining of the plenitude. "This chair shall be my state," proclaims Falstaff, improvising the king's part, "this dagger my sceptre, and this cushion my crown." Hal's cool rejoinder cuts deftly at both his real and his surrogate father: "Thy state is taken for a join'd-stool, thy golden sceptre for a leaden dagger, and thy precious rich crown for a pitiful bald crown" (2.4.378–82). Hal is the prince and principle of falsification – he is himself a counterfeit companion, and he reveals the emptiness in the world around him. "Dost thou hear, Hal?" Falstaff implores, with the sheriff at the door. "Never call a true piece of gold a counterfeit. Thou art essentially made, without seeming so" (2.4.491–93). The words, so oddly the reverse of the ordinary advice to beware of accepting the counterfeit for reality, attach themselves to both Falstaff and Hal: do not denounce me to the law for I, Falstaff, am genuinely your adoring friend and not merely a parasite; and also, do not think of yourself, Hal, as a mere pretender, do not imagine that your value depends upon falsification.

The "true piece of gold" is alluring because of the widespread faith that it has an intrinsic value, that it does not depend upon the stamp of authority and hence cannot be arbitrarily duplicated or devalued, that it is indifferent to its circumstances, that it cannot be robbed of its worth. This is the fantasy of identity that Falstaff holds out to Hal and that Hal empties out, as he empties out Falstaff's pockets. "What hast thou found?" "Nothing but papers, my lord" (2.4.532–3).[39] Hal is an anti-Midas: everything he touches turns to dross. And this devaluation is the source of his own sense of value, a value not intrinsic but contingent, dependent upon the circulation of counterfeit coin and the subtle manipulation of appearances:

> And like bright metal on a sullen ground,
> My reformation, glitt'ring o'er my fault,
> Shall show more goodly and attract more eyes
> Than that which hath no foil to set it off.
> I'll so offend, to make offense a skill,
> Redeeming time when men think least I will.
>   (1.2.212–17)

Such lines, as Empson remarks, "cannot have been written without bitterness against the prince," yet the bitterness is not incompatible with an "ironical acceptance" of his authority.[40] The dreams of plenitude are not abandoned altogether – Falstaff in particular has an imaginative life that overflows the confines of the play itself – but the daylight world of *1 Henry IV* comes to seem increasingly one of counterfeit, and hence one governed by Bolingbroke's cunning (he sends "counterfeits" of himself out onto the battlefield) and by Hal's calculations. A "starveling" – fat Falstaff's word for Hal – triumphs in a world of scarcity. Though we can perceive at every point, through our own constantly shifting allegiances, the potential instability of the structure of power that has Henry IV and his son at the pinnacle and Robin Ostler, who "never joy'd since the price of oats rose" (2.1.12–13), near the bottom, Hal's "redemption" is as inescapable and inevitable as the outcome of those practical jokes the madcap prince is so fond of playing. Indeed, the play insists, this redemption is not something toward which the action moves but something that is happening at every moment of the theatrical representation.

The same yoking of the unstable and the inevitable may be seen in the play's acts of *recording*, that is, the moments in which we hear voices that seem to dwell outside the realms ruled by the potentates of the land. These voices exist and have their apotheosis in Falstaff, but their existence proves to be utterly bound up with Hal, contained politically by his purposes as they are justified aesthetically by his involvement. The perfect emblem of this containment is Falstaff's company, marching off to Shrewsbury: "discarded unjust servingmen, younger sons to younger brothers, revolted tapsters, and ostlers trade-fall'n, the cankers of a calm world and a long peace" (4.2.27–30). As many a homily would tell us, these are the very types of Elizabethan subversion – the masterless men who rose up periodically in desperate protests against their social superiors. A half century later they would swell the ranks of the New Model Army and be disciplined into a revolutionary force. But here they are pressed into service as defenders of the established order, "good enough to toss," as Falstaff tells Hal, "food for powder, food for powder" (4.2.65–6). For power as well as powder, and we may add that this food is produced as well as consumed by the great.

Shakespeare gives us a glimpse of this production in the odd little scene in which Hal, with the connivance of Poins, reduces the puny tapster Francis to the mechanical repetition of the word "Anon":

> *Prince:* Nay, but hark you, Francis: for the sugar thou gavest me, 'twas a pennyworth, was't not?
> *Francis:* O Lord, I would it had been two!
> *Prince:* I will give thee for it a thousand pound. Ask me when thou wilt, and thou shalt have it.
> *Poins:* *(Within)* Francis!
> *Francis:* Anon, anon.
> *Prince:* Anon, Francis? No, Francis; but tomorrow, Francis; or, Francis, a' Thursday; or indeed, Francis, when thou wilt.
>
> (2.4.58–67)

The Bergsonian comedy in such a moment resides in Hal's exposing a drastic reduction of human possibility: "That ever this fellow should have fewer words than a parrot," he says at the scene's end, "and yet the son of a woman!" (2.4.98–9). But the chief interest for us resides in Hal's producing the very reduction he exposes. The fact of this production, its theatrical demonstration, implicates Hal not only in the linguistic poverty upon which he plays but in the poverty of the five years of apprenticeship Francis has yet to serve: "Five year!" Hal exclaims, "by'r lady, a long lease for the clinking of pewter" (2.4.45–6). And as the prince is implicated in the production of this oppressive order, so is he implicated in the impulse to abrogate it: "But, Francis, darest thou be so valiant as to play the coward with thy indenture, and show it a fair pair of heels and run from it?" (2.4.46–8).

It is tempting to think of this particular moment – the prince awakening the apprentice's discontent – as linked darkly with some supposed uneasiness in Hal about his own apprenticeship.[41] The momentary glimpse of a revolt against authority is closed off at once, however, with a few obscure words calculated to return Francis to his trade without enabling him to understand why he must return to it:

> *Prince:*   Why then your brown bastard is your only drink! for look you, Francis, your white canvas doublet will sully. In Barbary, sir, it cannot come to so much.
> *Francis:* What, sir?
> *Poins:*   (*Within*) Francis!
> *Prince:*   Away, you rogue, dost thou not hear them call?
>
> (2.4.73–79)

If Francis takes the earlier suggestion, robs his master and runs away, he will find a place for himself, the play implies, only as one of the "revolted tapsters" in Falstaff's company, men as good as dead long before they march to their deaths as upholders of the crown. Better that he should follow the drift of Hal's deliberately mystifying words and continue to clink pewter. As for the prince, his interest in the brief exchange, beyond what we have already sketched, is suggested by his boast to Poins moments before Francis enters: "I have sounded the very base-string of humility. Sirrah, I am sworn brother to a leash of drawers, and can call them all by their christen names, as Tom, Dick, and Francis" (2.4.5–8). The prince must sound the base-string of humility if he is to play all of the chords and hence be the master of the instrument, and his ability to conceal his motives and render opaque his language offers assurance that he himself will not be played on by another.

I have spoken of such scenes in *1 Henry IV* as resembling what in Harriot's text I have called *recording*, a mode that culminates for Harriot in a glossary, the beginnings of an Algonquian–English dictionary, designed to facilitate further acts of recording and hence to consolidate English power in Virginia. The resemblance may be seen most clearly perhaps in Hal's own glossary of tavern slang: "They call drinking deep, dyeing scarlet, and when you breathe in your watering, they cry 'hem!' and bid you play it off. To conclude, I am so good a proficient in one quarter of an hour, that I can drink with any tinker in his own language during my life" (2.4.15–20). The potential value of these lessons, the functional interest to power of recording the speech of an "under-skinker" and his mates, may be glimpsed in the expressions of loyalty that Hal laughingly recalls: "They take it already upon their salvation, that . . . when I am King of England I shall command all the good lads in Eastcheap" (2.4.9–15).

It may be objected that there is something slightly absurd in likening such moments to aspects of Harriot's text; *1 Henry IV* is a play, not a tract for potential investors in a colonial scheme, and the only values we may be sure Shakespeare had in mind, the argument would go, are theatrical values. But theatrical values do not exist in a realm of privileged literariness, of textual or even institutional self-referentiality. Shakespeare's theater was not isolated by its wooden walls, nor did it merely reflect social and ideological forces that lay entirely outside it: rather the Elizabethan and Jacobean theater was itself a *social event* in reciprocal contact with other social events.

One might add that *1 Henry IV* itself insists upon the impossibility of sealing off the interests of the theater from the interests of power. Hal's characteristic activity is playing or, more precisely, theatrical improvisation – his parts include his father, Hotspur, Hotspur's wife, a thief in buckram, himself as prodigal, and himself as penitent – and he fully understands his own behavior through most of the play as a role that he is performing. We might expect that this role playing gives way at the end to his true identity: "I shall hereafter," Hal has promised his father, "Be more myself" (3.2.92–3). With the killing of Hotspur, however, Hal clearly does not reject all theatrical masks but rather replaces one with another. "The time will come," Hal declares midway through the play, "That I shall make this northren youth exchange/His glorious deeds for my indignities" (3.2.144–6); when that time *has* come, at the play's close, Hal hides with his "favors" (that is, a scarf or other emblem, but the word *favor* also has in the sixteenth century the sense of "face") the dead Hotspur's "mangled face" (5.4.96), as if to mark the completion of the exchange.

Theatricality, then, is not set over against power but is one of power's essential modes. In lines that anticipate Hal's promise, the angry Henry IV tells Worcester, "I will from henceforth rather be myself,/Mighty and to be fear'd, than my condition" (1.3.5–6). "To be oneself" here means to perform one's part in the scheme of power rather than to manifest one's natural disposition, or what we would normally designate as the very core of the self. Indeed it is by no means clear that such a thing as a natural disposition exists in the play except as a theatrical fiction: we recall that in Falstaff's hands the word *instinct* becomes histrionic rhetoric, an improvised excuse for his flight from the masked prince. "Beware instinct – the lion will not touch the true prince. Instinct is a great matter; I was now a coward on instinct. I shall think the better of myself, and thee, during my life; I for a valiant lion, and thou for a true prince" (2.4.271–5). Both claims – Falstaff's to natural valor, Hal's to legitimate royalty – are, the lines darkly imply, of equal merit.

Again and again in *1 Henry IV* we are tantalized by the possibility of an escape from theatricality and hence from the constant pressure of improvisational power, but we are, after all, in the theater, and our pleasure depends upon there being no escape, and our applause ratifies the triumph of our confinement. The play operates in the manner of its central character, charming us with its visions of breadth and solidarity, "redeeming" itself in the end by betraying our hopes, and earning with this betrayal our slightly anxious admiration. Hence the odd balance in this play of spaciousness – the constant multiplication of separate, vividly realized realms – and militant claustrophobia: the absorption of all of these realms by a power at once vital and impoverished. The balance is almost perfect, as if Shakespeare had somehow reached through in *1 Henry IV* to the very center of the system of opposed and interlocking forces that held Tudor society together.

III

When we turn, however, to the plays that continue the chronicle of Hal's career, *2 Henry IV* and *Henry V*, we find not only that the forces balanced in the earlier play have pulled apart – the claustrophobia triumphant in *2 Henry IV*, the spaciousness triumphant in *Henry V*[42] – but that from this new perspective the familiar view of *1 Henry IV* as a perfectly poised play must be revised. What appeared as "balance" may on closer inspection seem like radical instability tricked out as moral or aesthetic order; what appeared as clarity may seem now like a conjurer's trick concealing confusion in order to buy time and stave off the collapse of an illusion.[43] Not waving but drowning.

In *2 Henry IV* the characteristic operations of power are less equivocal than they had been in the preceding play: there is no longer even the lingering illusion of distinct realms, each with its own system of values, its soaring visions of plenitude, and its bad dreams. There is manifestly a single system now, one based on predation and betrayal. Hotspur's intoxicating dreams of honor are dead, replaced by the cold rebellion of cunning but impotent schemers. The warm, roistering noise overheard in the tavern – noise that seemed to signal a subversive alternative to rebellion – turns out to be the sound of a whore and a bully beating a customer to death. And Falstaff, whose earlier larcenies were gilded by fantasies of innate grace, now talks of turning diseases to commodity (1.2.248).

Only Prince Hal seems in this play less meanly calculating, subject now to fits of weariness and confusion, though this change serves less to humanize him (as Auerbach argued in a famous essay) than to make it clear that the betrayals are systematic. They happen to him and for him. He need no longer soliloquize his intention to "falsify men's hopes" by selling his wastrel friends: the sale will be brought about by the structure of things, a structure grasped in this play under the twinned names of time and necessity. So too there is no longer any need for heroic combat with a dangerous, glittering enemy like Hotspur (the only reminder of whose voice in this play is Pistol's parody of Marlovian swaggering); the rebels are deftly, if ingloriously, dispatched by the false promises of Hal's younger brother, the primly virtuous John of Lancaster. To seal his lies, Lancaster swears fittingly "by the honor of my blood" (4.2.55) – the cold blood, as Falstaff observes of Hal, that he inherited from his father.

The recording of alien voices – the voices of those who have no power to leave literate traces of their existence – continues in this play, but without even the theatrical illusion of princely complicity. The king is still convinced that his son is a prodigal and that the kingdom will fall to ruin after his death – perhaps he finds a peculiar consolation in the thought – but it is no longer Hal alone who declares (against all appearances) his secret commitment to disciplinary authority. Warwick assures the king that the prince's interests in the good lads of Eastcheap are entirely what they should be:

> The Prince but studies his companions
> Like a strange tongue, wherein, to gain the language,
> 'Tis needful that the most immodest word
> Be look'd upon and learnt, which once attain'd,
> Your Highness knows, comes to no further use
> But to be known and hated. So, like gross terms,
> The Prince will in the perfectness of time
> Cast off his followers, and their memory
> Shall as a pattern or a measure live,
> By which his Grace must mete the lives of other,
> Turning past evils to advantages.
>
> (4.4.68–78)

At first the language analogy likens the prince's low-life excursions to the search for proficiency: perfect linguistic competence, the "mastery" of a language, requires the fullest possible vocabulary. But the darkness of Warwick's words – "to be known and hated" – immediately pushes the goal of Hal's linguistic researches beyond proficiency. When in *1 Henry IV* Hal boasts of his mastery of tavern slang, we are allowed for a moment at least to imagine that we are witnessing a social bond, the human fellowship of the extremest top and bottom of society in a homely ritual act of drinking together. The play may make it clear, as I have argued, that well-defined political interests are involved, but these interests may be bracketed, if only briefly, for the pleasure of imagining what Victor Turner calls "communitas" – a union based on the momentary breaking of the hierarchical order that normally governs a community.[44] And even when we pull back from this spacious sense of union, we are permitted for much of the play to take pleasure at least in Hal's surprising skill, the proficiency he rightly celebrates in himself.

To learn another language is to acknowledge the existence of another people and to acquire the ability to function, however crudely, in another social world. Hal's remark about drinking with any tinker in his own language suggests, if only jocularly, that for him the lower classes are virtually another people, an alien tribe – immensely more populous than his own – within the kingdom. That this perception extended beyond the confines of Shakespeare's play is suggested by the evidence that middle- and upper-class English settlers in the New World regarded the American Indians less as another race than as a version of their own lower classes; one man's tinker is another man's Indian.[45]

If Hal's glossary initially seems to resemble Harriot's practical word list in the *Brief and True Report*, with its Algonquian equivalents for *fire, food, shelter*, Warwick's account of Hal's intentions suggests a deeper resemblance to a different kind of glossary, one more specifically linked to the attempt to understand and control the lower classes. I refer to the sinister glossaries appended to sixteenth-century accounts of criminals and vagabonds. "Here I set before the good reader the lewd, lousy language of these loitering lusks and lazy lorels," announces Thomas Harman as he introduces (with a comical flourish designed to display his own rhetorical gifts) what he claims is an authentic list, compiled at great personal cost.[46] His pamphlet, *A Caveat for Common Cursitors*, is the fruit, he declares, of personal research, difficult because his informants are "marvellous subtle and crafty." But "with fair flattering words, money, and good cheer," he has learned much about their ways, "not without faithful promise made unto them never to discover their names or anything they showed me" (p. 82). Harman cheerfully goes on to publish what they showed him, and he ends his work not only with a glossary of "peddler's French" but with an alphabetical list of names, so that the laws made for "the extreme punishment" of these wicked idlers may be enforced.

It is not clear that Harman's subjects – upright men, doxies, Abraham men, and the like – bear any more relation to social reality than either Doll Tearsheet or Mistress Quickly.[47] Much of the *Caveat*, like the other cony-catching pamphlets of the period, has the air of a jest book: time-honored tales of tricksters and rogues, dished out as realistic observation. (It is not encouraging that the rogues' term for the stocks in which they were punished, according to Harman, is "the harmans.") But Harman is concerned to convey at least the impression of accurate observation and recording – clearly, this was among the book's selling points – and one of the principal rhetorical devices he uses to do so is the spice of betrayal: he repeatedly calls attention to his solemn promises never to reveal anything he has been told, for his breaking of his word assures the accuracy and importance of what he reveals.

A middle-class Prince Hal, Harman claims that through dissembling he has gained access to a world normally hidden from his kind, and he will turn that access to the advantage of the kingdom by helping his readers to identify and eradicate the dissemblers in their midst. Harman's own personal interventions – the acts of detection and apprehension he proudly reports (or invents) – are not enough; only his book can fully expose the cunning sleights of the rogues and thereby induce the justices and shrieves to be more vigilant and punitive. Just as theatricality is thematized in the *Henry IV* plays as one of the crucial agents of royal power, so in *A Caveat for Common Cursitors* (and in much of the cony-catching literature of the period in England and France) printing is represented in the text itself as a force for social order and the detection of criminal fraud. The printed book can be widely disseminated and easily revised, so that the vagabonds' names and tricks may be known before they themselves arrive at an honest citizen's door; as if this mobility were not tangible enough, Harman claims that when his pamphlet was only halfway printed, his printer helped him apprehend a particularly sly "counterfeit crank" – a pretended epileptic. In Harman's account the printer turns detective, first running down the street to apprehend the dissembler, then on a subsequent occasion luring him "with fair allusions" (p. 116) and a show of charity into the hands of the constable. With such lurid tales Harman literalizes the power of the book to hunt down vagabonds and bring them to justice.

The danger of such accounts is that the ethical charge will reverse itself, with the forces of order – the people, as it were, of the book – revealed as themselves dependent on dissembling and betrayal and the vagabonds revealed either as less fortunate and well-protected imitators of their betters or, alternatively, as primitive rebels against the hypocrisy of a cruel society. Exactly such a reversal seems to occur again and again in the rogue literature of the period, from the doxies and morts who answer Harman's rebukes with unfailing, if spare, dignity to the more articulate defenders of vice elsewhere who insist that their lives are at worst imitations of the lives of the great:

> Though your experience in the world be not so great as mine [says a cheater at dice], yet am I sure ye see that no man is able to live an honest man unless he have some privy way to help himself withal, more than the world is witness of. Think you the noblemen could do as they do, if in this hard world they should maintain so great a port only upon their rent? Think you the lawyers could be such purchasers if their pleas were short, and all their judgements, justice and conscience? Suppose ye that offices would be so dearly bought, and the buyers so soon enriched, if they counted not pillage an honest point of purchase? Could merchants, without lies, false making their wares, and selling them by a crooked light, to deceive the chapman in the thread or colour, grow so soon rich and to a baron's possessions, and make all their posterity gentlemen?[48]

Though these reversals are at the very heart of the rogue literature, it would be as much of a mistake to regard their intended effect as subversive as to regard in a similar light the comparable passages – most often articulated by Falstaff – in Shakespeare's histories. The subversive voices are produced by and within the affirmations of order; they are powerfully registered, but they do not undermine that order. Indeed, as the example of Harman – so much cruder than Shakespeare – suggests, the order is neither possible nor fully convincing without both the presence and perception of betrayal.

This dependence on betrayal does not prevent Harman from leveling charges of hypocrisy and deep dissembling at the rogues and from urging his readers to despise and prosecute them. On the contrary, Harman's moral indignation seems paradoxically heightened by his own implication in the deceitfulness that he condemns, as if the rhetorical violence of the condemnation cleansed him of any guilt. His broken promises are acts of civility, necessary strategies for securing social well-being. The "rowsy, ragged rabblement of rakehells" has put itself outside the bounds of civil conversation; justice consists precisely in taking whatever measures are necessary to eradicate them. Harman's false oaths are the means of identifying and ridding the community of the purveyors of false oaths. The pestilent few will "fret, fume, swear, and stare at this my book," in which their practices, disclosed after they had received fair promises of confidentiality, are laid open, but the majority will band together in righteous reproach: "The honourable will abhor them, the worshipful will reject them, the yeomen will sharply taunt them, the husbandmen utterly defy them, the labouring men bluntly chide them, the women with clapping hands cry out at them" (p. 84). To like reading about vagabonds is to hate them and to approve of their ruthless betrayal.

"The right people of the play," a gifted critic of 2 Henry IV observes, "merge into a larger order; the wrong people resist or misuse that larger order."[49] True enough, but like Harman's community of vagabond-haters, the "larger order" of the Lancastrian state in this play seems to batten on the breaking of oaths. Shakespeare does not shrink from any of the felt nastiness implicit in this sorting out of the right people and the wrong people; he takes the discursive mode that he could have found in Harman and a hundred other texts and intensifies it, so that the founding of the modern state, like the self-fashioning of the modern prince, is shown to be based upon acts of calculation, intimidation, and deceit. And these acts are performed in an entertainment for which audiences, the subjects of this very state, pay money and applaud.

There is, throughout *2 Henry IV*, a sense of constriction that is only intensified by the obsessive enumeration of details: "Thou didst swear to me upon a parcel-gilt goblet, sitting in my Dolphin chamber, at the round table by a sea-coal fire, upon Wednesday in Wheeson week ..." (2.1.86–9). We may find, in Justice Shallow's garden, a few twilight moments of release from this oppressive circumstantial and strategic constriction, but Falstaff mercilessly deflates them – and the puncturing is so wonderfully adroit, so amusing, that we welcome it: "I do remember him at Clement's Inn, like a man made after supper of a cheese-paring. When 'a was naked, he was for all the world like a fork'd redish, with a head fantastically carv'd upon it with a knife" (3.2.308–12).

What remains is the law of nature: the strong eat the weak. Yet this is not quite what Shakespeare invites the audience to affirm through its applause. Like Harman, Shakespeare refuses to endorse so baldly cynical a conception of the social order; instead actions that should have the effect of radically undermining authority turn out to be the props of that authority. In this play, even more cruelly than in *1 Henry IV*, moral values – justice, order, civility – are secured through the apparent generation of their subversive contraries. Out of the squalid betrayals that preserve the state emerges the "formal majesty" into which Hal at the close, through a final, definitive betrayal – the rejection of Falstaff – merges himself.

There are moments in *Richard II* when the collapse of kingship seems to be confirmed in the discovery of the physical body of the ruler, the pathos of his creatural existence:

> throw away respect,
> Tradition, form, and ceremonious duty,
> For you have but mistook me all this while.
> I live with bread like you, feel want,
> Taste grief, need friends: subjected thus,
> How can you say to me I am a king?
>   (3.2.172–7)

By the close of *2 Henry IV* such physical limitations have been absorbed into the ideological structure, and hence justification, of kingship. It is precisely because Prince Hal lives with bread that we can understand the sacrifice that he and, for that matter, his father have made. Unlike Richard II, Henry IV articulates this sacrifice not as a piece of histrionic rhetoric but as a private meditation, the innermost thoughts of a troubled, weary man:

> Why rather, sleep, liest thou in smoky cribs,
> Upon uneasy pallets stretching thee,
> And hush'd with buzzing night-flies to thy slumber,
> Than in the perfum'd chambers of the great,
> Under the canopies of costly state,
> And lull'd with sound of sweetest melody?
>
> (3.1.9–14)

Who knows? Perhaps it is even true; perhaps in a society in which the overwhelming majority of men and women had next to nothing, the few who were rich and powerful did lie awake at night. But we should understand that this sleeplessness was not a well-kept secret: the sufferings of the great are one of the familiar themes in the literature of the governing classes in the sixteenth century.[50] Henry IV speaks in soliloquy, but as is so often the case in Shakespeare, his isolation only intensifies the sense that he is addressing a large audience: the audience of the theater. We are invited to take measure of his suffering, to understand – here and elsewhere in the play – the costs of power. And we are invited to understand these costs in order to ratify the power, to accept the grotesque and cruelly unequal distribution of possessions: everything to the few, nothing to the many. The rulers earn, or at least pay for, their exalted position through suffering, and this suffering ennobles, if it does not exactly cleanse, the lies and betrayals upon which this position depends.

As so often, Falstaff parodies this ideology, or rather – and more significantly – presents it as humbug *before* it makes its appearance as official truth. Called away from the tavern to the court, Falstaff turns to Doll and Mistress Quickly and proclaims sententiously: "You see, my good wenches, how men of merit are sought after. The undeserver may sleep when the man of action is call'd on" (2.4.374–7). Seconds later this rhetoric – marked out as something with which to impress whores and innkeepers to whom one owes money one does not intend to pay – recurs in the speech and, by convention of the soliloquy, the innermost thoughts of the king.

This staging of what we may term anticipatory, or proleptic, parody is a major structural principle of Shakespeare's play. Its effect is not (as with straightforward parodies) to ridicule the claims of high seriousness but rather to mark them as slightly suspect and to encourage guarded skepticism. Thus in the wake of Falstaff's burlesque of the weariness of the virtuous, the king's insomniac pathos reverberates hollowness as well as poignancy. At such moments *2 Henry IV* seems to be testing and confirming a dark and disturbing hypothesis about the nature of monarchical power in England: that its moral authority rests upon a hypocrisy so deep that the hypocrites themselves believe it. "Then (happy) low, lie down!/Uneasy lies the head that wears a crown" (3.1.30–1): so the old pike tells the young dace. But the old pike actually seems to believe in his own speeches, just as he may believe that he never really sought the crown, "But that necessity so bow'd the state/That I and greatness were compell'd to kiss" (3.1.73–4). Our privileged knowledge of the network of state betrayals and privileged access to Falstaff's cynical wisdom can make this opaque hypocrisy transparent. Yet even with *2 Henry IV*, where the lies and the self-serving sentiments are utterly inescapable, where the illegitimacy of legitimate authority is repeatedly demonstrated, where the whole state seems – to adapt More's phrase – a conspiracy of the great to enrich and protect their interests under the name of commonwealth, even here the state, watchful for signs of sedition on the stage, was not prodded to intervene. We may choose to attribute this apparent somnolence to incompetence or corruption, but the linkages I have sketched between the history plays and the discursive practices represented by Harriot and Harman suggest another explanation. Once again, though in a still more iron-age spirit than at the close of *1 Henry IV*, the play appears to ratify the established order, with the new-crowned Henry V merging his body into "the great body of our state," with Falstaff despised and rejected, and with Lancaster – the coldhearted betrayer of the rebels – left to admire his still more coldhearted brother: "I like this fair proceeding of the King's" (5.5.97).[51]

The mood at the close remains, to be sure, an unpleasant one – the rejection of Falstaff has been one of the nagging "problems" of Shakespeare criticism – but the discomfort only serves to verify Hal's claim that he has turned away his former self. If there is frustration at the harshness of the play's end, the frustration confirms a carefully plotted official strategy whereby subversive perceptions are at once produced and contained:

> My father is gone wild into his grave;
> For in his tomb lie my affections,
> And with his spirits sadly I survive,
> To mock the expectation of the world,
> To frustrate prophecies, and to rase out
> Rotten opinion. . . .
>
> (5.2.123–8)

IV

The first part of *Henry IV* enables us to feel at moments that we are like Harriot, surveying a complex new world, testing upon it dark thoughts without damaging the order that those thoughts would seem to threaten. The second part of *Henry IV* suggests that we are still more like the Indians, compelled to pay homage to a system of beliefs whose fraudulence only confirms their power, authenticity, and truth. The concluding play in the series, *Henry V*, insists that we have all along been both colonizer and colonized, king and subject. The play deftly registers every nuance of royal hypocrisy, ruthlessness, and bad faith – testing, in effect, the proposition that successful rule depends not upon sacredness but upon demonic violence – but it does so in the context of a celebration, a collective panegyric to "This star of England," the charismatic leader who purges the commonwealth of its incorrigibles and forges the martial national state.

By yoking together diverse peoples – represented in the play by the Welshman Fluellen, the Irishman Macmorris, and the Scotsman Jamy, who fight at Agincourt alongside the loyal Englishmen – Hal symbolically tames the last wild areas in the British Isles, areas that in the sixteenth century represented, far more powerfully than any New World people, the doomed outposts of a vanishing tribalism.[52] We might expect then that in *Henry V* the mode that I have called recording would reach its fullest flowering, and in a sense it does. The English allies are each given a distinct accentual notation – "'a utt'red as prave words at the pridge as you shall see in a summer's day"; "By Chrish law, 'tish ill done! The work ish give over"; "It sall be vary gud, gud feith, gud captens bath, and I sall quit you with gud leve" – a notation that helped determine literary representations of the stock Welshman, Irishman, and Scotsman for centuries to come. But their distinctness is curiously formal, a collection of mechanistic attributes recalling the heightened but static individuality of Jonson's humorous grotesques.

The verbal tics of such characters interest us because they represent not what is alien but what is predictable and automatic. They give pleasure because they persuade an audience of its own mobility and complexity; even a spectator gaping passively at the play's sights and manipulated by its rhetoric is freer than these puppets jerked on the strings of their own absurd accents. Only Fluellen (much of the time an exuberant, bullying prince-pleaser) seems at one moment to articulate perceptions that lie outside the official line, and he arrives at these perceptions not through his foreignness but through his relentless pursuit of classical analogies. Teasing out a Plutarch-like parallel between Hal and "Alexander the Pig" – "There is a river in Macedon, and there is also moreover a river at Monmouth," and so forth – Fluellen reaches the observation that Alexander "did, in his ales and his angers, look you, kill his best friend, Clytus." Gower quickly intervenes: "Our King is not like him in that; he never kill'd any of his friends." But Fluellen persists: "as Alexander kill'd his friend Clytus, being in his ales and his cups; so also Harry Monmouth, being in his right wits and his good judgments, turn'd away the fat knight with the great belly doublet. He was full of jests, and gipes, and knaveries, and mocks – I have forgot his name." Gower provides it: "Sir John Falstaff" (4.7.26–51).

The moment is potentially devastating. The comparison with drunken Alexander focuses all our perceptions of Hal's sober cold-bloodedness, from his rejection of Falstaff – "The King has kill'd his heart" (2.1.88) – to his responsibility for the execution of his erstwhile boon companion Bardolph. The low-life characters in the earlier plays had been the focus of Hal's language lessons, but as Warwick had predicted, the prince studied them as "gross terms," no sooner learned than discarded.

The discarding in *Henry V* is not an attractive sight but is perfectly consistent with the practice we have analyzed in Harman's *Caveat*. Indeed in a direct recollection of the cony-catching literature, Fluellen learns that Pistol, whom he had thought "as valiant a man as Mark Antony" (3.6.13–14), is "a rogue, that now and then goes to the wars, to grace himself at his return into London under the form of a soldier" (3.6.67–9). "You must learn to know such slanders of the age," remarks Gower in a line that could serve as Harman's epigraph, "or else you may be marvellously mistook" (3.6.79–81). And how does Fluellen learn that Pistol is one of the slanders of the age? What does Pistol do to give himself away? He passionately pleads that

Fluellen intervene to save Bardolph, who has been sentenced to die for stealing a "pax of little price." "Let gallows gape for dog, let man go free," rages Pistol, "And let not hemp his windpipe suffocate" (3.6.42–3). Fluellen refuses; Bardolph hangs; and this attempt to save his friend's life marks Pistol as a "rascally, scald, beggarly, lousy, pragging knave" (5.1.5–6). By contrast, Hal's symbolic killing of Falstaff – which might have been recorded as a bitter charge against him – is advanced by Fluellen as the climactic manifestation of his virtues. No sooner is it mentioned than the king himself enters in triumph, leading his French prisoners. This entrance, with its military "Alarum" followed by a royal "Flourish," is the perfect emblematic instance of a potential dissonance being absorbed into a charismatic celebration. The betrayal of friends does not subvert but rather sustains the moral authority and the compelling glamour of power. That authority, as the play defines it, is precisely the ability to betray one's friends without stain.

If neither the English allies nor the low-life characters seem to fulfill adequately the role of aliens whose voices are "recorded," *Henry V* apparently gives us a sustained, even extreme, version of this practice in the dialogue of the French characters, dialogue that is in part presented untranslated in the performance. This dialogue includes even a language lesson, the very emblem of "recording" in the earlier plays. Yet like the English allies, the French enemies say remarkably little that is alien or disturbing in relation to the central voice of authority in the play. To be sure, several of the French nobles contemptuously dismiss Hal as "a vain, giddy, shallow, humorous youth" (2.4.28), but these terms of abuse are outmoded; it is as if news of the end of *1 Henry IV* or of its sequel had not yet crossed the Channel. Likewise, the easy French assumption of cultural and social superiority to the English – "The emptying of our fathers' luxury, / Our scions, put in wild and savage stock" (3.5.6–7) – is voiced only to be deflated by the almost miraculous English victory. The glamour of French aristocratic culture is not denied (see, for example, the litany of noble names beginning at 3.5.40), but it issues in overweening self-confidence and a military impotence that is explicitly thematized as sexual impotence. The French warriors "hang like roping icicles / Upon our houses' thatch," while the English "Sweat drops of gallant youth in our rich fields!" (3.5.23–5). In consequence, complains the Dauphin,

> Our madams mock at us, and plainly say
> Our mettle is bred out, and they will give
> Their bodies to the lust of English youth.
>
> (3.5.28–30)

Thus the affirmation of French superiority is immediately reprocessed as an enhancement of English potency. By the play's close, with a self-conscious gesture toward the conventional ending of a comedy, the sexualized violence of the invasion is transfigured and tamed in Hal's wooing of Princess Katherine: "I love France so well that I will not part with a village of it; I will have it all mine. And, Kate, when France is mine and I am yours, then yours is France and you are mine" (5.2.173–6). Acknowledgment of the other has now issued in the complete absorption of the other.

As for the language lesson, it is no longer Hal but the French princess who is the student. There is always a slight amusement in hearing one's own language spoken badly, a gratifying sense of possessing effortlessly what for others is a painful achievement. This sense is mingled at times with a condescending encouragement of the childish efforts of the inept learner, at times with delight at the inadvertent absurdities or indecencies into which the learner stumbles. (I spent several minutes in Bergamo once convulsing passersby with requests for directions to the Colleone Chapel. It was not until much later that I realized that I was pronouncing it the "Coglioni" – "Balls" – Chapel.) In *Henry V* the pleasure is intensified because the French princess is by implication learning English as a consequence of the successful English invasion, an invasion graphically figured as a rape. And the pleasing sense of national and specifically male superiority is crowned by the comic spectacle of the obscenities into which the princess is inadvertently led.[53]

If the subversive force of "recording" is substantially reduced in *Henry V*, the mode I have called explaining is by contrast intensified in its power to disturb. The war of conquest that Henry V launches against the French is depicted as carefully founded on acts of "explaining." The play opens with a notoriously elaborate account of the king's genealogical claim to the French throne, and, as in the comparable instances in Harriot, this ideological justification of English policy is an unsettling mixture of "impeccable" reasoning (once its initial premises are accepted) and gross self-interest.[54] In the ideological apologies for absolutism, the self-interest of the monarch and the interest of the nation are identical, and both in turn are secured by God's overarching design. Hence Hal's personal triumph at Agincourt is represented as the nation's triumph, which in turn is represented as God's triumph. When the deliciously favorable kill ratio – ten thousand French dead compared to twenty-nine English[55] – is reported to the king, he immediately gives "full trophy, signal, and ostent," as the Chorus later puts it, to God: "Take it, God, / For it is none but thine!" (4.8.11–12).

Hal evidently thinks this explanation of the English victory – this translation of its cause and significance from human to divine agency – needs some reinforcement:

> And be it death proclaimed through our host
> To boast of this, or take that praise from God
> Which is his only.
>
> (4.8.114–16)

By such an edict God's responsibility for the slaughter of the French is enforced, and with it is assured at least the glow of divine approval over the entire enterprise, from the complex genealogical claims to the execution of traitors, the invasion of France, the threats leveled against civilians, the massacre of the prisoners. Yet there is something disconcerting as well as reinforcing about this draconian mode of ensuring that God receive credit: with a strategic circularity at once compelling and suspect, God's credit for the killing can be guaranteed only by the threat of more killing. The element of compulsion would no doubt predominate if the audience's own survival were at stake – the few Elizabethans who openly challenged the theological pretensions of the great found themselves in deep trouble – but were the stakes this high in the theater? Was it not possible inside the playhouse walls to question certain claims elsewhere unquestionable?

A few years earlier, at the close of *The Jew of Malta*, Marlowe had cast a witheringly ironic glance, worthy of Machiavelli, at the piety of the triumphant: Ferneze's gift to God of the "trophy, signal, and ostent" of the successful betrayal of Barabas is the final bitter joke of a bitter play. Shakespeare does not go so far. But he does take pains to call attention to the problem of invoking a God of battles, let alone enforcing the invocation by means of the death penalty. On the eve of Agincourt, the soldier Williams had responded unenthusiastically to the disguised king's claim that his cause was good:

> But if the cause be not good, the King himself hath a heavy reckoning to make, when all those legs, and arms, and heads, chopp'd off in a battle, shall join together at the latter day and cry all, "We died at such a place" – some swearing, some crying for a surgeon, some upon their wives left poor behind them, some upon the debts they owe, some upon their children rawly left. I am afeard there are few die well that die in a battle; for how can they charitably dispose of any thing, when blood is their argument? (4.1.134–43)

To this the king replies with a string of awkward "explanations" designed to show that "the King is not bound to answer the particular endings of his soldiers" (4.1.155–6) – as if death in battle were a completely unforeseen accident or, alternatively, as if each soldier killed were being punished by God for a hidden crime or, again, as if war were a religious blessing, an "advantage" to a soldier able to "wash every mote out of his conscience" (4.1.179–80). Not only are these explanations mutually contradictory, but they cast long shadows on the king himself. For in the wake of this scene, as the dawn is breaking, Hal pleads nervously with God not to think – at least "not to-day" – upon the crime from which he has benefited: his father's deposition and killing of Richard II. The king calls attention to all the expensive and ingratiating ritual acts that he has instituted to compensate for the murder of the divinely anointed ruler – reinterment of the corpse, five hundred poor "in yearly pay" to plead twice daily for pardon, two chantries where priests say mass for Richard's soul – and he promises to do more. Yet in a moment that anticipates Claudius's inadequate repentance of old Hamlet's murder, inadequate since he is "still possess'd/Of those effects" for which the crime was committed (*Hamlet* 3.3.53–4), Hal acknowledges that these expiatory rituals and even "contrite tears" are worthless:

> Though all that I can do is nothing worth,
> Since that my penitence comes after all,
> Imploring pardon.
>
> (4.1.303–5)[56]

If by nightfall Hal is threatening to execute anyone who denies God full credit for the astonishing English victory, the preceding scenes would seem to have fully exposed the ideological and psychological mechanisms behind such compulsion, its roots in violence, magical propitiation and bad conscience. The pattern disclosed here is one we have glimpsed in *2 Henry IV*: we witness an anticipatory subversion of each of the play's central claims. The archbishop of Canterbury spins out an endless public justification for an invasion he has privately confessed would relieve financial pressure on the church; Hal repeatedly warns his victims that they are bringing pillage and rape upon themselves, but he speaks as the head of the invading army that is about to pillage and rape them; Gower claims that the king has ordered the killing of the prisoners in retaliation for the attack on the baggage train, but we have just been shown that the king's order preceded that attack.[57] Similarly, Hal's meditation on the sufferings of the great – "What infinite heart's ease / Must kings neglect, that private men enjoy!" (4.1.236–7) – suffers from his being almost single-handedly responsible for a war that by his own earlier account and that of the enemy is causing immense civilian misery. And after watching a scene in which anxious, frightened troops sleeplessly await the dawn, it is difficult to be fully persuaded by Hal's climactic vision of the "slave" and "peasant" sleeping comfortably, little knowing "What watch the King keeps to maintain the peace" (4.1.283).

This apparent subversion of the monarch's glorification has led some critics since Hazlitt to view the panegyric as bitterly ironic or to argue, more plausibly, that Shakespeare's depiction of Henry V is radically ambiguous.[58] But in the light of Harriot's *Brief and True Report*, we may suggest that the subversive doubts the play continually awakens originate paradoxically in an effort to intensify the power of the king and his war. The effect is bound up with the reversal that we have noted several times – the great events and speeches all occur twice: the first time as fraud, the second as truth. The intimations of bad faith are real enough, but they are deferred – deferred until after Essex's campaign in Ireland, after Elizabeth's reign, after the monarchy itself as a significant political institution. Deferred indeed even today, for in the wake of full-scale ironic readings and at a time when it no longer seems to matter very much, it is not at all clear that *Henry V* can be successfully performed as subversive.

The problem with any attempt to do so is that the play's central figure seems to feed on the doubts he provokes. For the enhancement of royal power is not only a matter of the deferral of doubt: the very doubts that Shakespeare raises serve not to rob the king of his charisma but to heighten it, precisely as they heighten the theatrical interest of the play; the unequivocal, unambiguous celebrations of royal power with which the period abounds have no theatrical force and have long since fallen into oblivion. The charismatic authority of the king, like that of the stage, depends upon falsification.

The audience's tension, then, enhances its attention; prodded by constant reminders of a gap between real and ideal, the spectators are induced to make up the difference, to invest in the illusion of magnificence, to be dazzled by their own imaginary identification with the conqueror. The ideal king must be in large part the invention of the audience, the product of a will to conquer that is revealed to be identical to a need to submit. *Henry V* is remarkably self-conscious about this dependence upon the audience's powers of invention. The prologue's opening lines invoke a form of theater radically unlike the one that is about to unfold: "A kingdom for a stage, princes to act, / And monarchs to behold the swelling scene!" (3–4). In such a theater-state there would be no social distinction between the king and the spectator, the performer and the audience; all would be royal, and the role of the performance would be to transform not an actor into a king but a king into a god: "Then should the warlike Harry, like himself, / Assume the port of Mars" (5–6). This is in effect the fantasy acted out in royal masques, but Shakespeare is intensely aware that his play is not a courtly entertainment, that his actors are "flat unraised spirits," and that his spectators are hardly monarchs – "gentles all," he calls them, with fine flattery.[59] "Let us," the prologue begs the audience, "On your imaginary forces work. . . . For 'tis your thoughts that now must deck our kings" (17–18, 28). This "must" is cast in the form of an appeal and an apology – the consequence of the miserable limitations of "this unworthy scaffold" – but the necessity extends, I suggest, beyond the stage: all kings are "decked" out by the imaginary forces of the spectators, and a sense of the limitations of king or theater only excites a more compelling exercise of those forces.

Power belongs to whoever can command and profit from this exercise of the imagination, hence the celebration of the charismatic ruler whose imperfections we are invited at once to register and to "piece out" (Prologue, 23). Hence too the underlying complicity throughout these plays between the prince and the playwright, a complicity complicated but never effaced by a strong counter-current of identification with Falstaff. In Hal, Shakespeare fashions a compelling emblem of the playwright as sovereign "juggler," the minter of counterfeit coins, the genial master of illusory subversion and redemptive betrayal. To understand Shakespeare's conception of Hal, from rakehell to monarch, we need in effect a poetics of Elizabethan power, and this in turn will prove inseparable, in crucial respects, from a poetics of the theater. Testing, recording, and explaining are elements in this poetics, which is inseparably bound up with the figure of Queen Elizabeth, a ruler without a standing army, without a highly developed bureaucracy, without an extensive police force, a ruler whose power is constituted in theatrical celebrations of royal glory and theatrical violence visited upon the enemies of that glory. Power that relies on a massive police apparatus, a strong middle-class nuclear family, an elaborate school system, power that dreams of a panopticon in which the most intimate secrets are open to the view of an invisible authority – such power will have as its appropriate aesthetic form the realist novel;[60] Elizabethan power, by contrast, depends upon its privileged visibility. As in a theater, the audience must be powerfully engaged by this visible presence and at the same time held at a respectful distance from it. "We princes," Elizabeth told a deputation of Lords and Commons in 1586, "are set on stages in the sight and view of all the world."[61]

Royal power is manifested to its subjects as in a theater, and the subjects are at once absorbed by the instructive, delightful, or terrible spectacles and forbidden intervention or deep intimacy. The play of authority depends upon spectators – "For 'tis your thoughts that now must deck our kings" – but the performance is made to seem entirely beyond the control of those whose "imaginary forces" actually confer upon it its significance and force. These matters, Thomas More imagines the common people saying of one such spectacle, "be king's games, as it were stage plays, and for the more part played upon scaffolds. In which poor men be but the lookers-on. And they that wise be will meddle no farther."[62] Within this theatrical setting, there is a notable insistence upon the paradoxes, ambiguities, and tensions of authority, but this apparent production of subversion is, as we have already seen, the very condition of power. I should add that this condition is not a theoretical necessity of theatrical power in general but a historical phenomenon, the particular mode of this particular culture. "In sixteenth century England," writes Clifford Geertz, comparing Elizabethan and Majapahit royal progresses, "the political center of society was the point at which the tension between the passions that power excited and the ideals it was supposed to serve was screwed to its highest pitch. . . . In fourteenth century Java, the center was the point at which such tension disappeared in a blaze of cosmic symmetry."[63]

It is precisely because of the English form of absolutist theatricality that Shakespeare's drama, written for a theater subject to state censorship, can be so relentlessly subversive: the form itself, as a primary expression of Renaissance power, helps to contain the radical doubts it continually provokes. Of course, what is for the state a mode of subversion contained can be for the theater a mode of containment subverted: there are moments in Shakespeare's career – King Lear is the greatest example[64] – when the process of containment is strained to the breaking point. But the histories consistently pull back from such extreme pressure. Like Harriot in the New World, the Henry plays confirm the Machiavellian hypothesis that princely power originates in force and fraud even as they draw their audience toward an acceptance of that power. And we are free to locate and pay homage to the plays' doubts only because they no longer threaten us.[65] There is subversion, no end of subversion, only not for us.

NOTES

1 John Bakeless, *The Tragicall History of Christopher Marlowe*, 2 vols. (Cambridge, Mass.: Harvard University Press, 1942), 1:111. *Juggler* is a richly complex word, including in its range of associations con man, cheap entertainer, magician, trickster, storyteller, conjurer, actor, and dramatist.
2 On Harriot, see especially *Thomas Harriot, Renaissance Scientist*, ed. John W. Shirley (Oxford: Clarendon Press, 1974); Muriel Rukeyser, *The Traces of Thomas Harriot* (New York: Random House, 1970); and Jean Jacquot, "Thomas Harriot's Reputation for Impiety," *Notes and Records of the Royal Society* 9 (1952): 164–87. Harriot himself appears to have paid close attention to his reputation; see David B. Quinn and John W. Shirley, "A Contemporary List of Hariot References," *Renaissance Quarterly* 22 (1969): 9–26.
3 John Aubrey, *Brief Lives*, 2 vols., ed. Andrew Clark (Oxford: Clarendon Press, 1898), 1:286.
4 For the investigation of Ralegh, see *Willobie His Avisa* (1594), ed. G. B. Harrison (London: John Lane, 1926), app. 3, pp. 255–71; for Oliver's story, see Ernest A. Strathmann, *Sir Walter Ralegh: A Study in Elizabethan Skepticism* (New York: Columbia University Press, 1951), p. 50.

5 There are, to be sure, some evangelical professions of having been *saved* from atheism. On treason see Lacey Baldwin Smith, "English Treason Trials and Confessions in the Sixteenth Century," *Journal of the History of Ideas* 15 (1954): 471–98.

6 See, for example, the story William Strachey borrows from Henri Estienne's commentary on Herodotus: "Pope Leo the 10. answered Cardinall Bembo that alleadged some parte of the Ghospell vnto him: 'Lord Cardinall, what a wealth this fable of Iesus Christ hath gotten vs?'" (William Strachey, *The Historie of Travell into Virginia Britania* [1612], ed. Louis B. Wright and Virginia Freund, Hakluyt Society 2d ser., no. 103 [London, 1953], p. 101).

7 Jacquot, "Thomas Harriot's Reputation for Impiety," p. 167. In another official record, Popham is reported to have said ominously, "You know what men say of *Hereiat*" (John W. Shirley, "Sir Walter Ralegh and Thomas Harriot," in *Thomas Harriot, Renaissance Scientist*, p. 27). The logic (if that is the word for it) would seem to be this: since God clearly supports the established order of things and punishes offenders with eternal torments, a criminal must be someone who has been foolishly persuaded that God does not exist. The alternative theory posits wickedness, a corruption of the will so severe as to lead people against their own better knowledge into the ways of crime. The two arguments are often conflated, since atheism is the heart of the greatest wickedness, as well as the greatest folly.

8 Northrop Frye, *On Shakespeare* (New Haven: Yale University Press, 1986), p. 10 (see also p. 60: "Shakespeare's social vision is a deeply conservative one"); Franco Moretti, "'A Huge Eclipse': Tragic Form and the Deconsecration of Sovereignty," in *The Power of Forms in the English Renaissance*, ed. Stephen Greenblatt (Norman, Okla.: Pilgrim Books, 1982), p. 31. On the histories as occasioning an interrogation of ideology, see Jonathan Dollimore and Alan Sinfield, "History and Ideology: The Instance of *Henry V*," in John Drakakis, *Alternative Shakespeares* (London: Methuen, 1985), pp. 205–27.

9 Here is how Richard Baines construes Marlowe's version of this argument: "He affirmeth . . . That the first beginning of Religioun was only to keep men in awe. That it was an easy matter for Moyses being brought vp in all the artes of the Egiptians to abuse the Jewes being a rude & grosse people" (C. F. Tucker Brooke, *The Life of Marlowe* (London: Methuen, 1930), app. 9, p. 98). For other versions, see Strathmann, *Sir Walter Ralegh*, pp. 70–2, 87.

10 "To come to those who have become princes through their own merits and not by fortune, I regard as the greatest, Moses, Cyrus, Romulus, Theseus, and their like. And although one should not speak of Moses, he having merely carried out what was ordered him by God, still he deserves admiration, if only for that grace which made him worthy to speak with God. But regarding Cyrus and others who have acquired or founded kingdoms, they will all be found worthy of admiration; and if their particular actions and methods are examined they will not appear very different from those of Moses, although he had so great a Master [che ebbe si gran precettore]" (Niccolò Machiavelli, *The Prince*, trans. Luigi Ricci, revised E. R. P. Vincent (New York: Random House, 1950), p. 20). Christian Detmold translated the *Discourses*, in the same volume.

The delicate ironies here are intensified in the remarks on ecclesiastical principalities:

> They are acquired either by ability or by fortune; but are maintained without either, for they are sustained by ancient religious customs, which are so powerful and of such quality, that they keep their princes in power in whatever manner they proceed and live. These

princes alone have states without defending them, have subjects without governing them, and their states, not being defended are not taken from them; their subjects not being governed do not resent it, and neither think nor are capable of alienating themselves from them. Only those principalities, therefore, are secure and happy. But as they are upheld by higher causes, which the human mind cannot attain to, I will abstain from speaking of them; for being exalted and maintained by God, it would be the work of a presumptuous and foolish man to discuss them. (*The Prince*, pp. 41–2)

The sly wit of this passage depends not only on the subtle mockery but also on the possibility that the "ancient religious customs" are in fact politically efficacious.

11 Kyd, in Brooke, *Life of Marlowe*, app. 12, p. 107; Parsons, in Strathmann, *Sir Walter Ralegh*, p. 25.

12 Quoted in Jean Jacquot, "Ralegh's 'Hellish Verses' and the 'Tragicall Raigne of Selimus,'" *Modern Language Review* 48 (1953): 1.

13 This is the suggestion of Pierre Lefranc, *Sir Walter Ralegh, Ecrivain* (Quebec: Armand Colin, 1968), pp. 673–4; Lefranc gives a slightly different version of the verses (app. N, p. 673).

For a popular instance of Ralegh's reputation as a freethinker, see the poem circulated against him, with the refrain "Damnable friend of hell, / Mischievous Matchivell" (in Lefranc, p. 667). I should add that Ralegh was famous for a theatrical manner, so that it may have seemed all the more plausible to attach to his name verses from a play.

14 Thomas Harriot, *A briefe and true report of the new found land of Virginia: of the commodities there found and to be raysed, as well marchantable, as others for victuall, building and other necessarie uses for those that are and shal be the planters there; and of the nature and manners of the naturall inhabitants* (London, 1588), in *The Roanoke Voyages, 1584–1590*, 2 vols., ed. David Beers Quinn, Hakluyt Society 2d ser. no. 104 (London, 1955), p. 375.

The illustrated edition of this account includes John White drawings of these priests and of the ceremonies over which they presided, along with a striking drawing of a dancing figure called "the conjurer." "They have commonly conjurers or jugglers," Harriot's annotation explains, "which use strange gestures, and often contrary to nature in their enchantments: For they be very familiar with devils, of whom they enquire what their enemies do, or other such things.... The Inhabitants give great credit unto their speech, which oftentimes they find to be true" (Thomas Harriot, *A Briefe and True Report*, facsimile of the 1590 Theodor De Bry edition (New York: Dover, 1972), p. 54). I will refer to this edition in my text as De Bry.

In the next generation, William Strachey would urge that when the colonists have the power, they should "performe the same acceptable service to god, that Iehu king of Israell did when he assembled all the priests of Baal, and slue them to the last man in their owne Temple" (*Historie of Travell*, p. 94).

The best introduction to the current scholarship on the Algonquians of southern New England is Bruce G. Trigger, ed., *Handbook of North American Indians*, vol. 15, *Northeast* (Washington, DC: Smithsonian, 1978).

15 Harriot goes on to note that the disciplinary force of religious fear is supplemented by secular punishment: "although notwithstanding there is punishment ordained for malefactours, as stealers, whoremoonger, and other sortes of wicked doers; some punished with death, some with forfeitures, some with beating, according to the greatnes of the factes" (De Bry, p. 26).

16   See Karen Ordahl Kupperman, *Settling with the Indians: The Meeting of English and Indian Cultures in America, 1580–1640* (Totowa, NJ: Rowman and Littlefield, 1975).

17   I should add that it quickly became a rhetorical trope to describe the mass of Europeans as little better than or indistinguishable from American savages.

18   *Discourses*, p. 148. The context of this observation is the continuing discussion of Numa's wisdom in feigning divine authority: "It is true that those were very religious times, and the people with whom Numa had to deal were very untutored and superstitious, which made it easy for him to carry out his designs, being able to impress upon them any new form. . . . I conclude that the religion introduced by Numa into Rome was one of the chief causes of the prosperity of that city" (pp. 147–8).

19   When in 1590 the Flemish publisher Theodor De Bry reprinted Harriot's *Briefe and True Report*, he made this belief explicit: along with engravings of John White's brilliant Virginia drawings, De Bry's edition includes five engravings of the ancient Picts, "to showe how that the Inhabitants of the great Bretannie haue bin in times past as sauuage as those of Virginia" (De Bry, p. 75).

20   In his notes to the John White engravings, Harriot also records his hopes for a widespread Algonquian conversion to Christianity:

> Thes poore soules haue none other knowledge of god although I thinke them verye Desirous to know the truthe. For when as wee kneeled downe on our knees to make our prayers vnto god, they went abowt to imitate vs, and when they saw we moued our lipps, they also dyd the like. Wherfore that is verye like that they might easelye be brought to the knowledge of the gospel. God of his mercie grant them this grace. (De Bry, p. 71)

21   In Richard Hakluyt, *The Principal Navigations, Voyages, Traffiques, and Discoveries of the English Nation*, 12 vols. (Glasgow: James Maclehose and Sons, 1903–5), 10:54.

22   The situation is parodied in Shakespeare's *Tempest* when the drunken Caliban, rebelling against Prospero, sings:

> No more dams I'll make for fish,
>   Nor fetch in firing
>   At requiring,
> Nor scrape trenchering, nor wash dish.
>   (2.2.180–3)

23   For an alternative explanation of the principal sources of the Europeans' apparent apathy, see Karen Ordahl Kupperman, "Apathy and Death in Early Jamestown," *Journal of American History 66* (1979): 24–40. Kupperman argues that there are significant parallels between the deaths of early colonists and the deaths of American prisoners in Korean prison camps.

24   On these catalogs, see Wayne Franklin, *Discoverers, Explorers, Settlers: The Diligent Writers of Early America* (Chicago: University of Chicago Press, 1979), pp. 69–122.

25   Quoted in Edward Rosen, "Harriot's Science: The Intellectual Background," in Shirley, *Thomas Harriot, Renaissance Scientist*, p. 4.

26   Donald Friedman, private correspondence. Friedman continues: "A point that follows is that Harriot's awareness of 'subversion' might, by this token, be cast in the mode of 'what else can you expect of heathen?' "

27   Francis Bacon, *The New Organon*, bk. 1, aphorism 129, in *Francis Bacon: A Selection of His Works*, ed. Sidney Warhaft (New York: Odyssey, 1965), p. 373. I am indebted for this reference to James Carson.

28   For a further instance of the term *juggler* used of English technology in the New World, see William Wood, *New Englands Prospect* (London, 1634), p. 78; quoted in Karen Ordahl Kupperman, "English Perceptions of Treachery, 1583–1640: The Case of the American 'Savages,'" *Historical Journal* 20 (1977): 263–87.

29   In Spenser, this primitive propensity toward idolatrous worship plays into the wicked hands of the Catholic Church, and there may be some echoes of this preoccupation in Harriot's text where it would provide further insulation against awareness of a radical self-indictment. The fetishism of religious objects, the confusion of the spiritual and the material, is a frequent Protestant accusation against Catholicism, as is the charge that subtle priests cynically foster idolatry to control the people. In his notes to the White illustrations, Harriot remarks that the Algonquians sometimes have two or three "idols in their churches . . . which they place in a dark corner where they show terrible"; he notes that the priest who guards the bones of the dead chieftains "mumbleth his prayers night and day"; and he describes the posts around which the Indians dance as "carved with heads like to the faces of Nuns covered with their veils" (De Bry, pp. 71–2). This is the familiar language of Protestant polemics, and it may imply that the English will be saving the Algonquians not only from their own false worship but from the oddly cognate false worship spread by the Catholic Spanish and French. But it should be noted that Harriot does not push the resemblance between Indian and Catholic priests very hard.

30   John Calvin, *Institutes of the Christian Religion*, 2 vols., ed. John T. McNeill, trans. Ford Lewis Battles, Library of Christian Classics, vols. 20–1 (Philadelphia: Westminster Press, 1960), 1:1.3.2, pp. 44–5. I am indebted for this and the following reference to John Coolidge.

31   Richard Hooker, *Works*, 3 vols., ed. John Keble (Oxford: Oxford University Press, 1836), 2:5.1.3, p. 21.

32   J. G. A. Pocock, *The Machiavellian Moment: Florentine Political Thought and the Atlantic Republican Tradition* (Princeton: Princeton University Press, 1975).

33   Cf. Walter Bigges's narrative of Drake's visit to Florida in 1586: "The wilde people at first comminge of our men died verie fast and saide amongst themselues, It was the Inglisshe God that made them die so faste" (in Quinn, *The Roanoke Voyages* 1:306).

34   The search for atheists offers a parallel: atheism is the cause of treason, and the occurrence of treason is itself evidence for the existence of atheism.

35   We should note, however, that the conception of "invisible bullets" implies intention and hence morality.

36   Guido Calabresi and Philip Bobbitt, *Tragic Choices* (New York: W. W. Norton, 1978), p. 195. The term *tragic* is misleading, I think, since the same strategies may be perceived in situations that do not invoke the generic expectations or constraints of tragedy.

37   John Upton, *Critical Observations on Shakespeare* (1748), in *Shakespeare: The Critical Heritage*, ed. Brian Vickers, vol. 3, *1733–1752* (London: Routledge and Kegan Paul, 1975), p. 297; Maynard Mack, introduction to the Signet Classic edition of *1 Henry IV* (New York: New American Library, 1965), p. xxxv.

38   Who is the "we" in these sentences? I refer both to the stage tradition of the play and to the critical tradition. This does not mean that the play cannot be staged as a bitter assault upon Hal, but such a staging will struggle against the current that has held sway since the play's inception and indeed since the formation of the whole ideological myth of Prince Hal.

39   In the battle of Shrewsbury, when Falstaff is pretending he is dead, Hal, seeing the
      body of his friend, thinks with an eerie symbolic appropriateness of having the
      corpse literally emptied. As Hal exits, Falstaff rises up and protests. If Falstaff is an
      enormous mountain of flesh, Hal is the quintessential thin man: "you starveling,"
      Falstaff calls him (2.4.244). From Hal's point of view, Falstaff's fat prevents him
      from having any value at all: "there's no room for faith, truth, nor honesty in this
      bosom of thine; it is all fill'd up with guts and midriff" (3.3.153–5).
      Here and throughout the discussion of *1 Henry IV*, I am indebted to Edward Snow.

40   William Empson, *Some Versions of Pastoral* (London: Chatto and Windus, 1968),
      p. 103.

41   See S. P. Zitner, "Anon, Anon; or, a Mirror for a Magistrate," *Shakespeare Quarterly*
      19 (1968): 63–70.

42   More accurately, the ratios are redistributed. For example, *Henry V* insists that the
      world represented in the play is extraordinarily spacious, varied, and mobile, while
      the stage itself is cramped and confining:

> Can this cockpit hold
> The vasty fields of France? Or may we cram
> Within this wooden O the very casques
> That did affright the air at Agincourt?
> (Prologue, 11–14)

The Chorus calls attention to this contradiction to exhort the audience to
transcend it "In the quick forge and working-house of thought" (5.0.23). We have
to do not with a balance of forces but with an imbalance that must be rectified by
the labor of the imagination:

> Piece out our imperfections with your thoughts;
> Into a thousand parts divide one man,
> And make imaginary puissance.
> (Prologue, 23–5)

43   What we took to be the "center" may be part of the remotest periphery. More
      unsettling still, topographic accounts of both theater and power may be illusions:
      there may be no way to locate oneself securely in relation to either.

44   See, for example, Victor Turner, *Drama, Fields, and Metaphors: Symbolic Action in
      Human Society* (Ithaca: Cornell University Press, 1974).

45   The evidence is amply documented by Karen Kupperman, *Settling with the Indians.*

46   Thomas Harman, *A Caueat or Warening, for Commen Cursetors Vulgarely Called
      Vagabones* (1566), in *Cony-Catchers and Bawdy Baskets*, ed. Gamini Salgado
      (Middlesex: Penguin, 1972), p. 146.

47   On the problems of Elizabethan representations of the underworld, see A. L. Beier,
      Masterless Men: The Vagrancy Problem in England, 1560–1640 (London: Methuen,
      1985).

48   [Gilbert Walker?] *A manifest detection of the moste vyle and detestable use of Diceplay*
      (c. 1552), in Salgado, *Cony-Catchers and Bawdy Baskets*, pp. 42–3.

49   Norman N. Holland, in the Signet Classic edition of *2 Henry IV* (New York: New
      American Library, 1965), p. xxxvi.

50   See Frank Whigham, *Ambition and Privilege: The Social Tropes of Elizabethan Courtesy
      Theory* (Berkeley: University of California Press, 1984).

51 The public response to betrayal is extremely difficult to measure. Lawrence Stone suggests that there is a transition in the early years of the seventeenth century: "Up to the end of the sixteenth century men saw nothing dishonorable in attacking by surprise with superior forces, and nothing in hitting a man when he was down. By the second decade of the seventeenth century, however, such behaviour was becoming discreditable and is much less frequently met with" (Lawrence Stone, *The Crisis of the Aristocracy, 1558–1641*, abridged edition (New York: Oxford University Press, 1967), p. 109).

52 The presence of the Irishman among the English forces is especially significant since as the Chorus points out, an English expeditionary army was attempting at the moment of the play to subjugate the Irish. It is not the least of the play's bitter historical ironies that in four hundred years this attempt has not become an anachronism.

53 It would not have escaped at least some members of an Elizabethan audience that an English gentleman or woman would have been far more likely to learn French than a Frenchman English. The language lesson, Steven Mullaney suggests, is Shakespeare's "rearward glance at the improprieties that occupied the ambivalent center of Hal's prodigality." Whereas in the first and second parts of *Henry IV*, the recording of the language of the other has an element of tragedy, its equivalent in *Henry V* has only the spirit of French farce (Steven Mullaney, "Strange Things, Gross Terms, Curious Customs: The Rehearsal of Cultures in the Late Renaissance," *Representations* 3 (1983): 63–4).

54 "This does not sound like hypocrisy or cynicism. The Archbishop discharges his duty faithfully, as it stands his reasoning is impeccable.... Henry is not initiating aggression" (J. H. Walter, in the Arden edition of *King Henry V* (London: Methuen, 1954), p. xxv).

55 The kill ratio is highly in the English favor in all accounts, but Shakespeare adopts from Holinshed the most extreme figure. Holinshed himself adds that "other writers of greater credit affirm that there were slain above five or six hundred" Englishmen (Holinshed, in the Oxford Shakespeare edition of *Henry V*, ed. Gary Taylor (Oxford: Oxford University Press, 1984), p. 308). Similarly, Shakespeare makes no mention of the tactical means by which the English army achieved its victory. The victory is presented as virtually miraculous.

56 In a long appendix to his edition of *Henry V*, Gary Taylor attempts to defend his emendation of "all" to "ill" in these lines, on the grounds that an interpretation along the lines of Claudius's failed repentance would be difficult for an actor to communicate and, if communicated, would make "the victory of Agincourt morally and dramatically incomprehensible" (Taylor, p. 298). The interpretive framework that I am sketching in this chapter should make the Folio's reading fully comprehensible; the effect of the victory is, by my account, intensified by the play's moral problems.

57 Taylor makes a subtle and, I think, implausible attempt to reduce the unintended irony of Gower's line, "wherefore the King, most worthily, hath caus'd every soldier to cut his prisoner's throat" (4.7.8–10): "Gower is not saying (as all editors and critics seem to have understood him) 'the king *caused* the prisoners to be executed because of the attack on the baggage train' but 'given the barbarity of the subsequent French conduct, the king *has* quite justifiably *caused* the death of his prisoners' " (Taylor, p. 243). Even were we to understand the line in Taylor's sense, it would open a moral problem still worse than the political problem that has been resolved.

58 See the illuminating discussion in Norman Rabkin, *Shakespeare and the Problem of Meaning* (Chicago: University of Chicago Press, 1981), pp. 33–62.

59 This is flattery carefully echoed in Hal's promise to his troops on the eve of Agincourt that "be he ne'er so vile,/This day shall gentle his condition" (4.3.62–3). The promise is silently forgotten after the battle.

60 For a brilliant exploration of this hypothesis, see D. A. Miller, "The Novel and the Police," in *Glyph* 8 (1981): 127–47.

61 Quoted in J. E. Neale, *Elizabeth I and Her Parliaments, 1584–1601*, 2 vols. (London: Cape, 1965), 2:119. For the complex relation between theater and absolutism, see Stephen Orgel, *The Illusion of Power: Political Theater in the English Renaissance* (Berkeley: University of California Press, 1975); Jonathan Goldberg, *James I and the Politics of Literature: Jonson, Shakespeare, Donne, and Their Contemporaries* (Baltimore: Johns Hopkins University Press, 1983); Jonathan Dollimore, *Radical Tragedy: Religion, Ideology, and Power in the Drama of Shakespeare and His Contemporaries* (Brighton: Harvester, 1983); Greenblatt, *The Power of Forms in the English Renaissance*; Steven Mullaney, "Lying like Truth: Riddle, Representation, and Treason in Renaissance England," *ELH* 47 (1980): 32–47; Paola Colaiacomo, "Il teatro del principe," *Calibano* 4 (1979): 53–98; Christopher Pye, "The Sovereign, the Theater, and the Kingdome of Darknesse: Hobbes and the Spectacle of Power," *Representations* 8 (1984):85–106.

62 *The History of King Richard III*, ed. R. S. Sylvester, in *The Complete Works of St. Thomas More*, vol. 3 (New Haven: Yale University Press, 1963), p. 80.

63 Clifford Geertz, "Centers, Kings, and Charisma: Reflections on the Symbolics of Power," in *Culture and Its Creators: Essays in Honor of Edward Shils*, ed. Joseph Ben David and Terry Nichols Clark (Chicago: University of Chicago Press, 1977), p. 160.

64 The nameless servant in *Lear* who can no longer endure what he is witnessing and who heroically stabs his master Cornwall, the legitimate ruler of half of England, inhabits a different political world from the one sketched here, a world marked out by Shakespeare as tragic.

65 Perhaps we should imagine Shakespeare writing at a moment when none of the alternatives for a resounding political commitment seemed satisfactory; when the pressure to declare himself unequivocally an adherent of one or another faction seemed narrow, ethically coarse, politically stupid; when the most attractive political solution seemed to be to keep options open and the situation fluid.

7

THE IMPROVISATION OF POWER

Spenser and Marlowe are, from the perspective of this study, mighty opposites, poised in antagonism as radical as that of More and Tyndale in the 1530s. If Spenser sees human identity as conferred by loving service to legitimate authority, to the yoked power of God and the state, Marlowe sees identity established at those moments in which order – political, theological, sexual – is violated. If repetition for Spenser is an aspect of the patient labor of civility, for Marlowe it is the means of constituting oneself in an anonymous void. If Spenser's heroes strive for balance and control, Marlowe's strive to shatter the restraints upon their desires. If in Spenser there is fear of the excess that threatens to engulf order and seems to leave an ineradicable taint on temperance itself, in Marlowe there is fear of the order that threatens to extinguish excess and seems to have always already turned rebellion into a tribute to authority. If Spenser writes for an aristocratic and upper-middle-class audience in a self-consciously archaizing manner, thereby participating in the decorative revival of feudal trappings that characterized Elizabethan courtly ritual,[1] Marlowe writes for the new public theater in a blank verse that must have seemed, after the jog-trot fourteeners of the preceding decades, like reality itself. If Spenser holds up his "other world" to the gaze of power and says, "Behold! This rich beauty is your own face," Marlowe presents *his* and says, "Behold! This tragi-comic, magnificent deformity is how you appear in my rich art." If Spenser's art constantly questions its own status in order to protect power from such questioning, Marlowe undermines power in order to raise his art to the status of a self-regarding, self-justifying absolute.

There is not, of course, anything in Spenser or Marlowe comparable to the violent polemical exchange between More and Tyndale, but there is at least one resonant moment of conjunction that will serve to exemplify the opposition I have just sketched here. In book 1, canto 7 of *The Faerie Queene*, dismayed by the news that Redcrosse has been overthrown by the giant Orgoglio, Una providentially encounters Prince Arthur, the embodiment of Magnificence – the virtue, according to the letter to Ralegh, that "is the perfection of all the rest,

This chapter in this form was first published in *Renaissance Self-Fashioning: From More to Shakespeare* (1980, pp. 222–54).

and containeth in it them all." This is Arthur's first appearance in the poem, and
there follows an elaborate description of his gorgeous armor, a description that
includes the following stanza on his helmet's crest:

> Vpon the top of all his loftie crest,
> A bunch of haires discolourd diuersly,
> With sprincled pearle, and gold full richly drest,
> Did shake, and seem'd to daunce for iollity,
> Like to an Almond tree ymounted hye
> On top of greene *Selinis* all alone,
> With blossomes braue bedecked daintily;
> Whose tender locks do tremble euery one
> At euery little breath, that vnder heauen is blowne.
>
> (1.7.32)

As early as the late eighteenth century, a reader records his surprise to find this
passage almost verbatim in part 2 of *Tamburlaine*.[2] It occurs in the scene in which
Tamburlaine is drawn on stage in his chariot by the captive kings, "with bits in
their mouths," the stage direction tells us, "reins in his left hand, in his right hand
a whip, with which he scourgeth them." Exulting in his triumphant power,
Tamburlaine baits his captives, hands over the weeping royal concubines to
satisfy the lust of his common soldiers, and – his own erotic satisfaction –
imagines his future conquests:

> Through the streets with troops of conquered kings,
> I'll ride in golden armor like the Sun,
> And in my helm a triple plume shall spring,
> Spangled with Diamonds dancing in the air,
> To note me Emperor of the three-fold world,
> Like to an almond tree ymounted high,
> Upon the lofty and celestial mount,
> Of ever green *Selinus* quaintly decked
> With blooms more white than *Hericina's* brows,
> Whose tender blossoms tremble every one,
> At every little breath that thorough heaven is blown.
>
> (4.3.4094–113)

What is sung by Spenser in praise of Arthur is sung by Tamburlaine in praise of
himself; the chivalric accoutrement, an emblem of Arthur's magnanimous
knighthood is here part of Tamburlaine's paean to his own power lust. Lines
that for Spenser belong to the supreme figure of civility, the chief upholder of the
Order of Maidenhead, the worshipful servant of Gloriana, for Marlowe belong to
the fantasy life of the Scythian Scourge of God. Marlowe's scene is self-consciously emblematic, as if it were a theatrical improvisation in the Spenserean
manner, but now with the hero's place taken by a character who, in his sadistic
excess, most closely resembles Orgoglio.[3] And even as we are struck by the
radical difference, we are haunted by the vertiginous possibility of an underlying
sameness. What if Arthur and Tamburlaine are not separate and opposed? What if

they are two faces of the same thing, embodiments of the identical power? Tamburlaine's is the face Arthur shows to his enemies or, alternatively, Arthur's is the face Tamburlaine shows to his followers. To the Irish kern, Spenser's Prince of Magnanimity looks like the Scourge of God; to the English courtier, Marlowe's grotesque conquerer looks like the Faerie Queene.

How shall we characterize the power that possesses both faces and can pass from one to the other? In a famous passage in *The Prince*, Machiavelli writes that a prince must know well how to use both the beast and the man, and hence the ancients depicted Achilles and other heroes as educated by Chiron the centaur. This discussion is an early instance of the celebration of psychic mobility that has continued to characterize discussions of Western consciousness to the present time. Thus in his influential study of modernization in the Middle East, *The Passing of Traditional Society*, the sociologist Daniel Lerner defines the West as a "mobile society," a society characterized not only by certain enlightened and rational public practices but also by the inculcation in its people of a *"mobile sensibility* so adaptive to change that rearrangement of the self-system is its distinctive mode."[4] While traditional society, Professor Lerner argues, functions on the basis of a "highly constrictive personality" (p. 51), one that resists change and is incapable of grasping the situation of another, the mobile personality of Western society "is distinguished by a high capacity for identification with new aspects of his environment," for he "comes equipped with the mechanisms needed to incorporate new demands upon himself that arise outside of his habitual experience" (p. 49). Those mechanisms Professor Lerner subsumes under the single term *empathy*, which he defines as "the capacity to see oneself in the other fellow's situation" (p. 50). In the West, this capacity was fostered first by the physical mobility initiated by the Age of Exploration, then confirmed and broadened by the mass media. "These," he writes, "have peopled the daily world of their audience with sustained, even intimate, experience of the lives of others. 'Ma Perkins,' 'The Goldbergs,' 'I Love Lucy' – all these bring us friends we never met, but whose joys and sorrows we intensely 'share'" (p. 53). And the international diffusion of the mass media means a concomitant diffusion of psychic mobility and hence of modernization: "In our time, indeed, the spread of empathy around the world is accelerating" (p. 52).

To test the rate of this acceleration, Professor Lerner devised a set of questions that he and his assistants put to a cross-section of the inhabitants of the Middle East, to porters and cobblers, as well as grocers and physicians. The questions began, "If you were made editor of a newspaper, what kind of a paper would you run?" and I confess myself in complete sympathy with that class of respondents who, like one shepherd interviewed in a village near Ankara, gasped "My God! How can you say such a thing? . . . A poor villager . . . master of the whole world" (p. 24). Professor Lerner invariably interprets such answers as indicative of a constrictive personality incapable of empathy, but in fact the Turkish shepherd, with his Tamburlainian language, reintroduces the great missing term in the analysis of modernization, and that term is *power*. For my own part, I would like in this chapter to delineate the Renaissance origins of the "mobile sensibility" and, having done so, to shift the ground from "I Love Lucy" to *Othello* in order to demonstrate that what Professor Lerner calls "empathy," Shakespeare calls "Iago."

To help us return from the contemporary Middle East to the early seventeenth century, let us dwell for a moment on Professor Lerner's own concept of Renaissance origins: "Take the factor of physical mobility," he writes, "which initiated Western take-off in an age when the earth was underpopulated in terms of the world man-land ratio. Land was to be had, more or less, for the finding. The great explorers took over vast real estate by planting a flag; these were slowly filled with new populations over generations" (p. 65). It didn't exactly happen this way. Land does not become "real estate" quite so easily, and the under-population was not found but created by those great explorers. Demographers of Mesoamerica now estimate, for example, that the population of Hispaniola in 1492 was 7–8 million, perhaps as high as 11 million. Reduction to that attractive man-land ratio was startlingly sudden: by 1501, enslavement, disruption of agriculture, and, above all, European disease had reduced the population to some 700,000; by 1512, to 28,000.[5] The unimaginable massiveness of the death rate did not, of course, go unnoticed; European observers took it as a sign of God's determination to cast down the idolaters and open the New World to Christianity.

With the passage from the sociologist's bland world of ceremonial flag-planting in an empty landscape to violent displacement and insidious death, we have already moved toward Shakespeare's tragedy, and we move still closer if we glance at an incident recounted in 1525 by Peter Martyr in the Seventh Decade of *De orbe novo*. Faced with a serious labor shortage in the gold mines as a result of the decimation of the native population, the Spanish in Hispaniola began to raid neighboring islands. Two ships reached an outlying island in the Lucayas (now called the Bahamas) where they were received with awe and trust. The Spanish learned through their interpreters that the natives believed that after death their souls were first purged of their sins in icy northern mountains, then borne to a paradisal island in the south, whose beneficent, lame prince offered them innumerable pleasures: "the souls enjoy eternal delights, among the dancings and songs of young maidens, and among the embracements of their children, and whatsoever they loved heretofore; they babble also there, that such as grow old, wax young again, so that all are of like years full of joy and mirth."[6] When the Spanish understood these imaginations, writes Martyr, they proceeded to persuade the natives "that they came from those places, where they should see their parents, and children, and all their kindred and friends that were dead: and should enjoy all kind of delights, together with the embracements and fruition of beloved things" (p. 625). Thus deceived, the entire population of the island passed "singing and rejoicing," Martyr says, onto the ships and were taken to the gold mines of Hispaniola. The Spanish, however, reaped less profit than they had anticipated; when they grasped what had happened to them, the Lucayans, like certain German Jewish communities during the Crusades, undertook mass suicide: "becoming desperate, they either slew themselves, or choosing to famish, gave up their faint spirits, being persuaded by no reason, or violence, to take food" (p. 625).

Martyr, it appears, feels ambivalent about the story. He is certain that God disapproves of such treachery, since many of those who perpetrated the fraud subsequently died violent deaths; on the other hand, he opposes those who would free enslaved natives, since bitter experience has shown that even those Indians who have apparently been converted to Christianity will, given the slightest opportunity, revert to "their ancient and native vices" and turn savagely against those who had instructed them "with fatherly charity" (p. 627). But, for our purposes, Martyr's ambivalence is less important than the power of his story to evoke a crucial Renaissance mode of behavior that links Lerner's "empathy" and Shakespeare's Iago: I shall call that mode *improvisation*, by which I mean the ability both to capitalize on the unforeseen and to transform given materials into one's own scenario. The spur-of-the-moment quality of improvisation is not as critical here as the opportunistic grasp of that which seems fixed and established. Indeed, as Castiglione and others in the Renaissance well understood, the impromptu character of an improvisation is itself often a calculated mask, the product of careful preparation.[7] Conversely, all plots, literary and behavioral, inevitably have their origin in a moment prior to formal coherence, a moment of experimental, aleatory impulse in which the available, received materials are curved toward a novel shape. We cannot locate a point of pure premeditation or pure randomness. What is essential is the Europeans' ability again and again to insinuate themselves into the preexisting political, religious, even psychic structures of the natives and to turn those structures to their advantage. The process is as familiar to us by now as the most tawdry business fraud, so familiar that we assume a virtually universal diffusion of the necessary improvisational talent, but that assumption is almost certainly misleading. There are periods and cultures in which the ability to insert oneself into the consciousness of another is of relatively slight importance, the object of limited concern; others in which it is a major preoccupation, the object of cultivation and fear. Professor Lerner is right to insist that this ability is a characteristically (though not exclusively) Western mode, present to varying degrees in the classical and medieval world and greatly strengthened from the Renaissance onward; he misleads only in insisting further that it is an act of imaginative generosity, a sympathetic appreciation of the situation of the other fellow. For when he speaks confidently of the "spread of empathy around the world," we must understand that he is speaking of the exercise of Western power, power that is creative as well as destructive, but that is scarcely ever wholly disinterested and benign.

To return to the Lucayan story, we may ask ourselves what conditions exist in Renaissance culture that make such an improvisation possible. It depends first upon the ability and willingness to play a role, to transform oneself, if only for a brief period and with mental reservations, into another. This necessitates the acceptance of disguise, the ability to effect a divorce, in Ascham's phrase, between the tongue and the heart. Such role-playing in turn depends upon the transformation of another's reality into a manipulable fiction. The Spanish had to perceive the Indians' religious beliefs as illusions, "imaginations" as Martyr's English translator calls them. Lucayan society, Martyr observes, is based upon a principle of reverent obedience fostered by a set of religious fables that "are delivered by word of mouth and tradition from the Elders to the younger, for a most sacred and true history, insomuch as he who but seemed to think otherwise, should be thrust out of the society of men" (p. 623). The Lucayan king performs the supreme sacral functions and partakes fully in the veneration accorded to the idols, so that if he were to command one of his subjects to cast himself down from a precipice, the subject would immediately comply. The king uses this absolute power to ensure the just distribution, to families according to need, of the tribe's food, all of which is stored communally in royal granaries: "They had the golden age, *mine* and *thine*, the seeds of discord, were far removed from them" (p. 618). Martyr then perceives the social function of Lucayan religious concepts, the native apparatus for their transmission and reproduction, and the punitive apparatus for the enforcement of belief. In short, he grasps Lucayan religion as an ideology, and it is this perception that licenses the transformation of "sacred and true history" into "crafty and subtle imaginations" (p. 625) that may be exploited.

If improvisation is made possible by the subversive perception of another's truth as an ideological construct, that construct must at the same time be grasped in terms that bear a certain structural resemblance to one's own set of beliefs. An ideology that is perceived as entirely alien would permit no point of histrionic entry: it could be destroyed but not performed. Thus the Lucayan religion, in Martyr's account, is an anamorphic representation of Catholicism: there are "images" carried forth with solemn pomp on "the holy day of adoration"; worshipers kneel reverently before these images, sing "hymns," and make offerings, "which at night the nobles divide among them, as our priests do the cakes or wafers which women offer" (p. 622); there are "holy relics" about which the chief priest, standing in his "pulpit," preaches; and, as we have seen, there is absolution for sin, purgatory, and eternal delight in paradise. The European account of the native religion must have borne some likeness to what the Lucayans actually believed; why else would they have danced, singing and rejoicing, onto the Spanish ships? But it is equally important that the religion is conceived as analogous to Catholicism, close enough to permit improvisation, yet sufficiently distanced to protect European beliefs from the violence of fictionalization. The Spanish were not compelled to perceive their own religion as a manipulable human construct; on the contrary, the compulsion of their own creed was presumably strengthened by their contemptuous exploitation of an analogous symbolic structure.

This absence of reciprocity is an aspect of the total economy of the mode of improvisation that I have sketched here. For what we may see in the Lucayan story is an early manifestation of an exercise of power that was subsequently to become vastly important and remains a potent force in our lives: the ownership of another's labor conceived as involving no supposedly "natural" reciprocal obligation (as in feudalism) but rather functioning by concealing the very fact of ownership from the exploited who believe that they are acting freely and in their own interest. Of course, once the ships reached Hispaniola, this concealed ownership gave way to direct enslavement; the Spanish were not capable of continuing the improvisation into the very mines. And it is this failure to sustain the illusion that led to the ultimate failure of the enterprise, for, of course, the Spanish did not want dead Indians but live mineworkers. It would take other, subtler minds, in the Renaissance and beyond, to perfect the means to sustain indefinitely an indirect enslavement.

I have called improvisation a central Renaissance mode of behavior, but the example on which I have focused is located on a geographical margin and might only seem to bear out Immanuel Wallerstein's theory that Western Europe in the sixteenth century increasingly established its ownership of the labor and resources of those located in areas defined as peripheral.[8] But I would argue that the phenomenon I have described is found in a wide variety of forms closer to home. It may be glimpsed, to suggest two significant instances, in the relation of Tudor power to Catholic symbolism and the characteristic form of rhetorical education.

The Anglican Church and the monarch who was its Supreme Head did not, as radical Protestants demanded, eradicate Catholic ritual but rather improvised within it in an attempt to assume its power. Thus, for example, in the Accession Day celebration of 1590, we are told that the queen, sitting in the Tilt gallery,

> did suddenly hear a music so sweet and so secret, as every one thereat greatly marvelled. And hearkening to that excellent melody, the earth as it were opening, there appears a Pavilion, made of white Taffeta, being in proportion like unto the sacred Temple of the Virgins Vestal. This Temple seemed to consist upon pillars of porphyry, arched like unto a Church, within it were many lamps burning. Also, on the one side an Altar covered with cloth of gold; and thereupon two wax candles burning in rich candlesticks; upon the Altar also were laid certain Princely presents, which after by three Virgins were presented unto her Majesty.[9]

This secular epiphany permits us to identify two of the characteristic operations of improvisation: displacement and absorption. By displacement I mean the process whereby a prior symbolic structure is compelled to coexist with other centers of attention that do not necessarily conflict with the original structure but are not swept up in its gravitational pull; indeed, as here, the sacred may find itself serving as an adornment, a backdrop, an occasion for a quite secular phenomenon. By absorption I mean the process whereby a symbolic structure is taken into the ego so completely that it ceases to exist as an external phenomenon; in the Accession Day ceremony, instead of the secular prince humbling herself before the sacred, the sacred seems only to enhance the ruler's identity, to express her power.[10]

Both displacement and absorption are possible here because the religious symbolism was already charged with the celebration of power. What we are witnessing is a shift in the institution that controls and profits from the interpretation of such symbolism, a shift mediated in this instance by the classical scholarship of Renaissance humanism. The invocation of the Temple of the Vestal Virgins is the sign of that transformation of belief into ideology that we have already examined; the Roman mythology, deftly keyed to England's Virgin Queen, helps to fictionalize Catholic ritual sufficiently for it to be displaced and absorbed.

This enzymatic function of humanism leads directly to our second instance of domestic improvisation, for the cornerstone of the humanist project was a rhetorical education. In *The Tudor Play of Mind*, Joel Altman has recently demonstrated the central importance for English Renaissance culture of the *argumentum in utramque partem*, the cultivation of the scholar's power to speak equally persuasively for diametrically opposed positions. The practice permeated intellectual life in the early sixteenth century and was, Altman convincingly argues, one of the formative influences on the early drama.[11] It is in the spirit of such rhetorical mobility that Erasmus praises More, as we have seen, for his ability "to play the man of all hours with all men" and that Roper recalls the young More's dazzling improvisations in Cardinal Morton's Christmas plays.

The hagiographical bias of Roper's and most subsequent writing on More has concealed the extent to which this improvisational gift is closely allied to a control of power in the law courts and the royal service: the mystification of manipulation as disinterested empathy begins as early as the sixteenth century. As a corrective, we need only recall More's controversial works, such as *The Confutation of Tyndale's Answer*, whose recurrent method is through improvisation to transform the heretic's faith into a fiction, then absorb it into a new symbolic structure that will ridicule or consume it. Thus Tyndale had written:

> Sin we through fragility never so oft, yet as soon as we repent and come into the right way again, and unto the testament which God hath made in Christ's blood: our sins vanish away as smoke in the wind, and as darkness at the coming of light, or as thou cast a little blood or milk into the main sea.

More responds by maliciously improvising on Tyndale's text:

> Neither purgatory need to be feared when we go hence, nor penance need to be done while we be here, but sin and be sorry and sit and make merry, and then sin again and then repent a little and run to the ale and wash away the sin, think once on God's promise and then do what we list. For hoping sure in that, kill we ten men on a day, we cast but a little blood into the main sea.

Having thus made a part of his own, More continues by labeling Tyndale's argument about penance as "but a piece of his poetry" – an explicit instance of that fictionalization we have witnessed elsewhere – and concludes,

> Go me to Martin Luther. . . . While that friar lieth with his nun and woteth well he doth nought [i.e., knows he does evil], and saith still he doth well: let Tyndale tell me what repenting is that. He repenteth every morning, and to bed again every night; thinketh on God's promise first, and then go sin again upon trust of God's testament, and then he calleth it casting of a little milk into the main sea.[12]

Improvisation here obviously does not intend to deceive its original object but to work upon a third party, the reader, who might be wavering between the reformers and the Catholic Church. If the heretic speaks of sin redeemed by God's testament as milk, More returns that milk to sin, then surpasses the simple reversal by transforming it to semen, while he turns the sea that imaged for Tyndale the boundlessness of divine forgiveness into the sexual insatiability of Luther's nun.

These perversions of the reformer's text are greatly facilitated by the fact that the text was already immersed in an intensely charged set of metaphorical transformations – that is, More seizes upon the brilliant instability of Tyndale's prose with its own nervous passage from Christ's blood to sin conceived progressively as smoke, darkness, blood, and finally milk. More's artful improvisation makes it seem that murder and lust lay just beneath the surface of the original discourse, as a kind of dark subtext, and he is able to do so more plausibly because both violence and sexual anxiety are in fact powerful underlying forces in Tyndale's prose as in More's. That is, once again, there is a haunting structural homology between the improviser and his other.

I would hope that by now *Othello* seems virtually to force itself upon us as the supreme symbolic expression of the cultural mode I have been describing, for violence, sexual anxiety, and improvisation are the materials out of which the drama is constructed. To be sure, there are many other explorations of these materials in Shakespeare – one thinks of Richard III wooing Anne[13] or, in comedy, of Rosalind playfully taking advantage of the disguise that exile has forced upon her – but none so intense and radical. In Iago's first soliloquy, Shakespeare goes out of his way to emphasize the improvised nature of the villain's plot:

> Cassio's a proper man, let me see now,
> To get this place, and to make up my will,
> A double knavery . . . how, how? . . . let me see,
> After some time, to abuse Othello's ear,
> That he is too familiar with his wife:
> He has a person and a smooth dispose,
> To be suspected, fram'd to make women false:
> The Moor a free and open nature too,
> That thinks men honest that but seems to be so:
> And will as tenderly be led by the nose . . .
> As asses are.
> I ha't, it is engender'd; Hell and night
> Must bring this monstrous birth to the world's light.
> (1.3.390–402)[14]

We will try shortly to cast some light on why Iago conceives of his activity here as sexual; for the moment, we need only to observe all of the marks of the impromptu and provisional, extending to the ambiguity of the third-person pronoun: "to abuse Othello's ear / That he is too familiar with his wife." This ambiguity is felicitous; indeed, though scarcely visible at this point, it is the dark essence of Iago's whole enterprise which is, as we shall see, to play upon Othello's buried perception of his own sexual relations with Desdemona as adulterous.[15]

What I have called the marks of the impromptu extend to Iago's other speeches and actions through the course of the whole play. In act 2, he declares of his conspiracy, "'tis here, but yet confus'd; / Knavery's plain face is never seen, till us'd," and this half-willed confusion continues through the agile, hectic maneuvers of the last act until the moment of exposure and silence. To all but Roderigo, of course, Iago presents himself as incapable of improvisation, except in the limited and seemingly benign form of banter and jig.[16] And even here, he is careful, when Desdemona asks him to improvise her praise, to declare himself unfit for the task:

> I am about it, but indeed my invention
> Comes from my pate as birdlime does from frieze,
> It plucks out brain and all: but my Muse labours,
> And thus she is deliver'd.
>
> (2.1.125–8)

Lurking in the homely denial of ability is the image of his invention as birdlime, and hence a covert celebration of his power to ensnare others. Like Jonson's Mosca, Iago is fully aware of himself as an improviser and revels in his ability to manipulate his victims, to lead them by the nose like asses, to possess their labor without their ever being capable of grasping the relation in which they are enmeshed. Such is the relation Iago establishes with virtually every character in the play, from Othello and Desdemona to such minor figures as Montano and Bianca. For the Spanish colonialists, improvisation could only bring the Lucayans into open enslavement; for Iago, it is the key to a mastery whose emblem is the "duteous and knee-crooking knave" who dotes "on his own obsequious bondage" (1.1.45–6), a mastery invisible to the servant, a mastery, that is, whose character is essentially ideological. Iago's attitude toward Othello is nonetheless colonial: though he finds himself in a subordinate position, the ensign regards his black general as "an erring barbarian" whose "free and open nature" is a fertile field for exploitation. However galling it may be to him, Iago's subordination is a kind of protection, for it conceals his power and enables him to play upon the ambivalence of Othello's relation to Christian society: the Moor at once represents the institution and the alien, the conqueror and the infidel. Iago can conceal his malicious intentions toward "the thick-lips" behind the mask of dutiful service and hence prolong his improvisation as the Spaniards could not. To be sure, the play suggests, Iago must ultimately destroy the beings he exploits and hence undermine the profitable economy of his own relations, but that destruction may be long deferred, deferred in fact for precisely the length of the play.[17]

If Iago then holds over others a possession that must constantly efface the signs of its own power, how can it be established, let alone maintained? We will find a clue, I think, in what we have been calling the process of fictionalization that transforms a fixed symbolic structure into a flexible construct ripe for improvisational entry. This process is at work in Shakespeare's play, where we may more accurately identify it as *submission to narrative self-fashioning*. When in Cyprus Othello and Desdemona have been ecstatically reunited, Iago astonishes Roderigo by informing him that Desdemona is in love with Cassio. He has no evidence, of course – indeed we have earlier seen him "engender" the whole plot entirely out of his fantasy – but he proceeds to lay before his gull all of the circumstances that make this adultery plausible: "mark me, with what violence she first lov'd the Moor, but for bragging, and telling her fantastical lies; and she will love him still for prating?" (2.1.221–3). Desdemona cannot long take pleasure in her outlandish match: "When the blood is made dull with the act of sport, there should be again to inflame it, and give satiety a fresh appetite, loveliness in favor, sympathy in years, manners and beauties" (2.1.225–9). The elegant Cassio is the obvious choice: "Didst thou not see her paddle with the palm of his hand?" Iago asks. To Roderigo's objection that this was "but courtesy," Iago replies, "Lechery, by this hand: an index and prologue to the history of lust and foul thoughts" (2.1.251–5). The metaphor makes explicit what Iago has been doing all along: constructing a narrative into which he inscribes ("by this hand") those around him. He does not need a profound or even reasonably accurate understanding of his victims; he would rather deal in probable impossibilities than improbable possibilities. And it is eminently probable that a young, beautiful Venetian gentlewoman would tire of her old, outlandish husband and turn instead to the handsome, young lieutenant: it is, after all, one of the master plots of comedy.

What Iago as inventor of comic narrative needs is a sharp eye for the surfaces of social existence, a sense, as Bergson says, of the mechanical encrusted upon the living, a reductive grasp of human possibilities. These he has in extraordinarily full measure.[18] "The wine she drinks is made of grapes," he says in response to Roderigo's idealization of Desdemona, and so reduced, she can be assimilated to Iago's grasp of the usual run of humanity. Similarly, in a spirit of ironic connoisseurship, he observes Cassio's courtly gestures, "If such tricks as these strip you out of your lieutenantry, it had been better you had not kiss'd your three fingers so oft, which now again you are most apt to play the sir in: good, well kiss'd, an excellent courtesy" (2.1.171–5). He is watching a comedy of manners. Above all, Iago is sensitive to habitual and self-limiting forms of discourse, to Cassio's reaction when he has had a drink or when someone mentions Bianca, to Othello's rhetorical extremism, to Desdemona's persistence and tone when she pleads for a friend; and, of course, he is demonically sensitive to the way individuals interpret discourse, to the signals they ignore and those to which they respond.

We should add that Iago includes himself in this ceaseless narrative invention; indeed, as we have seen from the start, a successful improvisational career depends upon role-playing, which is in turn allied to the capacity, as Professor Lerner defines empathy, "to see oneself in the other fellow's situation." This capacity requires above all a sense that one is not forever fixed in a single, divinely sanctioned identity, a sense Iago expresses to Roderigo in a parodically sententious theory of self-fashioning: "our bodies are gardens, to the which our wills are gardeners, so that if we will plant nettles, or sow lettuce, set hyssop, and weed up thyme; supply it with one gender of herbs, or distract it with many; either to have it sterile with idleness, or manur'd with industry, why, the power, and corrigible authority of this, lies in our wills" (1.3.320–6). Confident in his shaping power, Iago has the role-player's ability to imagine his nonexistence so that he can

exist for a moment in another and as another. In the opening scene he gives voice
to this hypothetical self-cancellation in a line of eerie simplicity: "Were I the Moor,
I would not be Iago" (1.1.57). The simplicity is far more apparent than real. Is the
"I" in both halves of the line the same? Does it designate a hard, impacted self-
interest prior to social identity, or are there two distinct, even opposing selves?
Were I the Moor, I would not be Iago, because the "I" always loves itself and the
creature I know as Iago hates the Moor he serves or, alternatively, because as the
Moor I would be other than I am now, free of the tormenting appetite and
revulsion that characterize the servant's relation to his master and that constitute
my identity as Iago. I would be radically the same / I would be radically different;
the rapacious ego underlies all institutional structures / the rapacious ego is constituted by institutional structures.[19]

What is most disturbing in Iago's comically banal and fathomless expression –
as for that matter, in Professor Lerner's definition of empathy – is that the
imagined self-loss conceals its opposite: a ruthless displacement and absorption
of the other. Empathy, as the German *Einfühlung* suggests, may be a feeling of
oneself into an object, but that object may have to be drained of its own
substance before it will serve as an appropriate vessel. Certainly in *Othello*,
where all relations are embedded in power and sexuality, there is no realm
where the subject and object can merge in the unproblematic accord affirmed
by the theorists of empathy.[20] As Iago himself proclaims, his momentary identification with the Moor is a strategic aspect of his malevolent hypocrisy:

> In following him, I follow but myself.
> Heaven is my judge, not I for love and duty,
> But seeming so, for my peculiar end.
>   (1.1.58–60)

Exactly what that "peculiar end" is remains opaque. Even the general term
"self-interest" is suspect: Iago begins his speech in a declaration of self-interest –
"I follow him to serve my turn upon him" – and ends in a declaration of self-
division: "I am not what I am."[21] We tend, to be sure, to hear the latter as "I am
not what I seem," hence as a simple confirmation of his public deception. But
"I am not what I am" goes beyond social feigning: not only does Iago mask
himself in society as the honest ancient, but in private he tries out a bewildering
succession of brief narratives that critics have attempted, with notorious results, to
translate into motives. These inner narratives – shared, that is, only with the
audience – continually promise to disclose what lies behind the public deception,
to illuminate what Iago calls "the native act and figure" of his heart, and continually
fail to do so; or rather, they reveal that his heart is precisely a series of acts and
figures, each referring to something else, something just out of our grasp. "I am not
what I am" suggests that this elusiveness is permanent, that even self-interest,
whose transcendental guarantee is the divine "I am what I am," is a mask.[22]
Iago's constant recourse to narrative then is both the affirmation of absolute
self-interest and the affirmation of absolute vacancy; the oscillation between the
two incompatible positions suggests in Iago the principle of narrativity itself, cut

off from original motive and final disclosure. The only termination possible in his case is not revelation but silence.

The question remains why anyone would submit, even unconsciously, to Iago's narrative fashioning. Why would anyone submit to another's narrative at all? For an answer we may recall the pressures on all the figures we have considered in this study and return to our observation that there is a structural resemblance between even a hostile improvisation and its object. In *Othello* the characters have always already experienced submission to narrativity. This is clearest and most important in the case of Othello himself. When Brabantio brings before the Signiory the charge that his daughter has been seduced by witchcraft, Othello promises to deliver "a round unvarnish'd tale . . . /Of my whole course of love" (1.3.90–1), and at the heart of this tale is the telling of tales:

> Her father lov'd me, oft invited me,
> Still question'd me the story of my life,
> From year to year; the battles, sieges, fortunes,
> That I have pass'd:
> I ran it through, even from my boyish days,
> To the very moment that he bade me tell it.
>
> (1.3.128–33)

The telling of the story of one's life – the conception of one's life as a story[23] – is a response to public inquiry: to the demands of the Senate, sitting in judgment or, at the least, to the presence of an inquiring community. When, as recorded in the fourteenth-century documents Le Roy Ladurie has brilliantly studied, the peasants of the Languedoc village of Montaillou are examined by the Inquisition, they respond with a narrative performance: "About 14 years ago, in Lent, towards vespers, I took two sides of salted pork to the house of Guillaume Benet of Montaillou, to have them smoked. There I found Guillemette Benet warming herself by the fire, together with another woman; I put the salted meat in the kitchen and left."[24] And when the Carthaginian queen calls upon her guest to "tell us all things from the first beginning, Grecian guile, your people's trials, and then your journeyings," Aeneas responds, as he must, with a narrative of the destiny decreed by the gods.[25] So too Othello before the Senate or earlier in Brabantio's house responds to questioning with what he calls his "travel's history" or, in the Folio reading, as if noting the genre, his "traveler's history." This history, it should be noted, is not only of events in distant lands and among strange peoples: "I ran it through," Othello declares, from childhood "To the very moment that he bade me tell it." We are on the brink of a Borges-like narrative that is forever constituting itself out of the materials of the present instant, a narrative in which the storyteller is constantly swallowed up by the story. That is, Othello is pressing up against the condition of all discursive representations of identity. He comes dangerously close to recognizing his status as a text, and it is precisely this recognition that the play as a whole will reveal to be insupportable. But, at this point, Othello is still convinced that the text is his own, and he imagines only that he is recounting a lover's performance.

In the 45th sonnet of Sidney's *Astrophil and Stella*, Astrophil complains that while Stella is indifferent to the sufferings she has caused him, she weeps piteous tears at a fable of some unknown lovers. He concludes,

> Then think my dear, that you in me do read
> Of Lovers' ruin some sad Tragedy:
> I am not I, pity the tale of me.

In *Othello* it is Iago who echos that last line – "I am not what I am," the motto of the improviser, the manipulator of signs that bear no resemblance to what they profess to signify – but it is Othello himself who is fully implicated in the situation of the Sidney sonnet: that one can win pity for oneself only by becoming a tale of oneself, and hence by ceasing to be oneself. Of course, Othello thinks that he has triumphed through his narrative self-fashioning:

> she thank'd me,
> And bade me, if I had a friend that lov'd her,
> I should but teach him how to tell my story,
> And that would woo her. Upon this hint I spake:
> She lov'd me for the dangers I had pass'd,
> And I lov'd her that she did pity them.
>
> (1.3.163–8)

But Iago knows that an identity that has been fashioned as a story can be unfashioned, refashioned, inscribed anew in a different narrative: it is the fate of stories to be consumed or, as we say more politely, interpreted. And even Othello, in his moment of triumph, has a dim intimation of this fate: a half-dozen lines after he has recalled "the Cannibals, that each other eat," he remarks complacently, but with an unmistakable undertone of anxiety, that Desdemona would come "and with a greedy ear / Devour up my discourse" (1.3.149–50).

Paradoxically, in this image of rapacious appetite Othello is recording Desdemona's *submission* to his story, what she calls the consecration of her soul and fortunes "to his honors, and his valiant parts" (1.3.253). What he has both experienced and narrated, she can only embrace as narration:

> my story being done,
> She gave me for my pains a world of sighs;
> She swore i' faith 'twas strange, 'twas passing strange;
> 'Twas pitiful, 'twas wondrous pitiful;
> She wish'd she had not heard it, yet she wish'd
> That heaven had made her such a man.
>
> (1.3.158–63)[26]

It is, of course, characteristic of early modern culture that male submission to narrative is conceived as active, entailing the fashioning of one's own story (albeit within the prevailing conventions), and female submission as passive, entailing the entrance into marriage in which, to recall Tyndale's definition, the "weak vessel" is put "under the obedience of her husband, to rule her lusts and wanton appetites." As we have seen, Tyndale explains that Sara, "before she was married, was Abraham's sister, and equal with him; but, as soon as she was married, was in subjection, and became without comparison inferior; for so is the nature of wedlock, by the ordinance of God."[27] At least for the world of Renaissance patriarchs, this account is fanciful in its glimpse of an original equality; most women must have entered marriage, like Desdemona, directly from paternal domination. "I do perceive here a divided duty," she tells her father before the Venetian Senate; "you are lord of all my duty,"

> but here's my husband:
> And so much duty as my mother show'd
> To you, preferring you before her father,
> So much I challenge, that I may profess,
> Due to the Moor my lord.
> (1.3.185–9)[28]

She does not question the woman's obligation to obey, invoking instead only the traditional right to transfer her duty. Yet though Desdemona proclaims throughout the play her submission to her husband – "Commend me to my kind lord," she gasps in her dying words – that submission does not accord wholly with the male dream of female passivity. She was, Brabantio tells us,

> A maiden never bold of spirit,
> So still and quiet, that her motion
> Blush'd at her self,
> (1.3.94–6)

yet even this self-abnegation in its very extremity unsettles what we may assume was her father's expectation:

> So opposite to marriage, that she shunn'd
> The wealthy curled darlings of our nation.
> (1.2.67–8)

And, of course, her marriage choice is, for Brabantio, an act of astonishing disobedience, explicable only as the somnambulistic behavior of one bewitched or drugged. He views her elopement not as a transfer of obedience but as theft or treason or a reckless escape from what he calls his "guardage." Both he and Iago remind Othello that her marriage suggests not submission but deception:

> She did deceive her father, marrying you;
> And when she seem'd to shake and fear your looks,
> She lov'd them most.
> (3.3.210–11)[29]

As the sly reference to Othello's "looks" suggests, the scandal of Desdemona's marriage consists not only in her failure to receive her father's prior consent but in her husband's blackness. That blackness – the sign of all that the society finds frightening and dangerous – is the indelible witness to Othello's permanent status as an outsider, no matter how highly the state may value his services or how sincerely he has embraced its values.[30] The safe passage of the female from father to husband is irreparably disrupted, marked as an escape: "O heaven," Brabantio cries, "how got she out?" (1.1.169).

Desdemona's relation to her lord Othello should, of course, lay to rest any doubts about her proper submission, but it is not only Brabantio's opposition and Othello's blackness that raise such doubts, even in the midst of her intensest declarations of love. There is rather a quality in that love itself that unsettles the orthodox schema of hierarchical obedience and makes Othello perceive her submission to his discourse as a devouring of it. We may perceive this quality most clearly in the exquisite moment of the lovers' reunion on Cyprus:

> *Othello*: It gives me wonder great as my content
> To see you here before me: O my soul's joy,
> If after every tempest come such calmness,
> May the winds blow, till they have waken'd death,
> And let the labouring bark climb hills of seas,
> Olympus-high, and duck again as low
> As hell's from heaven. If it were now to die,
> 'Twere now to be most happy, for I fear
> My soul hath her content so absolute,
> That not another comfort, like to this
> Succeeds in unknown fate.
> *Desdemona*:   The heavens forbid
> But that our loves and comforts should increase,
> Even as our days do grow.
> *Othello*:   Amen to that, sweet powers!
> I cannot speak enough of this content,
> It stops me here, it is too much of joy.
>
> (2.1.183–97)[31]

Christian orthodoxy in both Catholic and Protestant Europe could envision a fervent mutual love between husband and wife, the love expressed most profoundly by Saint Paul in words that are cited and commented upon in virtually every discussion of marriage:

> So men are bound to love their own wives as their own bodies. He that loveth his own wife, loveth himself. For never did any man hate his own flesh, but nourisheth and cherisheth it, even as the Lord doth the congregation: for we are members of his body, of his flesh and of his bones. For this cause shall a man leave father and mother, and shall be joined unto his wife, and they two shall be one flesh. This mystery is great, but I speak of Christ and of the congregation.[32]

Building upon this passage and upon its source in *Genesis*, commentators could write, like the Reformer Thomas Becon, that marriage is a "high, holy, and blessed order of life, ordained not of man, but of God, yea and that not in this sinful world, but in paradise that most joyful garden of pleasure." But like the Pauline text itself, all such discussions of married love begin and end by affirming the larger order of authority and submission within which marriage takes its rightful place. The family, as William Gouge puts it, "is a little Church, and a little Commonwealth . . . whereby trial may be made of such as are fit for any place of authority, or of subjection in Church or Commonwealth."[33]

In Othello's ecstatic words, the proper sentiments of a Christian husband sit alongside something else: a violent oscillation between heaven and hell, a momentary possession of the soul's absolute content, an archaic sense of monumental scale, a dark fear – equally archaic, perhaps – of "unknown fate." Nothing *conflicts* openly with Christian orthodoxy, but the erotic intensity that informs almost every word is experienced in tension with it. This tension is less a manifestation of some atavistic "blackness" specific to Othello than a manifestation of the colonial power of Christian doctrine over sexuality, a power visible at this point precisely in its inherent limitation.[34] That is, we glimpse in this brief moment the *boundary* of the orthodox, the strain of its control, the potential disruption of its hegemony by passion. This scene, let us stress, does not depict rebellion or even complaint – Desdemona invokes "the heavens" and Othello answers, "Amen to that, sweet powers!" Yet the plural here eludes, if only slightly, a serene affirmation of orthodoxy: the powers in their heavens do not refer unmistakably to the Christian God, but rather are the nameless transcendent forces that protect and enhance erotic love. To perceive the difference, we might recall that if Augustine argues, against the gnostics, that God had intended Adam and Eve to procreate in paradise, he insists at the same time that our first parents would have experienced sexual intercourse without the excitement of the flesh. How then could Adam have had an erection? Just as there are persons, Augustine writes, "who can move their ears, either one at a time, or both together" and others who have "such command of their bowels, that they can break wind continuously at pleasure, so as to produce the effect of singing," so, before the Fall, Adam would have had fully rational, willed control of the organ of generation and thus would have needed no erotic arousal. "Without the seductive stimulus of passion, with calmness of mind and with no corrupting of the integrity of the body, the husband would lie upon the bosom of his wife," and in this placid union, the semen could reach the womb "with the integrity of the female genital organ being preserved, just as now, with that same integrity being safe, the menstrual flow of blood can be emitted from the womb of a virgin."[35] Augustine grants that even Adam and Eve, who alone could have done so, failed to experience this "passionless generation," since they were expelled from paradise before they had a chance to try it. Nevertheless, the ideal of Edenic placidity, untried but intended by God for mankind, remains as a reproach to all fallen sexuality, an exposure of its inherent violence.[36]

The rich and disturbing pathos of the lovers' passionate reunion in *Othello* derives then not only from our awareness that Othello's premonition is tragically accurate, but from a rent, a moving ambivalence, in his experience of the ecstatic moment itself. The "calmness" of which he speaks may express gratified desire, but, as the repeated invocation of death suggests, it may equally express the longing for a final *release* from desire, from the dangerous violence, the sense of extremes, the laborious climbing and falling out of control that is experienced in the tempest. To be sure, Othello *welcomes* this tempest, with its charge of erotic feeling, but he does so for the sake of the ultimate consummation that the experience can call into being: "If after every tempest come such calmness. ..." That which men most fear to look upon in the storm – death – is for Othello that which makes the storm endurable. If the death he invokes may figure not the release from desire but its fulfillment – for *death* is a common Renaissance term for orgasm – this fulfillment is characteristically poised between an anxious sense of self-dissolution and a craving for decisive closure. If Othello's words suggest an ecstatic acceptance of sexuality, an absolute content, they suggest simultaneously that for him sexuality is a menacing voyage to reach a longed-for heaven; it is one of the dangers to be passed. Othello embraces the erotic as a supreme form of romantic narrative, a tale of risk and violence issuing forth at last in a happy and final tranquillity.

Desdemona's response is in an entirely different key:

> The heavens forbid
> But that our loves and comforts should increase,
> Even as our days do grow.

This is spoken to allay Othello's fear, but may it not instead augment it? For if Othello characteristically responds to his experience by shaping it as a story, Desdemona's reply denies the possibility of such narrative control and offers instead a vision of unabating increase. Othello says "Amen" to this vision, but it arouses in him a feeling at once of overflowing and inadequacy:

> I cannot speak enough of this content,
> It stops me here, it is too much of joy.

Desdemona has once again devoured up his discourse, and she has done so precisely in bringing him comfort and content.[37] Rather than simply confirming male authority, her submission eroticizes everything to which it responds, from the "disastrous chances" and "moving accidents" Othello relates, to his simplest demands,[38] to his very mistreatment of her:

> my love doth so approve him,
> That even his stubbornness, his checks and frowns, –
> Prithee unpin me, – have grace and favour in them.
> (4.3.19–21)[39]

The other women in the play, Bianca and Emilia, both have moments of disobedience to the men who possess and abuse them – in the case of Emilia, it is a heroic disobedience for which she pays with her life.[40] Desdemona performs no such acts of defiance, but her erotic submission, conjoined with Iago's murderous cunning, far more effectively, if unintentionally, subverts her husband's carefully fashioned identity.

We will examine more fully the tragic process of this subversion, but it is important to grasp first that Othello's loss of himself – a loss depicted discursively in his incoherent ravings – arises not only from the fatal conjunction of Desdemona's love and Iago's hate, but from the nature of that identity, from what we have called his submission to narrative self-fashioning. We may invoke in this connection Lacan's observation that the source of the subject's frustration in psychoanalysis is ultimately neither the silence nor the reply of the analyst:

> Is it not rather a matter of frustration inherent in the very discourse of the subject? Does the subject not become engaged in an ever-growing dispossession of that being of his, concerning which – by dint of sincere portraits which leave its idea no less incoherent, of rectifications which do not succeed in freeing its essence, of stays and defenses which do not prevent his statue from tottering, of narcissistic embraces which become like a puff of air in animating it – he ends up by recognizing that this being has never been anything more than his construct in the Imaginary and that this construct disappoints all of his certitudes? For in this labor which he undertakes to reconstruct this construct *for another*, he finds again the fundamental alienation which made him construct it *like another one*, and which has always destined it to be stripped from him *by another*.[41]

Shakespeare's military hero, it may be objected, is particularly far removed from this introspective project, a project that would seem, in any case, to have little bearing upon any Renaissance text. Yet I think it is no accident that nearly every phrase of Lacan's critique of psychoanalysis seems a brilliant reading of *Othello*, for I would propose that there is a deep resemblance between the construction of the self in analysis – at least as Lacan conceives it – and Othello's self-fashioning. The resemblance is grounded in the dependence of even the innermost self upon a language that is always necessarily given from without and upon representation before an audience. I do not know if such are the conditions of human identity, apart from its expression in psychoanalysis, but they are unmistakably the conditions of theatrical identity, where existence is conferred upon a character by the playwright's language and the actor's performance. And in *Othello* these governing circumstances of the medium itself are reproduced and intensified in the hero's situation: his identity depends upon a constant performance, as we have seen, of his "story," a loss of his own origins, an embrace and perpetual reiteration of the norms of another culture. It is this dependence that gives Othello, the warrior and alien, a relation to Christian values that is the existential equivalent of a religious vocation; he cannot allow himself the moderately flexible adherence that most ordinary men have toward their own formal beliefs. Christianity is the alienating yet constitutive force in Othello's identity, and if we seek a discursive mode in the play that is the social equivalent of the experience Lacan depicts, we will find it in *confession*. Othello himself invokes before the Venetian Senate the absolute integrity of confession, conceived, it appears, not as the formal auricular rite of penitence but as a generalized self-scrutiny in God's presence:

> as faithful as to heaven
> I do confess the vices of my blood,

> So justly to your grave ears I'll present
> How I did thrive in this fair lady's love,
> And she in mine.
>
>   (1.3.123–36)[42]

The buried identification here between the vices of the blood and mutual
thriving in love is fully exhumed by the close of the play when confession has
become a virtually obsessional theme.[43] Theological and juridical confession are
fused in Othello's mind when, determined first to exact a deathbed confession,
he comes to take Desdemona's life:

> If you bethink yourself of any crime,
> Unreconcil'd as yet to heaven and grace,
> Solicit for it straight. . . .
> Therefore confess thee freely of thy sin,
> For to deny each article with oath
> Cannot remove, nor choke the strong conceit,
> That I do groan withal: thou art to die.
>
>   (5.2.26–8, 54–7)

The sin that Othello wishes Desdemona to confess is adultery, and her refusal to
do so frustrates the achievement of what in theology was called "a good,
complete confession."[44] He feels the outrage of the thwarted system that needs
to imagine itself merciful, sacramental, when it disciplines:

> thou dost stone thy heart,
> And makest me call what I intend to do
> A murder, which I thought a sacrifice.
>
>   (5.2.64–6)

We are at last in a position to locate the precise nature of the symbolic
structure into which Iago inserts himself in his brilliant improvisation: this
structure is the centuries-old Christian doctrine of sexuality, policed socially
and psychically, as we have already seen, by confession. To Iago, the Renaissance
skeptic, this system has a somewhat archaic ring, as if it were an earlier stage of
development which his own modern sensibility had cast off.[45] Like the Lucayan
religion to the conquistadors, the orthodox doctrine that governs Othello's
sexual attitudes – his simultaneous idealization and mistrust of women – seems
to Iago sufficiently close to be recognizable, sufficiently distant to be manipulable. We watch him manipulate it directly at the beginning of act 4, when he
leads Othello through a brutally comic parody of the late medieval confessional
manuals with their casuistical attempts to define the precise moment at which
venial temptation passes over into mortal sin:

> *Iago*: To kiss in private?
> *Othello*:   An unauthoriz'd kiss.
> *Iago*: Or to be naked with her friend abed,

> An hour, or more, not meaning any harm?
> *Othello*: Naked abed, Iago, and not mean harm?
> It is hypocrisy against the devil:
> They that mean virtuously, and yet do so,
> The devil their virtue tempts, and they tempt heaven.
> *Iago*: So they do nothing, 'tis a venial slip.
>
> (4.1.2–9)

Iago in effect assumes an extreme version of the laxist position in such manuals in order to impel Othello toward the rigorist version that viewed adultery as one of the most horrible of mortal sins, more detestable, in the words of the *Eruditorium penitentiale*, "than homicide or plunder," and hence formerly deemed punishable, as several authorities remind us, by death.[46] Early Protestantism did not soften this position. Indeed, in the mid-sixteenth century, Tyndale's erstwhile collaborator, George Joye, called for a return to the Old Testament penalty for adulterers. "God's law," he writes, "is to punish adultery with death for the tranquillity and commonwealth of His church." This is not an excessive or vindictive course; on the contrary, "to take away and to cut off putrified and corrupt members from the whole body, lest they poison and destroy the body, is the law of love."[47] When Christian magistrates leave adultery unpunished, they invite more betrayals and risk the ruin of the realm, for as Protestants in particular repeatedly observe, the family is an essential component of an interlocking social and theological network. Hence adultery is a sin with the gravest of repercussions; in the words of the great Cambridge Puritan William Perkins, it

> destroyeth the Seminary of the Church, which is *a godly seed* in the family, and it breaketh the covenant between the parties and God; it robs another of the precious ornament of chastity, which is a gift of the Holy Ghost; it dishonors their bodies and maketh them temples of the devil; and the Adulterer maketh his family a Stews.[48]

It is in the bitter spirit of these convictions that Othello enacts the grotesque comedy of treating his wife as a strumpet and the tragedy of executing her in the name of justice, lest she betray more men.

But we still must ask how Iago manages to persuade Othello that Desdemona has committed adultery, for all of the cheap tricks Iago plays seem somehow inadequate to produce the unshakable conviction of his wife's defilement that seizes Othello's soul and drives him mad. After all, as Iago taunts Othello, he cannot achieve the point of vantage of God whom the Venetian women let "see the pranks / They dare not show their husbands" (3.3.206–7):

> Would you, the supervisor, grossly gape on,
> Behold her topp'd?
>
> (3.3.401–2)

How then, without "ocular proof" and in the face of both love and common sense, is Othello so thoroughly persuaded? To answer this, we must recall the syntactic ambiguity we noted earlier – "to abuse Othello's ear, / That he is too familiar with his wife" – and turn to a still darker aspect of orthodox Christian doctrine, an aspect central both to the confessional system and to Protestant self-scrutiny. *Omnis amator feruentior est adulter,* goes the Stoic epigram, and Saint Jerome does not hesitate to draw the inevitable inference: "An adulterer is he who is too ardent a lover of his wife."[49] Jerome quotes Seneca: "All love of another's wife is shameful; so too, too much love of your own. A wise man ought to love his wife with judgment, not affection. Let him control his impulses and not be borne headlong into copulation. Nothing is fouler than to love a wife like an adultress.... Let them show themselves to their wives not as lovers, but as husbands."[50] The words echo through more than a thousand years of Christian writing on marriage, and, in the decisive form given them by Augustine and his commentators, remain essentially unchallenged by the leading continental Reformers of the sixteenth and early seventeenth century, by Tudor ecclesiastical authorities, and even by Elizabethan and Jacobean Puritans who sharply opposed so many conservative Anglican doctrines. There is, to be sure, in all shades of Protestantism an attack on the Catholic doctrine of celibacy and a celebration of married love, a celebration that includes acknowledgment of the legitimate role of sexual pleasure. But for Reformer as for Catholic, this acknowledgment is hedged about with warnings, and restrictions. The "man who shows no modesty or comeliness in conjugal intercourse," writes Calvin, "is committing adultery with his wife," and the *King's Book*, attributed to Henry VIII, informs its readers that in lawful matrimony a man may break the Seventh Commandment "and live unchaste with his own wife, if he do unmeasurably or inordinately serve his or her fleshly appetite or lust."[51]

In the Augustinian conception, as elaborated by Raymond of Peñaforte, William of Rennes, and others, there are four motives for conjugal intercourse: to conceive offspring; to render the marital debt to one's partner so that he or she might avoid incontinency; to avoid fornication oneself; and to satisfy desire. The first two motives are without sin and excuse intercourse; the third is a venial sin; the fourth – to satisfy desire – is mortal. Among the many causes that underlie this institutional hostility to desire is the tenacious existence, in various forms, of the belief that pleasure constitutes a legitimate release from dogma and constraint. Thus when asked by the Inquisition about her happy past liaison with the heretical priest of Montaillou, the young Grazide Lizier replies with naive frankness, "in those days it pleased me, and it pleased the priest, that he should know me carnally, and be known by me; and so I did not think I was sinning, and neither did he."[52] "With Pierre Clergue," she explains, "I liked it. And so it could not displease God. It was not a sin" (p. 157). For the peasant girl, apparently, pleasure was the guarantee of innocence: "But now, with him, it does not please me any more. And so now, if he knew me carnally, I should think it a sin" (p. 151). A comparable attitude, derived not from peasant culture but from the troubadours, evidently lies behind the more sophisticated courtship of Romeo: "Thus from my lips, by thine my sin is purged."[53]

It should not surprise us that churchmen, Catholic and Protestant alike, would seek to crush such dangerous notions, nor that they would extend their surveillance and discipline to married couples and warn that excessive pleasure in the marriage bed is at least a potential violation of the Seventh Commandment. "Nothing is more vile," says Raymond's influential *summa*, "than to love your wife in adulterous fashion."[54] The conjugal act may be without sin, writes the rigorist Nicolaus of Ausimo, but only if "in the performance of this act there is no enjoyment of pleasure."[55] Few *summas* and no marriage manuals take so extreme a position, but virtually all are in agreement that the active *pursuit* of pleasure in sexuality is damnable, for as Jacobus Ungarelli writes in the sixteenth century, those who undertake intercourse for pleasure "exclude God from their minds, act as brute beasts, lack reason, and if they begin marriage for this reason, are given over to the power of the devil."[56]

Confessors then must determine if the married penitent has a legitimate excuse for intercourse and if the act has been performed with due regard for "matrimonial chastity," while Protestants who have rejected auricular confession must similarly scrutinize their own behavior for signs that their pleasure has been too "spacious."[57] "Lust is more spacious than love," writes Alexander Niccoles in the early seventeenth century; it "hath no mean, no bound ... more deep, more dangerous than the Sea, and less restrained, for the Sea hath bounds, but it [lust] hath none."[58] Such unbounded love is a kind of idolatry, an encroachment upon a Christian's debt of loving obedience to God, and it ultimately destroys the marital relationship as well. Immoderate love, another Puritan divine warns, "will either be blown down by some storm or tempest of displeasure, or fall of itself, or else degenerate into jealousy, the most devouring and fretting canker that can harbor in a married person's breast."[59]

These anxieties, rich in implication for *Othello*, are frequently tempered in Protestant writings by a recognition of the joyful ardor of young married couples, but there remains a constant fear of excess, and, as Ambrose observed centuries earlier, even the most plausible excuse for sexual passion is shameful in the old: "Youths generally assert the desire for generation. How much more shameful for the old to do what is shameful for the young to confess."[60] Othello himself seems eager to ward off this shame; he denies before the Senate that he seeks

> To please the palate of my appetite,
> Nor to comply with heat, the young affects
> In me defunct. ...
>
> (1.3.262–4)[61]

But Desdemona makes no such disclaimer; indeed her declaration of passion is frankly, though by no means exclusively, sexual:

> That I did love the Moor, to live with him,
> My downright violence, and scorn of fortunes,
> May trumpet to the world: my heart's subdued
> Even to the utmost pleasure of my lord.
>
> (1.3.248–51)[62]

This moment of erotic intensity, this frank acceptance of pleasure and submission to her spouse's pleasure, is, I would argue, as much as Iago's slander the cause of Desdemona's death, for it awakens the deep current of sexual anxiety in Othello, anxiety that with Iago's help expresses itself in quite orthodox fashion as the perception of adultery.[63] Othello unleashes upon Cassio – "Michael Cassio, / That came a-wooing with you" (3.3.71–2) – the fear of pollution, defilement, brutish violence that is bound up with his own experience of sexual pleasure, while he must destroy Desdemona both for her excessive experience of pleasure and for awakening such sensations in himself. Like Guyon in the Bower of Bliss, Othello transforms his complicity in erotic excess and his fear of engulfment into a "purifying," saving violence:

> Like to the Pontic sea,
> Whose icy current and compulsive course
> Ne'er feels retiring ebb, but keeps due on
> To the Propontic and the Hellespont,
> Even so my bloody thoughts, with violent pace,
> Shall ne'er look back, ne'er ebb to humble love,
> Till that a capable and wide revenge
> Swallow them up.
>
>   (3.3.460–7)

His insupportable sexual experience has been, as it were, displaced and absorbed by the act of revenge which can swallow up not only the guilty lovers but – as the syntax suggests – his own "bloody thoughts."

Such is the achievement of Iago's improvisation on the religious sexual doctrine in which Othello believes; true to that doctrine, pleasure itself becomes for Othello pollution, a defilement of his property in Desdemona and in himself.[64] It is at the level of this dark, sexual revulsion that Iago has access to Othello, access assured, as we should expect, by the fact that beneath his cynical modernity and professed self-love Iago reproduces in himself the same psychic structure. He is as intensely preoccupied with adultery, while his anxiety about his own sexuality may be gauged from the fact that he conceives his very invention, as the images of engendering suggest, as a kind of demonic semen that will bring forth monsters.[65] Indeed Iago's discourse – his assaults on women, on the irrationality of eros, on the brutishness of the sexual act – reiterates virtually to the letter the orthodox terms of Ungarelli's attack on those who seek pleasure in intercourse.

The improvisational process we have been discussing depends for its success upon the concealment of its symbolic center, but as the end approaches this center becomes increasingly visible. When, approaching the marriage bed on which Desdemona has spread the wedding sheets, Othello rages, "Thy bed, lust stain'd, shall with lust's blood be spotted" (5.1.36), he comes close to revealing his tormenting identification of marital sexuality – limited perhaps to the night he took Desdemona's virginity – and adultery.[66] The orthodox element of this identification is directly observed –

> this sorrow's heavenly,
> It strikes when it does love —
> (5.2.21–2)

and on her marriage bed / deathbed Desdemona seems at last to pluck out the heart of the mystery:

Othello:	Think on thy sins.
Desdemona:	They are loves I bear to you.
Othello:	And for that thou diest.
Desdemona:	That death's unnatural, that kills for loving.

> (5.2.39–42)

The play reveals at this point not the unfathomable darkness of human motives but their terrible transparency, and the horror of the revelation is its utter inability to deflect violence. Othello's identity is entirely caught up in the narrative structure that drives him to turn Desdemona into a being incapable of pleasure, a piece of "monumental alabaster," so that he will at last be able to love her without the taint of adultery:

> Be thus, when thou art dead, and I will kill thee,
> And love thee after.
> (5.2.18–19)

It is as if Othello had found in a necrophilic fantasy the secret solution to the intolerable demands of the rigorist sexual ethic, and the revelation that Cassio has not slept with Desdemona leads only to a doubling of this solution, for the adulterous sexual pleasure that Othello had projected upon his lieutenant now rebounds upon himself.[67] Even with the exposure of Iago's treachery, then, there is for Othello no escape — rather a still deeper submission to narrative, a reaffirmation of the self as story, but now split suicidally between the defender of the faith and the circumcised enemy who must be destroyed. Lodovico's bizarrely punning response to Othello's final speech — "O bloody period!" — insists precisely upon the fact that it was a speech, that this life fashioned as a text is ended as a text.

To an envious contemporary like Robert Greene, Shakespeare seems a kind of green-room Iago, appropriating for himself the labors of others. In *Othello* Shakespeare seems to acknowledge, represent, and explore his affinity to the malicious improviser, but, of course, his relation to the theater and to his culture is far more complex than such an affinity could suggest. There are characters in his works who can improvise without tragic results, characters who can embrace a mobility of desire — one of whose emblems is the male actor playing a female character dressed up as a male — that neither Iago, nor Othello, nor Desdemona can endure. Destructive violence is not Shakespeare's only version of these materials, and even in *Othello*, Iago is not the playwright's only representation of himself. Still, at the least we must grant Robert Greene that it would have seemed fatal to be imitated by Shakespeare. He possessed a limitless talent for entering into the consciousness of another, perceiving its deepest structures as a manipulable fiction, reinscribing it into his own narrative form.[68] If in the late plays, he experiments with controlled disruptions of narrative, moments of eddying and ecstasy, these invariably give way to reaffirmations of self-fashioning through story.

Montaigne, who shares many of Shakespeare's most radical perceptions, invents in effect a brilliant mode of *non-narrative* self-fashioning: "I cannot keep my subject still. It goes along befuddled and staggering, with a natural drunkenness. I take it in this condition, just as it is at the moment I give my attention to it."[69] Shakespeare by contrast remains throughout his career the supreme purveyor of "empathy," the fashioner of narrative selves, the master improviser. Where Montaigne withdrew to his study, Shakespeare became the presiding genius of a popular, urban art form with the capacity to foster psychic mobility in the service of Elizabethan power; he became the principal maker of what we may see as the prototype of the mass media Professor Lerner so admires.

Finally, we may ask, is this service to power a function of the theater itself or of Shakespeare's relation to his medium? The answer, predictably, is both. The theater is widely perceived in the period as the concrete manifestation of the histrionic quality of life, and, more specifically, of power – the power of the prince who stands as an actor upon a stage before the eyes of the nation, the power of God who enacts His will in the Theater of the World. The stage justifies itself against recurrent charges of immorality by invoking this normative function: it is the expression of those rules that govern a properly ordered society and displays visibly the punishment, in laughter and violence, that is meted out upon those who violate the rules. Most playwrights pay at least professional homage to these values; they honor the institutions that enable them to earn their keep and give voice to the ideology that holds together both their "mystery" and the society at large.

In Marlowe, as we have seen, we encounter a playwright at odds with this ideology. If the theater normally reflects and flatters the royal sense of itself as national performance, Marlowe struggles to expose the underlying motives of any performance of power. If the theater normally affirms God's providence, Marlowe explores the tragic needs and interests that are served by all such affirmations. If the Elizabethan stage functions as one of the public uses of spectacle to impose normative ethical patterns on the urban masses, Marlowe enacts a relentless challenge to those patterns and undermines employment of rhetoric and violence in their service.

Shakespeare approaches his culture not, like Marlowe, as rebel and blasphemer, but rather as dutiful servant, content to improvise a part of his own within its orthodoxy. And if after centuries, that improvisation has been revealed to us as embodying an almost boundless challenge to the culture's every tenet, a devastation of every source, the author of *Othello* would have understood that such a revelation scarcely matters. After all, the heart of a successful improvisation lies in concealment, not exposure; and besides, as we have seen, even a hostile improvisation reproduces the relations of power that it hopes to displace and absorb. This is not to dismiss the power of hatred or the significance of distinctions – it matters a great deal whether Othello or Iago, the Lucayans or the Spaniards prevail – only to suggest the boundaries that define the possibility of any improvisational contact, even contact characterized by hidden malice.

I would not want to argue, in any event, that Shakespeare's relation to his culture is defined by hidden malice. Such a case can no doubt be made for many of the plays – stranger things have been said – but it will sound forced and unconvincing, just as the case for Shakespeare as an unwavering, unquestioning apologist for Tudor ideology sounds forced and unconvincing. The solution here is not, I suggest, that the truth lies somewhere in between. Rather the truth itself is radically unstable and yet constantly stabilized, as unstable as those male authorities that affirm themselves only to be undermined by subversive women and then to be reconstituted in a different guise. If any reductive generalization about Shakespeare's relation to his culture seems dubious, it is because his plays offer no single timeless affirmation or denial of legitimate authority and no central, unwavering authorial presence. Shakespeare's language and themes are caught up, like the medium itself, in unsettling repetitions, committed to the shifting voices and audiences, with their shifting aesthetic assumptions and historical imperatives, that govern a living theater.

Criticism can legitimately show – as I hope my discussion of *Othello* does – that Shakespeare relentlessly *explores* the relations of power in a given culture. That more than exploration is involved is much harder to demonstrate convincingly. If there are intimations in Shakespeare of a release from the complex narrative orders in which everyone is inscribed, these intimations do not arise from bristling resistance or strident denunciation – the mood of a Jaques or Timon. They arise paradoxically from a peculiarly intense *submission* whose downright violence undermines everything it was meant to shore up, the submission depicted not in Othello or Iago but in Desdemona. As both the play and its culture suggest, the arousal of intense, purposeless pleasure is only superficially a confirmation of existing values, established selves.[70] In Shakespeare's narrative art, liberation from the massive power structures that determine social and psychic reality is glimpsed in an *excessive* aesthetic delight, an erotic embrace of those very structures – the embrace of a Desdemona whose love is more deeply unsettling than even a Iago's empathy.

NOTES

1   On the feudal revival, see Arthur B. Ferguson, *The Indian Summer of English Chivalry* (Durham, NC: Duke University Press, 1960), Frances A. Yates, "Elizabethan Chivalry: The Romance of the Accession Day Tilts," in *Astraea: The Imperial Theme in the Sixteenth Century* (London: Routledge, 1975), pp. 88–111, and Roy Strong, *The Cult of Elizabeth: Elizabethan Portraiture and Pageantry* (London: Thames and Hudson, 1977).

2   John Steevens, cited in Spenser, *Variorum* 1:252.

3   It is not certain who borrowed from whom, though I think the dominant view, that Marlowe borrowed from Spenser, is quite likely. See chapter 5, note 2, above. For

188 SHAKESPEARE STUDIES

the parallels between Spenser and Marlowe, see also Charles Crawford, "Edmund Spenser, 'Locrine,' and 'Selimus,'" *Notes and Queries* (9th ser.) 7 (1901): 61–3, 101–3, 142–4, 203–5, 261–3, 324–5, 384–6.

4 Daniel Lerner, *The Passing of Traditional Society: Modernizing the Middle East* (New York: Free Press, 1958; rev. edn 1964), p. 49.

5 The figures are from Sherburne Cook and Woodrow W. Borah, *Essays in Population History: Mexico and the Caribbean* (Berkeley: University of California Press, 1971), pp. 376–411.

6 Peter Martyr (Pietro Martire d'Anghiera), *De Orbe Novo*, trans. M. Lok, p. 623. The Seventh Decade was finished in the middle of 1525. On Peter Martyr, see Henry R. Wagner, "Peter Martyr and His Works," *Proceedings of the American Antiquarian Society* 56 (1946): 238–88. There is a rather pallid modern translation of *De Orbe Novo* by Francis A. MacNutt (New York: Putnam's, 1912).

7 It is the essence of *sprezzatura* to create the impression of a spontaneous improvisation by means of careful rehearsals. Similarly, the early English drama often strove for this effect; see, for example, *Fulgens and Lucres* where the seemingly incidental conversation of "A" and "B" is fully scripted.

8 Immanuel Wallerstein, *The Modern World System*.

9 Roy Strong, *The Cult of Elizabeth: Elizabethan Portraiture and Pageantry*, p. 153.

10 As an example of the operation of displacement in the visual arts, one may consider Breughel's *Christ Bearing the Cross*, where the mourning figures from Van der Weyden's great *Descent from the Cross* are pushed out to the margin of the canvas and the swirling, festive crowd all but obscures Christ. Similarly, for absorption we may invoke Dürer's self-portrait of 1500, where the rigidly frontalized, verticalized, hieratic figure has taken into itself the Christ Pantocrator.

11 Joel B. Altman, *The Tudor Play of Mind*. See also Jackson I. Cope, *The Theater and the Dream: From Metaphor to Form in Renaissance Drama* (Baltimore: The Johns Hopkins University Press, 1973), esp. chaps. 4–6. Cope argues brilliantly for the central importance of improvisation in the drama of the Renaissance, but for him improvisation is in the service finally of "a real coherence" of "the eternal order" of the myths of renewal (p. 210). One passes, by means of an apparent randomness, a chaotic flux, to a buried but all-powerful form. Improvisation is the mask of providence, and Cope concludes his study with a discussion of *The Tempest* as a "mythic play" of natural resurrection and Christian doctrine. I would argue that the final effect of improvisation in Shakespeare is the reverse: we always begin with a notion of the inescapability of form, a sense that there are no surprises, that narrative triumphs over the apparent disruptions, that even the disruptions serve narrative by confirming the presence of the artist as a version of the presence of God. And through improvisation we pass, only partially and tentatively, to a sense that in the very acts of homage to the great formal structures, there open up small but constant glimpses of the limitations of those structures, of their insecurities, of the possibility of their collapse.

12 *Confutation*, 8:1, pp. 90–2. My attention was drawn to this passage by Professor Louis L. Martz who discussed it in a lecture at the Folger conference "Thomas More: The Man and His Age." On More's "art of improvisation" see Martz, "The Tower Works," in *St. Thomas More: Action and Contemplation*, pp. 63–5.

13 Richard III virtually declares himself an improviser: "I clothe my naked villainy / With odd old ends stol'n forth of holy writ" (1.3.335–6). He gives a fine demonstration of his agility when he turns Margaret's curse back on herself. Behind this

trick perhaps is the fact that there were in the popular culture of the Renaissance formulaic curses and satirical jigs into which any names could be fitted; see Charles Read Baskervill, *The Elizabethan Jig and Related Song Drama* (Chicago: University of Chicago Press, 1929), pp. 66–7.

14   All citations of *Othello* are to the Arden edition, ed. M. R. Ridley (Cambridge, Mass.: Harvard University Press, 1958). Iago's description of Cassio, "a finder out of occasions" (2.1.240–1), is a far more apt description of himself as an improviser.

15   This interpretation is argued powerfully in an unpublished essay, "On the Language of Sexual Pathology in *Othello*," by Edward Snow of George Mason University. A similar case is made by Arthur Kirsch in a sensitive psychoanalytic study, "The Polarization of Erotic Love in *Othello*" (*Modern Language Review* 73 (1978): 721–40). Kirsch suggests that what becomes insupportable for Othello is "the fulsomeness of his own sexual instincts and, as his verbal and physical decomposition suggests, his jealous rage against Cassio is ultimately a rage against himself which reaches back to the elemental and destructive triadic fantasies which at one stage in childhood govern the mind of every human being" (737).

16   Iago's performance here, which Desdemona unnervingly characterizes as "lame and impotent," is one of the ways in which he is linked to the playwright or at least to the Vice-like "presenter" of a play; see Bernard Spivack, *Shakespeare and the Allegory of Evil: The History of a Metaphor in Relation to His Major Villains* (New York: Columbia University Press, 1958).

17   One might argue that Shakespeare, like Marx, sees the exploiter as doomed by the fact that he must reduce his victim to nothingness, but where Marx derives a revolutionary optimism from this process, Shakespeare derives the tragic mood of the play's end.

18   For Iago's "corrosive habit of abstraction," see Maynard Mack, "The Jacobean Shakespeare: Some Observations on the Construction of the Tragedies," in *Stratford-upon-Avon Studies: Jacobean Theatre* 1 (1960), p. 18. For Iago as a "portrait of the artist," see Stanley Edgar Hyman, *Iago: Some Approaches to the Illusion of His Motivation* (New York: Atheneum, 1970), pp. 61–100.

19   The vertigo intensifies if we add the sly preceding line: "It is as sure as you are Roderigo, / Were I the Moor, I would not be Iago." One imagines that Roderigo would unconsciously touch himself at this point to make sure that he *is* Roderigo. Iago is a master of the vertiginous confounding of self and other, being and seeming:

> Men should be what they seem,
> Or those that be not, would they might seem none.
> (III, iii, 130–1)
> He's that he is; I may not breathe my censure,
> What he might be, if, as he might, he is not,
> I would to heaven he were!
> (IV, i, 267–9)

20   See, for example, Theodor Lipps:

> The specific characteristic of esthetic pleasure has now been defined. It consists in this: that it is the enjoyment of an object, which however, so far as it is the object of *enjoyment*, is not an object, but myself. Or, it is the enjoyment of the ego, which however, so far as it is esthetically enjoyed, is not myself but objective.

Now, all this is included in the concept empathy. It constitutes the very meaning of this concept. Empathy is the fact here established, that the object is myself and by the very same token this self of mine is the object. Empathy is the fact that the antithesis between myself and the object disappears, or rather does not yet exist. ("Empathy, Inner Imitation, and Sense-Feelings," in *A Modern Book of Esthetics*, ed. Melvin Rader (New York: Holt, Rinehart and Winston, 1960), p. 376.)

To establish this "fact," Lipps must posit a wholly a esthetic dimension and what he calls an "ideal," as opposed to a "practical" self. In *Othello* there is no realm of the purely esthetic, no space defined by the intersection of negative capability and the willing suspension of disbelief, and no separation of an "ideal" from a "practical" self.

21   To complicate matters further, both declarations occur in a cunning performance for his dupe Roderigo; that is, Iago is saying what he presumes Roderigo wants to believe.

22   Thus Iago invokes heaven as the judge of his self-interested hypocrisy, for *self* and *interest* as stable entities both rely ultimately upon an absolute Being.

23   Elsewhere too, Othello speaks as if aware of himself as a character: "Were it my cue to fight," he tells the incensed Brabantio and his own followers, "I should have known it, / Without a prompter" (1.2.83–4). His acceptance of the commission to fight the Turks is likewise couched in an inflated diction that suggests he is responding to a cue:

> The tyrant custom, most grave senators,
> Hath made the flinty and steel couch of war
> My thrice-driven bed of down: I do agnize
> A natural and prompt alacrity
> I find in hardness, and would undertake
> This present wars against the Ottomites.
> (1.3.229–34)

24   Emmanuel Le Roy Ladurie, *Montaillou: The Promised Land of Error*, trans. Barbara Bray (New York: Braziller, 1978), pp. 8–9. In a review essay, Natalie Zemon Davis calls attention to the narrative structure of the testimony, a structure she attributes not to the pressure of the Inquisition but to the form of village culture: "Some of these details were probably remembered over the decades – good memories are part of oral culture – but most form a reconstructed past: from a general memory of an event, a narrative is created that tells with verisimilitude how the events could have unfolded. The past is a story" ("Les Conteurs de Montaillou," *Annales: Economies, Sociétés, Civilisations* 34 (1979): 70). On narrativity as a mode, see Louis Marin, *Utopiques: jeux d'espaces*; Svetlana Alpers, "Describe or Narrate? A Problem in Realistic Representation," *New Literary History* 7 (1976–7): 15–41; Leo Bersani, "The Other Freud," *Humanities in Society* 1 (1978): 35–49.

25   *The Aeneid of Virgil*, trans. Allen Mandelbaum (New York: Bantam Books, 1972), bk. 1, lines 1049–51.

26   I very reluctantly accept the Quarto's *sighs* for the Folio's *kisses*; the latter need not, as editors sometimes claim, suggest an improbable immodesty but rather may express Othello's perception of Desdemona's nature, hence what her love has given him. Moreover, the frank eroticism of *kisses* is in keeping with Desdemona's own speeches; it is Othello who emphasizes a pity that she voices nowhere in the play itself. On the other hand, *sighs* admits a simpler reading and by no means excludes the erotic.

There is another interpretive problem in this speech that should be noted: the last two lines are usually taken as a continuation of Desdemona's actual response, as recalled by Othello. But they may equally be his interpretation of her feelings, in which case they may say far more about Othello than about Desdemona. A competent actor could suggest either possibility. There is a further ambiguity in the *her* of "made her such a man": I hear *her* as accusative, but the dative cannot be ruled out.

27 William Tyndale, *Obedience*, p. 171, and above, chapter 2.

28 Both the Folio and the Second Quarto read "You are the Lord of duty," but the paradox of an absolute duty that must nevertheless be divided is suggestive.

29 Iago is improvising on two earlier remarks of Brabantio:

> and she, in spite of nature,
> Of years, of country, credit, everything,
> To fall in love with what she fear'd to look on?
> (1.3.96–8)

and

> Look to her, Moor, have a quick eye to see:
> She has deceiv'd her father, may do thee.
> (1.3.292–3)

In a society deeply troubled by clandestine marriage, the circumstances of Desdemona's union already brand her as faithless, even at the moment Othello stakes his life upon her faith, while, quite apart from these circumstances, it would seem for the male psyche depicted in the play that the very act of leaving her father borders obscurely on sexual betrayal.

30 See George K. Hunter, "Othello and Colour Prejudice," *Proceedings of the British Academy 1967* 53 (1968): 139–63; Leslie A. Fielder, *The Stranger in Shakespeare* (New York: Stein & Day, 1972), chap. 3.

A measure of the complex significance of Othello's blackness may be taken from a glance at the competing interpretive possibilities of Desdemona's "I saw Othello's visage in his mind" (1.3.252):

> "Do not be surprised that I have married an older black man who looks to you grotesque and terrifying. I have married not a face, a complexion, but a mind: a resolute, Christian mind."
>
> "I saw Othello's valuation of himself, his internal image, the picture he has in his mind of his own face. I saw how much he had at stake in his narrative sense of himself, how much his whole existence depended upon this sense, and I was deeply drawn to this 'visage.'"
>
> "I saw Othello's visage – his blackness, his otherness – in his mind as well as his complexion: there is a unity in his being. I am subdued to precisely this quality in him."

31 Ridley, in the Arden edition, adheres to the Quarto's "calmness" at line 185. Most editors prefer the Folio's "calms."

32 Ephesians 5.28–32, as cited in the marriage liturgy (*The Book of Common Prayer 1559*, ed. John Booty (Charlottesville: University of Virginia Press, 1976), p. 297). The passage is quoted by Arthur Kirsch, "The Polarization of Erotic Love in

Othello," p. 721, who draws conclusions closely parallel to some of my own, though he differs in emphases and methodology.

33 Becon and Gouge are cited in William and Malleville Haller, "The Puritan Art of Love," *Huntington Library Quarterly* 5 (1941–2): 44–5, 46.

34 From its inception, Christianity competed fiercely with other sexual conceptions and practices. For a detailed and moving study of one episode in this struggle, see Le Roy Ladurie's *Montaillou*. Michel Foucault has attempted the beginnings of a modern history of the subject in *La volonté de savoir*.

35 *The City of God*, trans. Marcus Dods (New York: Modern Library, 1950), bk. 14, chap. 24, pp. 473–5.

36 For the inherent violence of sexuality, see Lucretius, *The Nature of the Universe*, trans. Ronald Latham (Baltimore: Penguin, 1951): "Lovers' passion is storm-tossed, even in the moment of fruition, by waves of delusion and incertitude. They cannot make up their mind what to enjoy first with eye or hand. They clasp the object of their longing so tightly that the embrace is painful. They kiss so fiercely that teeth are driven into lips. All this because their pleasure is not pure, but they are goaded by an underlying impulse to hurt the thing, whatever it may be, that gives rise to these budding shoots of madness" (pp. 163–4).

37 Richard Onorato has called my attention to the way Iago, who is watching this scene, subsequently uses the word *content*. 'nothing can, nor shall content my soul,' he tells himself, "Till I am even with him, wife, for wife" (2.1.293–4). Later, when under his influence Othello has bade "farewell content" (3.3.354), Iago proffers the consoling words, "Pray be content" (3.3.457).

38 When Othello asks Desdemona to leave him a little to himself, she replies, "Shall I deny you? no, farewell, my lord" (3.3.87).

39 "Prithee unpin me" requires that the actress, as she speaks these words, call attention to Desdemona's erotic submission to Othello's violence.

40 As Gabrielle Jackson pointed out to me, Emilia feels that she must explain her refusal to observe her husband's commands to be silent and go home:

> Good gentlemen, let me have leave to speak,
> 'Tis proper I obey him but not now:
> Perchance, Iago, I will ne'er go home.
> (5.2.196–8)

The moment is felt as a liberating gesture and redeems her earlier, compliant theft of the handkerchief, but it is both too late and fatal. The play does not hold out the wife's disobedience as a way of averting tragedy.

41 Jacques Lacan, *The Language of the Self: The Function of Language in Psychoanalysis*, trans. Anthony Wilden (Baltimore: The Johns Hopkins University Press, 1968), p. 11.

42 In effect, Othello invokes larger and larger spheres of self-fashioning: Othello to Desdemona, Othello to Desdemona and Brabantio, Othello to the Senate, Othello to heaven. We might add that the narrative element in formal auricular confession may have been heightened by the fact that confessors were instructed not to interrupt the penitent but to let him begin with a full and circumstantial account.

43 The word *confession* and its variants (*confess'd, confessions*) is repeated eighteen times in the course of the play, more often than in any other play in the canon.

44 See Thomas N. Tentler, *Sin and Confession on the Eve of the Reformation*, and chapter 2, above.

45 This is a frequent response in the literature of colonialism; we have encountered it in Spenser's *View of the Present State of Ireland*, where he sees the Irish as living in certain respects as the English did before the civilizing influence of the Norman Conquest.

46 Tentler, p. 229. The *Eruditorium penitentiale* points out that in cases of necessity it is possible to kill or steal justifiably, "but no one may fornicate knowingly without committing a mortal sin." Tentler observes, "This kind of thinking is an exaggeration even of medieval puritanism. Yet it is also true that the climate of religious opinion allowed and perhaps even encouraged such exaggerations."

Cf. Francis Dillingham, *Christian Oeconomy or Household Government* (London: John Tapp, 1609): "Julius Caesar made a law that if the husband or the wife found either in adultery, it should be lawful for the husband to kill the wife or the wife the husband. Death then by the light of nature is fit punishment for adulterers and adulteresses" (p. 13).

47 George Joye, *A Contrarye (to a certayne manis) Consultacion: That Adulterers ought to be punyshed wyth deathe. Wyth the solucions of his argumentes for the contrarye* (London: n.p., 1559?), pp. G4ᵛ, A4ᵛ.

> The sacred integrity therefore of this Christ's holy church, the inviolable honor of holy matrimony ordained of God, the preservation of the private and public peace, all honesty, godly zeal to virtue, to the salvation of our souls and to God's glory should constrain every Christian heart to counsel, to exhort and to excite all Christian magistrates to cut off this contagious canker of adultery from among us, lest in further creeping, . . . it daily corrupteth the whole body of this noble realm so that it else be at last so incurable that . . . neither the vice nor yet the just remedy will be suffered. (A6ᵛ)

The death penalty for adulterers was briefly adopted by the Puritan Parliament in the seventeenth century; see Keith Thomas, "The Puritans and Adultery: the Act of 1650 Reconsidered," in *Puritans and Revolutionaries: Essays in Seventeenth-Century History*, ed. Donald Pennington and Keith Thomas (Oxford: At the Clarendon Press, 1978), pp. 257–82.

48 William Perkins, *A Godly and Learned Exposition of Christs Sermon in the Mount* (Cambridge: Thomas Pierson, 1608), p. 111. See Robert V. Schnucker, "La position puritaine à l'égard de l'adultère," *Annales: Economies, Sociétés, Civilisations* 27 (1972): 1379–88.

49 Quoted, with a mass of supporting material, in John T. Noonan, Jr., *Contraception: A History of Its Treatment by the Catholic Theologians and Canonists* (Cambridge, Mass.: Harvard University Press, 1966), p. 80. The Stoic marital doctrine, Noonan observes, "joined the Stoic distrust of pleasure and the Stoic insistence on purpose" (p. 47); early Christians embraced the doctrine and hardened its formulation in combatting the gnostic sects.

50 Noonan, p. 47.

51 John Calvin, *Institutes of the Christian Religion*, bk. 2, chap. 8, section 44, quoted in Lawrence Stone, *The Family, Sex and Marriage in England 1500–1800*, p. 499; *The King's Book, or a Necessary Doctrine and Erudition for Any Christian Man* (1543), ed. T. A. Lacey (London: Society for Promoting Christian Knowledge, 1932), pp. 111–12. See likewise John Rogers, *The Glasse of Godly Loue* (1569), ed. Frederick J. Furnivall, New Shakespeare Society, ser. 6, no. 2 (London: N Trübner, 1876), p. 185:

> Also there ought to be a temperance between man and wife, for God hath ordained marriage for a remedy or medicine, to assuage the heart of the burning flesh, and for procreation, and not beastly for to fulfill the whole lusts of the devilish mind and wicked flesh; for, though ye have a promise that the act in marriage is not sin ... yet if ye take excess, or use it beastly, vilely, or inordinately, your mistemperance makes that ill which is good (being rightly used), and that which is clean, ye defile through your abusing of it.

In the seventeenth century, William Perkins informs his readers that the "holy manner" in marital intercourse involves moderation, "for even in wedlock, excess in lusts is not better than plain adultery before God." "This is the judgment of the ancient Church," notes Perkins, citing Ambrose and Augustine, "that Intemperance, that is, immoderate desire even between man and wife, is fornication" (*Christian Oeconomie*, trans. Thomas Pickering (London: Felix Kyngstone, 1609), pp. 113–14).

52 Le Roy Ladurie, *Montaillou*, p. 151. In fact the priest, who was, in Le Roy Ladurie's words, "an energetic lover and incorrigible Don Juan" (p. 154), held a somewhat different position. "One woman's just like another," he told Grazide's mother, "The sin is the same, whether she is married or not. Which is as much as to say that there is no sin about it at all" (p. 157). Le Roy Ladurie interprets his views on love as follows: "Starting from the Cathar proposition that 'any sexual act, even between married persons, is wrong,' he applied it to suit himself. Because everything was forbidden, one act was no worse than another" (pp. 158–9).

53 1.5.107. Le Roy Ladurie quotes from the *Brévaire d'amour.* "A lady who sleeps with a true lover is purified of all sins ... the joy of love makes the act innocent, for it proceeds from a pure heart" (p. 159).

See Friar Laurence's warnings to Romeo about excessive love:

> These violent delights have violent ends
> And in their triumph die, like fire and powder,
> Which, as they kiss, consume. ...
> Therefore love moderately: long love doth so.
> (2.6.9–14)

54 Tentler, p. 174.

55 Tentler, p. 181: "hoc est in executione ipsius actus nulla voluptatis delectatione teneatur."

56 Tentler, p. 183. According to the *King's Book*, over those who have violated married chastity, "the Devil hath power, as the angel Raphael said unto Thobit, They that marry in such wise that they exclude God out of their hearts, and give themselves unto their own carnal lusts, as it were an horse or a mule, which have no reason; upon such persons the Devil hath power" (p. 112).

For a humanist's version of these notions, see the following aphorisms from Juan Luis Vives's *Introductio ad Sapientam*:

> The pleasure of the body is, like the body itself, vile and brutal.
> Sensual delectation bores the soul and benumbs the intellect.
> Sensual delectation is like robbery, it vilifies the soul. This is the reason why even the most corrupted man seeks secrecy and abhors witnesses.
> Sensual pleasure is fleeting and momentaneous, totally beyond any control and always mixed with frustration.
> Nothing debilitates more the vigor of the our intellect than sexual pleasure.
> (Carlos G. Noreña, *Juan Luis Vives* (The Hague: Martinus Nijhoff, 1970), p. 211)

For an attenuated modern version, see the first televised speech delivered from the Sistine Chapel on 27 August 1978 by Pope John Paul I; the pope prayed that families "may be defended from the destructive attitude of sheer pleasure-seeking, which snuffs out life" (*S. F. Chronicle*, 28 August 1978, p. 1).

57   In the early seventeenth century, Samuel Hieron counsels married couples to recite the following prayer before going to bed: "Allay in us all sensual and brutish love, purifying and sanctifying our affections one towards another, that we may in nothing dishonor this honorable state, nor pollute the bed of marriage . . . but may use this thine ordinance in the holy sort, that carnal lusts may be slaked and subdued, nor increased or inflamed thereby" (*A Helpe Unto Devotion*, 3d edn (London: H.L., 1611), p. 411).

58   *A Discourse of Marriage and Wiving* (London, 1620), quoted in Ronald Mushat Frye, "The Teachings of Classical Puritanism on Conjugal Love," *Studies in the Renaissance* 2 (1955): 156–7.

59   William Whately, *A Bride-bush* (London, 1619), quoted in Frye, p. 156.

60   Noonan, p. 79.

61   A major textual crux, and I have taken the liberty, for the sake of clarity and brevity, to depart from Ridley's reading which is as follows:

> the young affects
> In my defunct, and proper satisfaction.

As Ridley says, "after all the discussion, Othello's meaning is moderately clear. He is too mature to be subjugated by physical desire"; but he goes on to read *proper* as "justifiable," where I would read it as "my own." Ridley's *moderately* should be emphasized.

62   Yet another crux: the Quarto reads "very quality" instead of "utmost pleasure." I find the latter more powerful and persuasive, particularly in the context of Desdemona's further mention (l. 255) of "The rites for which I love him."

Iago twice echoes Desdemona's declaration: "It was a violent commencement in her, and thou shalt see an answerable sequestration" (1.3.342–3) and again "Mark me with what violence she first loved the Moor" (2.1.221).

63   Desdemona is, in effect, a kind of mirror reversal of Cordelia: where the latter is doomed in the first act of the play by her refusal to declare her love, the former is doomed precisely for such a declaration.

Professor Spivack, along with most critics of the play, sees Iago as the enemy of the religious bond in marriage (pp. 49–50); I would argue that it is precisely the nature of this bond, as defined by rigorists, that torments Othello.

64   On "property" see Kenneth Burke, *A Grammar of Motives* (Berkeley: University of California Press, 1969): "Iago may be considered 'consubstantial' with Othello in that he represents the principles of jealousy implicit in Othello's delight in Desdemona as a private spiritual possession. Iago, to arouse Othello, must talk a language that Othello knows as well as he, a language implicit in the nature of Othello's love as the idealization of his private property in Desdemona. This language is the dialectical opposite of Othello's; but it so thoroughly shares a common ground with Othello's language that its insinuations are never for one moment irrelevant to Othello's thinking. Iago must be cautious in leading Othello to believe them as true: but Othello never for a moment doubts them as *values*" (p. 414). As so often happens, I discovered that Burke's brilliant sketch had anticipated the shape of

much of my argument. Burke has an essay on the ritual structure of the play in *Hudson Review* 4 (1951): 165–203.

65   I have read two powerful unpublished essays that analyze the male sexual anxieties in the play at a level prior to or beneath the social and doctrinal one discussed here: Edward Snow, "On the Language of Sexual Pathology in *Othello*" and C. L. Barber, "'I'll pour this pestilence into his ear'; *Othello* as a Development from Hamlet."

66   In act 4, Othello had first thought of poisoning Desdemona and then was persuaded by Iago to "strangle her in her bed, even the bed she hath contaminated" (4.1.203–4). The blood he fantasizes about later may be simply an expression of vionlence (as he had earlier declared, "I will chop her into messes" [4.1.196]), but it is tempting to see it as a projection of the blood that marked her loss of virginity and hence, in his disturbed formulation, as "lust's blood." For a sensitive exploration of the anxiety over virginity, staining, and impotence in *Othello*, see Stanley Cavell, "Epistemology and Tragedy: A Reading of *Othello*," *Daedalus* 108 (1979): 27–43.

67   Like Oedipus, Othello cannot escape the fact that it is he who has committed the crime and must be punished.

We should, in all fairness, call attention to the fact that Othello in the end views his wife as "chaste," but the language in which he does so reinforces the orthodox condemnation of pleasure:

> cold, cold my girl,
> Even like thy chastity.
> (5.2.276–7)

Indeed the identification of the coldness of death with marital chastity seems to me a *confirmation* of the necrophilic fantasy.

68   Shakespeare's talent for entering into the consciousness of others and giving supreme expression to incompatible perspectives has been a major preoccupation of criticism since Coleridge and Keats. For a recent exploration, see Norman Rabkin's concept of "complementarity": *Shakespeare and the Common Understanding* (New York: Free Press, 1967).

In *The Anxiety of Influence* (New York: Oxford University Press, 1973), Harold Bloom remarks, "Shakespeare is the largest instance in the language of a phenomenon that stands outside the concern of this book: the absolute absorption of the precursor" (p. 11).

69   "Of Repentance," in *The Complete Essays of Montaigne*, trans. Donald M. Frame (Stanford: Stanford University Press, 1958), pp. 610–11. It is hardly irrelevant for our purposes that Montaigne describes this method in an essay in which he rejects the confessional system.

70   On pleasure and the threat to established order, see Georges Bataille, *Death and Sensuality: A Study of Eroticism and the Taboo* (New York: Walker & Co., 1962), and Mikhail Bakhtin, *Rabelais and His World*, trans. Helene Iswolsky (Cambridge, Mass.: MIT Press, 1968).

See also Herbert Marcuse, *Eros and Civilization* (New York: Random House, 1955); Michel Foucault, *Discipline and Punish*; Leo Bersani, *A Future for Asyanax: Character and Desire in Literature* (Boston: Little, Brown and Company, 1976).

In work in progress, Jonathan Crewe of Berkeley is investigating comparable issues in the work of Thomas Nashe.

8

SHAKESPEARE AND THE EXORCISTS

Between the spring of 1585 and the summer of 1586, a group of English Catholic priests led by the Jesuit William Weston, alias Father Edmunds, conducted a series of spectacular exorcisms, principally in the house of a recusant gentleman, Sir George Peckham of Denham, Buckinghamshire. The priests were outlaws – by an act of 1585 the mere presence in England of a Jesuit or seminary priest constituted high treason – and those who sheltered them were guilty of a felony, punishable by death. Yet the exorcisms, though clandestine, drew large crowds, almost certainly in the hundreds, and must have been common knowledge to hundreds more. In 1603, long after the arrest and punishment of those involved, Samuel Harsnett, then chaplain to the bishop of London, wrote a detailed account of the cases, based on sworn statements taken from four of the demoniacs and one of the priests. It has been recognized since the eighteenth century that Shakespeare was reading Harsnett's book, *A Declaration of Egregious Popish Impostures*, as he was writing *King Lear*.[1]

The relation between these two texts enables us to glimpse with unusual clarity and precision the institutional negotiation and exchange of social energy. The link between *King Lear* and *A Declaration of Egregious Popish Impostures* has been known for centuries, but the knowledge has remained almost entirely inert, locked in the conventional pieties of source study. From Harsnett, we are told, Shakespeare borrowed the names of the foul fiends by whom Edgar, in his disguise as the bedlam beggar Poor Tom, claims to be possessed. From Harsnett too the playwright derived some of the language of madness, several of the attributes of hell, and a number of colorful adjectives. These and other possible borrowings have been carefully cataloged, but the question of their significance has been not only unanswered but, until recently, unasked.[2] For a long time the prevailing model for the study of literary sources, a model in effect parceled out between the old historicism and the new criticism, blocked such a question. As a freestanding, self-sufficient, disinterested art work produced by a solitary genius, *King Lear* has only an accidental relation to its sources: they provide a glimpse of the "raw material" that the artist fashioned. Insofar as this "material" is taken

This chapter was first published in this form in *Shakespearean Negotiations* (1988, pp. 94–128).

seriously at all, it is as part of the work's "historical background," a phrase that reduces history to a decorative setting or a convenient, well-lighted pigeonhole. But once the differentiations on which this model is based begin to crumble, then source study is compelled to change its character: history cannot simply be set against literary texts as either stable antithesis or stable background, and the protective isolation of those texts gives way to a sense of their interaction with other texts and hence of the permeability of their boundaries. "When I play with my cat," writes Montaigne, "who knows if I am not a pastime to her more than she is to me?"[3] When Shakespeare borrows from Harsnett, who knows if Harsnett has not already, in a deep sense, borrowed from Shakespeare's theater what Shakespeare borrows back? Whose interests are served by the borrowing? And is there a larger cultural text produced by the exchange?

Such questions do not lead, for me at least, to the *O altitudo!* of radical indeterminacy. They lead rather to an exploration of the institutional strategies in which both *King Lear* and Harsnett's *Declaration* are embedded. These strategies, I suggest, are part of an intense and sustained struggle in late sixteenth- and early seventeenth-century England to redefine the central values of society. Such a redefinition entailed transforming the prevailing standards of judgment and action, rethinking the conceptual categories by which the ruling elites constructed their world and which they attempted to impose on the majority of the population. At the heart of this struggle, which eventuated in a murderous civil war, was the definition of the sacred, a definition that directly involved secular as well as religious institutions, since the legitimacy of the state rested explicitly on its claim to a measure of sacredness. What is the sacred? Who defines and polices its boundaries? How can society distinguish between legitimate and illegitimate claims to sacred authority? In early modern England rivalry among elites competing for the major share of authority was characteristically expressed not only in parliamentary factions but also in bitter struggles over religious doctrine and practice.

Harsnett's *Declaration* is a weapon in one such struggle, the attempt by the established and state-supported Church of England to eliminate competing religious authorities by wiping out pockets of rivalrous charisma. Charisma, in Edward Shils's phrase, is "awe-arousing centrality,"[4] the sense of breaking through the routine into the realm of the "extraordinary" to make direct contact with the ultimate, vital sources of legitimacy, authority, and sacredness. Exorcism was for centuries one of the supreme manifestations in Latin Christianity of this charisma: "In the healing of the possessed," Peter Brown writes, "the *praesentia* of the saints was held to be registered with unfailing accuracy, and their ideal power, their *potentia*, shown most fully and in the most reassuring manner."[5] Reassuring, that is, not only or even primarily to the demoniac but to the community of believers who bore witness to the ritual and, indeed, through their tears and prayers and thanksgiving, participated in it. For unlike the sorcerer who practiced his art most frequently in the dark corners of the land, in remote rural hamlets and isolated cottages, the charismatic healer depended upon an audience: the great exorcisms of the late Middle Ages and early Renaissance took place at the heart of cities, in churches packed with spectators.

"Great troupes did daily flock thither," writes the Dominican exorcist Sebastian Michaelis about a series of exorcisms he conducted in Aix-en-Provence in the early seventeenth century, and they were, he argues, deeply moved by what they witnessed. Thus, for example, from the body of the young nun Louise, the demon Verrine cried out "with great and ghastly exclamations" that heretics and sinners would be deprived of the vision of God "for ever, for ever, for ever, for ever, for ever." The spectators were so "affrighted" with these words "that there gushed from their eyes abundance of tears, when they called to remembrance their offences which they had committed."[6]

As voluminous contemporary accounts declare, then, exorcisms were moving testimonials to the power of the true faith. But by the late sixteenth century in Protestant England neither the *praesentia* nor the *potentia* of the exorcist was reassuring to religious authorities, and the Anglican church had no desire to treat the urban masses to a spectacle whose edifying value had been called into question. Moving testimonials extorted from the devil himself – praise of the Virgin, awe in the presence of the Eucharist, acknowledgment of the authority of the pope – now seemed both fraudulent and treasonous, and the danger was as great when it came not from a Catholic healer but from a stubbornly nonconforming Protestant. Although the latter did not celebrate the power of the Virgin – when someone tried to invoke Mary's name at a Protestant exorcism, the presiding exorcist sternly rebuked him, "for there is no other name under Heaven, whereby we may challenge Salvation, but th' only name of Jesus Christ"[7] – he exalted the power of fasting and prayer and made it clear that this power did not depend upon a state-sponsored ecclesiastical hierarchy. The authorities could easily close the cathedrals to such sedition, but even relatively small assemblies in obscure private houses far from the cities had come to represent a threat.

In the *Declaration* Harsnett specifically attacks exorcism as practiced by Jesuits, but he had earlier leveled the same charges at a Puritan exorcist. And he does so not, as we might expect, to claim a monopoly on the practice for the Anglican Church but to expose exorcism itself as a fraud. On behalf of established religious and secular authority, Harsnett wishes to cap permanently the great rushing geysers of charisma released in rituals of exorcism. Spiritual *potentia* will henceforth be distributed with greater moderation and control through the whole of the Anglican hierarchy, at whose pinnacle sits the sole legitimate possessor of absolute charismatic authority, the monarch, Supreme Head of the Church in England.

The arguments that Harsnett marshals against exorcism have a rationalistic cast that may mislead us, for despite appearances we are not dealing with the proto-Enlightenment attempt to construct a rational faith. Harsnett denies the presence of the demonic in those whom Father Edmunds claimed to exorcise but finds it in the exorcists themselves: "And who was the devil, the broacher, herald, and persuader of these unutterable treasons, but *Weston* [alias Edmunds] the Jesuit, the chief plotter, and . . . all the holy Covey of the twelve devilish comedians in their several turns: for there was neither devil, nor urchin, nor Elf, but themselves" (pp. 154–5). Hence, writes Harsnett, the "Dialogue between *Edmunds*, & the devil" was in reality a dialogue between "the devil *Edmunds*, and *Edmunds* the devil, for he played both parts himself" (p. 86).

This strategy – the reinscription of evil onto the professed enemies of evil – is one of the characteristic operations of religious authority in the early modern period and has its secular analogues in more recent history when famous revolutionaries are paraded forth to be tried as counter-revolutionaries. The paradigmatic Renaissance instance is the case of the *benandanti*, analyzed brilliantly by the historian Carlo Ginzburg.[8] The *benandanti* were members of a northern Italian folk cult who believed that they went forth seasonally to battle with fennel stalks against their enemies, the witches. If the *benandanti* triumphed, their victory assured the peasants of good harvests; if they lost, the witches would be free to work their mischief. The Inquisition first became interested in the practice in the late sixteenth century; after conducting a series of lengthy inquiries, the Holy Office determined that the cult was demonic and in subsequent interrogations attempted, with some success, to persuade the witch-fighting *benandanti* that they were themselves witches.

Harsnett does not hope to persuade exorcists that they are devils; he wishes to expose their fraudulence and relies on the state to punish them. But he is not willing to abandon the demonic altogether, and it hovers in his work, half accusation, half metaphor, whenever he refers to Father Edmunds or the pope. Satan's function was too important for him to be cast off lightly by the early seventeenth-century clerical establishment. The same state church that sponsored the attacks on superstition in *A Declaration of Egregious Popish Impostures* continued to cooperate, if less enthusiastically than before, in the ferocious prosecutions of witches. These prosecutions, significantly, were handled by the secular judicial apparatus – witchcraft was a criminal offense like aggravated assault or murder – and hence reinforced rather than rivaled the bureaucratic control of authority. The eruption of the demonic into the human world was not denied altogether, but the problem would be processed through the proper secular channels. In cases of witchcraft, the devil was defeated in the courts through the simple expedient of hanging his human agents, not, as in cases of possession, compelled by a spectacular spiritual counterforce to speak out and depart.

Witchcraft then was distinct from possession, and though Harsnett himself is skeptical about accusations of witchcraft, his principal purpose is to expose a nexus of chicanery and delusion in the practice of exorcism.[9] By doing so he hopes to drive the practice out of society's central zone, to deprive it of its prestige, and to discredit its apparent efficacy.[10] In late antiquity, as Peter Brown has demonstrated, exorcism was based on the model of the Roman judicial system: the exorcist conducted a formal *quaestio* in which the demon, under torture, was forced to confess the truth.[11] Now, after more than a millennium, this power would once again be vested solely in the state.

Harsnett's efforts, backed by his powerful superiors, did seriously restrict the practice of exorcism. Canon 72 of the new Church Canons of 1604 ruled that henceforth no minister, unless he had the special permission of his bishop, was to attempt "upon any pretense whatsoever, whether of possession or obsession, by fasting and prayer, to cast out any devil or devils, under pain of the imputation of

imposture or cozenage and deposition from the ministry."[12] Since special permission was rarely, if ever, granted, in effect exorcism had been officially halted.
But it proved easier to drive exorcism from the center to the periphery than to
strip it entirely of its power. Exorcism had been a process of reintegration as well
as a manifestation of authority; as the ethnographer Shirokogorov observed of
the shamans of Siberia, exorcists could "master" harmful spirits and restore
"psychic equilibrium" to whole communities as well as to individuals.[13] The
pronouncements of English bishops could not suddenly banish from the land
inner demons who stood, as Peter Brown puts it, "for the intangible emotional
undertones of ambiguous situations and for the uncertain motives of refractory
individuals."[14] The possessed gave voice to the rage, anxiety, and sexual frustration that built up easily in the authoritarian, patriarchal, impoverished, and
plague-ridden world of early modern England. The Anglicans attempted to
dismantle a corrupt and inadequate therapy without effecting a new and successful cure. In the absence of exorcism Harsnett could offer the possessed only
the slender reed of Jacobean medicine; if the recently deciphered journal of the
Buckinghamshire physician Richard Napier is at all representative, doctors in the
period struggled to treat a significant number of cases of possession.[15]

But for Harsnett the problem does not really exist, for he argues that the great
majority of cases of possession are either fraudulent or subtly called into existence
by the ritual designed to treat them. Eliminate the cure and you eliminate the
disease. He is forced to concede that at some distant time possession and exorcism
were authentic, for Christ himself had driven a legion of unclean spirits out of a
possessed man and into the Gadarene swine (Mark 5:1–19); but the age of miracles
has passed, and corporeal possession by demons is no longer possible. The spirit
abroad is "the spirit of illusion" (*Discovery*, p. A3). Whether they profess to be
Catholics or Calvinists does not matter; all modern exorcists practice the same
time-honored trade: "the feat of juggling and deluding the people by counterfeit
miracles" (*Discovery*, p. A2). Exorcists sometimes contend, Harsnett acknowledges, that the casting out of devils is not a miracle but a wonder – "*mirandum &
non miraculum*" – but "both terms spring from one root of wonder or marvel: an
effect which a thing strangely done doth procure in the minds of the beholders,
as being above the reach of nature and reason" (*Discovery*, p. A4[r–v]).

The significance of exorcism, then, lies not in any intrinsic quality of the ritual or
in the character of the marks of possession but in the impression made upon the
minds of the spectators. In *The Discovery of Witchcraft* (1584), a remarkable book
that greatly influenced Harsnett, Reginald Scot detailed some of the means used
to shape this impression: the cunning manipulation of popular superstitions; the
exploitation of grief, fear, and credulity; the skillful handling of illusionistic
devices developed for the stage; the blending of spectacle and commentary; the
deliberate arousal of anxiety coupled with the promise to allay it. Puritan
exorcists throw themselves into histrionic paroxysms of prayer; Catholic exorcists
deploy holy water, smoldering brimstone, and sacred relics. They seem utterly
absorbed in the plight of the wretches who writhe in spectacular contortions,
vomit pins, display uncanny strength, foam at the mouth, cry out in weird voices.
But all of this apparent absorption in the supernatural crisis is an illusion; there is

nothing real out there on the bed, in the chair, on the pulpit. The only serious action is transpiring in the minds of the audience.

Hence the exorcists take care, notes Harsnett, to practice their craft only when there is "a great assembly gathered together," and the ritual is then explicitly presented to this assembly with a formal prologue:

> The company met, the *Exorcists* do tell them, *what a work of God they have in hand,* and after a long discourse, *how Sathan doth afflict the parties,* and *what strange things they shall see*: the said parties are brought forth, as it were a Bear to the stake, and being either bound in a chair, or otherwise held fast, they fall to their fits, and play their pranks point by point exactly, according as they have been instructed. (*Discovery,* p. 62)

What seems spontaneous is in fact carefully scripted, from the shaping of audience expectations to the rehearsal of the performers. Harsnett grants that to those who suspect no fraud the effect is extraordinarily powerful: "They are cast thereby into a wonderful astonishment" (*Discovery,* p. 70). Aroused by wonder to a heightened state of both attention and suggestibility, the beholders are led to see significance in the smallest gestures of the possessed and to apply that significance to their own lives. But the whole moving process is a dangerous fraud that should be exposed and punished in the courts.

To substantiate these charges the English church needed, in the language of spy stories, to "turn" one of the participants in the spectacle of possession and exorcism. In the mid-1590s the authorities were alerted to the activities of a charismatic Puritan healer named John Darrel. Through fasting and prayer he had helped to exorcise one Thomas Darling, popularly known as the Boy of Burton, and had then gone on to a still greater success in a case of mass possession, known as the Seven in Lancashire. Alarmed by this success, the authorities in 1598 found what they were looking for: William Sommers, aged twenty-one, an unstable musician's apprentice in Nottingham who was being exorcized by Darrel in a series of spectacular spiritual encounters. Under great pressure Sommers confessed to imposture and exposed – or claimed to expose – Darrel's secret methods: "As I did use any of the said gestures," testified Sommers, recalling his first manifestation in Nottingham of the symptoms of possession,

> Oh would M. Darrell say, to the standers by: see you not how he doth thus, and thus? These things signify that such and such sins do reign in this town. They also that were present having heard M. Darrell, would as I tossed with my hands, and tumbled up and down upon my bed presently collect and say: oh, he doth so for this sin, and so for that sin, whereby it came to pass, that I could do nothing in any of my fits, either that night or the day after, either stir my head, or any part of my body: look merrily, or sadly, sit or lie, speak or be silent, open or shut mine eyes, but some would still make an interpretation of it: as to be done by the Devil in me, to declare such sins in Nottingham, as they themselves imagined. (*Discovery,* p. 117)

Darrel denied ever offering an interpretation of Sommer's gestures, but he confirmed the nature of the performance:

This evening, he acted many sins by signs & gestures, most lively representing & shadowing, them out unto us: as namely brawling, quarreling, fighting, swearing, robbing by the highways, picking and cutting of purses, burglary, whoredom, pride in men and women, hypocrisy, sluggishness in hearing of the word, drunkenness, gluttony, also dancing with the toys thereunto belonging, the manner of Antic dancers, the games of dicing and carding, the abuse of the Viol, with other instruments. At the end of sundry of these, he laughed exceedingly, diverse times clapping his hands on his thighs for joy: percase to shadow out the delight, that both himself, and, sinners take in their sins. And at the end of some of them, as killing and stealing, he showed how he brought them to the Gallows, making a sign thereof. (*Discovery*, pp. 118–19)

According to Harsnett, on the Sunday following this display one of Darrel's colleagues delivered from the pulpit an "authentical reading" of the "dumb show," and this reading was in turn followed by a popular ballad: a campaign, in short, to extend the exorcist's influence beyond the immediate circle of beholders to both the elite and the masses. Harsnett, in response, participates in a massive counter-campaign to destroy this influence. Hounding or imprisoning Darrel was not enough, for persecution could easily heighten his popular appeal, and even were he conveniently to disappear, he would be succeeded by others. The exorcist had to be attacked where he had his power: in the minds of beholders or potential beholders.

Accounts of exorcism in the late sixteenth and early seventeenth centuries make it clear that the spectacle of the symptoms of demonic possession had a profoundly disturbing effect on those who witnessed them. The spectacle was evidently more than that of physical or psychic anguish; after all, the men and women of this period would have been accustomed and perhaps hardened to the sight of abject misery. Quite apart from the spectacle of public maimings and executions, an Elizabethan who survived to adolescence must have already been an aficionado of human wretchedness.

Demonic possession was something more: it was utterly strange – a fearful visitation of the perverted spiritual presences of the other world – and at the same time uncannily intimate, for if the demons were exotic tormenters with weird names, the victims were neighbors enduring their trials in altogether familiar surroundings. Hence the testimony taken from those who witnessed the sufferings combines the homely and the bizarre: an evil spirit that appeared in Suffolk became "a thick dark substance about a foot high, like to a sugar loaf, white on the top";[16] young Mary Glover's voice sounded to one witness like "the hissing of a violent *Squib*," to another like a "*Hen* that hat the *squack*," to a third like "the loathsome noise that a *Cat* maketh forcing to cast her gorge";[17] William Sommer's "entrails shot up & down like a weavers shuttle."[18] Sommers's cries seemed unutterably strange – he shrieked "with 3 several voices so hideously, and so terribly," a surgeon reports, "as they were not like any human creature" – but each of the witnesses seems to have tried immediately to place the extraordinary events in the context of the familiar. William Aldred, a preacher, reports that he stood in a crowd of about one hundred fifty persons and watched Sommers having his fits. What he noticed was Darrel praying and preaching; "then the whole congregation breaking their hitherto continued silence cried out all at once as it were with one voice unto the Lord, to relieve the distressed person: and within a quarter of an hour, or thereabouts it pleased God to hear their prayers." Joan Pie, the wife of Nottingham baker Robert Pie, also saw the fits; what she noticed was that suddenly Sommers "was plucked round upon a heap, as though his body had lain like a great brown loaf." Richard Mee, butcher, remarked that Sommers suddenly screeched "like a swine when he is in sticking."[19]

The domestication of the demonic (a zany Elizabethan version of *What Do People Do All Day?*) only serves to intensify for most of the witnesses the wonder of the supernatural visitation. Harsnett's task is to demolish this experience of wonder; he seeks to shine the sharp, clear light of ridicule on the exorcist's mysteries and thus to expose them as shabby tricks. Among the demoniac's most frightening symptoms was a running lump – variously described as resembling a kitten, a mouse, a halfpenny white loaf, a goose egg, a French walnut, and a hazelnut – that could be seen under the coverlet, moving across his body as he lay in a trance. One of the bystanders, apparently less awestruck than the rest, impulsively pounced on the lump and found that he had seized Sommers's hand. In his confession Sommers confirmed that he achieved his effect by no more complicated means than moving his fingers and toes under the coverlet. It seems impossible for this miserable expedient to produce so much as a frisson, but a skeptical witness, quoted by Harsnett, tried it out at home: "And it fell out to be so agreeable with that which the boy did, as my wife being in bed with me, was on the sudden in great fear, that *Somers* spirit had followed me" (*Discovery*, p. 240).

Held up to the light, the devil's coin is a pathetic counterfeit, fit only to frighten women and boys. Yet Harsnett is not content simply to publish Sommers's confession of fraud, in part, perhaps, because there was reason to believe that the confession was forced, in part because even if Sommers were proven to be a mere actor, other demoniacs clearly believed in all sincerity that they were possessed by devils. Moreover, the polemic had to be conducted with an odd blend of rhetorical violence and doctrinal caution. "If neither possession, nor witchcraft (contrary to that hath been so long generally & confidently affirmed)," wrote Darrel in his own defense, "why should we think that there are Devils? If no Devils, no God."[20]

No one in the Anglican church was prepared to deny the existence of Satan, any more than they were prepared to deny the existence of God. What role did Satan play then in the fraudulent dramas in which his name figured so prominently? In the case of Catholic exorcists, Harsnett is prepared to locate the demonic in the very figures who profess themselves to be the agents of God:

> Dissemblers, jugglers, impostors, players with God, his son, his angels, his saints: devisers of new devils, feigned tormentors of spirits, usurpers of the key of the bottomless pit, whippers, scourgers, batfoulers of fiends, Pandars, Ganimedeans, enhancers of lust, deflowerers of virgins, defilers of houses, uncivil, unmanly, unnatural venereans, offerers of their own mass to supposed devils, depravers of their own relics, applying them to unspeakable, detestable, monstrous deformities: prostituters of all the rites, ornaments, and ceremonies of their Church to impure

villainies: profaners of all parts of the service, worship, and honour of God: violators of tombs, sacrilegious, blasphemers of God, the blessed Trinity, and the virgin *Mary*, in the person of a counterfeit devil: seducers of subjects, plotters, conspirators, contrivers of bloody & detestable treasons, against their anointed Sovereign: it would pose all hell to sample them with such another dozen. (*Declaration*, pp. 160–1)

In short, they were Jesuits. But Darrel was a Protestant and, by all accounts, a man of austere and upright life. If he could not be portrayed as the devil incarnate, where was the devil to be found? One answer, proposed by Harsnett's allies John Deacon and John Walker, was that Satan could produce the *illusion* of demonic possession.

> The *Devil* (being always desirous to work among the dear children of *God* the greatest *disturbance* that may be, and finding withal some such lewd disposed *person* as is naturally inclined to all manner of *knaveries*) he taketh the opportunity of so fit a *subject*, and worketh so cunningly upon the *corruption* of *that lewd persons nature*, as the *party* himself is easily brought to believe, and to bear others also in hand, that he is (in deed and in truth) *essentially possessed of Satan*.[21]

The problem with this argument is that it undermines the clarity and force of the confession of fraudulence the authorities had worked so hard to obtain. That confession was intended to establish a fixed, stable opposition between counterfeit – the false claim of demonic agency – and reality: the unblinking, disenchanted grasp of the mechanics of illusion mongering. Now after all the devil is discovered hovering behind the demoniac's performance. And if the Prince of Darkness is actually present, then the alleged evidence of fraudulence need not trouble the exorcist. For as Satan in possessing someone has sought to hide himself under the cover of human agency, so when detected he may wish to convince observers that the signs of possession are counterfeits. "Sathan in his subtlety," argued Darrel, "hath done in the boy some sleight and trifling things, at divers times, of purpose to deceive the beholders, and to bear them in hand, that he did never greater things in him: thereby to induce them to think, that he was a counterfeit" (*Discovery*, p. 231).[22]

If Satan can counterfeit counterfeiting, there can be no definitive confession, and the prospect opens of an infinite regress of disclosure and uncertainty. "How shall I know that this is thou *William Somers*?" asked Darrel, after the boy confessed to fraud. At first Sommers had been possessed only in body; now, said the exorcist, he is "also possessed in soul" (*Discovery*, p. 186). As Harsnett perceives, this "circular folly" at the heart of the practice of exorcism prevents a decisive judicial falsification. What Harsnett needs is not further evidence of fraud in particular cases – for such evidence can always be subverted by the same strategy of demonic doubt – but a counter-strategy to disclose fraudulence *always and everywhere*: in every gesture of the demoniac, in every word and deed of the exorcist. To demystify exorcism definitively, Harsnett must demonstrate not only why the ritual was so empty but why it was so effective, why beholders could be induced to believe that they were witnessing the ultimate confrontation between good and evil, why a few miserable shifts could produce the experience of horror and wonder. He must identify not merely the specific institutional motives behind exorcism – the treasonous designs of the Catholic Church or the seditious mischief of self-styled Protestant saints – but the source of the extraordinary power in exorcism itself, a power that seems to transcend the specific and contradictory ideological designs of its practitioners. He needs an explanatory model, at once metaphor and analytical tool, by which all beholders will see fraud where once they saw God. Harsnett finds that explanatory model in *theater*.[23]

Exorcisms, Harsnett argues, are stage plays, most often tragicomedies, that cunningly conceal their theatrical inauthenticity and hence deprive the spectators of the rational disenchantment that frames the experience of a play. The audience in a theater knows that its misrecognition of reality is temporary, deliberate, and playful; the exorcist seeks to make the misrecognition permanent and invisible. Harsnett is determined to make the spectators see the theater around them, to make them understand that what seems spontaneous is rehearsed, what seems involuntary carefully crafted, what seems unpredictable scripted.

Not all of the participants themselves may fully realize that they are in a stage play. The account in *A Declaration of Egregious Popish Impostures* presents the exorcists, Father Edmunds and his cohorts, as self-conscious professionals and the demoniacs (mostly impressionable young servingwomen and unstable, down-at-heels young gentlemen) as amateurs subtly drawn into the demonic stage business. Those selected to play the possessed in effect learn their roles without realizing at first that they are roles.

The priests begin by talking conspicuously about successful exorcisms abroad and describing in lurid detail the precise symptoms of the possessed. They then await occasions on which to improvise: a servingman "being pinched with penury, & hunger, did lie but a night, or two, abroad in the fields, and being a melancholic person, was scared with lightning, and thunder, that happened in the night, & lo, an evident sign, that the man was possessed" (p. 24); a dissolute young gentleman "had a spice of the *Hysterica passio*" or, as it is popularly called, "the Mother" (p. 25),[24] and that too is a sign of possession. An inflamed toe, a pain in the side, a fright taken from the sudden leaping of a cat, a fall in the kitchen, an intense depression following the loss of a beloved child – all are occasions for the priests to step forward and detect the awful presence of the demonic, whereupon the young "scholars," as Harsnett wryly terms the naive performers, "*frame* themselves jump and fit unto the Priests humors, to mop, mow, jest, rail, rave, roar, commend & discommend, and as the priests would have them, upon fitting occasions (according to the difference of times, places, and comers in) in all things to play the devils accordingly" (p. 38).

To glimpse the designing clerical playwright behind the performance is to transform terrifying supernatural events into a human strategy. One may then glimpse the specific material and symbolic interests served by this particular strategy, above all by its clever disguising of the fact that it is a strategy.

The most obvious means by which the authorities of the English church and state could make manifest the theatricality of exorcism was the command performance: the ability to mime the symptoms at will would, it was argued, decisively prove the possession a counterfeit. Hence we find the performance test frequently applied in investigations of alleged supernatural visitations. In the 1590s, for example, Ann Kerke was accused of bewitching a child to death and casting the child's sister into a fit that closely resembled that of a demoniac: "her mouth being drawn aside like a purse, her teeth gnashing together, her mouth foaming, and her eyes staring."[25] The judge, Lord Anderson, ordered the sister to "show how she was tormented: she said she could not shew it, but when the fit was on her" (p. 100). The reply was taken to be strong corroboration of the authenticity of the charge, and Anne Kerke was hanged.

A similar, if subtler, use of the performance test occurs in the early 1620s. Thomas Perry, known as the Boy of Bilson, would fall into fits upon hearing the opening verse from the Gospel of John; other verses from Scriptures did not have the same effect. Three Catholic priests were called in to exorcise the evil spirit that possessed him. During the boy's fit – watched by a large crowd – one of the priests commanded the devil "to show by the sheet before him, how he would use one dying out of the Roman Catholic Church? who very unwillingly, yet at length obeyed, tossing, plucking, haling, and biting the sheet, that it did make many to weep and cry forth."[26] A similar but still fiercer demonstration was evoked in response to the names Luther, Calvin, and Fox. Then, predictably, the priest commanded the devil "to show what power he had on a good Catholic that died out of mortal sin? he thrust down his arms, trembled, holding down his head, and did no more" (p. 51).[27] The Catholics triumphantly published an account of the case, *A Faithful Relation*.

English officials, understandably annoyed by such propaganda, remanded Perry to the custody of the bishop of Coventry and Lichfield. To test if the boy was authentically possessed or "an execrable wretch, who playest the devils part," the Bishop read aloud the verse that set off the symptoms; the boy fell into fits. When the boy recovered, the bishop told him that he would read the same verse in Greek; once again the boy fell into fits. But in fact the Bishop had not read the correct verse, and the boy had been tricked into performance. Since the Devil was "so ancient a scholar as of almost 6000 years standing" (p. 59), he should have known Greek. The possession was proved to be a counterfeit, and the boy, it is said, confessed that he had been instructed by an old man who promised that he would no longer have to go to school.

The Protestants now produced their own account of the case, *The Boy of Bilson; or, A True Discovery of the Late Notorious Impostures of Certain Romish Priests in Their Pretended Exorcism.* "Although these and the like pranks have been often hissed of[f] the Stage, for stale and gross forgeries," the author declares, since the Catholics have ventured to publish their version, it is necessary to set the record straight. A reader of the Catholic account should understand

> that he hath seen a *Comedy*, wherein the Actors, which present themselves, are these, A crafty *old man*, teaching the feats and pranks of counterfeiting a person *Demoniacal* and possessed of the *Devil*; the next, a most docible, subtle, and expert young *Boy*, far more dextrous in the Practique part, than his Master was in the Theory; after him appear three Romish *Priests*, the Authors of seducement,

conjuring their only imaginary *Devils*, which they brought with them; and lastly, a *Chorus* of credulous people easily seduced, not so much by the subtlety of those *Priests*, as by their own sottishness. (p. 9)

Performance kills belief; or rather acknowledging theatricality kills the credibility of the supernatural. Hence in the case of William Sommers the authorities not only took the demoniac's confession of fraud but also insisted that he perform his simulated convulsions before the mayor and three aldermen of Nottingham. If he could act his symptoms, then the possession would be decisively falsified. Darrel countered that "if he can act them all in such manner and form as is deposed, then he is, either still possessed, or more than a man: for no humans power can do the like."[28] But the officials denied that the original performances themselves, stripped of the awe that the spectators brought to them, were particularly impressive. Sommers's possession, Harsnett had said, was a "dumb show" that depended upon an interpretive supplement, a commentary designed at once to intensify and control the response of the audience by explicating both the significance and the relevance of each gesture. Now the state would in effect seize control of the commentary and thereby alter the spectators' perceptions. Sommers's audience would no longer see a demoniac; they would see someone playing a demoniac. Demonic possession would become theater.

After the civic officials had satisfied themselves that Sommers's possession was a theatrical imposture, an ecclesiastical commission was convened to view a repeat performance. In a bizarre twist, however, Sommers unexpectedly with-drew his confession before the startled commissioners, and he signaled this withdrawal by falling into spectacular fits before the moment appointed for the performance. The commissioners, unprepared to view these convulsions as a deliberate or self-conscious exhibition, declared that they were evidently of supernatural origin. But in less than two weeks, before the mayor and two justices, the wretched Sommers, under renewed state pressure, reaffirmed his confession of fraud, and a few days later he once again "proved" his claim by simulating fits, this time before the assize judge. The next step might have been to ask a court of law to determine whether Sommers's expressly simulated fits were identical to those he underwent when he was not confessing imposture. But the authorities evidently regarded this step, which Darrel himself demanded,[29] as too risky; instead, without calling Sommers to appear, they first obtained a conviction of the exorcist on charges of imposture and then launched a national campaign to persuade the public that possession and exorcism were illicit forms of theater.

Sommers's oscillation between the poles of authenticity and illusion are for Harsnett an emblem of the maddening doubleness implicit in the theatricality of exorcism: its power to impose itself on beholders and its half-terrifying, half-comic emptiness. Exorcists could, of course, react by demonizing the theater: Puritans like Darrel argued at length that the playhouse was Satan's temple, while the Jesuit exorcists operating clandestinely in England implied that theatrical representations of the devil in mystery plays were not mere imitations of reality but lively images based on a deep bond of resemblance. When in the 1580s a devil possessing Sara Williams refused to tell his name, the exorcist, according to the Catholic *Book of Miracles*, "caused to be drawn upon a piece of paper, the picture of a vice in a play, and the same to be burned with hallowed brimstone, whereat the devil cried out as being grievously tormented."[30] Harsnett remarks in response that "it was a pretty part in the old Church-plays, when the nimble Vice would skip up nimbly like Jacke an Apes into the devils neck, and ride the devil a course, and belabour him with his wooden dagger, til he made him roar, whereat the people would laugh to see the devil so vice-haunted" (pp. 114–15). Sara's devils, he concludes contemptuously, "be surely some of those old vice-haunted cashiered wooden-beaten devils, that were wont to frequent the stages ... who are so scared with the *Idea* of a vice, & a dagger, as they durst never since look a paper-vice in the face" (p. 115). For Harsnett the attempt to demonize the theater merely exposes the theatricality of the demonic; once we acknowledge this theatricality, he suggests, we can correctly perceive the actual genre of the performance: not tragedy but farce.

The theatricality of exorcism, to which the *Declaration* insistently calls attention, has been noted repeatedly by modern ethnographers who do not share Harsnett's reforming zeal or his sense of outrage.[31] In an illuminating study of possession among the Ethiopians of Gondar, Michel Leiris notes that the healer carefully instructs the *zâr*, or spirit, who has seized on someone how to behave: the types of cries appropriate to the occasion, the expected violent contortions, the "decorum," as Harsnett would put it, of the trance state.[32] The treatment is in effect an initiation into the performance of the symptoms, which are then cured precisely because they conform to the stereotype of the healing process. One must not conclude, writes Leiris, that there are no "real" – that is, sincerely experienced – cases of possession, for many of the patients (principally young women and slaves) seem genuinely ill, but at the same time no cases are exempt from artifice (pp. 27–8). Between authentic possession, spontaneous and involuntary, and inauthentic possession, simulated to provide a show or to extract some material or moral benefit, there are so many subtle shadings that it is impossible to draw a firm boundary (pp. 94–5). Possession in Gondar *is* theater, but theater that cannot confess its own theatrical nature, for this is not "theater played" (*théâtre joué*) but "theater lived" (*théâtre vécu*), lived not only by the spirit-haunted actor but by the audience. Those who witness a possession may at any moment be themselves possessed, and even if they are untouched by the *zâr*, they remain participants rather than passive spectators. For the theatrical performance is not shielded from them by an impermeable membrane; possession is extraordinary but not marginal, a heightened but not separate state. In possession, writes Leiris, the collective life itself takes the form of theater (p. 96).

Precisely those qualities that fascinate and charm the ethnographer disgust the embattled clergyman: where Leiris can write of "authentic" possession in the unspoken assurance that none of his readers actually believe in the existence of "zârs," Harsnett, granted no such assurance and culturally threatened by the alternative vision of reality, struggles to prove that possession is by definition inauthentic; where the former sees a complex ritual integrated into the social process, the latter sees "a *Stygian* comedy to make silly people afraid" (p. 69);

where the former sees the theatrical expression of collective life, the latter sees the theatrical promotion of specific and malevolent institutional interests. And where Leiris's central point is that possession is a theater that does not confess its own theatricality, Harsnett's concern is to enforce precisely such a confession: the last 112 pages of *A Declaration of Egregious Popish Impostures* reprint the "several Examinations, and confessions of the parties pretended to be possessed, and dispossessed by *Weston* the Jesuit, and his adherents: set down word for word as they were taken upon oath before her Majesty's Commissioners for causes Ecclesiastical" (p. 172). These transcripts prove, according to Harsnett, that the solemn ceremony of exorcism is a "play of sacred miracles," a "wonderful pageant" (p. 2), a "devil Theater" (p. 106).

The confession of theatricality, for Harsnett, demolishes exorcism. Theater is not the disinterested expression of the popular spirit but the indelible mark of falsity, tawdriness, and rhetorical manipulation. And these sinister qualities are rendered diabolical by the very concealment of theatricality that so appeals to Leiris. The spectators do not know that they are responding to a powerful, if sleazy, tragicomedy; their tears and joy, their transports of "commiseration and compassion" (p. 74), are rendered up not to a troupe of acknowledged players but to seditious Puritans or to the supremely dangerous Catholic Church. For Harsnett the theatrical seduction is not merely a Jesuitical strategy; it is the essence of the church itself: Catholicism is a "Mimic superstition" (p. 20).[33]

Harsnett's response is to try to drive the Catholic Church into the theater, just as during the Reformation Catholic clerical garments – the copes and albs and amices and stoles that were the glories of medieval textile crafts – were sold to the players. An actor in a history play taking the part of an English bishop could conceivably have worn the actual robes of the character he was representing. Far more than thrift is involved here. The transmigration of a single ecclesiastical cloak from the vestry to the wardrobe may stand as an emblem of the more complex and elusive institutional exchanges that are my subject: a sacred sign, designed to be displayed before a crowd of men and women, is emptied, made negotiable, traded from one institution to another. Such exchanges are rarely so tangible; they are not usually registered in inventories, not often sealed with a cash payment. Nonetheless they occur constantly, for through institutional negotiation and exchange differentiated expressive systems, distinct cultural discourses, are fashioned.

What happens when the piece of cloth is passed from the Church to the playhouse? A consecrated object is reclassified, assigned a cash value, transferred from a sacred to a profane setting, deemed suitable for the stage. The theater company is willing to pay for the object not because it contributes to naturalistic representation but because it still bears a symbolic value, however attenuated. On the bare Elizabethan stage costumes were particularly important – companies were willing to pay more for a good costume than for a good play – and that importance in turn reflected the culture's fetishistic obsession with clothes as a mark of status and degree. And if for the theater the acquisition of clerical garments was a significant appropriation of symbolic power, why would the Church part with that power? Because for the Anglican polemicists, as for a long

tradition of moralists in the West, the theater signifies the unscrupulous manipulation for profit of popular faith; the cynical use of setting and props to generate
unthinking consent; the external and trivialized staging of what should be deeply
inward; the tawdry triumph of spectacle over reason; the evacuation of the divine
presence from religious mystery, leaving only vivid but empty ceremonies; the
transformation of faith into bad faith.[34] Hence selling Catholic vestments to the
players was a form of symbolic aggression: a vivid, wry reminder that Catholicism, as Harsnett puts it, is "the Pope's playhouse."[35]

This blend of appropriation and aggression is similarly at work in the transfer of
possession and exorcism from sacred to profane representation. *A Declaration of
Egregious Popish Impostures* takes pains to identify exorcism not merely with "the
theatrical" – a category that scarcely exists for Harsnett – but with the actual
theater; at issue is not so much a metaphorical concept as a functioning institution. For if Harsnett can drive exorcism into the theater – if he can show that the
stately houses in which the rituals were performed were playhouses, that the
sacred garments were what he calls a "lousy holy wardrobe" (p. 78), that the
terrifying writhings were simulations, that the uncanny signs and wonders were
contemptible stage tricks, that the devils were the "cashiered wooden-beaten"
Vices from medieval drama (p. 115), and that the exorcists were "vagabond
players, that coast from Town to Town" (p. 149) – then the ceremony and
everything for which it stands will, as far as he is concerned, be emptied out. And
with this emptying out Harsnett will have driven exorcism from the center to the
periphery – in the case of London quite literally to the periphery, where
increasingly stringent urban regulation had already driven the public playhouses.

In this symbolically charged zone of pollution, disease, and licentious entertainment Harsnett seeks to situate the practice of exorcism.[36] What had once
occurred in solemn glory at the very center of the city would now be staged
alongside the culture's other vulgar spectacles and illusions. Indeed the sense of
the theater's tawdriness, marginality, and emptiness – the sense that everything
the players touch is rendered hollow – underlies Harsnett's analysis not only of
exorcism but of the entire Catholic Church. Demonic possession is a particularly
attractive cornerstone for such an analysis, not only because of its histrionic
intensity but because the theater itself is by its nature bound up with possession.
Harsnett did not have to believe that the cult of Dionysus out of which the Greek
drama evolved was a cult of possession; even the ordinary and familiar theater of
his own time depended upon the apparent transformation of the actor into the
voice, the actions, and the face of another.

II

With his characteristic opportunism and artistic self-consciousness, Shakespeare
in his first known play, *The Comedy of Errors* (1590), was already toying with the
connection between theater, illusion, and spurious possession. Antipholus of
Syracuse, accosted by his twin's mistress, imagines that he is encountering the
devil: "Sathan, avoid. I charge thee tempt me not" (4.3.48). The Ephesian

Antipholus's wife, Adriana, dismayed by the apparently mad behavior of her husband, imagines that the devil has possessed him, and she dutifully calls in an exorcist: "Good Doctor Pinch, you are a conjurer,/Establish him in his true sense again." Pinch begins the solemn ritual:

> I charge thee, Sathan, hous'd within this man,
> To yield possession to my holy prayers,
> And to thy state of darkness hie thee straight:
> I conjure thee by all the saints in heaven!
> (4.4.54–7)

But he is interrupted with a box on the ears from the outraged husband: "Peace, doting wizard, peace! I am not mad." For the exorcist, such denials only confirm the presence of an evil spirit: "the fiend is strong within him" (4.4.107). At the scene's end, Antipholus is dragged away to be "bound and laid in some dark room."

The false presumption of demonic possession in *The Comedy of Errors* is not the result of deception; it is an instance of what Shakespeare's source calls a "suppose" – an attempt to make sense of a series of bizarre actions gleefully generated by the comedy's screwball coincidences. Exorcism is the straw people clutch at when the world seems to have gone mad. In *Twelfth Night*, written some ten years later, Shakespeare's view of exorcism, though still comic, has darkened. Possession now is not a mistaken "suppose" but a fraud, a malicious practical joke played on Malvolio. "Pray God he be not bewitch'd!" (3.4.101) Maria piously exclaims at the sight of the cross-gartered, leering gull, and when he is out of earshot, Fabian laughs: "If this were play'd upon a stage now, I could condemn it as an improbable fiction" (3.4.127–8).[37] The theatrical self-consciousness is intensified when Feste the clown is brought in to conduct a mock exorcism: "I would I were the first that ever dissembled in such a gown" (4.2.5–6), he remarks sententiously as he disguises himself as Sir Topas the curate. If the jibe had a specific reference for the play's original audience, it would be to the Puritan Darrel, who had only recently been convicted of dissembling in the exorcism of Sommers. Now, the scene would suggest, the tables are being turned on the self-righteous fanatic. "Good Sir Topas," pleads Malvolio, "do not think I am mad; they have laid me here in hideous darkness." "Fie, thou dishonest Sathan!" Feste replies; "I call thee by the most modest terms, for I am one of those gentle ones that will use the devil himself with courtesy" (4.2.29–33).

By 1600, then, Shakespeare had clearly marked out possession and exorcism as frauds, so much so that in *All's Well That Ends Well* a few years later he could casually use the term *exorcist* as a synonym for illusion monger: "Is there no exorcist / Beguiles the truer office of mine eyes?" cries the King of France when Helena, whom he thought dead, appears before him; "Is't real that I see?" (5.3.304–6). When in 1603 Harsnett was whipping exorcism toward the theater, Shakespeare was already at the entrance to the Globe to welcome it.

Given Harsnett's frequent expressions of the "antitheatrical prejudice," this welcome may seem strange, but in fact nothing in *A Declaration of Egregious Popish*

Impostures necessarily implies hostility to the theater as a professional institution. It was Darrel, not Harsnett, who represented an implacable threat to the theater, for where the Anglican polemicist saw the theatrical in the demonic, the Puritan polemicist saw the demonic in the theatrical: "The Devil," wrote Stephen Gosson, "is the efficient cause of plays."[38] Harsnett's work attacks a form of theater that pretends it is not entertainment but sober reality; his polemic virtually depends upon the existence of an officially designated commercial theater, marked off openly from all other forms and ceremonies of public life precisely by virtue of its freely acknowledged fictionality. Where there is no pretense to truth, there can be no *imposture*: this argument permits so ontologically anxious a figure as Sir Philip Sidney to defend poetry – "Now for the poet, he nothing affirms, and therefore never lieth."

In this spirit Puck playfully defends *A Midsummer Night's Dream*:

> If we shadows have offended,
> Think but this, and all is mended,
> That you have but slumb'red here
> While these visions did appear.
> And this weak and idle theme,
> No more yielding but a dream.
>   (5.1.423–8)

With a similarly frank admission of illusion Shakespeare can open the theater to Harsnett's polemic. Indeed, as if Harsnett's momentum carried *him* into the theater along with the fraud he hotly pursues, Shakespeare in *King Lear* stages not only exorcism, but Harsnett *on* exorcism: "Five fiends have been in poor Tom at once: of lust, as Obidicut; Hobbididence, prince of dumbness; Mahu, of stealing; Modo, of murder; Flibbertigibbet, of mopping and mowing, who since possesses chambermaids and waiting-women" (4.1.58–63).[39]

Those in the audience who had read Harsnett's book or heard of the notorious Buckinghamshire exorcisms would recognize in Edgar's lines an odd joking allusion to the chambermaids, Sara and Friswood Williams, and the waiting woman, Ann Smith, principal actors in Father Edmunds's "devil Theater." The humor of the anachronism here is akin to that of the Fool's earlier quip, "This prophecy Merlin shall make, for I live before his time" (3.2.95–6); both sallies of wit show a cheeky self-consciousness that dares deliberately to violate the historical setting to remind the audience of the play's conspicuous doubleness, its simultaneous distance and contemporaneity.

A Declaration of Egregious Popish Impostures supplies Shakespeare not only with an uncanny anachronism but also with the model for Edgar's histrionic disguise. For it is not the *authenticity* of the demonology that the playwright finds in Harsnett – the usual reason for authorial recourse to a specialized source (as, for example, to a military or legal handbook) – but rather the inauthenticity of a theatrical role. Shakespeare appropriates for Edgar a documented fraud, complete with an impressive collection of what the *Declaration* calls "uncouth non-significant names" (p. 46) that have been made up to sound exotic and that carry with them a faint but ineradicable odor of spuriousness.

In Sidney's *Arcadia*, which provided the outline of the Gloucester subplot, the good son, having escaped his father's misguided attempt to kill him, becomes a soldier in another land and quickly distinguishes himself. Shakespeare insists not only on Edgar's perilous fall from his father's favor but upon his marginalization: Edgar becomes the possessed Poor Tom, the outcast with no possibility of working his way back toward the center. "My neighbors," writes John Bunyan in the 1660s, "were amazed at this my great conversion from prodigious profaneness to something like a moral life; and truly so well they might for this my conversion was as great as for a Tom of Bethlem to become a sober man."[40] Although Edgar is only a pretend Tom o' Bedlam and can return to the community when it is safe to do so, the force of Harsnett's argument makes mimed possession even more marginal and desperate than the real thing.

Indeed Edgar's desperation is bound up with the stress of "counterfeiting," a stress he has already noted in the presence of the mad and ruined Lear and now, in the lines I have just quoted, feels more intensely in the presence of his blinded and ruined father. He is struggling with the urge to stop playing or, as he puts it, with the feeling that he "cannot daub it further" (4.1.52). Why he does not simply reveal himself to Gloucester at this point is unclear. "And yet I must" is all he says of his continued disguise, as he recites the catalog of devils and leads his despairing father off to Dover Cliff.[41]

The subsequent episode – Gloucester's suicide attempt – deepens the play's brooding upon spurious exorcism. "It is a good *decorum* in a Comedy," writes Harsnett, "to give us empty names for things, and to tell us of strange Monsters within, where there be none" (p. 142); so too the "Miracle-minter" Father Edmunds and his fellow exorcists manipulate their impressionable gulls: "The priests do report often in their patients hearing the dreadful forms, similitudes, and shapes, that the devils use to depart in out of those possessed bodies . . . : and this they tell with so grave a countenance, pathetical terms, and accommodate action, as it leaves a very deep impression in the memory, and fancy of their actors" (pp. 142–3). Thus by the power of theatrical suggestion the anxious subjects on whom the priests work their charms come to believe that they too have witnessed the devil depart in grotesque form from their own bodies, whereupon the priests turn their eyes heavenward and give thanks to the Blessed Virgin. In much the same manner Edgar persuades Gloucester that he stands on a high cliff, and then, after his credulous father has flung himself forward, Edgar switches roles and pretends that he is a bystander who has seen a demon depart from the old man:

> As I stood here below, methought his eyes
> Were two full moons; he had a thousand noses,
> Horns welk'd and waved like the enridged sea.
> It was some fiend; therefore, thou happy father,
> Think that the clearest gods, who make them honors
> Of men's impossibilities, have preserved thee.
>
> (4.6.69–74)

Edgar tries to create in Gloucester an experience of awe and wonder so intense that it can shatter his suicidal despair and restore his faith in the benevolence of the gods: "Thy life's a miracle" (4.6.55), he tells his father.[42] For Shakespeare as for Harsnett this miracle minting is the product of specifically histrionic manipulations; the scene at Dover is a disenchanted analysis of both religious and theatrical illusions. Walking about on a perfectly flat stage, Edgar does to Gloucester what the theater usually does to the audience: he persuades his father to discount the evidence of his senses – "Methinks the ground is even" – and to accept a palpable fiction: "Horrible steep" (4.6.3). But the audience at a play never absolutely accepts such fictions: we enjoy being brazenly lied to, we welcome for the sake of pleasure what we know to be untrue, but we withhold from the theater the simple assent we grant to everyday reality. And we enact this withholding when, depending on the staging, either we refuse to believe that Gloucester is on a cliff above Dover Beach or we realize that what we thought was a cliff (in the convention of theatrical representation) is in reality flat ground.

Hence in the midst of the apparent convergence of exorcism and theater, we return to the difference that enables *King Lear* to borrow comfortably from Harsnett: the theater elicits from us complicity rather than belief. Demonic possession is responsibly marked out for the audience as a theatrical fraud, designed to gull the unsuspecting: monsters such as the fiend with the thousand noses are illusions most easily imposed on the old, the blind, and the despairing; evil comes not from the mysterious otherworld of demons but from this world, the world of court and family intrigue. In *King Lear* there are no ghosts, as there are in *Richard III, Julius Caesar*, or *Hamlet*; no witches, as in *Macbeth*; no mysterious music of departing daemons, as in *Antony and Cleopatra*.

King Lear is haunted by a sense of rituals and beliefs that are no longer efficacious, that have been *emptied out*. The characters appeal again and again to the pagan gods, but the gods remain utterly silent.[43] Nothing answers to human questions but human voices; nothing breeds about the heart but human desires; nothing inspires awe or terror but human suffering and human depravity. For all the invocation of the gods in *King Lear*, it is clear that there are no devils.

Edgar is no more possessed than the sanest of us, and we can see for ourselves that there was no demon standing by Gloucester's side. Likewise Lear's madness has no supernatural origin; it is linked, as in Harsnett, to *hysterica passio*, exposure to the elements, and extreme anguish, and its cure comes at the hands not of an exorcist but of a doctor. His prescription involves neither religious rituals (as in Catholicism) nor fasting and prayer (as in Puritanism) but tranquilized sleep:

> Our foster-nurse of nature is repose,
> The which he lacks; that to provoke in him
> Are many simples operative, whose power
> Will close the eye of anguish.
>
> (4.4.12–15)[44]

King Lear's relation to Harsnett's book is one of reiteration then, a reiteration that signals a deeper and unexpressed institutional exchange. The official church dismantles and cedes to the players the powerful mechanisms of an unwanted and dangerous charisma; in return the players confirm the charge that those mechanisms are theatrical and hence illusory. The material structure of Elizabethan and Jacobean public theaters heightened this confirmation; unlike medieval drama, which was more fully integrated into society, Shakespeare's drama took place in carefully demarcated playgrounds. *King Lear* offers a double corroboration of Harsnett's arguments. Within the play, Edgar's possession is clearly designated as a fiction, and the play itself is bounded by the institutional signs of fictionality: the wooden walls of the play space, payment for admission, known actors playing the parts, applause, the dances that followed the performance.

The theatrical confirmation of the official position is neither superficial nor unstable. And yet, I want now to suggest, Harsnett's arguments are alienated from themselves when they make their appearance on the Shakespearean stage. This alienation may be set in the context of a more general observation: the closer Shakespeare seems to a source, the more faithfully he reproduces it on stage, the more devastating and decisive his transformation of it. Let us take, for a small initial instance, Shakespeare's borrowing from Harsnett of the unusual adjective *corky* – that is, sapless, dry, withered. The word appears in the *Declaration* in the course of a sardonic explanation of why, despite the canonist Mengus's rule that only old women are to be exorcised, Father Edmunds and his crew have a particular fondness for tying in a chair and exorcising young women. Along with more graphic sexual innuendos, Harsnett observes that the theatrical role of a demoniac requires "certain actions, motions, distortions, dislocations, writhings, tumblings, and turbulent passions . . . not to be performed but by suppleness of sinews. . . . It would (I fear me) pose all the cunning Exorcists, that are this day to be found, to teach an old corky woman to writhe, tumble, curvet, and fetch her morris gambols" (p. 23).

Now Shakespeare's eye was caught by the word "corky," and he reproduces it in a reference to old Gloucester. But what had been a flourish of Harsnett's typically bullying comic style becomes part of the horror of an almost unendurable scene, a scene of torture that begins when Cornwall orders his servant to take the captive Gloucester and "Bind fast his corky arms" (3.7.29). The note of bullying humor is still present in the word, but it is present in the character of the torturer.

This one-word instance of repetition as transvaluation may suggest in the smallest compass what happens to Harsnett's work in the course of *Lear*. The *Declaration*'s arguments are loyally reiterated, but in a curiously divided form. The voice of skepticism is assimilated to Cornwall, to Goneril, and above all to Edmund, whose "naturalism" is exposed as the argument of the younger and illegitimate son bent on displacing his legitimate older brother and eventually on destroying his father. The fraudulent possession and exorcism are given to the legitimate Edgar, who is forced to such shifts by the nightmarish persecution directed against him. Edgar adopts the role of Poor Tom not out of a corrupt will to deceive but out of a commendable desire to survive. Modo, Mahu, and the rest are fakes, exactly as Harsnett said they were, but Edgar's impostures are the venial sins of a will to endure. And even "venial sins" is too strong: the clever inventions enable a decent and unjustly persecuted man to live. Similarly, there is no grotesque monster standing on the cliff with Gloucester – there is not even a cliff – but only Edgar, himself hunted down like an animal, trying desperately to save his father from suicidal despair.

All of this has an odd and unsettling resemblance to the situation of the Jesuits in England, if viewed from an unofficial perspective.[45] The resemblance does not necessarily resolve itself into an allegory in which Catholicism is revealed to be the persecuted legitimate elder brother forced to defend himself by means of theatrical illusions against the cold persecution of his skeptical bastard brother Protestantism. But the possibility of such a radical undermining of the orthodox position exists, and not merely in the cool light of our own historical distance. In 1610 a company of traveling players in Yorkshire included *King Lear* and *Pericles* in a repertoire that included a "St. Christopher Play" whose performance came to the attention of the Star Chamber. The plays were performed in the manor house of a recusant couple, Sir John and Lady Julyan Yorke, and the players themselves and their organizer, Sir Richard Cholmeley, were denounced for recusancy by their Puritan neighbor, Sir Posthumus Hoby.[46] It is difficult to resist the conclusion that someone in Stuart Yorkshire believed that *King Lear*, despite its apparent staging of a fraudulent possession, was not hostile, was strangely sympathetic even, to the situation of persecuted Catholics. At the very least, we may suggest, the current of sympathy is enough to undermine the intended effect of Harsnett's *Declaration*: an intensified adherence to the central system of official values. In Shakespeare, the realization that demonic possession is a theatrical imposture leads not to a clarification – the clear-eyed satisfaction of the man who refuses to be gulled – but to a deeper uncertainty, a loss of moorings, in the face of evil.

"Let them anatomize Regan," Lear raves, "see what breeds about her heart. Is there any cause in nature that make these hard hearts?" (3.6.76–8). We know that there is no cause *beyond* nature; the voices of evil in the play – "Thou, Nature, art my goddess"; "What need one?"; "Bind fast his corky arms" – do not well up from characters who are possessed. I have no wish to live in a culture where men believe in devils; I fully grasp that the torturers of this world are all too human. Yet Lear's anguished question insists on the pain this understanding brings, a pain that reaches beyond the king. Is it a relief to understand that the evil was not visited upon the characters by demonic agents but released from the structure of the family and the state by Lear himself?

Edgar's pretended demonic possession, by ironic contrast, is homiletic; the devil compels him to acts of self-punishment, the desperate masochism of the very poor, but not to acts of viciousness. Like the demoniacs who in Harsnett's contemptuous account praise the Mass and the Catholic Church, Poor Tom gives a highly moral performance: "Take heed o' th' foul fiend. Obey thy parents, keep thy word's justice, swear not, commit not with man's sworn spouse, set not thy sweet heart on proud array. Tom's a-cold" (3.4.80–3). Is it a relief to know that Edgar only mimes this little sermon?

All attempts by the characters to explain or relieve their sufferings through the invocation of transcendent forces are baffled. Gloucester's belief in the influence of "these late eclipses in the sun and moon" (1.2.103) is dismissed decisively, even if the spokesman for the dismissal is the villainous Edmund. Lear appeals almost constantly to the gods:

> O Heavens!
> If you do love old men, if your sweet sway
> Allow obedience, if you yourselves are old,
> Make it your cause; send down, and take my part.
>   (2.4.189–92)

But his appeals are left unanswered. The storm in the play seems to several characters to be of more than natural intensity, and Lear above all tries desperately to make it *mean* something (as a symbol of his daughters' ingratitude, a punishment for evil, a sign from the gods of the impending universal judgment), but the thunder refuses to speak. When Albany calls Goneril a "devil" and a "fiend" (4.2.59, 66), we know that he is not identifying her as a supernatural being – it is impossible, in this play, to witness the eruption of the denizens of hell into the human world – just as we know that Albany's prayer for "visible spirits" to be sent down by the heavens "to tame these vild offenses" (4.2.46–47) will be unanswered.

In *King Lear*, as Harsnett says of the Catholic Church, "neither God, Angel, nor devil can be gotten to speak" (p. 169). For Harsnett this silence betokens a liberation from lies; we have learned, as the last sentence of his tract puts it, "to loathe these despicable Impostures and return unto the truth" (*Declaration*, p. 171). But for Shakespeare the silence leads to the desolation of the play's close:

> Lend me a looking-glass,
> If that her breath will mist or stain the stone,
> Why then she lives.
>   (5.3.262–4)

The lines voice a hope that has repeatedly tantalized the audience: a hope that Cordelia will not die, that the play will build toward a revelation powerful enough to justify Lear's atrocious suffering, that we are in the midst of what the Italians called a *tragedia di fin lieto*, that is, a play in which the villains absorb the tragic punishment while the good are wondrously restored.[47] Lear appeals, in effect, to the conventions of this genre. The close of a tragicomedy frequently requires the audience to will imaginatively a miraculous turn of events, often against the evidence of its senses (as when the audience persuades itself that the two actors playing Viola and Sebastian in *Twelfth Night* really *do* look identical, in spite of the ocular proof to the contrary, or when at the close of *The Winter's Tale* the audience accepts the fiction that Hermione is an unbreathing statue in order to experience the wonder of her resurrection). But the close of *King Lear* allows an appeal to such conventions only to reverse them with bitter irony: to believe Cordelia dead, the audience, insofar as it can actually see what is occurring onstage, must work against the evidence of its own senses. After all, the actor's breath would have misted the stone, and the feather held to Cordelia's mouth must have stirred. But we remain convinced that Cordelia is, as Lear first says, "dead as earth."

In the wake of Lear's first attempt to see some sign of life in Cordelia, Kent asks, "Is this the promis'd end?" Edgar echoes the question: "Or image of that horror?" And Albany says, "Fall, and cease!" By itself Kent's question has an oddly literary quality, as if he were remarking on the end of the play, either wondering what kind of ending this is or implicitly objecting to the disastrous turn of events. Edgar's response suggests that the "end" is the end of the world, the Last Judgment, here experienced not as a "promise" – the punishment of the wicked, the reward of the good – but as a "horror." But like Kent, Edgar is not certain about what he is seeing: his question suggests that he may be witnessing not the end itself but a possible "image" of it, while Albany's enigmatic "Fall, and cease!" empties even that image of significance. The theatrical means that might have produced a "counterfeit miracle" out of this moment are abjured; there will be no imposture, no histrionic revelation of the supernatural.

Lear repeats this miserable emptying out of the redemptive hope in his next lines:

> This feather stirs, she lives! If it be so,
> It is a chance which does redeem all sorrows
> That ever I have felt.
>
> (5.3.266–8)

Deeply moved by the sight of the mad king, a nameless gentleman had earlier remarked,

> Thou hast one daughter
> Who redeems nature from the general curse
> Which twain have brought her to.
>
> (4.6.205–7)

Now in Lear's words this vision of universal redemption through Cordelia is glimpsed again, intensified by the king's conscious investment in it.

What would it mean to "redeem" Lear's sorrows? To buy them back from the chaos and brute meaninglessness they now seem to signify? To reward the king with a gift so great that it outweighs the sum of misery in his entire long life? To reinterpret his pain as the necessary preparation – the price to be paid – for a consummate bliss? In the theater such reinterpretation would be represented by a spectacular turn in the plot – a surprise unmasking, a sudden reversal of fortunes, a resurrection – and this dramatic redemption, however secularized, would almost invariably recall the consummation devoutly wished by centuries of Christian believers. This consummation had in fact been represented again and again in medieval Resurrection plays, which offered the spectators ocular proof that Christ had risen.[48] Despite the pre-Christian setting of Shakespeare's play, Lear's craving for just such proof – "This feather stirs, she lives!" – would seem to evoke precisely this theatrical and religious tradition, but only to reveal itself, in C. L. Barber's acute phrase, as "post-Christian."[49] *If it be so:* Lear's sorrows are not redeemed; nothing can turn them into joy, but the forlorn hope of an impossible redemption persists, drained of its institutional and doctrinal significance, empty and vain, cut off even from a theatrical realization, but like the dream of exorcism, ineradicable.

The close of *King Lear* in effect acknowledges that it can never satisfy this dream, but the acknowledgment must not obscure the play's having generated the craving for such satisfaction. That is, Shakespeare does not simply inherit and make use of an anthropological given; rather, at the moment when the official religious and secular institutions are, for their own reasons, abjuring the ritual they themselves once fostered, Shakespeare's theater moves to appropriate it. Onstage the ritual is effectively contained in the ways we have examined, but Shakespeare intensifies as a theatrical experience the need for exorcism, and his demystification of the practice is not identical in its interests to Harsnett's.

Harsnett's polemic is directed toward a bracing anger against the lying agents of the Catholic Church and a loyal adherence to the true established Church of England. He writes as a representative of that true church, and this institutional identity is reinforced by the secular institutional imprimatur on the confessions that are appended to the *Declaration*. The joint religious and secular apparatus works to strip away imposture and discover the hidden reality that is, Harsnett says, the theater. Shakespeare's play dutifully reiterates this discovery: when Lear thinks he has found in Poor Tom "the thing itself," "unaccommodated man," he has in fact found a man playing a theatrical role. But if false religion is theater, and if the difference between true and false religion is the presence of theater, what happens when this difference is enacted in the theater?

What happens, as we have already begun to see, is that the official position is *emptied out*, even as it is loyally confirmed. This "emptying out" resembles Brecht's "alienation effect" and, even more, Althusser and Macheray's "internal distantiation." But the most fruitful terms for describing the felt difference between Shakespeare's art and the religious ideology to which it gives voice are to be found, I think, in the theological system to which Harsnett adhered. What is the status of the Law, asks Hooker, after the coming of Christ? Clearly the Savior effected the "evacuation of the Law of Moses." But did that abolition mean "that the very name of Altar, of Priest, of Sacrifice itself, should be banished out of the world"? No, replies Hooker; even after evacuation, "the words which were do continue: the only difference is, that whereas before they had a literal, they now have a metaphorical use, and are as so many notes of remembrance unto us, that what they did signify in the letter is accomplished in the truth."[50] Both exorcism and Harsnett's own attack on exorcism undergo a comparable process of evacuation and transformed reiteration in *King Lear*. Whereas before they had a literal, they now have a literary use and are as so many notes of remembrance unto us, that what they did signify in the letter is accomplished – with a drastic swerve from the sacred to the secular – in the theater.

Edgar's possession is a theatrical performance exactly in Harsnett's terms, but there is no saving institution, purged of theater, against which it may be set, nor is there a demonic institution that the performance may be shown to serve. On the contrary, Edgar mimes in response to a free-floating, contagious evil more terrible than anything Harsnett would allow. For Harsnett the wicked are corrupt individuals in the service of a corrupt church; in *King Lear* neither individuals nor institutions can adequately contain the released and enacted wickedness; the force of evil in the play is larger than any local habitation or name. In this sense, Shakespeare's tragedy reconstitutes as theater the demonic principle demystified by Harsnett. Edgar's fraudulent, histrionic performance is a response to this principle: evacuated rituals, drained of their original meaning, are preferable to no rituals at all.

Shakespeare does not counsel, in effect, that for the dream of a cure one accept the fraudulent institution as true – that is the argument of the Grand Inquisitor. He writes for the greater glory and profit of the theater, a fraudulent institution that never pretends to be anything but fraudulent, an institution that calls forth what is not, that signifies absence, that transforms the literal into the metaphorical, that evacuates everything it represents. By doing so the theater makes for itself the hollow round space within which it survives. The force of *King Lear* is to make us love the theater, to seek out its satisfactions, to serve its interests, to confer on it a place of its own, to grant it life by permitting it to reproduce itself over generations. Shakespeare's theater has outlived the institutions to which it paid homage, has lived to pay homage to other, competing, institutions that in turn it seems to represent and empty out. This complex, limited institutional independence, this marginal and impure autonomy, arises not out of an inherent, formal self-reflexiveness but out of the ideological matrix in which Shakespeare's theater is created and re-created.

Further institutional strategies lie beyond a love for the theater. In a move that Ben Jonson rather than Shakespeare seems to have anticipated, the theater itself comes to be emptied out in the interests of reading. In the argument made famous by Charles Lamb and Coleridge, and reiterated by Bradley, theatricality must be discarded to achieve absorption, and Shakespeare's imagination yields forth its sublime power not to a spectator but to one who, like Keats, sits down to reread *King Lear*. Where institutions like the King's Men had been thought to generate their texts, now texts like *King Lear* appear to generate their institutions. The commercial contingency of the theater gives way to the philosophical necessity of literature.

Why has our culture embraced *King Lear*'s massive display of mimed suffering and fraudulent exorcism? Because the judicial torture and expulsion of evil have for centuries been bound up with the display of power at the center of society. Because we no longer believe in the magical ceremonies through which devils were once made to speak and were driven out of the bodies of the possessed. Because the play recuperates and intensifies our need for these ceremonies, even though we do not believe in them, and performs them, carefully marked out for us as frauds, for our continued consumption. Because with our full complicity Shakespeare's company and scores of companies that followed have catered profitably to our desire for spectacular impostures.

And also, perhaps, because the Harsnetts of the world would free us from the oppression of false belief only to reclaim us more firmly for the official State Church, and the "solution" – confirmed by the rechristening, as it were, of the devil as the pope – is hateful. Hence we embrace an alternative that seems to confirm the official line, and thereby to take its place in the central system of values, yet at the same time works to unsettle all official lines.[51] Shakespeare's theater empties out the center that it represents and in its cruelty – Edmund, Goneril, Regan, Cornwall, Gloucester, Cordelia, Lear: all dead as earth – paradoxically creates in us the intimation of a fullness that we can savor only in the conviction of its irremediable loss:

> we that are young
> Shall never see so much, nor live so long.

NOTES

1   Samuel Harsnett, *A Declaration of egregious Popish Impostures, to withdraw the harts of her Maiesties Subiects from their allegeance, and from the truth of Christian Religion professed in England, under the pretence of casting out deuils* (London: Iames Roberts, 1603). Harsnett's influence is noted in Lewis Theobald's edition of Shakespeare, first published in 1733. Shakespeare is likely to have known one of the principal exorcists, Robert Dibdale, the son of a Stratford Catholic family linked to the Hathaways.

     On the clandestine exorcisms I am particularly indebted to D. P. Walker, *Unclean Spirits: Possession and Exorcism in France and England in the Late Sixteenth and Early Seventeenth Centuries* (Philadelphia: University of Pennsylvania Press, 1981).

2   A major exception, with conclusions different from my own, has recently been published: John L. Murphy, *Darkness and Devils: Exorcism and "King Lear"* (Athens: Ohio University Press, 1984). Murphy's study, which he kindly allowed me to read in galleys after hearing the present chapter delivered as a lecture, argues that exorcism is an aspect of clandestine political and religious resistance to Queen Elizabeth's rule. For thoughtful comments on Murphy's book by an expert on Harsnett, see F. W. Brownlow's review in *Philological Quarterly* 65 (1986): 131–3. See also, for interesting reflections, William Elton, *"King Lear" and the Gods* (San Marino, Calif.: Huntington Library, 1966). For useful accounts of Harsnett's relation to *Lear*, see *Narrative and Dramatic Sources of Shakespeare*, 8 vols., ed. Geoffrey Bullough (London: Routledge and Kegan Paul, 1958–75), 7:299–302; Kenneth Muir, "Samuel Harsnett and *King Lear*," *Review of English Studies* 2 (1951): 11–21, and Muir's edition of *Lear*, New Arden text (Cambridge, Mass.: Harvard University Press, 1952), pp. 253–6.

3   Michel de Montaigne, "Apology for Raymond Sebond," in *Complete Essays*, trans. Donald M. Frame (Stanford: Stanford University Press, 1948), p. 331.

4   Edward Shils, *Center and Periphery: Essays in Macrosociology* (Chicago: University of Chicago Press, 1975), p. 257.

5   Peter Brown, *The Cult of the Saints: Its Rise and Function in Latin Christianity* (Chicago: University of Chicago Press, 1981), p. 107.

6   Sebastian Michaelis, *The Admirable Historie of the Possession and Conversion of a Penitent Woman*, trans. W. B. (London: William Aspley, 1613), p. 21. Mass exorcism was a particularly important phenomenon in sixteenth- and early seventeenth-century France. See Michel de Certeau, *La Possession de Loudun*, Collection Archive Series no. 37 (Paris: Gallimard, 1980); Robert Mandrou, *Magistrats et sorciers en France au*

XVIIe siècle (Paris: Seuil, 1980); Robert Muchembled, *La Culture populaire et culture des élites* (Paris: Flammarion, 1977); Jonathan L. Pearl, "French Catholic Demonologists and Their Enemies in the Late Sixteenth and Early Seventeenth Centuries," *Church History* 52 (1983): 457–67; Henri Weber, "L'Exorcisme à la fin du seizième siècle, instrument de la Contre Réforme et spectacle baroque," *Nouvelle Revue du seizième siècle* 1 (1983): 79–101. For a comparison between exorcism in France and in England, see D. P. Walker, *Unclean Spirits*, and my own article, "Loudun and London," *Critical Inquiry* 12 (1986): 326–46. I have incorporated some pages from this article in the present chapter.

7 *A Booke Declaringe the Fearfull Vexasion of one Alexander Nyndge. Beynge moste Horriblye tormented wyth an euyll Spirit* (London: Thomas Colwell, 1573), p. Biiii^r.

8 Carlo Ginzburg, *I benandanti: Recerche sulla stregoneria e sui culti agrari tra cinquecento e seicento* (Turin: Einaudi, 1966).

9 For Harsnett's comments on witchcraft, see *Declaration*, pp. 135–6. The relation between demonic possession and witchcraft is complex. John Darrel evidently had frequent recourse, in the midst of his exorcisms, to accusations of witchcraft whose evidence was precisely the demonic possessions; Harsnett remarks wryly that "of all the partes of the tragicall Comedie acted between him and *Somers*, there was no one Scene in it, wherein *M. Darrell* did with more courage and boldnes acte his part, then in this of the discouerie of witches" (*A Discovery of the Fraudulent Practises of J. Darrel . . . concerning the pretended possession and dispossession of W. Somers, etc.* [1599], p. 142). There is a helpful discussion of possession and witchcraft, along with an important account of Harsnett and Darrel, in Keith Thomas, *Religion and the Decline of Magic* (London: Weidenfeld and Nicolson, 1971).

10 I borrow the phrase "central zone" from Edward Shils, for whom it is coterminous with society's central value system, a system constituted by the general standards of judgment and action and affirmed by the society's elite (*Center and Periphery*, p. 3). At the heart of the central value system is an affirmative attitude toward authority, which is endowed, however indirectly or remotely, with a measure of sacredness. "By their very possession of authority," Shils writes, elites "attribute to themselves an essential affinity with the sacred elements of their society, of which they regard themselves as the custodians" (p. 5).

11 Brown, *Cult of the Saints*, pp. 109–11.

12 Thomas, *Religion and the Decline of Magic*, p. 485. "This effectively put an end to the practice," Thomas writes, "at least as far as conforming members of the Anglican Church were concerned."

13 S. M. Shirokogorov, *The Psycho-Mental Complex of the Tungus* (Peking: Routledge, 1935), p. 265.

14 Brown, *Cult of the Saints*, p. 110.

15 Michael MacDonald, *Mystical Bedlam* (Cambridge: Cambridge University Press, 1981). See also MacDonald's "Religion, Social Change, and Psychological Healing in England, 1600–1800," in *The Church and Healing*, ed. W. J. Shiels, Studies in Church History 19 (Oxford: Basil Blackwell, 1982); H. C. Erik Midelfort, "Madness and the Problems of Psychological History in the Sixteenth Century," *Sixteenth Century Journal* 12 (1981): 5–12.

16 *A Report Contayning a brief Narration of certain diuellish and wicked witcheries, practized by Olisse Barthram alias Doll Barthram in the Country of Suffolke*, bound with *The Triall of Maist. Dorrell, or A Collection of Defences against Allegations not yet suffered to receive convenient answere* (1599), p. 94.

17   Iohn Swan, *A True and Briefe Report. of Mary Glovers Vexation* (1603), p. 42.

18   *The Triall of Maist. Dorrell*, p. 29.

19   Quoted in [John Darrel,] *A Briefe Narration of the possession, dispossession, and repossession of William Sommers* (1598), pp. Diiv, Ciiiiv.

20   *The Triall of Maist. Dorrell*, p. 8.

21   John Deacon and John Walker, *A Summarie Answere to al the material points in any of Master Darel his bookes* (London: George Bishop, 1601), pp. 237–38.

22   Harsnett sees this argument as a variant on the exorcists' general rule that "when the deuilles are cast out of man, they endeuoure by all the means they can, to perswade, that hee was neuer in them: that so the partie being vnthankefull to God for his deliuerance, they might the better reenter into him" (*Discovery*, p. 72). Harsnett cites the important exorcism manual by R. F. Hieronymus Mengus [Girolamo Menghi], *Flagellum Daemonum* (Bologna, 1582).

23   In 1524 Erasmus satirized exorcism by depicting it not simply as a fraud but as a play in five acts (*Exorcismus, sive spectrum*, in *The Colloquies of Erasmus*, trans. Craig R. Thompson (Chicago: University of Chicago Press, 1965), pp. 231–7). The play, in Erasmus's account, is an elaborate practical joke played on a character called Faunus, a gullible and pretentious parish priest who is cleverly induced to be an unwitting actor in an outlandish and grotesque theatrical performance. The representation of the demonic is spurious, but its effect on the victim of the joke is alarmingly real: "So thoroughly did this fancy obsess him that he dreamt of nothing but specters and evil spirits and talked of nothing else. His mental condition carried over into his very countenance, which became so pale, so drawn, so downcast that you would have said he was a ghost, not a man" (p. 237). A successful demon play can fashion the dreams of its victims, and illusions can inscribe themselves in the very bodies of those who believe in them.

        The colloquy ostensibly celebrates the histrionic cunning of the jokers, but Erasmus makes it clear that there are larger institutional implications: a gifted director, an unscrupulous actor who has "perfect control of his expression," and a few props suffice not only to create an intense illusion of the demonic among large numbers of spectators but also to entice the gullible into participating in a play whose theatricality they cannot acknowledge. The defense against such impostures is a widespread public recognition of this theatricality and a consequent skepticism: "Up to this time I haven't, as a rule, had much faith in popular tales about apparitions," one of Erasmus's speakers concludes, "but hereafter I'll have even less" (p. 237).

24   See Edmund Jorden, *A briefe discourse of a disease Called the Suffocation of the Mother* (London, 1603).

25   *A Report Contayning a brief Narration of certain diuellish and wicked witcheries*, pp. 99–100.

26   [Richard Baddeley,] *The Boy of Bilson, or A True Discovery of the Late Notorious Impostvres of Certaine Romish Priests in their pretended Exorcisme, or expulsion of the Diuell out of a young Boy, named William Perry, sonne of Thomas Perry of Bilson* (London: F. K., 1622), p. 51. Baddeley is quoting from the Catholic account of the events, which, in order to dispute, he reprints: *A Faithful Relation of the Proceedings of the Catholicke Gentlemen with the Boy of Bilson; shewing how they found him, on what termes they meddled with him, how farre they proceeded with him, and in what case, and for what cause they left to deale further with him* (in Baddeley, pp. 45–54).

27   In both England and France the reliability of the devil's testimony was debated extensively. "We ought not to beleeue the Diuell," writes the exorcist and inquisi-

tor Sebastian Michaelis, "yet when hee is compelled to discourse and relate a truth, then wee should feare and tremble, for it is a token of the wrath of God" (*Admirable Historie of the Possession and Conversion of a Penitent Woman*, p. C7v). Michaelis's long account of his triumph over a devil named Verrine was published, the translator claims, to show "that the Popish Priests, in all Countries where men will beleeue them, are vniforme & like vnto themselues, since that which was done couertly in England, in the daies of Queene *Elizabeth*, by the Deuils of *Denham* in *Sara Williams* and her fellowes, is now publikely taken vp elsewhere by men of no small ranke" (A4r). This seems to me a disingenuous justification for publishing, without further annotation or qualification, over five hundred pages of Catholic apologetics, but obviously the Jacobean licensing authorities accepted the explanation.

28 [Darrel,] *A Briefe Narration of the possession, dispossession, and repossession of William Sommers*, p. Biiv.

29 "Let him be brought before some indifferent persons, let the depositions be read, and let him act the same in such maner, and forme as is deposed, by naturall, or artificiall power, then Mr. Dorrell will yeeld that he did conterfeit. It he cannot, (as vndoubtedlie he cannot,) then pleade no longer for the Deuill; but punish that imp of Satan as a wicked lier, and blasphemer of the mightie worke of God" (*Briefe Narration*, p. Biiv).

30 *Booke of Miracles*, quoted in Harsnett, *Declaration*, pp. 113–14.

31 In Haiti, for example, an individual possessed by a *loa*, or spirit, is led to the vestry of the sanctuary, where he chooses the costume appropriate to the particular spirit that has possessed him; dressed in this costume – for Baron Saturday, a black suit, starched cuffs, top hat, and white gloves; for the peasant god Zaka, a straw hat, pouch, and pipe; and so forth – he returns to the clearing and performs for the assembled crowd the appropriate mimes, monologues, and dances (Alfred Metraux, "Dramatic Elements in Ritual Possession," *Diogenes* 11 (1964): 18–36). In Sri Lanka, exorcisms integrate feasting, the making of ritual offerings, dancing, the singing of sacred texts, drumming, masking, and the staging of improvised, frequently obscene, comedies. The comedies are at once explicitly theatrical and integral to the healing process.

In a major study of exorcism rituals performed in and near the town of Galle in southern Sri Lanka, Bruce Kapferer observes that demons in Sinhalese culture are understood to operate by means of illusions; the disorder and suffering that these illusions occasion are combated by spectacular demystifying counter-illusions. Hence exorcists "consider their healing rites to be elaborate tricks which they play on demons": to induce demons to treat the illusory as reality is to gain control over them (Bruce Kapferer, *A Celebration of Demons: Exorcism and the Aesthetics of Healing in Sri Lanka* (Bloomington: Indiana University Press, 1983), p. 112). Demonic possession has disturbed a hierarchical order that must be restored by humiliating the demons and returning them to their rightful subordinate position in the order of things. This restoration is achieved through ceremonies that "place major aesthetic forms into relation and locate them at points when particular transformations in meaning and experience are understood by exorcists to be occurring or are to be effected" (p. 8). The ceremonies transform demonic identity into normal social identity; the individual is returned to himself and hence to his community whose solidarity is not only mirrored but constituted by the aesthetic experience. Exorcists then are "the masters of illusion" (p. 113), and their histrionic skills do not arouse doubts about their authenticity but heighten confidence in their powers.

For further reflections on demonic possession, see Ernst Arbman, *Ecstasy or Religious Trance* (Norstedts: Svenska Bokforlaget, 1963), 3 vols., esp. chapter 9; *Disguises of the Demonic: Contemporary Perspectives on the Power of Evil*, ed. Alan M. Olson (New York: Association Press, n.d.); I. M. Lewis, *Ecstatic Religion: An Anthropological Study of Spirit Possession and Shamanism* (Harmondsworth: Penguin, 1971).

32 Michel Leiris, *La Possession et ses aspects théâtraux chez les Ethiopiens de Gondar* (Paris: Plon, 1958).

33 This argument has the curious effect of identifying all exorcisms, including those conducted by nonconformist preachers, with the pope. On attacks on the Catholic church as a theater, see Jonas Barish, *The Antitheatrical Prejudice* (Berkeley: University of California Press, 1981), pp. 66–131 passim.

34 At least since Plato there has been a powerful tendency to identify the stage with unreality, debased imitation, and outright counterfeiting. Like the painter, says Socrates in the *Republic*, the tragic poet is an imitator of objects that are themselves imitations and hence "thrice removed from the king and from the truth" (597e). Though this position had its important Christian adherents, it is not, of course, the only intellectual current in the West; not only do medieval mystery plays depend upon a conviction that dramatic performance does not contradict religious truth, but the Mass itself appears to have been conceived by several important medieval thinkers as analogous to theatrical representation. For further discussion, see my "Loudun and London," pp. 328–9.

35 *Discovery*, p. A3r. As Catholic priests "have transformed the celebrating of the Sacrament of the *Lords supper* into a *Masse-game*, and all other partes of the *Ecclesiasticall service* into *theatricall sights*," writes another sixteenth-century Protestant polemicist, "so, in steede of *preaching the word*, they caused it to be played" (John Rainolds, cited in Barish, *The Antitheatrical Prejudice*, p. 163).

36 Harsnett was not alone, of course. See, for example, John Gee: "The Jesuits being or having Actors of such dexterity, I see no reason but that they should set up a company for themselves, which surely will put down The Fortune, Red-Bull, Cock-pit, and Globe" (John Gee, *New Shreds of the Old Snare* [London, 1624]). I owe this reference, along with powerful reflections on the significance of the public theater's physical marginality, to Steven Mullaney.

37 This sentiment could serve as the epigraph to both of Harsnett's books on exorcism; it is the root perception from which most of Harsnett's rhetoric grows.

38 Stephen Gosson, *Plays Confuted in Five Actions* (c. 1582), cited in E. K. Chambers, *The Elizabethan Stage*, 4 vols. (Oxford: Clarendon, 1923), 4:215.

39 These lines were included in the quarto but omitted from the folio. For the tangled textual history, see Michael J. Warren, "Quarto and Folio *King Lear*, and the Interpretation of Albany and Edgar," in *Shakespeare: Pattern of Excelling Nature*, ed. David Bevington and Jay L. Halio (Newark: University of Delaware Press, 1978), pp. 95–107; Steven Urkowitz, *Shakespeare's Revision of "King Lear"* (Princeton: Princeton University Press, 1980); and Gary Taylor, "The War in *King Lear*," *Shakespeare Survey* 33 (1980): 27–34. Presumably, by the time the folio appeared, the point of the allusion to Harsnett would have been lost, and the lines were dropped.

40 John Bunyan, *Grace Abounding to the Chief of Sinners*, ed. Roger Sharrock (London: Clarendon Press, 1966), p. 15.

41 Edgar's later explanation – that he feared for his father's ability to sustain the shock of an encounter – is, like so many explanations in *King Lear*, too little, too late. On

this characteristic belatedness as an element of the play's greatness, see Stephen Booth, "*King Lear*," "*Macbeth*," *Indefinition, and Tragedy* (New Haven: Yale University Press, 1983).

42 On "counterfeit miracles" produced to arouse awe and wonder, see especially Harsnett, *Discovery*, Epistle to the Reader.

43 Words, signs, gestures that claim to be in touch with super-reality, with absolute goodness and absolute evil, are exposed as vacant – illusions manipulated by the clever and imposed on the gullible.

44 This is, in effect, Edmund Jorden's prescription for cases such as Lear's, in *A briefe discourse of a disease.*

45 "It is even possible," writes Peter Milward, S.J., "that the lot of such priests as Weston and Dibdale provided Shakespeare with a suggestion for his portrayal of Edgar in hiding" (*Shakespeare's Religious Background* (London: Sidgwick and Jackson, 1973), p. 54). But I cannot agree with Milford's view that Shakespeare continually "laments 'the plight of his poor country' since the day Henry VIII decided to break with Rome" (p. 224).

46 On the Yorkshire performance, see John Murphy, *Darkness and Devils*, pp. 93–118.

47 In willing this disenchantment against the evidence of our senses, we pay tribute to the theater. Harsnett has been twisted around to make this tribute possible. Harsnett several times characterizes exorcism as a "tragicomedy" (*Discovery*, p. 142; *Declaration*, p. 150). On Harsnett's conception of tragicomedy, see Herbert Berry, "Italian Definitions of Tragedy and Comedy Arrive in England," *Studies in English Literature* 14 (1974): 179–87.

48 O. B. Hardison, Jr., *Christian Rite and Christian Drama in the Middle Ages: Essays in the Origin and Early History of Modern Drama* (Baltimore: Johns Hopkins University Press, 1965), esp. pp. 220–52.

49 C. L. Barber, "The Family in Shakespeare's Development: Tragedy and Sacredness," in *Representing Shakespeare: New Psychoanalytic Essays*, ed. Murray M. Schwartz and Coppélia Kahn (Baltimore: Johns Hopkins University Press, 1980), p. 196.

50 Richard Hooker, *Laws of Ecclesiastical Polity*, 1:582–3. This truth, which is the triumph of the metaphorical over the literal, confers on the church the liberty to use certain names and rites, even though they have been abolished. The entire passage in Hooker is powerfully suggestive for understanding the negotiation between the domain of literature and the domain of religion:

> They which honour the Law as an image of the wisdom of God himself, are notwithstanding to know that the same had an end in Christ. But what? Was the Law so abolished with Christ, that after his ascension the office of Priests became immediately wicked, and the very name hateful, as importing the exercise of an ungodly function? No, as long as the glory of the Temple continued, and till the time of that final desolation was accomplished, the very Christian Jews did continue with their sacrifices and other parts of legal service. That very Law therefore which our Saviour was to abolish, did not *so soon* become unlawful to be observed as some imagine; nor was it afterwards unlawful *so far*, that the very name of Altar, of Priest, of Sacrifice itself, should be banished out of the world. For though God do now hate sacrifice, whether it be heathenish or Jewish, so that we cannot have the same things which they had but with impiety; yet unless there be some greater let than the only evacuation of the Law of Moses, the names themselves may (I hope) be retained without sin, in respect of that proportion which things established by our Saviour have unto them which by him are abrogated. And so throughout all the writings of the ancient Fathers we see that the words which were do continue; the only difference is,

that whereas before they had a literal, they now have a metaphorical use, and are so many notes of remembrance unto us, that what they did signify in the letter is accomplished in the truth. And as no man can deprive the Church of this liberty, to use names whereunto the Law was accustomed, so neither are we generally forbidden the use of things which the Law hath; though it neither command us any particular rite, as it did the Jews a number and the weightiest which it did command them are unto us in the Gospel prohibited. (4.11.10)

For the reference to Hooker I am indebted to John Coolidge.

51   "Truth to tell," writes Barthes, "the best weapon against myth is perhaps to mythify it in its turn, and to produce an *artificial myth*: and this reconstituted myth will in fact be a mythology" (Roland Barthes, *Mythologies*, trans. Annette Lavers (New York: Hill and Wang, 1972), p. 135).

9

MARTIAL LAW IN THE LAND OF COCKAIGNE

I want to begin this chapter with a sermon that Hugh Latimer, the great Protestant divine martyred during the reign of Mary Tudor, delivered before the Lady Catharine Bertie, duchess of Suffolk, in 1552. In the course of expounding his text, the Lord's Prayer, Latimer tells of something that happened many years before in Cambridge. He had gone with Thomas Bilney – the man who converted Latimer and who was himself martyred in the later years of Henry VIII's rule – to the town prison to urge the condemned to acknowledge their faults and to bear patiently their punishments. Among the prisoners was a pregnant woman who had been convicted of murdering one of her children. The woman claimed that the child had been sick for a year and had died of natural causes. Her husband being away, she alone witnessed the death. She went, she said, to her neighbors and friends to seek their help to prepare the child for burial, but it was harvest time and no one was at home. Therefore alone, "in an heaviness and trouble of spirit," she made the necessary preparations and buried the dead. But when her husband returned home, he – who "loved her not; and therefore . . . sought means to make her out of the way" – accused her of murdering the child.[1] The accusation was believed by the Cambridge jury, and the woman was sentenced to be executed, the execution being delayed only until such time as she delivered her baby.

When Latimer spoke with her in prison, the woman steadfastly maintained her innocence, and after "earnest inquisition" he came to believe her story. Immediately thereafter it chanced that he was called to Windsor to preach before Henry VIII. After the sermon the king graciously strolled with the minister in a gallery. Latimer knelt, told the woman's story, begged the king for a royal pardon on her behalf, and received it. He returned to Cambridge, pardon in hand, but he kept it hidden, exhorting the woman to confess the truth. She held fast to her professions of innocence.

In due time the woman had her baby, and Latimer consented to be its godfather. The moment had thus come for the woman's execution, and she was in an agony of apprehension. But she was fearful, Latimer found, not because

This chapter was first published in this form in *Shakespearean Negotiations* (1988, pp. 129–63).

she was about to die but because she would die without being "churched" – that is, without the Catholic rite of purification based on the Jewish rituals tradition-ally held after childbirth (or menstruation) to cleanse the woman of the stain associated with any blood or discharge. "For she thought," writes Latimer, "that she should have been damned, if she should suffer without purification."

Latimer and Bilney then set about to disabuse her of this doctrinal error. They explained that the law of purification "was made unto the Jews, and not unto us; and that women lying in child-bed be not unclean before God." Significantly, Latimer opposed not the ritual of purification but only the belief that such a ritual cleanses women of sin, for women, he argues, "be as well in the favour of God before they be purified as after." Purification is not a theological but rather "a civil and politic law, made for natural honesty sake; signifying, that a woman before the time of her purification, that is to say, as long as she is a green woman, is not meet to do such acts as other women, nor to have company with her husband: for it is against natural honesty, and against the commonwealth." Only when the poor prisoner accepted this doctrinal point and agreed that she could go to her death unchurched and still receive salvation did Latimer produce the royal pardon and let her go.

I want to suggest that this little story reveals characteristic Renaissance beliefs and practices, and I propose to begin by noting some aspects of the gender relations it sketches.

First, we encounter the story as an allegorically charged but "real-life" tale about a woman, a tale that Latimer relates in a sermon originally delivered before another woman. As such, perhaps it subtly suggests, in the presence of a social superior, Latimer's moral superiority and power and so reestablishes male dom-inance in a moment of apparent inferiority.[2]

Second, the story could perhaps have been told about a male prisoner in the grip of a comparable "superstition" – let us imagine, for example, that he feared damnation if he did not have auricular confession and absolution prior to execution – but the prisoner's being female manifestly enhances its special symbolic charge. The woman's body after childbirth is polluted in "nature" and in the commonwealth but not in the eyes of God: hence she can exemplify directly and in the flesh the crucial theological distinction between, on the one hand, the domain of law and nature and, on the other, the order of grace and salvation. The distinction applies to all of humanity, but the male body passes through no fully comparable moments of pollution.[3]

Third, the particular suitability of the woman's body for this theological allegory rests on an implied Pauline syllogism, conveniently reinforced by Latimer's saving of the woman: the woman is to the man as the man is to God. And this syllogism intersects with other implied analogical relations: the woman is to the man as the simple peasant is to the gentleman and as the prisoner is to the free man.

Fourth, Latimer functions as part of a highly educated, male, professional elite that takes power over the woman away from her husband and lodges it in the punishing and pardoning apparatus of the state. The husband, as Latimer tells the story, had thought he could use that apparatus as an extension of his own power, but instead a gap is disclosed between patriarchal authority in the marital relation and patriarchal authority in the society at large.[4]

Fifth, the male professional elite, whether constituted as a body of jurists, theologians, or physicians, attempts to regulate the female body: to identify its periods of untouchability or pollution, to cleanse it of its stains, to distinguish between "superstitious" practices and those conducive to public health. What we are witnessing is an instance of transcoding and naturalization: Latimer attempts to transfer the practice of purification from the religious to the civil sphere.[5] He goes out of his way to distinguish an appeal to "natural honesty" – that is, the demands of cleanliness, decorum, and health – from "superstition": thus he denies that before purification a woman sheds a malign influence on the objects about her and denounces those who "think they may not fetch fire nor any thing in that house where there is a green woman." Such folk beliefs are for Latimer part of the orbit of Catholicism and pose a threat to the commonwealth far greater than any posed by a "green woman." The religious rituals to ward off defilement are themselves defiling and must be cleansed by driving them out of the precinct of the sacred and into the realm of the secular.

Rituals of purification thus transcoded from the religious to the civil sphere serve to shape certain late sixteenth- and early seventeenth-century representations, in particular theatrical representations, of women. Thus, for example, Hermione in Shakespeare's *Winter's Tale* complains bitterly that her husband has denied her "The child-bed privilege ... which 'longs/To women of all fashion" (3.2.103–4) and has brutally hurried her into "th' open air, before" she has "got strength of limit." Leontes has denied his wife the "child-bed privilege" because he believes that her adulterous body is defiled beyond redemption; she is, he is convinced, permanently and irreparably stained. Her sullying, as he perceives it, of the "purity and whiteness" of his sheets threatens to defile him as well, and he imagines that he can save himself only by denouncing, and destroying her. The secularized ritual is disrupted by a primal male nausea at the thought of the female body, the nausea most fully articulated in *King Lear* :

> But to the girdle do the gods inherit,
> Beneath is all the fiends': there's hell, there's darkness,
> There is the sulphurous pit, burning, scalding,
> Stench, consumption. Fie, fie, fie! pah, pah!
> Give me an ounce of civet; good apothecary,
> Sweeten my imagination.
>
> $(4.6.126-31)$[6]

In *The Winter's Tale* this nausea appears to be awakened in some obscure way by Hermione's pregnancy, as if what it revealed was beyond the power of any ritual to cleanse. The play suggests that Leontes is horribly staining himself, and its last act movingly depicts a ceremony conducted by a woman, Paulina, to cleanse the king. *The Winter's Tale* then at once symbolically rehearses and reverses the ritual pattern that we glimpse in Latimer: the tainting of the female, her exclusion from the social contacts that normally govern her sex, and her ultimate reintegration into a renewed community.

We could go on to look at other instances of the "green woman" and the tainted man in Renaissance drama, but for an understanding of the circulation of social energy the representational content of Latimer's story is less resonant than its strategic practice. Latimer and Bilney choose to leave the poor prisoner hanging, as it were, until she has accepted the doctrinal point: "So we travailed with this woman till we brought her to a good trade; and at the length showed her the king's pardon and let her go." A student of Shakespeare will immediately think of *Measure for Measure* where in the interest of moral reformation, Duke Vincentio, disguised as a holy friar, forces Claudio to believe that he is about to be executed – indeed forces virtually all of the major characters to face dreaded punishments – before he pardons everyone.

The resemblance between the tales arises not because Latimer's sermon is one of Shakespeare's sources but because Latimer is practicing techniques of arousing and manipulating anxiety, and these techniques are crucial elements in the representational technology of the Elizabethan and Jacobean theater.[7]

English dramatists developed extraordinary mastery of these techniques; indeed one of the defining characteristics of the dramaturgy of Marlowe and Shakespeare, as opposed to that of their medieval predecessors, is the startling increase in the level of represented and aroused anxiety. There is, to be sure, fear and trembling in the mysteries and moralities of the fifteenth and early sixteenth centuries, but a dread bound up with the fate of particular situated individuals is largely absent, and the audience shares its grief and joy in a collective experience that serves either to ward off or to absorb private emotions. Marlowe's *Faustus*, by contrast, though it appears conventional enough in its plot and overarching religious ideology, seems like a startling departure from everything that has preceded it precisely because the dramatist has heightened and individuated anxiety to an unprecedented degree and because he has contrived to implicate his audience as individuals in that anxiety.

Not all theatrical spectacles in the late sixteenth century are equally marked by the staging of anxiety: both civic pageantry and the masque are characterized by its relative absence. But in the public theater the manipulation of anxiety plays an important part and is brought to a kind of perfection in Shakespeare. This is obviously and overwhelmingly the case in the tragedies: *Othello*, for example, remorselessly heightens audience anxiety, an anxiety focused on the audience's inability to intervene and stop the murderous chain of lies and misunderstandings. But it is equally the case, in a different register, in the comedies. The pleasures of love, courtship, music, dance, and poetry in these plays are continually seasoned by fear, grief, and the threat of shame and death. The comedy of *The Comedy of Errors*, for example, floats buoyantly on a sea of epistemological and ontological confusion that is represented as having potentially fatal consequences. The audience's anxiety at these consequences, and for that matter at its own confusion, is different from that in a tragedy but is nonetheless an important element in the aesthetic experience. We could argue that anxiety in the comedies is an emotion experienced only by the characters and not by the audience, that comic pleasure lies in contemplating the anxiety of others. But this Hobbesian account does not do justice to the currents of sympathy in the plays and overlooks Shakespeare's efforts to make us identify powerfully with the dilemmas that his characters face. A sardonic detachment, such as one feels in response to a play like Ben Jonson's *Every Man in His Humour*, is not called forth by *The Merchant of Venice* or *Twelfth Night*, plays in which the audience's pleasure clearly depends upon a sympathetic engagement with the characters' situation and hence the acceptance of a measure of anxiety.[8]

It is worth stressing, however, that the audience accepts theatrical anxiety for the sake of pleasure, since this pleasure enables us to make an important distinction between the manipulation of anxiety in the theater and the comparable practice in Latimer.[9] The dramatist may have a palpable ideological purpose, generating anxiety, for example, to persuade women to submit to their husbands, or to warn men against paranoid suspicions of women, or to persuade subjects to obey even corrupt authority rather than risk rebellion. But in the public theater such purposes are subordinated to the overriding need to give pleasure. Anxiety takes its place alongside other means – erotic arousal, the excitement of spectacle, the joys of exquisite language, the satisfaction of curiosity about other peoples and places, and so forth – that the players employ to attract and satisfy their customers. The whole point of anxiety in the theater is to make it give such delight that the audience will pay for it again and again.[10] And this delight seems bound up with the marking out of theatrical anxiety as represented anxiety – not wholly real, either in the characters onstage or in the audience.[11]

Latimer, by contrast, insists that the anxiety in which he traffics is real. He does not, as far as we can tell, withhold the prisoner's pardon to heighten her subsequent pleasure; his purpose rather is to use her anxiety as a tool to transform her attitude toward what he regards as superstition.[12] Why should anxiety be used for this purpose? The answer perhaps seemed too obvious for Latimer to articulate: anxiety, in the form of threats of humiliation and beating, had long been used as an educative tool. To be sure, the threat of hanging goes well beyond what Shakespeare's Duke Vincentio in *Measure for Measure* calls "the threat'ning twigs of birch" (1.3.24), but Latimer presumably believes that at moments of crisis, moments beyond hope itself, men and women have to face the truth; their defenses are down, and they are forced to confront their salvation or perdition.[13] Latimer may also believe that we are all in effect under a death sentence from which we can be redeemed only by a mysterious and gratuitous act of pardon from God. The situation of the Cambridge prisoner is that of all mankind: hence the appropriateness of the story in a sermon on the Lord's Prayer. If he risked presumptuously casting himself or Henry VIII in the role of God, he could have appealed in good conscience to his certainty that he was God's humble servant. And if he seemed cruel, he could have told himself that he too would prefer death to doctrinal error. "Be of good comfort, Master Ridley, and play the man," Latimer was to say as the flames rose around his feet. "We shall this day light such a candle, by God's grace, in England, as I trust shall never be put out."

Latimer's last words, as the martyrologist Foxe reports them, move us beyond anxiety to the still point of absolute faith, but very few sixteenth-century Englishmen succeeded in reaching that point. (I doubt that many sixteenth-century Englishmen *wanted* to reach that point.) Those who governed the

Church had to be content that the faithful remain in a condition of what we may call salutary anxiety, and those who governed the state actively cultivated that condition. For the ruling elite believed that a measure of insecurity and fear was a necessary, healthy element in the shaping of proper loyalties, and Elizabethan and Jacobean institutions deliberately evoked this insecurity. Hence the Church's constant insistence upon the fear and trembling, the sickness unto death, that every Christian should experience; hence too the public and increasingly spectacular character of the punishments inflicted by the state.

At his accession to the English throne, in response to a murky conspiracy known as the Bye Plot, James I staged a particularly elaborate display of the techniques of salutary anxiety. Two of the alleged conspirators — the priests Watson and Clarke — were tortured horribly, "to the great discontent of the people," writes one observer, "who now think that matters were not so heinous as were made show of."[14] As usual, the dismembered bodies were stuck on the city gates. A week later another conspirator, George Brooke, was executed, and then after several more days, the sheriff led to the scaffold Lords Grey and Cobham and Sir Gervase Markham, who had also been condemned to die. Markham, who had hoped for a reprieve, looked stunned with horror. After a delay, the sheriff told him that since he seemed ill prepared to face death, he would be granted a two-hour reprieve; similar delays were granted to Grey and Cobham. The prisoners were then assembled together on the scaffold, "looking strange one upon the other," wrote Dudley Carleton, who witnessed the scene, "like men beheaded, and met again in the other world." At this point the sheriff made a short speech, asking the condemned if the judgments against them were just. When the wretches assented, he proclaimed that the merciful king had granted them their lives.[15]

The florid theatricality of the occasion was not lost on Carleton; the three men, he observed, were "together on the stage as use is at the end of the play." And in his letter granting the reprieve, James himself seems to confirm Carleton's perception. The king suggests that his clemency is in part a response to the "hearty and general . . . applause" given him on his entry into England, applause in which "all the kin, friends, and allies" of the condemned participated.[16] The cheering had stopped after the first three executions, for if some anxiety is salutary, it may also go too far and evoke not obedience but a sullen withdrawal into discontented silence or even an outburst of rash rebellion. These scenarios are at most only partially and superficially in the control of the authorities; if at such times the prince seems to manipulate the anxieties of others, he inevitably discloses his own half-buried fears.[17] The executioner held up Brooke's severed head and cried, "God save the king!" But the cry "was not seconded," Carleton notes, "by the voice of any one man but the sheriff." The spectators to the display of royal clemency, on the other hand, once again found their voices, for their anxiety had been turned into gratitude: "There was then no need to beg a *plaudite* of the audience," remarks Carleton, "for it was given with such hues and cries, that it went down from the castle into the town, and there began afresh."[18] So too the audience may have cheered the flurry of pardons in the last act of *Measure for Measure*.

But why should Renaissance England have been institutionally committed to the arousal of anxiety? After all, there was plenty of anxiety without the need of such histrionic methods; like other European countries of the period, England had experienced a population growth that put a heavy strain on food supplies, and the struggle for survival was intensified by persistent inflation, unemployment, and epidemic disease. But perhaps precisely because this anxiety was pervasive and unavoidable, those in power wanted to incorporate it ideologically and manage it. Managed insecurity may have been reassuring both to the managers themselves and to those toward whom the techniques were addressed.

Public maimings and executions were designed to arouse fear and to set the stage for the royal pardons that would demonstrate that the prince's justice was tempered with mercy.[19] If there were only fear, the prince, it was said, would be deemed a tyrant; if there were only mercy, it was said that the people would altogether cease to be obedient. Similarly, religious anxiety was welcomed, even cultivated, as the necessary precondition of the reassurance of salvation. William Tyndale suggested that St Paul had written the Epistle to the Romans precisely to generate a suffering that could then be joyously relieved: "For except thou have born the cross of adversity and temptation, and hast felt thyself brought unto the very brim of desperation, yea, and unto hell-gates, thou canst never meddle with the sentence of predestination without thine own harm."[20]

What would be the harm? Why shouldn't the order of things be simply revealed without the prior generation of anxiety? Because, answers Tyndale, unless one is "under the cross and suffering of tribulation," it is impossible to contemplate that order "without secret wrath and grudging inwardly against God"; that is, "it shall not be possible for thee to think that God is righteous and just." Salutary anxiety, then, blocks the anger and resentment that would well up against what must, if contemplated in a secure state, seem an unjust order. And the great virtue of the technique is that it blocks *secret* wrath and *inward* grudging – that is, it does not merely suppress the expression of undesirable responses but represses those responses at their source, so that potential anger gives way to obedience, loyalty, and admiration.

Renaissance England had a subtle conception of the relation between anxiety and the fashioning of the individual subject, and its governing institutions developed discursive and behavioral strategies to implement this conception by arousing anxiety and then transforming it through pardon into gratitude, obedience, and love. These strategies were implicated from their inception in the management of spectacles and the fashioning of texts; that is, they are already implicated in cultural practices that are essential to the making and staging of plays. There was no need in this case for special modifications to adapt the techniques of salutary anxiety to the theater. Indeed the theater is a virtual machine for deploying these techniques in a variety of registers, from the comic anxiety that gives way to the clarification and release of marriage to the tragic anxiety that is at once heightened and ordered by the final solemnity of death. It is not surprising that the disguised duke of *Measure For Measure*, who fuses the strategies of statecraft and religion, has also seemed to many critics an emblem of the playwright.

This perception seems to me fundamentally correct, but it is complicated by what happens to the techniques of salutary anxiety when they are transferred to the stage. Even as it is evoked with extraordinary technical skill, salutary anxiety is emptied out in the service of theatrical pleasure. This emptying out through representation enables Shakespeare at once to identify the playwright with the mastery of salutary anxiety and to subject that mastery to complex ironic scrutiny. If Shakespeare in *Measure for Measure* seems to represent the protagonist's task as inflicting anxiety for ideological purposes, he also clearly calls that task into question. In a scene that particularly recalls Latimer's story, the disguised duke pays a pastoral visit to "the afflicted spirits" in the town prison. "Do me the common right," he asks the provost,

> To let me see them, and to make me know
> The nature of their crimes, that I may minister
> To them accordingly.
>
> (2.3.5–8)

"Repent you," he asks the pregnant Juliet, who has been imprisoned for fornication, "of the sin you carry?" The question, collapsing the sin and its fruit into one another, is a harsh one, but the prisoner replies serenely: "I do; and bear the shame most patiently." Sensing an unwelcome doctrinal slippage in the shift from sin to shame, Duke Vincentio proposes to teach the unfortunate Juliet

> how you shall arraign your conscience,
> And try your penitence, if it be sound,
> Or hollowly put on.

"I'll gladly learn," Juliet replies, and the remainder of the short scene provides a revealing glimpse of the duke's methods and interests:

Duke: Love you the man that wrong'd you?
Juliet: Yes, as I love the woman that wrong'd him.
Duke: So then it seems your most offenseful act Was mutually committed?
Juliet: Mutually.
Duke: Then was your sin of heavier kind than his.
Juliet: I do confess it, and repent it, father.
Duke: 'Tis meet so, daughter, but lest you do repent
         As that the sin hath brought you to this shame,
         Which sorrow is always toward ourselves, not heaven,
         Showing we would not spare heaven as we love it
         But as we stand in fear –
Juliet: I do repent me as it is an evil,
         And take the shame with joy.
Duke: There rest.
         Your partner, as I hear, must die to-morrow,
         And I am going with instruction to him.
         Grace go with you, *Benedicite!*

> *Juliet:*　Must die to-morrow? O injurious love,
> 　　　　That respites me a life whose very comfort
> 　　　　Is still a dying horror!
> *Provost:*　　　　　　　　　'Tis pity of him.

$$(2.3.24\text{--}42)$$

The duke's questioning of the prisoner is based upon the medieval distinction between *attrition* and *contrition*. As one fourteenth-century theologian puts it, "When the will of a man clinging to sin is overcome by fear and by consideration of the punishment owed for sin, and on account of this recoils from sin, he is said to be 'attrite'; but when not only from fear of punishment, but also from love of eternal life he totally recoils from sin by fully detesting it, he is called 'contrite.' "[21] Juliet interrupts and in effect silences the duke's attempt to draw this doctrinal distinction:

> I do repent me as it is an evil,
> And take the shame with joy.

These words may express a perfect contrition, but they may also signal a quiet rejection of the whole system for which the duke speaks. "I do repent me as it is an evil" – but is it an evil? The provost had remarked of Claudio that he was "a young man/More fit to do another such offense/Than die for this" (2.3.13–15). "And take the shame with joy": earlier Juliet referred to her unborn child as "the shame." If she is still doing so, then her words affirm not repentance but love for her child. In either case, Juliet's words here and throughout the exchange are remarkable for their tranquillity. Each of Duke Vincentio's questions would seem to be an attempt to awaken an instructive anxiety, but the attempt appears to fail.

In response to Juliet's words the duke can only reply, "There rest." But as if this "rest" contradicts his own interest in arousing rather than allaying anxiety, he immediately continues by casually informing Juliet that the man she loves will be executed the next day. Her response provides ample evidence of anxiety, but that anxiety does not appear to serve an orthodox ideological purpose:

> 　　　　O injurious love,
> That respites me a life whose very comfort
> Is still a dying horror!

Again the words are ambiguous (and emendations have been proposed), but Juliet appears either to be calling into question the divine love about which the duke has just been lecturing her or the human love whose fruit – the baby she carries in her womb – has presumably afforded her a "respite" from the execution to which her conviction for fornication would have doomed her. In either case, the anxiety she is expressing simply brushes aside the theological categories the duke had taken it upon himself to instill in her.

None of the duke's other attempts to awaken anxiety and to shape it into what he regards as a proper attitude has the desired effect. When Claudio voices what sounds like an admirable acceptance of his situation – "I have hope to live, and am prepar'd to die" – Duke Vincentio replies, "Be absolute for death: either death or life/Shall thereby be the sweeter" (3.1.4–6). Here the duke would appear to be molding Claudio's emotions into philosophical detachment, but the strategy fails since Claudio almost immediately abandons his detachment and frantically sues for life. We may say that the duke has succeeded in raising Claudio's anxiety level, but the moral purpose for which he set out to do so seems to have collapsed.

The duke had embarked on his course because Vienna seemed insufficiently anxious in the presence of authority:

> Now, as fond fathers,
> Having bound up the threat'ning twigs of birch,
> Only to stick it in their children's sight
> For terror, not to use, in time the rod
> Becomes more mock'd than fear'd; so our decrees,
> Dead to infliction, to themselves are dead,
> And liberty plucks justice by the nose;
> The baby beats the nurse, and quite athwart
> Goes all decorum.
>
>   (1.3.23–31)

But at the close of the play, society at large seems singularly unaffected by the renewed exercise in anxiety. The magnificent emblems of indifference are the drunken Barnadine and the irrepressible Lucio: if they are any indication, the duke's strategy has not changed the structure of feeling or behavior in Vienna in the slightest degree. All that it has done is to offer the spectators pleasure in the spectacle. But that pleasure is precisely Shakespeare's professional purpose, and his ironic reflections on salutary anxiety do not at all diminish his commitment to it as a powerful theatrical technique.

II

When near the close of his career Shakespeare reflected upon his own art with still greater intensity and self-consciousness than in *Measure for Measure*, he once again conceived of the playwright as a princely creator of anxiety. But where in *Measure for Measure* disguise is the principal emblem of this art, in *The Tempest* the emblem is the far more potent and disturbing power of magic. Prospero's chief magical activity throughout *The Tempest* is to harrow the other characters with fear and wonder and then to reveal that their anxiety is his to create and allay. The spectacular storm in the play's first scene gives way to Miranda's empathic agitation: "O! I have suffered/With those that I saw suffer.... O, the cry did knock/Against my very heart." "The direful spectacle of the wrack," replies Prospero,

> which touch'd
> The very virtue of compassion in thee,

> I have with such provision in mine art
> So safely ordered that there is no soul –
> No, not so much perdition as an hair
> Betid to any creature in the vessel
> Which thou heardst cry, which thou saw'st sink.
>
> (1.2.26–32)

Miranda has been treated to an intense experience of suffering and to a still more intense demonstration of her father's power, the power at once to cause such suffering and to cancel it. Later in the play the threat of "perdition" – both loss and damnation – will be concentrated against Prospero's enemies, but it is important to recall that at the start the management of anxiety through the "provision" of art is practiced upon Prospero's beloved daughter. Her suffering is the prelude to the revelation of her identity, as if Prospero believes that this revelation can be meaningful only in the wake of the amazement and pity he artfully arouses. He is setting out to fashion her identity, just as he is setting out to refashion the inner lives of his enemies, and he employs comparable disciplinary techniques.

With his daughter, Prospero's techniques are mediated and softened: she suffers at the sight of the sufferings of unknown wretches. With his enemies the techniques are harsher and more direct – the spectacle they are compelled to watch is not the wreck of others but of their own lives. In one of the play's most elaborate scenes, Prospero stands above the stage, invisible to those below him, and conjures up a banquet for Alonso, Antonio, Sebastian, and their party; when they move toward the table, Ariel appears like a Harpy and, with a clap of his wings and a burst of thunder and lightning, makes the table disappear. Ariel then solemnly recalls their crimes against Prospero and sentences the guilty in the name of the powers of Destiny and Fate:

> Thee of thy son, Alonso,
> They have bereft; and do pronounce by me
> Ling'ring perdition (worse than any death
> Can be at once).
>
> (3.3.75–8)

Prospero is delighted at Ariel's performance:

> My high charms work,
> And these, mine enemies, are all knit up
> In their distractions. They now are in my pow'r.
>
> (3.3.88–90)

To compel others to be "all knit up/In their distractions," to cause a paralyzing anxiety, is the dream of power, a dream perfected over bitter years of exile.[22] But as we have already seen, the artful manipulation of anxiety is not only the manifestation of aggression; it is also a strategy for shaping the inner lives of others and for fashioning their behavior. Hence we find Prospero employing the strategy not only upon those he hates but upon his daughter and upon the man whom he has chosen to be his daughter's husband. Ferdinand and Miranda fall in love instantly – "It goes on, I see,/As my soul prompts it" (1.2.420–1), remarks Prospero – but what is missing from their love is precisely the salutary anxiety that Prospero undertakes to impose: "this swift business/I must uneasy make, lest too light winning/Make the prize light" (1.2.451–3). To Miranda's horror, he accuses Ferdinand of treason and employs his magic charms once again to cause a kind of paralysis: "My spirits," exclaims Ferdinand, "as in a dream, are all bound up" (1.2.487). The rituals of humiliation and suffering through which Prospero makes Ferdinand and Miranda pass evidently have their desired effect: at the end of the play the couple displayed to the amazed bystanders are revealed to be not only in a state of love but in a state of symbolic war. The lovers, you will recall, are discovered playing chess, and Miranda accuses Ferdinand of cheating. The deepest happiness is represented in this play as a state of playful tension.

Perhaps the supreme representation of this tension in *The Tempest* is to be found not in Prospero's enemies or in his daughter and son-in-law but in himself. The entire action of the play rests on the premise that value lies in controlled uneasiness, and hence that a direct reappropriation of the usurped dukedom and a direct punishment of the usurpers has less moral and political value than an elaborate inward restaging of loss, misery, and anxiety. Prospero directs this restaging not only against the others but also – even principally – against himself. That is, he arranges for the reenactment in a variety of registers and through different symbolic agents of the originary usurpation, and in the play's most memorable yet perplexing moment, the princely artist puts himself through the paralyzing uneasiness with which he has afflicted others. The moment to which I refer is that of the interrupted wedding masque. In the midst of the climactic demonstration of Prospero's magical powers, the celebration of the paradisal "green land" where spring comes at the very end of harvest, Prospero suddenly starts, breaks off the masque, and declares that he had "forgot that foul conspiracy / Of the beast Caliban and his confederates/Against my life" (4.1.139–41).

In recalling the conspiracy, Prospero clearly exhibits signs of extreme distress: Ferdinand is struck by the "passion/That works him strongly," and Miranda says that "never till this day" has she seen him "touch'd with anger, so distemper'd" (4.1.143–5). Noticing that Ferdinand looks "in a mov'd sort," as if he were "dismay'd," Prospero tells him to "be cheerful" and informs him that "Our revels now are ended." The famous speech that follows has the effect of drastically evacuating the masque's majestic vision of plenitude. "Let me live here ever," the delighted Ferdinand had exclaimed, enchanted by the promise of an aristocrat's equivalent of the Land of Cockaigne:

> Honor, riches, marriage-blessing,
> Long continuance, and increasing,
> Hourly joys be still upon you!
>   (4.1.106–8)

But Prospero now explains that the beneficent goddesses "Are melted into air, into thin air" (4.1.150). What had seemed solid is "baseless"; what had seemed enduring ("the great globe itself")

> shall dissolve,
> And like this insubstantial pageant faded
> Leave not a rack behind.
>   (4.1.154–6)

Prospero offers this sublime vision of emptiness to make Ferdinand feel "cheerful" – secure in the consciousness that life is a dream. It is difficult to believe in the effectiveness of these professed attempts at reassurance: like Duke Vincentio's religious consolations in *Measure for Measure*, they seem suited more to heighten anxiety than to allay it. The ascetic security Prospero articulates has evidently not stilled his own "beating mind":

> Sir, I am vex'd;
> Bear with my weakness, my old brain is troubled.
> Be not disturb'd with my infirmity.
>   (4.1.158–60)

Since Prospero's art has in effect created the conspiracy as well as the defense against the conspiracy, and since the profession of infirmity comes at the moment of his greatest strength, we may conclude that we are witnessing the practice of salutary anxiety operating at the center of the play's world, in the consciousness of Prospero himself, magician, artist, and prince. This does not mean that Prospero's anxiety about the conspiracy, about his enemies and servants and daughter, about his own inward state is not genuinely felt, nor does it mean that he is in absolute, untroubled control either of the characters whom he has brought onto the island or of himself. Rapt in his own magical vision of bounteousness, he has forgotten a serious threat to his life: "The minute of their plot/Is almost come" (4.1.141–2). But it is important to take seriously his deep complicity in his present tribulations, for only by actively willing them can he undo the tribulations that he unwillingly and unwittingly brought about years before. At that time, absorbed in his occult studies, he had been unaware of the dangers around him; now as the condition of a return to his dukedom, he himself brings those dangers to the center of his retreat. This center, whether we regard it as emblematic of the dominant religious, aesthetic, or political institution, is not the still point in a turbulent world but the point at which the anxieties that shape the character of others are screwed up to their highest pitch. Precisely from that point – and as a further exemplification of the salutary nature of anxiety – reconciliation and pardon can issue forth. This pardon is not a release from the power in which Prospero holds everyone around him but, as with Latimer and James I, its ultimate expression.[23]

Shakespeare goes beyond Latimer and James, however, in envisaging a case in which anxiety does not appear to have its full redeeming effect, a case in which the object of attention refuses to be fashioned inwardly, refuses even to acknowledge guilt, and yet is pardoned. The generosity of the pardon in this instance is

inseparable from a demonstration of supreme force. "For you, most wicked sir,"
Prospero says to his brother Antonio,

> whom to call brother
> Would even infect my mouth, I do forgive
> Thy rankest fault – all of them; and require
> My dukedom of thee, which perforce, I know
> Thou must restore.
>
> (5.1.130–4)

Antonio's silence at this point suggests that he remains unrepentant, but it also
expresses eloquently the paralysis that is the hallmark of extreme anxiety. It has
been argued convincingly that the truculence of the villains at the close of the play
marks the limit of Prospero's power – as Prospero's failure to educate Caliban has
already shown, the strategy of salutary anxiety cannot remake the inner life of
everyone – yet at the very moment the limit is marked, the play suggests that it is
relatively inconsequential. It would no doubt be preferable to receive the appropriate signs of inward gratitude from everyone, but Prospero will have to content
himself in the case of Antonio with the full restoration of his dukedom.[24]

III

What I have been describing here is the theatrical appropriation and staging of a
sixteenth- and seventeenth-century social practice. But the strategy of salutary
anxiety is not simply reflected in a secondhand way by the work of art, because
the practice itself is already implicated in the artistic traditions and institutions out
of which this particular representation, The Tempest, has emerged. Latimer may
have been indifferent or hostile to the drama and to literature in general, but his
tale of the Cambridge prisoner seems shaped by literary conventions, earlier tales
of wronged innocence and royal pardons. And if the practice he exemplifies helps
to empower theatrical representations, fictive representations have themselves
helped to empower his practice.[25] So too Dudley Carleton, watching men about
to go to their deaths, thinks of the last act of a play, and when a pardon is granted,
the spectators applaud. This complex circulation between the social dimension of
an aesthetic strategy and the aesthetic dimension of a social strategy is difficult to
grasp because the strategy in question has an extraordinarily long and tangled
history, one whose aesthetic roots go back at least as far as Aristotle's Poetics. But
we may find a more manageable, though still complex, model in the relation
between The Tempest and one of its presumed sources, William Strachey's
account of the tempest that struck an English fleet bound for the fledgling colony
at Jamestown.[26]

   Strachey's account, with its bravura description of a violent storm at sea and its
tale of Englishmen providentially cast ashore on an uninhabited island rumored
to be devil haunted, is likely, along with other New World materials, to have
helped shape The Tempest. The play was performed long before Strachey's

narrative was printed in Purchas's *Pilgrims* as "A true reportory of the wrack, and redemption of Sir Thomas Gates Knight," but scholars presume that Shakespeare read a manuscript version of the work, which takes the form of a confidential letter written to a certain "noble lady."[27] My interest is not the particular verbal echoes, which have been painstakingly researched since Malone in 1808 first called attention to them, but the significance of the relation between the two texts, or rather between the institutions that the texts serve. For it is important to grasp that we are dealing not with the reflections of isolated individuals musing on current events but with expressions whose context is corporate and institutional.

William Strachey was a shareholder and secretary of the Virginia Company's colony at Jamestown; his letter on the events of 1609–10 was unpublished until 1625, not for want of interest but because the Virginia Company was engaged in a vigorous propaganda and financial campaign on behalf of the colony, and the company's leaders found Strachey's report too disturbing to allow it into print. Shakespeare too was a shareholder in a joint-stock company, the King's Men, as well as its principal playwright and sometime actor; *The Tempest* also remained unpublished for years, again presumably not for want of interest but because the theater company resisted losing control of its playbook. Neither joint-stock company was a direct agent of the crown: despite the legal fiction that they were retainers of the monarch, the King's Men could not have survived through royal patronage alone, and they were not in the same position of either dependence or privilege as other household servants; the crown had deliberately withdrawn from the direction of the Virginia Company. Royal protection and support, of course, remained essential in both cases, but the crown would not assume responsibility, nor could either company count on royal financial support in times of need. Committed for their survival to attracting investment capital and turning a profit, both companies depended on their ability to market stories that would excite, interest, and attract supporters. Both Strachey and Shakespeare were involved in unusually direct and intricate ways in every aspect of their companies' operations: Strachey as shareholder, adventurer, and eventually secretary; Shakespeare as shareholder, actor, and playwright. Because of these multiple positions, both men probably identified intensely with the interests of their respective companies.

I want to propose that the relation between the play and its alleged source is a relation between joint-stock companies.[28] I do not mean that there was a direct, contractual connection.[29] As we have already seen with Latimer, the transfer of cultural practices and powers depends not upon contracts but upon networks of resemblance. In the case of Strachey and Shakespeare, there *are*, in point of fact, certain intriguing institutional affiliations: as Charles Mills Gayley observed many years ago, a remarkable number of social and professional connections link Shakespeare and the stockholders and directors of the Virginia Company; moreover, Strachey in 1605 wrote a prefatory sonnet commending Jonson's *Sejanus* and in 1606 is listed as a shareholder in an acting company known as the Children of the Queen's Revels, the company that had taken over the Blackfriars Theater from Richard Burbage.[30] Still, I should emphasize that these affiliations do not amount to a direct transfer of properties; we are dealing with a system of mimetic rather than contractual exchange. The conjunction of Strachey's unpublished letter and Shakespeare's play signals an institutional circulation of culturally significant narratives. And as we shall see, this circulation has as its central concern the public management of anxiety.

Strachey tells the story of a state of emergency and a crisis of authority. The "unmerciful tempest" that almost sank Sir Thomas Gates's ship, the *Sea Venture*, provoked an immediate collapse of the distinction between those who labor and those who rule, a distinction, we should recall, that is at the economic and ideological center of Elizabethan and Jacobean society:

> Then men might be seen to labour, I may well say, for life, and the better sort, even our Governour, and Admiral themselves, not refusing their turn. . . . And it is most true, such as in all their life times had never done hours work before (their minds now helping their bodies) were able twice forty eight hours together to toil with the best, (in Purchas, 19:9–11)

"The best" – the violence of the storm has turned Strachey's own language upside down: now it is the common seamen, ordinarily despised and feared by their social superiors, who are, as the Romans called their aristocrats, the *optimi viri*, the best of men.[31] Indeed the storm had quite literally a leveling force: while the governor was "both by his speech and authority heartening every man unto his labour," a great wave "struck him from the place where he sat, and groveled him, and all us about him on our faces, beating together with our breaths all thoughts from our bosoms, else then that we were now sinking" (p. 10).

Even after the ship had run aground in the Bermudas and the one hundred fifty men, women, and children on board had been saved, the crisis of authority was not resolved; indeed it only intensified then, not because of a leveling excess of anxiety but because of its almost complete absence in the colonists. The alarm of the rulers makes itself felt in quirks of Strachey's style. He reports, for example, that many palmettos were cut down for their edible tops, but the report has a strange nervous tone, as the plants are comically turned into wealthy victims of a popular uprising: "Many an ancient Burgher was therefore heaved at, and fell not for his place, but for his head: for our common people, whose bellies never had ears, made it no breach of Charity in their hot bloods and tall stomachs to murder thousands of them" (p. 19).

The strain registered here in the tone stands for concerns that are partially suppressed in the published text, concerns that are voiced in a private letter written in December 1610 by Richard Martin, secretary of the Virginia Company in London, to Strachey, who was by then in Jamestown. Martin asks Strachey for a full confidential report on

> the nature & quality of the soil, & how it is like to serve you without help from hence, the manners of the people, how the Barbarians are content with your being there, but especially how our own people do brook their obedience, how they endure labor, whether willingly or upon constraint, how they live in the exercise of Religion, whether out of conscience or for fashion, And generally what ease you have in the government there, & what hope of success.[32]

Here the deepest fears lie not with the human or natural resources of the New World but with the discipline of the English colonists and common seamen. And the principal questions – whether obedience is willing or forced, whether religious observance is sincere or feigned – suggest an interest in inner states, as if the shareholders in the Virginia Company believed that only with a set of powerful inward restraints could the colonists be kept from rebelling at the first sign of the slippage or relaxation of authority. The company had an official institutional interest in shaping and controlling the minds of its own people. But the Bermuda shipwreck revealed the difficulty of this task as well as its importance: set apart from the institutional and military safeguards established at Jamestown, Bermuda was an experimental space, a testing ground where the extent to which disciplinary anxiety had been internalized by the ordinary venturers could be measured.

The results were not encouraging. As Strachey and others remark, Bermuda was an extraordinarily pleasant surprise: the climate was healthful, the water was pure, there were no native inhabitants to contend with, and, equally important, there was no shortage of food. Tortoises – "such a kind of meat, as a man can neither absolutely call Fish nor Flesh" (p. 24)[33] – were found in great number, and the skies were dark with great flocks of birds:

> Our men found a pretty way to take them, which was by standing on the Rocks or Sands by the Sea side, and hollowing, laughing, and making the strangest out-cry that possibly they could: with the noise whereof the Birds would come flocking to that place, and settle upon the very arms and head of him that so cried, and still creep nearer and nearer, answering the noise themselves: by which our men would weigh them with their hands, and which weighed heaviest they took for the best and let the others alone. (Purchas, 19:22–3)

Even to us, living for the most part in the confident expectation of full bellies, this sounds extraordinary enough; to seventeenth-century voyagers, whose ordinary condition was extreme want and who had dragged themselves from the violent sea onto an unknown shore with the likely prospect of starvation and death, such extravagant abundance must have seemed the fantastic realization of old folk dreams of a land where the houses were roofed with pies and the pigs ran about with little knives conveniently stuck in their precooked sides. In this Land of Cockaigne setting, far removed not only from England but from the hardships of Jamestown, the authority of Sir Thomas Gates and his lieutenants was anything but secure. For the perception that Bermuda was a providential deliverance contained within it a subversive corollary: why leave? why press on to a hungry garrison situated in a pestiferous swamp and in grave tension with the surrounding Algonquian tribesmen?[34]

According to Strachey, Gates was initially concerned less about his own immediate authority than about the possible consequences of his absence in Virginia. The *Sea Venture* had come to grief in the tempest, but Gates thought (correctly, as it happened) that the other two vessels might have reached their destination, and this thought brought not only consolation but anxiety, which focused, in characteristic Renaissance fashion, on the ambitions of the younger generation. Fearful about "what innovation and tumult might happily [haply] arise, among the younger and ambitious spirits of the new companies to arrive in Virginia" (p. 26) in his absence, Gates wished to construct new ships as quickly as possible to continue on to Jamestown, but the sailors and the colonists alike began to grumble at this plan. In Virginia, they reasoned, "nothing but wretchedness and labour must be expected, with many wants and a churlish entreaty"; in Bermuda, all things "at ease and pleasure might be enjoyed" (p. 29) without hardship or threatening. There is, at least as Strachey reports it, virtually no internalization of the ideology of colonialism; the voyagers appear to think of themselves as forced to endure a temporary exile from home. As long as "they were (for the time) to lose the fruition both of their friends and Country, as good, and better it were for them, to repose and seat them where they should have the least outward wants the while" (p. 29). And to this dangerous appeal – the appeal, in Strachey's words, of "liberty, and fulness of sensuality" (p. 35) – was added a still more dangerous force: religious dissent.

Arguments against leaving Bermuda began to be voiced not only among the "idle, untoward, and wretched number of the many" (p. 29) but among the educated few. One of these, Stephen Hopkins,

> alleged substantial arguments, both civil and divine (the Scripture falsely quoted) that it was no breach of honesty, conscience, nor Religion, to decline from the obedience of the Governour, or refuse to go any further, led by his authority (except it so pleased themselves) since the authority ceased when the wrack was committed, and with it, they were all then freed from the government of any man. (pp. 30–1)

Hopkins evidently accepted the governor's authority as a contractual obligation that continued only so long as the enterprise remained on course. Once there was a swerve from the official itinerary, that authority, not granted a general or universal character, lapsed, and the obedience of the subject gave way to the will and pleasure of each man.[35] We cannot know, of course, if Hopkins said anything so radical, but this is how his "substantial arguments, both civil and divine," sounded to those in command. In Strachey's account, at least, the shipwreck had led to a profound questioning of authority that seems to anticipate the challenge posed by mid-seventeenth-century radicals like Winstanley. What are the boundaries of authority? What is the basis of its claim to be obeyed? How much loyalty does an individual owe to a corporation?

When the seditious words were reported to Gates, the governor convened a martial court and sentenced Hopkins to death, but the condemned man was so tearfully repentant that he received a pardon. This moving scene – the saving public display of anxiety – evidently did not settle the question of authority, however, for shortly after, yet another mutiny arose, this time led by a gentleman named Henry Paine. When Paine was warned that he risked execution for "insolency," he replied, Strachey reports,

> with a settled and bitter violence, and in such unreverent terms, as I should offend the modest ear too much to express it in his own phrase; but its contents were, how that the Governour had no authority of that quality, to justify upon any one

(how mean soever in the colony) an action of that nature, and therefore let the Governour (said he) kiss, &c. (p. 34)

When these words, "with the omitted additions," were reported, the governor, "who had now the eyes of the whole Colony fixed upon him," condemned Paine "to be instantly hanged; and the ladder being ready, after he had made many confessions, he earnestly desired, being a Gentleman, that he might be shot to death, and towards the evening he had his desire, the Sun and his life setting together" (p. 34). "He had his desire" – Strachey's sarcasm is also perhaps the representation of what those in authority regarded as an intolerable nonchalance, a refusal to perform those rituals of tearful repentance that apparently saved Hopkins's life. In effect Paine is killed to set an example, condemned to die for cursing authority, for a linguistic crime, for violating discursive decorum, for inadequate anxiety in the presence of power.

In his narrative, Strachey represents the norms Paine has challenged by means of his "&c." – the noble lady to whom he is writing, like Mr. Kurtz's intended, must be sheltered from the awful truth, here from the precise terms of the fatal irreverent challenge to authority. The suppression of the offending word enacts in miniature the reimposition of salutary anxiety by a governor "so solicitous and careful, whose both example . . . and authority, could lay shame, and command upon our people" (p. 28). The governor is full of care – therefore resistant to the lure of the island – and he manages, even in the midst of a paradisal plenty, to impose this care upon others. When the governor himself writes to a fellow officer explaining why all of the colonists must be compelled to leave the island, he invokes not England's imperial destiny or Christianity's advancement but the Virginia Company's investment: "The meanest in the whole Fleet stood the Company in no less than twenty pounds, for his own personal Transportation, and things necessary to accompany him" (p. 36). On the strength of this compelling motive, new ships were built, and in an impressive feat of navigation, the whole company finally reached Jamestown.

Upon their arrival Gates and his people found the garrison in desperate condition – starving, confused, terrorized by hostile and treacherous Indians, and utterly demoralized. In Gates's view, the problem was almost entirely one of discipline, and he addressed it by imposing a set of "orders and instructions" upon the colony that transformed the "government" of Jamestown "into an absolute command." The orders were published in 1612 by Strachey as the *Laws Divine, Moral, and Martial*, an exceptionally draconian code by which whipping, mutilation, and the death penalty might be imposed for a wide range of offenses, including blasphemy, insubordination, even simple criticism of the Virginia Company and its officers. These orders, the first martial law code in America, suspended the traditional legal sanctions that governed the lives of Englishmen, customary codes based on mutual constraints and obligations, and instituted in their stead the grim and self-consciously innovative logic of a state of emergency. The company's claim upon the colonists had become total. The group that had been shipwrecked in Bermuda passed from dreams of absolute freedom to the imposition of absolute control.

Such then were the narrative materials that passed from Strachey to Shake-speare, from the Virginia Company to the King's Men: a violent tempest, a providential shipwreck on a strange island, a crisis in authority provoked by both danger and excess, a fear of lower-class disorder and upper-class ambition, a triumphant affirmation of absolute control linked to the manipulation of anxiety and to a departure from the island. But the swerve away from these materials in *The Tempest* is as apparent as their presence: the island is not in America but in the Mediterranean; it is not uninhabited – Ariel and Caliban (and, for that matter, Sycorax) were present before the arrival of Prospero and Miranda; none of the figures are in any sense colonists; the departure is for home rather than a colony and entails not an unequivocal heightening of authority but a partial diminution, signaled in Prospero's abjuration of magic.

> I'll break my, staff,
> Bury it certain fadoms in the earth,
> And deeper than did ever plummet sound
> I'll drown my book.
>
> (5.1.54–7)[36]

If the direction of Strachey's narrative is toward the promulgation of the martial law codes, the direction of *The Tempest* is toward forgiveness. And if that forgiveness is itself the manifestation of supreme power, the emblem of that power remains marriage rather than punishment.

The changes I have sketched are signs of the process whereby the Bermuda narrative is made negotiable, turned into a currency that may be transferred from one institutional context to another. The changes do not constitute a coherent critique of the colonial discourse, but they function as an unmooring of its elements so as to confer upon them the currency's liquidity. Detached from their context in Strachey's letter, these elements may be transformed and recombined with materials drawn from other writers about the New World who differ sharply from Strachey in their interests and motives – Montaigne, Sylvester Jourdain, James Rosier, Robert Eden, Peter Martyr – and then integrated in a dramatic text that draws on a wide range of discourse, including pastoral and epic poetry, the lore of magic and witchcraft, literary romance, and a remarkable number of Shakespeare's own earlier plays.

The ideological effects of the transfer to *The Tempest* are ambiguous. On the one hand, the play seems to act out a fantasy of mind control, to celebrate absolute patriarchal rule, to push to an extreme the dream of order, epic achievement, and ideological justification implicit in Strachey's text. The lower-class resistance Strachey chronicles becomes in Shakespeare the drunken rebellion of Stephano and Trinculo, the butler and jester who, suddenly finding themselves freed from their masters, are drawn to a poor man's fantasy of mastery: "the King and all our company else being drown'd, we will inherit here" (2.2.174–5). Similarly, the upper-class resistance of Henry Paine is transformed into the murderous treachery of Sebastian, in whom the shipwreck arouses dreams of an escape from subordination to his older brother, the king of Naples, just as Antonio had escaped subordination to his older brother Prospero:

> *Sebastian:*   I remember
> You did supplant your brother Prospero.
> *Antonio:*   True.
> And look how well my garments sit upon me,
> Much feater than before. My brother's servants
> Were then my fellows, now they are my men.
>   (2.1.270–4)

By invoking fratricidal rivalry here Shakespeare is not only linking the Strachey materials to his own long-standing theatrical preoccupations but also supplementing the contractual authority of a governor like Sir Thomas Gates with the familial and hence culturally sanctified authority of the eldest son. To rise up against such a figure, as Claudius had against old Hamlet or Edmund against Edgar, is an assault not only on a political structure but on the moral and natural order of things: it is an act that has, as Claudius says, "the primal eldest curse upon't." The assault is magically thwarted by Ariel, the indispensable agent of Prospero's "art"; hence that art, potentially a force of disorder, spiritual violence, and darkness, is confirmed as the agent of legitimacy. Through his mastery of the occult, Prospero withholds food from his enemies, spies upon them, listens to their secret conversations, monitors their movements, blocks their actions, keeps track of their dealings with the island's native inhabitant, torments and disciplines his servants, defeats conspiracies against his life. A crisis of authority – deposition from power, exile, impotence – gives way through the power of his art to a full restoration. From this perspective Prospero's magic is the romance equivalent of martial law.

Yet *The Tempest* seems to raise troubling questions about this authority. The great storm with which the play opens has some of the leveling force of the storm that struck the *Sea Venture*. To be sure, unlike Strachey's gentlemen, Shakespeare's nobles refuse the boatswain's exasperated demand that they share the labor, "Work you then," but their snarling refusal – "Hang, cur! hang, you whoreson, insolent noisemaker!" (1.1.42–4) – far from securing their class superiority, represents them as morally beneath the level of the common seamen.[37] Likewise, Shakespeare's king, Alonso, is not "groveled" by a wave, but – perhaps worse – he is peremptorily ordered below by the harried boatswain: "What cares these roarers for the name of king? To cabin! silence! trouble us not" (1.1.16–18). And if we learn eventually that these roarers are in fact produced *by* a king – in his name and through his command of a magical language – this knowledge does not altogether cancel our perception of the storm's indifference to the ruler's authority and the idle aristocrat's pride of place.

The perception would perhaps be overwhelmed by the display of Prospero's power were it not for the questions that are raised about this very power. A Renaissance audience might have found the locus of these questions in the ambiguous status of magic, an ambiguity deliberately heightened by the careful parallels drawn between

Prospero and the witch Sycorax and by the attribution to Prospero of claims made by Ovid's witch Medea. But for a modern audience, at least, the questions center on the figure of Caliban, whose claim to the legitimate possession of the island – "This island's mine by Sycorax my mother" (1.2.331) – is never really answered, or rather is answered by Prospero only with hatred, torture, and enslavement.[38] Though he treats Caliban as less than human, Prospero finally expresses, in a famously enigmatic phrase, a sense of connection with his servant-monster, standing anxious and powerless before him: "this thing of darkness I / Acknowledge mine" (5.1.275–76). He may intend these words only as a declaration of ownership, but it is difficult not to hear in them some deeper recognition of affinity, some half-conscious acknowledgment of guilt. At the play's end the princely magician appears anxious and powerless before the audience to beg for indulgence and freedom.

As the epilogue is spoken, Prospero's magical power and princely authority – figured in the linked abilities to raise winds and to pardon offenders – pass, in a startling display of the circulation of social energy, from the performer onstage to the crowd of spectators. In the play's closing moments the marginal, vulnerable actor, more than half-visible beneath the borrowed robes of an assumed dignity, seems to acknowledge that the imaginary forces with which he has played reside ultimately not in himself or in the playwright but in the multitude. The audience is the source of his anxiety, and it holds his release quite literally in its hands: without the crowd's applause his "ending is despair" (Epilogue, 15). This admission of dependence includes a glance at the multitude's own vulnerability:

> As you from crimes would pardon'd be,
> Let your indulgence set me free.
> (Epilogue, 19–20)

But it nonetheless implicates the prince as well as the player in the experience of anxiety and the need for pardon.

Furthermore, even if we may argue that such disturbing or even subversive reflections are contained within the thematic structure of the play, a structure that seems to support the kind of authority served by Strachey, we must acknowledge that the propagandists for colonization found little to admire in the theater. That is, the most disturbing effects of the play may have been located not in what may be perceived in the text by a subtle interpreter – implied criticisms of colonialism or subversive doubts about its structures of authority – but in the phenomenon of theatrical representation itself. In 1593 Sir Thomas Smith reminded each captain in Virginia that his task was "to lay the foundation of a good and . . . an eternal colony for your posterity, not a May game or stage play."[39] Festive, evanescent, given over to images of excess, stage plays function here as the symbolic opposite to the lasting colony. So too in a sermon preached in London in 1610 to a group of colonists about to set out for Virginia, William Crashaw declared that the enemies of the godly colony were the devil, the pope, and the players – the latter angry "because we resolve to suffer no Idle persons in Virginia."[40] Similarly, at the end of the martial law text, Strachey records an exceptionally long prayer that he claims was "duly said Morning and Evening upon the Court of Guard, either by the Captain of the watch himself, or by some one of his principal officers." If Strachey is right, twice a day the colonists would have heard, among other uplifting sentiments, the following:

> Whereas we have by undertaking this plantation undergone the reproofs of the base world, insomuch as many of our own brethren laugh us to scorn, O Lord we pray thee fortify us against this temptation: let *Sanballat, & Tobias*, Papists & players, & such other *Ammonites & Horonites* the scum & dregs of the earth, let them mock such as help to build up the walls of Jerusalem, and they that be filthy, let them be filthy still.[41]

Even if the content of a play seemed acceptable, the model of entertainment itself was the enemy of the colonial plantation.

IV

What then is the relation between the theater and the surrounding institutions? Shakespeare's play offers us a model of unresolved and unresolvable doubleness: the island in *The Tempest* seems to be an image of the place of pure fantasy, set apart from surrounding discourses; and it seems to be an image of the place of power, the place in which all individual discourses are organized by the half-invisible ruler. By extension art is a well-demarcated, marginal, private sphere, the realm of insight, pleasure, and isolation; and art is a capacious, central, public sphere, the realm of proper political order made possible through mind control, coercion, discipline, anxiety, and pardon. The aesthetic space – or, more accurately, the commercial space of the theatrical joint-stock company – is constituted by the simultaneous appropriation of and swerving from the discourse of power.

And this doubleness in effect produces two different accounts of the nature of mimetic economy. In one account, aesthetic representation is unlike all other exchanges because it takes nothing; art is pure plenitude. Everywhere else there is scarcity: wretches cling to "an acre of barren ground, long heath, brown furze, any thing" (1.1.66–7), and one person's gain is another's loss. In works of art, by contrast, things can be imitated, staged, reproduced without any loss or expense; indeed what is borrowed seems enhanced by the borrowing, for nothing is used up, nothing fades. The magic of art resides in the freedom of the imagination and hence in liberation from the constraints of the body. What is produced elsewhere only by intense labor is produced in art by a magical command whose power Shakespeare figures in Ariel's response to Prospero's call:

> All hail, great master, grave sir, hail! I come
> To answer thy best pleasure; be't to fly,
> To swim, to dive into the fire, to ride
> On the curl'd clouds. To thy strong bidding, task
> Ariel, and all his quality.
>
> (1.2.189–93)

This account of art as pure plenitude is perhaps most perfectly imaged in Prospero's wedding masque, with its goddesses and nymphs and dancing reapers, its majestic vision of

> Barns and garners never empty;
> Vines with clust'ring bunches growing,
> Plants with goodly burthen bowing.
>   (4.1.111–13)

But the prayer at the end of the martial law code reminds us that there is another version of mimetic economy, one in which aesthetic exchanges, like all other exchanges, always involve loss, even if it is cunningly hidden; in which aesthetic value, like all other value, actively depends upon want, craving, and absence; in which art itself – fantasy ridden and empty – is the very soul of scarcity. This version too finds its expression in *The Tempest* in the high cost Prospero has paid for his absorption in his secret studies, in Ariel's grumblings about his "pains" and "toil," and in the sudden vanishing – "to a strange, hollow, and confused noise" – of the masque that had figured forth plenitude and in Prospero's richly anxious meditation on the "baseless fabric" of his own glorious vision.

It is this doubleness that Shakespeare's joint-stock company bequeathed to its cultural heirs. And the principal beneficiary in the end was not the theater but a different institution, the institution of literature. Shakespeare served posthumously as a principal shareholder in this institution as well – not as a man of the theater but as the author of the book. During Shakespeare's lifetime, the King's Men showed no interest in and may have actually resisted the publication of a one-volume collection of their famous playwright's work; the circulation of such a book was not in the interests of their company. But other collective enterprises, including the educational system in which this study is implicated, have focused more on the text than on the playhouse.

For if Shakespeare himself imagined Prospero's island as the great Globe Theater, succeeding generations found that island more compactly and portably figured in the bound volume. The passage from the stage to the book signals a larger shift from the joint-stock company, with its primary interest in protecting the common property, to the modern corporation, with its primary interest in the expansion and profitable exploitation of a network of relations. Unlike the Globe, which is tied to a particular place and time and community, unlike even the traveling theater company, with its constraints of personnel and stage properties and playing space, the book is supremely portable. It may be readily detached from its immediate geographical and cultural origins, its original producers and consumers, and endlessly reproduced, circulated, exchanged, exported to other times and places.[42]

The plays, of course, continue to live in the theater, but Shakespeare's achievement and the cult of artistic genius erected around the achievement have become increasingly identified with his collected works. Those works have been widely acknowledged as the central literary achievement of English culture. As such they served – and continue to serve – as a fetish of Western civilization, a fetish Caliban curiously anticipates when he counsels Stephano and Trinculo to cut Prospero's throat:[43]

> Remember
> First to possess his books; for without them
> He's but a sot, as I am; nor hath not
> One spirit to command: they all do hate him
> As rootedly as I. Burn but his books.
> (3.2.91–95)

I want to close with a story that provides an oddly ironic perspective on Caliban's desire and exemplifies the continued doubleness of Shakespeare in our culture: at once the embodiment of civilized recreation, freed from the anxiety of rule, and the instrument of empire. The story is told by H. M. Stanley – the journalist and African explorer of "Doctor Livingstone, I presume?" fame – in his account of his journeyings through what he calls "the dark continent." In May 1877 he was at a place called Mowa in central Africa. I will let him tell the story in his own words:

> On the third day of our stay at Mowa, feeling quite comfortable amongst the people, on account of their friendly bearing, I began to write down in my note-book the terms for articles in order to improve my already copious vocabulary of native words. I had proceeded only a few minutes when I observed a strange commotion amongst the people who had been flocking about me, and presently they ran away. In a short time we heard war-cries ringing loudly and shrilly over the table-land. Two hours afterwards, a long line of warriors, armed with muskets, were seen descending the table-land and advancing towards our camp. There may have been between five hundred and six hundred of them. We, on the other hand, had made but few preparations except such as would justify us replying to them in the event of the actual commencement of hostilities. But I had made many firm friends amongst them, and I firmly believed that I would be able to avert an open rupture.
>
> When they had assembled at about a hundred yards in front of our camp, Safeni [the chief of another tribe with whom Stanley had become friendly] and I walked up towards them, and sat down midway. Some half-dozen of the Mowa people came near, and the shauri began.
>
> "What is the matter, my friends?" I asked. "Why do you come with guns in your hands in such numbers, as though you were coming to fight? Fight! Fight us, your friends! Tut! this is some great mistake, surely."
>
> "Mundelé," replied one of them, . . . "our people saw you yesterday make marks on some tara-tara" (paper). "This is very bad. Our country will waste, our goats will die, our bananas will rot, and our women will dry up. What have we done to you, that you should wish to kill us? We have sold you food, and we have brought you wine, each day. Your people are allowed to wander where they please, without trouble. Why is the Mundelé so wicked? We have gathered together to fight you if you do not burn that tara-tara now before our eyes. If you burn it we go away, and shall be friends as heretofore."
>
> I told them to rest there, and left Safeni in their hands as a pledge that I should return. My tent was not fifty yards from the spot, but while going towards it my

brain was busy in devising some plan to foil this superstitious madness. My notebook contained a vast number of valuable notes; plans of falls, creeks, villages,
sketches of localities, ethnological and philological details, sufficient to fill two
octavo volumes – everything was of general interest to the public. I could not
sacrifice it to the childish caprice of savages. As I was rummaging my book box,
I came across a volume of Shakespeare (Chandos edition), much worn and well
thumbed, and which was of the same size as my field-book; its cover was similar
also, and it might be passed for the note-book provided that no one remembered
its appearance too well. I took it to them.
"Is this the tara-tara, friends, that you wish burnt?"
"Yes, yes, that is it!"
"Well, take it, and burn it or keep it."
"M-m. No, no, no. We will not touch it. It is fetish. You must burn it."
"I! Well, let it be so. I will do anything to please my good friends of Mowa."
      We walked to the nearest fire. I breathed a regretful farewell to my genial
companion, which during many weary hours of night had assisted to relieve my
mind when oppressed by almost intolerable woes, and then gravely consigned the
innocent Shakespeare to the flames, heaping the brush-fuel over it with ceremo-
nious care.
      "Ah-h-h," breathed the poor deluded natives, sighing their relief. "The Mundelé
is good – is very good. He loves his Mowa friends. There is no trouble now,
Mundelé. The Mowa people are not bad." And something approaching to a cheer
was shouted among them, which terminated the episode of the Burning of Shakespeare.[44]

Stanley's precious notebook, with its sketches and ethnographic and philologic
details, survived then and proved invaluable in charting and organizing the Belgian
Congo, perhaps the most vicious of all of Europe's African colonies. As Stanley had
claimed, everything was indeed of general interest to the public. After Stanley's
death, the notebooks passed into the possession of heirs and then for many years
were presumed lost. But they were rediscovered at the time of the Congo
independence celebrations and have recently been edited. Their publication
revealed something odd: while the notebook entry for his stay at Mowa records
that the natives were angry at his writing – "They say I made strong medicine to kill
their country" – Stanley makes no mention of the burning of Shakespeare.[45]
Perhaps, to heighten that general interest with which he was so concerned, he
made up the story. He could have achieved his narrative effect with only two
books: Shakespeare and the Bible. And had he professed to burn the latter to save
his notebook, his readers would no doubt have been scandalized.
      For our purposes, it doesn't matter very much if the story "really" happened.
What matters is the role Shakespeare plays in it, a role at once central and
expendable – and, in some obscure way, not just expendable but exchangeable
for what really matters: the writing that more directly serves power. For if at
moments we can convince ourselves that Shakespeare *is* the discourse of power,
we should remind ourselves that there are usually other discourses – here the
notes and vocabulary and maps – that are instrumentally far more important. Yet
if we try then to convince ourselves that Shakespeare is marginal and untainted
by power, we have Stanley's story to remind us that without Shakespeare we

wouldn't have the notes. Of course, this is just an accident – the accident of the books' resemblance – but then why was Stanley carrying the book in the first place?

For Stanley, Shakespeare's theater had become a book, and the book in turn had become a genial companion, a talisman of civility, a source not of salutary anxiety but of comfort in adversity. The anxiety in his account – and it is not salutary – is among the natives, and it is relieved only when, as Caliban had hoped, the book is destroyed. But the destruction of one book only saves another, more practical, more deadly. And when he returned to London or New York, Stanley could always buy another copy (Chandos edition) of his genial companion.

NOTES

1 "First Sermon on the Lord's Prayer," in *The Works of Hugh Latimer*, 2 vols., ed. George Elwes Corrie, Parker Society (Cambridge: Cambridge University Press, 1844), 1:335. Though her mother was a near relation of Catherine of Aragon, the duchess of Suffolk was a staunch Protestant who went into exile during the reign of Mary Tudor.

   Latimer's rhetorical occasion for relating this story is an odd one: he is commenting on the appropriateness of addressing God as "our father," since God "hath a fatherly and loving affection towards us, far passing the love of bodily parents to their children." Latimer then cites a passage from Isaiah in which the prophet asks rhetorically, in speaking of God's love, "Can a wife forget the child of her womb, and the son whom she hath borne?" Isaiah uses the image of a wife, Latimer remarks, "because women most commonly are more affected towards their children than men be." He then recalls with horror that under the devil's influence some women have in fact killed their own children, but he warns his listeners not to believe every story of this kind that they hear. And he proceeds to support this warning with the story of the Cambridge woman.

2 Alternatively, we might say that Latimer occupies a peculiarly intermediate position, anticipating that occupied by the players: at once free and constrained, the strutting master of the scene and the social inferior, the charismatic object of intense cathexis and the embodiment of dependence.

3 The closest parallel, I suppose, would be nocturnal emissions, about which there is a substantial literature in the Middle Ages and early modern period, but I am not sure a story about them would have been suitable for the duchess of Suffolk.

4 The gap is, at this point, a very small one, and on her release from prison the woman may well have been sent back to her husband. Latimer does not bother to say, presumably because the woman's fate was irrelevant to his homiletic point.

5 Though the justification for a transfer (as opposed to a simple elimination) is left vague, perhaps to spare the sensibility of the duchess of Suffolk, Latimer may believe that for some time after childbirth the woman's body is tainted – hence "a green woman," as in green or tainted meat – and that in the interest of public health she should not be permitted contact, in particular sexual contact, with others. Or perhaps he simply believes that a woman still weakened from the ordeal of childbirth – hence a different meaning for "green woman," as in a green or fresh wound – should be spared the normal demands on her energies.

6   See similarly Spenser's account of Duessa (*Faerie Queene* 1.8.46–8). There are many medical as well as literary and theological reflections on the innate filthiness of women.

7   The sermon is probably not a source for *Measure for Measure*, though it is intriguing that another, more famous, sermon by Latimer – the first of the "Sermons on the Card" – includes an emblematic story that bears a certain resemblance to Shakespeare's play. The king in Latimer's fable accepts into his favor "a mean man," "not because this person hath of himself deserved any such favour, but that the king casteth this favour unto him of his own mere motion and fantasy." The man thus favored is appointed "the chief captain and defender of his town of Calais," but he treacherously violates his trust (*The Works of Hugh Latimer* 1:4–5).

8   Although one can readily imagine a detached response to a Shakespearean comedy, such a response would signal the failure of the play to please or a refusal of the pleasure the play was offering.

9   This is, however, only a *working* distinction, to mark an unstable, shifting relation between anxiety and pleasure. Anxiety and pleasure are not the same, but they are not simple opposites. Anxiety in the presence of real bodies put at real risk is a source of pleasure for at least some of the spectators, whereas in the theater pleasure in imaginary situations is not entirely unmixed with (and does not entirely absorb and transform) anxiety. Even if we discount the rhetorical exaggerations of that anxiety in a literary criticism that often speaks of the excruciating pain and difficulty of spectatorship (or reading), we must acknowledge that Shakespeare often arouses considerable anxiety. Still, we must also acknowledge that for the collective body of spectators the ratio of anxiety to pleasure in the theater was likely to have differed from that outside its walls.

10 Theatrical anxiety must not only give pleasure in the theater but generate a longing for the theater in those who have left its precincts. If large numbers of potential spectators feel they can get what they need in other places, they will not take the trouble to return. The point is obvious but still worth remarking, since we are likely to forget, first, that Elizabethan and Jacobean public theaters had extremely large capacities (as high as two thousand spectators) and hence expected to draw substantial crowds and, second, that it was by no means simple to attend most of the theaters. A trip to the Globe took a good part of the day and involved considerable expense, including transportation by boat and refreshments. The theater had to contrive to make potential spectators think, and think frequently, "I wish I were at the theater." To do so, it could advertise through playbills and processions, but it could also count on deep associations: that is, certain anxieties would remind one of the theater where those same anxieties were turned to the service of pleasure.

11 The very point of theatrical anxiety may be that it is not "real" – that is, we are not threatened, there are no consequences in the real world to fortune or station or life, and so forth. But this formulation is at best only a half-truth, since at the level of feelings it is not always so easy to distinguish between the anxiety generated by a literary experience and the anxiety generated by events in one's own life.

12 He does, however, in some sense tell the story for his hearers' pleasure as well as instruction, and I think it is important to resist making too sharp a distinction between the purely theatrical uses of anxiety and the uses elsewhere in the culture. The distinction is practical and relative: no less important for that, but not to be construed as a theoretical necessity.

13   His strategy may also derive from a late-medieval clerical preoccupation with the
      distinction between *attrition* and *contrition*. The former was a change in behavior
      caused by the buffets of fortune and the hope of escaping punishment through a
      prudent repentance; the latter was a more authentic repentance rooted not in
      calculation but in grief. Latimer may have felt that only when the woman was at
      the point of death could she experience a genuine contrition. I discuss below an
      instance of this distinction in *Measure for Measure*.

14   It is worth reflecting on the implications of this casual remark: "the people" appear
      to believe that there is an inverse relation between the severity of the punishment
      and the heinousness of the crime.

15   For an account of the scene, see Catherine Drinker Bowen, *The Lion and the Throne:
      The Life and Times of Sir Edward Coke* (Boston: Little, Brown and Company, 1956),
      pp. 220–2.

16   For the text of James's letter, see *Letters of King James VI and I*, ed. G. P. V. Akrigg
      (Berkeley: University of California Press, 1984), pp. 218–19.

17   James himself was one of the most notoriously anxious monarchs in British history,
      and with good reason. In the event, his son, as well as his mother and father, met a
      violent end.

18   Dudley Carleton's letter, dated December 11, 1603, is reprinted in Thomas Birch,
      The Court and Times of James the First, 2 vols. (London: Henry Colburn, 1849), 1:27–
      32. Carleton suggests that Sir Walter Ralegh, who had also been convicted in the
      Bye Plot, was the particular object of the king's techniques of anxiety arousal.
      Ralegh was to be executed on the following Monday and was watching the scene
      on the scaffold from a window in his cell. "Raleigh, you must think," writes
      Carleton, "had hammers working in his head, to beat out the meaning of this
      strategem" (31). In a comparable last-minute reprieve, James suspended Ralegh's
      execution as well; Ralegh was kept prisoner (and was considered to be legally dead)
      for thirteen years until, in the wake of the Guiana fiasco, he was executed (tech-
      nically on the original charge from 1603) in 1618.

19   Their popularity as spectacle suggests that the fear was to some degree pleasurable to
      the onlookers, whether, as Hobbes argued, because they delighted in not being
      themselves the victims or, as official spokesmen claimed, because the horror was
      produced by a higher order whose interests it served. In either case, the experience,
      it was assumed, would make the viewers more obedient subjects.

20   Quoted in my *Renaissance Self-Fashioning: From More to Shakespeare* (Chicago:
      University of Chicago Press, 1980), p. 103.

21   Durandus of St. Pourçain, quoted in Thomas N. Tentler, *Sin and Confession on the
      Eve of the Reformation* (Princeton: Princeton University Press, 1977), p. 251. Tentler
      observes that this psychologizing of the distinction is not characteristic of the
      medieval *summae* for confessors; the crucial distinction rather was between sorrow
      that was imperfect and sorrow that had been formed by grace and hence was
      perfect. In either case the limitation – and perhaps the cunning – of the distinction
      is that it is virtually impossible to establish with any confidence.

22   Recall Carleton's description of the expression on the faces of the Bye Plot
      conspirators as they were assembled together on the scaffold.

23   On the significance of pardon as a strategy in Renaissance monarchies, see Natalie
      Zemon Davis, *Fiction in the Archives* (Stanford: Stanford University Press, forthcom-
      ing). Davis's wonderful book, which she graciously allowed me to read in manu-
      script, shows that the system of pardons in France generated a remarkable range of

narratives. Though the English legal system differed in important ways from the French, pardon played a significant, if more circumscribed, role. Shakespeare seems to have deliberately appropriated for *The Tempest* the powerful social energy of princely pardons.

24 In this regard Prospero resembles less a radical reformer like Latimer than a monarch like Queen Elizabeth: a ruler who abjured the complete inquisitorial control of the inner life and settled when necessary for the outward signs of obedience.

    For a brilliant discussion of Prospero's relations with Antonio, see the introduction to the Oxford Shakespeare edition of *The Tempest*, ed. Stephen Orgel (Oxford: Oxford University Press, 1987). Throughout this chapter, I have profited from Orgel's introduction, which he kindly showed me in advance of its publication.

25 I am trying to resist here the proposition that Latimer's story is the actual practice that is then represented in works of art, and hence that in it we encounter the basis in reality of theatrical fictions. Even if we assume that the events in Cambridge occurred exactly as Latimer related them – and this is a large assumption based on a reckless act of faith – those events seem saturated with narrative conventions. It is not only that Latimer lives his life as if it were material for the stories he will tell in his sermons but that the actions he reports are comprehensible only if already fashioned into a story.

26 On Strachey's career, see S. G. Culliford, *William Strachey, 1572–1621* (Charlottesville: University Press of Virginia, 1965). See also Charles Richard Sanders, "William Strachey, the Virginia Colony, and Shakespeare," *Virginia Magazine* 57 (1949): 115–32. Sanders notes that "many of the eighteenth and nineteenth century Stracheys became servants of the East India Company" (118).

27 William Strachey, in Samuel Purchas, *Hakluytus Posthumus or Purchas His Pilgrimes*, 20 vols. (Glasgow: James Maclehose and Sons, 1905–7), 19:5–72. It seems worth remarking the odd coincidence between this circumstance and Latimer's presenting his sermon also to a noble lady. Men in this period often seem to shape their experiences in the world to present them as instruction or entertainment to powerfully placed ladies. The great Shakespearean exploration of this social theme is *Othello*.

28 On joint-stock companies in the early modern period, see William Robert Scott, *The Constitution and Finance of English, Scottish, and Irish Joint-Stock Companies to 1720*, 3 vols. (Cambridge: Cambridge University Press, 1912). On the theater and the marketplace, see the excellent book by Jean-Christophe Agnew, *Worlds Apart: The Market and the Theater in Anglo-American Thought, 1550–1750* (Cambridge: Cambridge University Press, 1986).

29 Indeed the demand for such connections, a demand almost always frustrated in the early modern period, has strengthened the case for the formalist isolation of art.

30 Charles Mills Gayley, *Shakespeare and the Founders of Liberty in America* (New York: Macmillan, 1917); William Strachey, *The Historie of Travell into Virginia Britania* (1612), ed. Louis B. Wright and Virginia Freund, Hakluyt Society 2d ser., no. 103 (London, 1953), p. xix.

31 Detestation of the sailors is a common theme in the travel literature of the period. One of the strongest elements of an elitist utopia in *The Tempest* is the fantasy that the sailors will in effect be put to sleep for the duration of the stay on the island, to be awakened only to labor on the return voyage.

32 Quoted in the introduction to *The Historie of Travell into Virginia Britania*, p. xxv.

33 I quote these lines because they may have caught Shakespeare's attention: "What have we here?" asks Trinculo, catching sight of Caliban, "a man or a fish? dead or

alive? A fish, he smells like a fish" (2.2.24–6). Prospero in exasperation calls Caliban a tortoise (1.2.316).

34 The promotional literature written on behalf of the Virginia Company prior to the voyage of 1609 makes it clear that there was already widespread talk in England about the hardships of the English colonists. No one on the *Sea Venture* is likely to have harbored any illusions about conditions at Jamestown.

35 The office of governor was created by the royal charter of 1609. The governor replaced the council president as the colony's chief executive. He was granted the right to "correct and punishe, pardon, governe, and rule all such the subjects of us ... as shall from time to time adventure themselves ... thither," and he was empowered to impose martial law in cases of mutiny or rebellion (quoted in *The Three Charters of the Virginia Company of London, with Seven Related Documents, 1606–1621*, ed. S. F. Bemiss, Jamestown 350th Anniversary Historical Booklet 4 [Williamsburg, Va., 1957], p. 52). See Warren M. Billings, "The Transfer of English Law to Virginia, 1606–1650," in *The Westward Enterprise: English Activities in Ireland, the Atlantic, and America, 1480–1650*, ed. K. R. Andrews, N. P. Canny, and P. E. H. Hair (Liverpool: Liverpool University Press, 1978), pp. 214ff.

36 Leaving the island is not in itself, as is sometimes claimed, an abjuration of colonialism: as we have seen in the case of Bermuda, the enforced departure from the island signals the resumption of the colonial enterprise. On the other hand, insofar as *The Tempest* conflates the Bermuda and Virginia materials, the departure for Italy – and by implication England – would necessitate abandoning the absolute rule that had been established under martial law.

37 The noblemen's pride is related to the gentlemanly refusal to work that the leaders of the Virginia Company bitterly complained about. The English gentlemen in Jamestown, it was said, preferred to die rather than lift a finger to save themselves. So too when the boatswain urges Antonio and Sebastian to get out of the way or to work, Antonio answers, "We are less afraid to be drown'd than thou art" (1.1.44–5).

38 For acute observations on the parallels with Sycorax, see Stephen Orgel, "Prospero's Wife," *Representations* 8 (1985): 1–13; among the many essays on Caliban is one of my own: "Learning to Curse: Aspects of Linguistic Colonialism in the Sixteenth Century," in *First Images of America: The Impact of the New World on the Old*, 2 vols., ed. Fredi Chiappelli (Berkeley: University of California Press, 1976), 2:561–80.

39 Quoted in Nicholas Canny, "The Permissive Frontier: The Problem of Social Control in English Settlements in Ireland and Virginia, 1550–1650," in *The Westward Enterprise*, p. 36.

40 William Crashaw, *A sermon preached in London before the right honorable the Lord Lawarre, Lord Governour and Captaine Generall of Virginia ... at the said Lord Generall his leave taking of England ... and departure for Virginea, Febr. 21, 1609* (London, 1610), pp. H1v–H1r. The British Library has a copy of Strachey's *Lawes Diuine, Morall and Martiall* with a manuscript inscription by the author to Crashaw; see Sanders, "William Strachey, the Virginia Colony, and Shakespeare," p. 121.

41 William Strachey, *For the Colony in Virginea Britannia. Lawes Diuine, Morall and Martiall, &c.* (London: Walter Burre, 1612), in Peter Force, *Tracts and Other Papers, Relating Principally to the Origin, Settlement, and Progress of the Colonies in North America, from the Discovery to the Year 1776*, 4 vols. (Washington, DC, 1836–46), 3:67.

42 In our century the market for Shakespeare as book has come to focus increasingly upon adolescents in colleges and universities who are assigned expensive texts

furnished with elaborate critical introductions and editorial apparatus. On the ideological implications of Shakespeare in the curriculum, see Alan Sinfield, "Give an account of Shakespeare and Education, showing why you think they are effective and what you have appreciated about them. Support your comments with precise references," in *Political Shakespeare: New Essays in Cultural Materialism*, ed. Jonathan Dollimore and Alan Sinfield (Manchester: Manchester University Press, 1985), pp. 134–57.

43 But if Shakespeare's works have become a fetish, they are defined for their possessors not by their magical power to command but by their freedom from the anxieties of rule. They are the emblems of cultivation, civility, recreation, but they are not conceived of as direct agents in the work of empire.

44 Henry M. Stanley, *Through the Dark Continent*, 2 vols. (New York: Harper and Brothers, 1878), 2:384–86. I owe this story to Walter Michaels, who found it quoted by William James in a footnote. James's interest was aroused by what he saw as primitive literalism. The natives' oral culture makes it impossible for them to understand writing. They cannot distinguish between books that are reproducible and books that are unique, or for that matter between fiction and field notes, and because of this inability they cannot identify what was at least the immediate threat to their culture. In making the book a fetish they fail to make the necessary distinction between fantasy and truth, a distinction whose origins reside in texts like *The Tempest*, that is, in texts that thematize a difference between the island of art and the mainland of reality.

It is difficult to gauge how much of this analysis is only James's own fantasy. The natives may not actually have been incapable of making such a distinction. It is interesting, in this regard, that they are said to be carrying muskets, so there must already have been a history of involvement with Arabs or Europeans, a history that Stanley, making much of his role as explorer, represses. It is noteworthy too that as Stanley warms to his story, his natives increasingly speak in the racist idiom familiar from movies like *King Kong:* "M-m. No, no, no." And it is also possible, as I have already suggested, to see in Stanley the actual fetishism of the book: the attribution of power and value and companionship to the dead letter. In Stanley's reverie Shakespeare becomes a friend who must be sacrificed (as Stanley seems prepared to sacrifice Safeni) to protect the colonial project. Shakespeare is thus indispensable in two ways – as a consolation in the long painful trials of empire and as a deceptive token of exchange.

45 *The Exploration Diaries of H. M. Stanley*, ed. Richard Stanley and Alan Neame (New York: Vanguard Press, 1961), p. 187. Many of the journal entries that Stanley professes to transcribe in *Through the Dark Continent* are in fact invented: "The so-called 'extracts from my diary' in *Through the Dark Continent*," the editors remark, "are hardly more than a device for varying the typeface, for they are quite as deliberately composed as the rest of the narrative" (p. xvi). I should add that the day after the burning of his "genial companion," Stanley lost his close friend and associate Frank Pocock, who drowned when his canoe overturned. There is an odd sense of a relation between the loss of these two friends, as if Stanley viewed the burning of the one and the drowning of the other as linked sacrifices for the cause of empire.

Part IV

OCCASIONAL PIECES

10

PROLOGUE TO *HAMLET IN PURGATORY*

THIS IS a book about the afterlife of Purgatory, the echoes of its dead name. Specifically, it is about the traces of Purgatory in *Hamlet* (1601). Thus described, my project seems very tightly focused, but since Purgatory was a creation of Western Christendom as a whole, I found I could not neatly restrict my account, geographically or culturally: Ireland plays an important role, as do France, Italy, and Germany. But my principal concern is with England; to understand what Shakespeare inherited and transformed, we need to understand the way in which Purgatory, the middle space of the realm of the dead, was conceived in English texts of the later Middle Ages and then attacked by English Protestants of the sixteenth and early seventeenth centuries. That attack, as we will see, focused on the imagination: Purgatory, it was charged, was not simply a fraud; it was a piece of poetry. The terms of this attack in turn, I will argue, facilitated Shakespeare's crucial appropriation of Purgatory in *Hamlet*.

As such sketches often do, this one reverses the order in which this book actually evolved. I began with the notion of writing a book about Shakespeare as a Renaissance conjurer. By the term "conjurer" I simply mean someone who has the power to call forth or make contact through language with those things – voices, faces, bodies, and spirits – that are absent. Shakespeare possessed this power to an extraordinary degree, and I wanted to explore some of its sources. I made starts in several different directions: an essay on *Macbeth* and Shakespeare's great contemporary, Reginald Scot, who blamed witchcraft persecutions on a misplaced faith in poets' metaphors; an essay on the peculiar absence in Shakespeare's drama, even in a play like *King Lear* about extreme old age, of what we would term "natural death;" several essays on Shakespeare's theatrical appropriation of the Eucharist.[1] Above all, I found myself drawn again and again to the weird, compelling ghost in *Hamlet*, and I set aside the overarching project to concentrate on that single figure.

My goal was not to understand the theology behind the ghost; still less, to determine whether it was "Catholic" or "Protestant." My only goal was to immerse myself in the tragedy's magical intensity. It seems a bit absurd to bear

This chapter was first published in *Hamlet in Purgatory* (2001, pp. 3–9).

witness to the intensity of *Hamlet*; but my profession has become so oddly diffident and even phobic about literary power, so suspicious and tense, that it risks losing sight of – or at least failing to articulate – the whole reason anyone bothers with the enterprise in the first place. The ghost in *Hamlet* is like none other – not only in Shakespeare but in any literary or historical text that I have ever read. It does not have very many lines – it appears in three scenes and speaks only in two – but it is amazingly disturbing and vivid. I wanted to let the feeling of this vividness wash over me, and I wanted to understand how it was achieved.

I believe that nothing comes of nothing, even in Shakespeare. I wanted to know where he got the matter he was working with and what he did with that matter. And so the broad inquiry that had come to focus more and more sharply on one figure in a single play spread out once again to encompass a dauntingly large field. Many of the key features of this field – the "poetics" of Purgatory in England and the struggle over its existence – do not align themselves conveniently with elements in *Hamlet* or in any of Shakespeare's plays. For example, Prince Hamlet does not worry that he, like his father, may serve a prison term in Purgatory (though he does worry that his soul might go to Hell), and Shakespeare never in his career seems drawn to the argument that ghost stories were cynical devices wielded by wolvish priests to extract wealth from the gullible. But I believe strongly that the historical and contextual work that literary critics do succeeds only if it acquires its own compelling imaginative interest, a powerful gravitational pull that makes it feel almost wrenching to turn back to the thing that was the original focus of interest. And paradoxically it is this independent interest – the fascination that I at least have found in Saint Patrick's Purgatory and *The Gast of Gy* and the *Supplication of Souls*, along with trentals, indulgences, chantries, and requiem masses – that makes the whole subject seem worthy of *Hamlet*.

For even when in the course of this book I seem to be venturing far away from *Hamlet*, the play shapes virtually everything I have to say. This is in part because *Hamlet* has made so central a contribution to what Joel Fineman calls "the subjectivity effect" in Western consciousness that it has helped to condition the sensibilities of its readers and auditors.[2] In part, too, it is because my interest in what years ago I called a cultural poetics, adapting the term from Clifford Geertz, requires a certain hermeneutical patience, a willingness to suspend direct literary analysis, in order to examine more thoroughly what had been treated as mere background for the canonical work of art. If we are in part the unintended consequences of *Hamlet*, Shakespeare's play, I will suggest, is in part one of the unintended consequences of the theological struggles with which much of this book will be concerned. But for this book to work properly, the reader should understand literary analysis, and specifically the analysis of *Hamlet*, to be suspended in another sense as well, that is, distributed in tiny, almost invisible particles throughout my account.

A few years ago, as a fellow at the Wissenschaftskolleg in Berlin, I had a conversation with an urbane Islamicist who was maintaining eloquently that one must put aside one's family and group identifications, no matter how powerful they may be, in order to think and speak as a rational person. I agreed with him, but I found myself thinking, and not for the first time, how slyly amusing and acute Plato was in the *Ion* in pointing to the tension between the work of the rational philosopher and the work of the rhapsode or, let us say, the literary critic. I know, in any case, that I am incapable of simply bracketing my own origins; rather, I find myself trying to transform them, most often silently and implicitly, into the love I bring to my work.

Let me on this occasion be explicit. My father was born in the late nineteenth century. I was the child of what I used to think of as his old age but that I have now, at my point in life, come to think of, rather, as his vigorous middle age. I saw him, in any case, as embodying the life experience not of the generation directly behind me but of two generations back. His own childhood memories seemed to have a quite unusual, almost eerie distance from my life-world. Hence, for example, he told me that when he was very young, he was taken, along with the other boys in his Hebrew school class (his *cheder*) to the apartment of a Jewish railway worker who had been struck and killed by a train. The little children were told by their teacher, whom I can only imagine as a madman, to stand around the mangled corpse – which was placed on great cakes of ice, since it was the summer in Boston and very hot – and to recite the psalms, while the man's wife wailed inconsolably in a corner.

Initiated, perhaps, by this traumatic experience, my father was obsessed throughout his life with death. His own father had died dreadfully, clinging to his son and begging for help, and my father carried the scars of that experience with him ever after. The effect on him was not exactly melancholy, but rather something like a strange blend of wonder and denial. The wonder had a specific origin: my grandfather had died in New York, where my father had taken him in a desperate, last-ditch search for medical treatment. My father then had to bring the body back to Boston by train. The coffin was in the baggage car, and my father was sitting quietly weeping in the club car, when, in New Haven, Connecticut, the entire chorus line of the Ziegfield Follies climbed on board. The chorus girls, leggy, buxom, bejeweled, bedecked in feather boas and wide-brimmed hats, sweetly crowded around my weeping father, kissing and hugging him and trying to cheer him up. It was perhaps my father's purest encounter with the wonderful power of *eros* over *thanatos*.

To this experience of wonder my father conjoined denial. He kept us from celebrating his birthday, refused to retire, working until the week before he died in his eighty-seventh year, and lied about his age even when he entered the hospital. But when we read his will, we found that he had, after all, been thinking about his death. He had left a sum of money to an organization that would say kaddish for him – kaddish being the Aramaic prayer for the dead, recited for eleven months after a person's death and then on certain annual occasions. The prayer is usually said by the deceased's immediate family and particularly by his sons – in Yiddish a son could actually be called a *kaddish*, so that a childless man could be said to die without leaving a *kaddish*. Evidently, my father did not trust either my older brother or me to recite the prayer for him. The effect the bequest had on me, perhaps perversely, was to impel me to do so, as if in a blend of love and spite.

I did not until that moment know that Jews had anything like chantries, and I realized that I did not know why Jews prayed for the dead at all. After all, biblical Judaism has only what seems like a vague and imaginatively impoverished account of the afterlife. The Hebrew Bible speaks of a place called *sheol*, often translated by Christians as "Hell," but it is not a place of torture and has very few of the features of the Christian or classical underworld.[3] It seems to be associated not with torment (or purgation) but rather with privation or depression. "Are not my days few?" complains Job; "cease then, and let me alone, that I may take comfort a little, Before I go whence I shall not return, even to the land of darkness and the shadow of death; A land of darkness, as darkness itself; and of the shadow of death, without any order, and where the light is as darkness" (Job 10:20–2). The phrase "without any order" links this netherworld not with a prison house or penal colony – we are immensely distant conceptually from Dante's circles – but with the state of things before the Creation, when "the earth was without form, and void; and darkness was upon the face of the deep" (Gen. 1:2). The overall focus in the Hebrew Scriptures is not on assuring oneself a more favorable location in this melancholy kingdom, but rather on valuing life: "For him that is joined to all the living there is hope," as Ecclesiastes puts it, "for a living dog is better than a dead lion" (9:4).

There are, however, some biblical expressions, especially in the Psalter, of a hope to be liberated from *sheol*: "Like sheep they are laid in the grave; death shall feed on them; and the upright shall have dominion over them in the morning; and their beauty shall consume in the grave from their dwelling. But God will redeem my soul from the power of the grave: for he shall receive me. Selah" (Ps. 49:14–15). Or again, "For thou wilt not leave my soul in hell; neither wilt thou suffer thine Holy One to see corruption. Thou wilt shew me the path of life: in thy presence is fullness of joy; at thy right hand there are pleasures for evermore" (Ps. 16:10–11). This faith in the possibility of resurrection – and the Jewish liturgy to this day praises God for raising the dead to life – still does not explain why Jews would offer prayers for the dead.

The answer seems to be that the kaddish, as we know it, is relatively recent. In a sermon preached at St Paul's on May 21, 1626, John Donne notes that God gave his chosen people, through Moses and Aaron, the most elaborate directions for every aspect of their lives: "what they should eat, what they should wear, how often they should wash, what they should do, in every religious, in every civil action." Yet, Donne continues, "never, never any mention, any intimation, never any approach, any inclination, never any light, no nor any shadow, never any color, any colorableness of any command of prayer for the Dead." There was, to be sure, an ancient custom of remembering the dead, on Yom Kippur, as part of the general ritual of atonement, and there was also a long-standing Hebrew custom of giving alms to the poor or to charitable institutions in memory of the dead. But the Jews adopted prayers for the dead, Donne argues, from the pagans: "After the Jews had been a long time conversant amongst the Gentiles, and that as fresh water approaching the Sea, contracts a saltish, a brackish taste, so the Jews received impressions of the customs of the Gentiles, who were ever naturally inclined to this mis-devotion, and left-handed piety, of praying for the Dead."[4]

In fact, though the left-handed piety of the pagans may be the ultimate origin of praying for the dead, the Jews may well have adopted it from the Christians. The recitation of the mourner's kaddish seems to have originated in the Rhineland in the twelfth century, after the horrors of the First and Second Crusade. In the wake of the mass murders and suicides, the Ashkenazim evidently began to keep memorial books, *Memorbucher*, in which the martyrs, along with benefactors of the community and other worthies, were commemorated. The inscriptions in these books were linked to the kaddish, and, eventually, the recitation of this prayer was generalized to include all of the dead.

In a recent, often haunting meditation on the kaddish, Leon Wieseltier acknowledges that the recitation of the mourner's kaddish thus originated precisely at the time that Christianity in the West formalized the practice of praying for the dead in order to alleviate their sufferings in Purgatory. "Yet this is, as I say, a coincidence," Wieseltier insists; "I do not believe for a minute that the one was the cause of the other."[5] It is not my intention to dispute this flat claim, nor do I have the scholarship to do so, but if it were a coincidence, it would be an almost miraculous one, since many of the texts that Wieseltier cites bear a startling resemblance to the exempla and scholastic arguments of the medieval and early modern Christians among whom the Jews were dwelling. I suspect, rather, that the long, twisting path that leads back from my father and forefathers passes through the Christianity that seemed to them the embodiment of otherness.[6]

Very few Jews were dwelling among the Christians in early modern England; the entire community had been officially expelled in 1290.[7] But Donne speaks as if he had personally witnessed them saying the kaddish: "This is true which I have seen," he tells his London congregation, "that the Jews at this day continue it in practice; For when one dies, for some certain time after, appointed by them, his son or some other near in blood or alliance, comes to the Altar, and there saith and doth something in the behalf of his dead father, or grandfather respectively."[8]

This practice, then, which with a lightly ironic piety I, who scarcely know how to pray, undertook for my own father, is the personal starting point for what follows.

NOTES

1   "Shakespeare Bewitched," in *New Historical Literary Study: Essays on Reproducing Texts, Representing History*, ed. Jeffrey N. Cox and Larry J. Reynolds (Princeton: Princeton University Press, 1993), pp. 108–35; "The Eating of the Soul," *Representations* 48 (1994): 97–116; "La souris mangeuse d'hostie: les miettes du repas eucharistique," *Traverses* 5 (1993): 42–54, revised as "The Mousetrap," in *Practicing New Historicism* [with Catherine Gallagher] (Chicago: University of Chicago Press, 2000); "Remnants of the Sacred in Early Modern England," in *Subject and Object in Renaissance Culture*, ed. Margreta de Grazia, Maureen Quilligan, and Peter Stallybrass (Cambridge: Cambridge University Press, 1996), pp. 337–45.
2   Joel Fineman, *The Subjectivity Effect in Western Literary Tradition* (Cambridge: MIT Press, 1991).

3   See Saul Lieberman, *Texts and Studies* (New York: Ktav Publishing House, 1974), esp. pp. 29–56, 235–72.

4   *The Sermons of John Donne*, ed. Evelyn M. Simpson and George R. Potter, 10 vols. (Berkeley and Los Angeles: University of California Press, 1954), 7:168–69. Donne's text is 1 Cor. 15:29: "Else, what shall they do which are baptized for the dead? If the dead rise not at all, why are they then baptized for the dead?" His purpose is to disprove the Catholic claim that "this Baptisme for the Dead must necessarily prove Purgatory, and their Purgatory" (165).

5   Leon Wieseltier, *Kaddish* (New York: Knopf, 1998), p. 194.

6   The complex relations between Judaism and Christianity – relations that by no means always display the priority of Israel – have recently been illuminated by, among others, Ivan Marcus, *Rituals of Childhood: Jewish Acculturation in Medieval Europe* (New Haven: Yale University Press, 1996). and Daniel Boyarin, *Dying for God: Martyrdom and the Making of Christianity and Judaism* (Stanford: Stanford University Press, 1999).

7   For a fascinating argument about the small number of Jews who were living in early modern England, see James Shapiro, *Shakespeare and the Jews* (New York: Columbia University Press, 1996).

8   7:169. Donne traveled abroad on several occasions, including a voyage in 1619, as chaplain with Viscount Doncaster, that took him to Germany and the Netherlands, where he would have had ample opportunity to observe Jewish worship.

11

CHINA: VISITING RITES

The academic delegation that met me at Beijing Airport at the start of my six-week stay in the People's Republic of China was like the bomber crew in a World War II movie: each chosen to embody a significant group in the great collective enterprise. But where the choices in the American movie were ethnic – an Irish gunner, an Italian navigator, and so forth – the Chinese choices were generational. The senior member of the delegation – both in age and authority – was Zhang Wen-Xiang, a dignified Shakespeare scholar in his late sixties, with close-cropped gray hair, elegant features, and exquisite, Oxford-accented English. Next to him, waving enthusiastically as I came through customs, stood Liu Jing-Lian ("Sounds like 'Jingle' – 'Jingle Bells,' " he said), in his late forties, thin enough for his belt to lap around him twice and in a perpetual state of harried excitement and anxiety. Liu had just returned from two years in the United States as a visiting professor, and spoke rapid, idiomatic American English, laced with occasional Anglicisms that were the legacy of his original training ("My dear fellow, be careful not to be ripped off"). Half-hidden behind Liu was a third greeter, Wu Zi-Teng, about thirty, solidly built, with a broken nose, a ready laugh, and – though he too was a member of the English Department at Beijing University – very shaky English. He was introduced to me as Xiao Wu, "Little Wu."

There was a fourth person who had come to the airport to fetch me: the taxi driver. He was missing several teeth, spoke no English, and seemed irritated that his May Day was being wasted in this way. Or so at least I interpreted his mad, incessant honking at anything and nothing in particular – a bicyclist 50 yards away, a donkey cart on the other side of the road, a peasant pulling a nightsoil wagon – until I realized that all Chinese drivers keep a heavy hand on the horn.

As we drove along, we reviewed the terms of my visit: over the next three weeks, I would give six lectures to the faculty and students in the English Department at Beijing University. Four of the lectures would be on Shakespeare, two on contemporary American literature; I could also conduct several informal seminars. Most of the lectures would be in the evening, so that I would have

This chapter was first published in *Raritan*, Vol. 2, No. 4 (Spring, 1983): 1–23.

plenty of time to poke around Beijing or take side trips, and I could have a car and driver whenever I wished. My audience would be most interested in current trends in criticism and literature. The Cultural Revolution had brought education to a halt for ten years, and it was time now to catch up in every field. There would be no need for a translator, for I would be lecturing to advanced students and to faculty; the problem would not be proficiency in language, but accessibility of ideas.

The car turned in through a gate, past a bayonet-bearing soldier. "Is this Beijing University?" "No," said Liu, "This is the Friendship Hotel where you will be staying." But I had been told that I would be staying on the campus of the university where I could easily see students and faculty informally. "This is much nicer; you'll be more comfortable here."

"I'd rather be on the campus."

"Here you have two rooms and a private bath; you'll be more comfortable."

"I don't mind staying in one room. On the campus it will be easy to meet people. Isn't the Friendship Hotel a place where Chinese visitors have to sign in at the gate?"

"Yes, but here you will have a TV in your room."

"Oh, that doesn't matter, I don't watch much TV at home."

"Here you'll be more comfortable."

Xiao Wu looked around my rooms at the Friendship Hotel with an admiration I later came to understand; he and his wife lived on the campus in a room less than half the size of my sitting room. They did their cooking on a tiny charcoal brazier outside their door, and shared a toilet and shower with dozens of others on their long corridor. Zhang and Liu knew that American academics lived like princes, and they glanced about with the complacent assurance that these accommodations could not be *vastly* below my expectations. The four of us sat in overstuffed armchairs and sipped tea.

In the late afternoon, after the three had left, I decided to go out for a walk. I passed three white-jacketed attendants refilling the large thermoses provided in each room for tea, two other attendants sorting out the laundry, an attendant in charge of the keys, three desk clerks, and two doormen: I was now out not of the hotel but only of my building, one of a dozen or more in the enormous complex built by the Russians in the 1950s to house "Foreign Experts." Then past the infirmary, the tennis courts, the swimming pool (not open until the official start of summer, June 1, though it was already searingly hot), the dining hall, the taxi office, the guard house, the gatehouse, the soldier again – and finally I was out on the street. I saw now more clearly what I had glimpsed through the curtained windows of the taxi: I was in the middle of an enormous suburb of huge apartment blocks, small factories, and nondescript building sites. A few streets away were several tiny shops with a handful of people squatting outside them on the dirt sidewalk selling peanuts, pumpkin seeds, and garlic shoots. No other street life was visible. I came to what appeared to be a pleasant park, but when I tried to walk through the gate I was stopped. In my halting Chinese – the fruit of three months of cramming – I asked to enter and was refused. This was People's University, and I needed special permission to visit. As I walked away, a young man came up to me, his face already betraying the effort to form an English sentence:

"Is this your first visit to China?"

I told him it was; he was pleased. He smiled and said, "Welcome to our factory!"

Next morning, in the company of Liu, I went off for some sight-seeing; once again we had a driver and official car, this time a large black Warszawa. The car, honking steadily, pulled rapidly out of the Friendship Hotel and forced two women off their bicycles, scattering their belongings. The women cursed; the driver laughed. In a country without private cars, riding around in the back of a Warszawa makes one feel like an eighteenth-century French nobleman running his carriage through the crowds or, alternatively, like the Pope. Neither role suited me. Buses were preferable, but they are astonishingly crowded, and in boarding them the normally disciplined Chinese release an impressively anarchic spirit. (Zhang said that manners had deteriorated under the Gang of Four; the one TV show I watched, however, tried to blame the problem on Western corruption. The pushers and shovers on the screen all wore bell-bottom trousers and leather jackets.)

The solution to getting around Beijing is a bicycle, and when I managed to borrow one for the duration of my stay, my sense of the city was entirely transformed. The endless sprawl of half-finished construction – for Beijing has grown from six million to ten million inhabitants in little more than a decade – was less numbing when viewed from the midst of a stream of thousands of bicyclists; I could easily pedal around blocks of factories and put together like a puzzle multiple glimpses of the former temples that now housed the machinery; the obsessive thoroughness with which almost everything in the city is walled no longer seemed so daunting; most important, it was simple now to get off the main streets and into the tiny *hutongs*, or alleys, that run between the low gray courtyard houses with their graceful tiled roofs, ornamented doorposts, and quiet interiors. Even with eight families to a courtyard, there are too many people in Beijing for one-story housing, and these structures are rapidly being ripped down and replaced with large ugly apartment blocks. But for the moment there are still great networks of *hutongs*, and even in their dilapidated state, with piles of rubble by the walls and the courtyards half-filled with brick sheds jerry-built to accommodate the swelling populations, the old houses have an austere beauty intensified by the major aesthetic principle of contemporary Beijing: sensory deprivation.

A week after my arrival, I had lunch in a traditional courtyard house with Lin Zhi-Xiao, an old and distinguished novelist to whom I had been given an introduction by an American friend. Situated near the back gate of the Imperial Palace, this complex of courtyards had been built in the last century by one of the Empress Dowager's eunuchs. Lin had bought the house before Liberation and had raised his children there, but during the Cultural Revolution the Red Guards occupied the courtyard, confined Lin and his wife to a single, small room, and moved in several poor families. In the last few years there have been major government efforts to restore losses suffered during the years of upheaval, but it is politically and socially impossible to relocate the poor. Still, Lin and his wife have managed to recover several rooms, and I had already seen enough to know that by Chinese standards this was an exceptionally spacious apartment: a handsome living room with fine old cabinets packed with books, a carved wooden sofa, separate tables for eating and conversation, plus a narrow kitchen, a small bedroom, even a tiny study.

Lin had lived in England in the late thirties and forties; he had known Leonard and Virginia Woolf and others in Bloomsbury; he was suave, urbane, steeped in Western culture. Despite his perfectly orthodox politics, he was an obvious target for the xenophobic Red Guards. I asked him how he had managed to keep his belongings through the Cultural Revolution. He had taken the furniture apart, he replied, and hidden it away, along with his books, in a space between two walls. Some things, however, had been too dangerous to keep: he had burned the manuscripts of four novels. "No point in keeping them, no point at all."

Over a long, wonderful lunch – shrimp with peanuts, cold meats, "thousand-year-old eggs," pork with garlic shoots, and a delicious "river duck" that stared at me mournfully from the plate – Lin and I had a wide-ranging conversation, from his recollections of childhood and of the Woolfs, to contemporary American and Chinese culture, from modern painting to international politics. Like many Chinese I met, Lin was supremely gracious, witty, even intimate; I felt we were speaking utterly frankly. Yet as the afternoon wore on, I had an odd feeling which I was to experience several other times in China: a feeling that this moving and convincing intimacy was an elegant conjuring trick. Lin would lean forward and tell me, in confidential tones, things that I knew were utterly conventional, so that I began to lose touch with the markers by which we normally define the boundary between authenticity and illusion.

Uneasy, I told Lin two stories that I had heard during the past week. I carefully altered the names and precise circumstances, as I am doing right now, and I realized that I myself was beginning to replicate the calculated and illusory frankness that was making me uneasy.

The first story involved a young Chinese scientist whom I had met through an American friend teaching at a Beijing research institute. My friend told this scientist that the new and extremely expensive piece of equipment his unit had just purchased was hopelessly difficult to maintain, and, moreover, that all the important work to be done on it had already been done. The scientist said he knew this very well himself, but that the equipment had been ordered by the head of the unit, and consequently there had been no way to stop the decision, or even to argue strenuously against it. Their budget would now be exhausted for years, and they would go through the motions of pointless research.

The second story involved a young academic who had been working for three years on a linguistics project and then had been transferred, on a day's notice and without the possibility of appeal, to an entirely different project, the compiling of a dictionary. At first he hated the project, but gradually, over a year and a half, he had developed, almost in spite of himself, an interest in the intellectual problems raised by the dictionary. Then quite suddenly he was told that a teacher was needed at a new institute, and he was again transferred. This time, he said bitterly, he would no longer commit himself – he would only do what the job absolutely demanded and nothing more. He was "finished."

Lin sighed, "These stories are true; such things do happen, and frequently at that." Then bending toward me and lowering his voice: "What we need to do is to replace the old cadres with new, bright, up-to-date cadres." The idea was scarcely surprising; I had read it two days before in a speech by Premier Deng, duly reprinted in *China Daily*. I observed that even if such replacement were carried out (itself extremely difficult), it would leave the basic structure of things entirely intact, and young cadres before too long would become old cadres. "What we need," Lin repeated, "are younger cadres."

Perhaps this is what he actually believed, just as he may even have believed that contemporary Chinese literature was, as he said, "wonderful and exciting." And even if he believed otherwise, what right had I to expect that he would say so to me? It was not his caution – if that is what it was – that surprised me, but his exquisite miming of candor.

In the midst of this perfect courtesy – the consummate achievement of those whom the Chinese are said to call "barbarian handlers" – I found myself longing, perversely perhaps, to break through to something clear and unequivocal. Once on a visit to Datong, a bleak, coal-mining town on the Mongolian border where there are ancient and remarkably beautiful Buddhist rock carvings, I allowed this longing to get the better of me. I had gone to the Public Security Office to request permission to climb Wu Tai Shan, a Buddhist holy mountain. (I had earlier received permission to climb Tai Shan, a sacred peak in Shandong Province, and so I did not anticipate problems.)

"Wu Tai Shan is too far away," I was told by the cadre. "It's difficult to reach by train or bus."

"That's okay; I'll hire a taxi."

"But there is no place to stay on the top of Wu Tai Shan."

"I don't intend to climb to the top, and I'll have the taxi take me back to Datong."

"But there are no restaurants on Wu Tai Shan."

"I'll carry food with me."

"But there are only three monasteries open on Wu Tai Shan."

"I'll look at those and then enjoy the scenery."

"Wu Tai Shan is closed to foreigners."

What had I accomplished by not stopping at the first polite answer? After that experience I resolved to content myself with indirection, but the irritable reaching after unequivocal truths was difficult to suppress.

"What interests you most about the study of Shakespeare?" I asked an assistant professor who had written his dissertation on the comedies.

"The universal values."

"Which universal values?"

"Those everywhere expressed in Shakespeare's plays."

"But why did you choose to study Shakespeare in particular?"

"I was assigned to study him."

Assigned. This is not, one must understand, said casually; the assignments are major life decisions that remain in force indefinitely – until the next assignment. Perhaps this partly explains the craving for nameless universal values; it does not matter what you study if you always find the same thing.

But do Chinese scholars always find the same thing? "Do you never feel the distance, the foreignness, of your subject?" I asked Qin You-Shi, a strange, sardonic, brilliant young professor.

"I had wanted to study phonetics," he replied, "but there was no room for me. When I was assigned to study Shakespeare, I felt at first like a young woman who has been married against her will to a hideous old man; at first she bemoans her fate, but gradually she becomes accustomed to it."

Zhang laughed when Qin made his remark and said that the analogy was absurd. But how did he, I asked, deal with the distance between Shakespeare and Chinese culture? After all, he had earlier complained that Americans were obsessed with sex and violence. True enough, but these obsessions, I suggested, are neither new nor exclusively American; they are already articulated in Shakespeare's plays which Zhang too professed to admire for their universal values. "What do you do," I asked, "with all those moments in Shakespeare? What do you do with lines like Othello's: 'Thy bed, lust stained, shall with lust's blood be spotted?' "

He smiled. "I ignore them."

This was the reply of someone who had not been assigned to study Western literature, someone whose perfect English and elegant manner bespoke a world far different from that invoked by his wrinkled Mao jacket and faded, threadbare trousers. Revolutions must always divide generations; the abyss separating Zhang and others of his age from their younger colleagues is truly startling. At a banquet given for me, one of the senior professors, a cherubic old man named Leng Zi-Xing, proposed endless toasts to Yale where we had both been students, some forty years apart. We drank to Chauncy Brewster Tinker (long dead when I arrived), to the Sterling Library, to the Elizabethan Club, to the elms that have by now all succumbed to blight. As we laughed and drank, Leng looked into my eyes with a peculiar look I encountered at several other moments in China: a blend of cordiality and detached assessment. The old man, I felt, was measuring the distance between his knowledge of the human condition and mine. Mine fell far short, I'm afraid, but I thought of the Yiddish proverb, "Spare us what we can learn to endure."

At another dinner, this time not at a fancy restaurant but in a bleak concrete shack, Hua Zi-Fang, a frail, wonderfully hospitable professor who, as a young man, had been at Harvard, showed me a book inscribed to him by the eminent Shakespeare scholar, George Lyman Kittredge. His wife Xue Bao-Chai had a still more precious memento: at my urging, she showed me her family album. It began with a yellowed nineteenth-century photograph of her famous, enlightened grandfather, by whom she had been raised: a young man poised for his first trip outside of China and obviously self-conscious about his Western suit and the wig beneath which he had tucked his queue. There followed baby pictures in the background of which one could glimpse the Shanghai mansion, vaguely Tudor, in which she had been raised; pictures of her friends from the missionary school to which she had been sent; pictures of her, wearing chic Western clothes, as a radicalized student at Beijing University in the early thirties. Tucked away unmounted at the end of the album were a set of photographs from the 1950s of her grandfather and Mao, strolling together in conversation by the Temple of Heaven. I did not ask why she had not mounted these, but I did ask why she had carefully cut and discarded all but the heads of her friends in the pictures from the 1920s and 1930s. "During the Cultural Revolution, I could not hide my origins," she said, "but if the album had fallen into the hands of unfriendly people, I did not wish to incriminate my friends by preserving pictures of them in bourgeois dress."

The fear was not ungrounded. Hua and Xue both suffered terribly during the Cultural Revolution: their possessions were seized, their children taken from them, their names vilified. There were beatings, imprisonment, hard labor. Xue's impressive connections were useless; indeed they were the cause of the persecutions, along with her high culture, her membership in the intelligentsia, her impeccable, missionary-school English. Zhang was savagely treated – over five years in what he called a "concentration camp" – and Leng Zi-Xing, the jovial drinker of toasts to Mother Yale, had spent the better part of a decade hauling night-soil on a commune in the north.

Near the end of my trip, in Shanghai, I gave a single lecture at Fudan University. The occasion was marked by the customary rituals of hospitality, which always included introductions to the senior members of the department. This formality is tied not only to the traditional Chinese respect for the old but to the fact that the present regime, in making reparations for the disasters inflicted by the Gang of Four, has installed in high positions those who suffered during the Cultural Revolution. But at Fudan, I was introduced to only one old man, Wang Xi-Teng. When I remarked on this at dinner, I was told that many of the professors in the English Department had committed suicide – ten in all – and that several others had been beaten to death. Shanghai was the fervent center of the Cultural Revolution.

To be old and a professor of English in China is to be a survivor. Not only had most such people, in the eyes of the Red Guard, been born into the wrong class, not only had they elected a profession in which they were removed from workers, soldiers, and peasants, but they had all committed a cultural crime, a crime confessed in the very subject they had chosen to study. An American friend who lived in China during the Cultural Revolution told me that she heard a strange sound outside her apartment one day and went to look: it was the sound of Western records – Bach, Mozart, Beethoven – being thrown from windows into the courtyard below.

The senior generation of literary intellectuals were nightmarishly vulnerable to attack at that time, even if they had unswervingly followed the twisting ideological currents of postliberation China. The generation below them – men and women now in their late forties and fifties – were slightly less vulnerable, if only because in 1965 they had not yet attained positions of authority, and because most of them had originally had less access to Western culture. In fact, they seemed less the repositories of that culture than its managerial assistants. But the young teachers I was meeting had the least access of all: in virtually every case their education had been drastically curtailed; they had spent two or three years in school doing nothing but political agitation and "self-criticism" (universally described as excruciatingly boring); and when the schools themselves were shut down, they had been sent to the countryside or factories to work.

Xiao Wu, the young man who had greeted me at the airport and whom I came to know quite well, laughed when he recalled the Cultural Revolution: "I ran around in the streets shouting that teachers were running dogs of U.S. imperialism. I was a Red Guard, you see, and now I'm a teacher myself." How had he made the change, I asked, and how – since he had grown up in a peasant family in remote Gansu province – had he come to Beijing? After all, mobility of this kind, from country to city, from fields to university, is immensely difficult in China. In the early 1970s, Wu said, he had been assigned to work in a machine-tool factory where his job included directing the weekly political meetings at which the latest government directives and exhortations were read. (These meetings continue to be held throughout China – in the universities, on Wednesday afternoons.) Near the close of the Cultural Revolution, when the regime took its first steps toward reconstruction of the shattered university system, an order came from the central government to choose from the factory's sixteen hundred workers one man and one woman to be sent to Beijing to learn English.

"I had no real interest in learning English," Xiao Wu said with a smile, "but I wanted to get to Beijing, so I applied." Most of his friends applied too, but his political job enabled him to know the right line to take.

"What was the line?"

"I don't remember."

"Sure you do. Let me guess, and you tell me if I'm close. 'I want to learn English in order to promote the development and perfection of socialist politics and to struggle against imperialism. My only concern is to serve Marxism-Leninism-Mao Zedong thought. I will never use my knowledge of English to separate myself from the people.' "

Uproarious laughter. "That's right! That's exactly right!"

Were his friends – and as I asked this I thought of David Copperfield's warehouse mates, Mick Waller and Mealy Potatoes – disappointed and resentful that they were not chosen? "Of course."

Those in Wu's position – the "worker-soldier-peasant students" who came to the university without any real high school education – hold enviable jobs compared with many of their peers, but in the context of the universities and institutes in which they teach, they are at a distinct disadvantage. Far more than their elders (those, at least, who survived), they bear the visible scars of the Cultural Revolution. For they have had painfully little access to the subjects they are assigned to study and teach, and they are treated with condescension both by their elders and by the new generation of post-Cultural Revolution students that is just now emerging. At the present time there is a popular mania in China for learning English, and in this climate those whose education was irreparably damaged by the Cultural Revolution are made to seem backward and dull. There are university lecturers in English whose command of the language is far exceeded by young workers whose passion is for poring over tattered dictionaries and chatting up foreign visitors. An eighteen-year-old who once helped me on a Beijing trolley told me that she was a telephone operator and had learned her excellent English by listening in on all conversations in that language. "May I ask you a question?" an earnest young textile worker said to me at 6:30 one morning by the lake in Hangzhou. A crowd of fifteen or twenty others on their way to work instantly gathered around us. "What is the difference, please, between algae and kelp?"

Ten years ago Xiao Wu and his friends at a comparable age were shouting slogans about long-nosed foreign devils. It seems unlikely now that they will ever catch up either with their elders or with the younger students who have already surpassed their command of English.

"Is it hard to learn Swedish?" Xiao Wu asked me one day. "If I could learn Swedish I would be one of the only people in China to know the language, and I might have a chance to be sent abroad."

The deep rifts that divide the generations in China posed a dilemma for me. To whom should my lectures be addressed? At what level should I make entry into my subject? What issues was it important to discuss? What model for literary study was I going to project, and whose interests would it serve? The questions were scarcely of major importance in themselves, but they were linked to issues of very real significance. For literature and literary criticism have no autonomy, in theory or practice, in China; they are intimately and inextricably bound up with the state. The traditional Confucian conception of literature was already deeply ethical and social, and this conception was then simultaneously confirmed and radicalized in Mao's "Talks on Literature and Art at the Yenan Forum." In these statements, delivered forty years ago at an embattled moment and since elevated into national dogma, Mao declared that in judging a literary work, political criteria come first and artistic second, that a work's historical progressiveness and the author's attitude to the people are measures by which to judge a work's relative value; that writers must promote the cause of socialism and integrate themselves with the masses.

After the downfall of the Gang of Four, some oblique criticism of Mao's position – or, in the euphemistic language of Chinese politics, of "Leftist misinterpretation" of Mao's position – has been aired. The political test, it was charged, had been too rigidly and crudely applied, and, in the words of a *People's Daily* commentary, there had been "a tendency to create artistic and literary works by formula." But just at the time of my visit to China, there was a reaction against this criticism, and a fierce struggle – still unresolved – emerged between those who wished to challenge or at least modify Mao's principles and those who wished to reaffirm them. The principal battleground is the artist's right to represent characters with mixed motives and to expose serious problems in the contemporary Chinese situation. For a brief period artists were encouraged to write denunciations of the Cultural Revolution, but the literary establishment has started once again to demand a more positive vision: "Having abolished exploitation," write Ding Zhenhai and LiZhun in the May 27, 1982, *China Daily*, "China is a society where the people control state power. Life has more and more of the new and the beautiful, and representing this aspect should be the major task of writers and artists.... Some recent works ignore this. They are shallow, incorrect in ideology and artistic expression, and leave bad influences on society." Artists and writers, the article concludes, "must adopt a correct standpoint, be aware of their responsibility to socialism and create works which play positive roles."

These arguments would seem to touch only contemporary literature (and thus leave at least my Shakespeare lectures undisturbed), but they have a strong historical dimension as well. For Marxism lays claim to identifying the "progressive" forces in any historical period, and hence the political test can be applied to the artists of the past. In the prevailing "moderate" mood, this principle leads less to a rejection of major figures in the European literary tradition than to a search for the radical politics of every great writer. With English literature this is a particularly thankless task; there are a few great radicals, to be sure, but they are outnumbered by writers who at least presented themselves as upholders of the values of the ruling elite. Often these apparently conservative artists produced works whose effect is far more corrosive and challenging to the dominant social order than the forthright denunciations of self-conscious revolutionaries, but at least until recently the Chinese seemed to need evidence of a more straightforward political engagement. Thus, if a Chinese scholar did not wish to scrap most of the tradition altogether, he had to indulge in what might be generously called acts of historical imagination. A single example: Shakespeare, declares the two-volume Chinese literary history assigned to undergraduates, always allied himself with the oppressed masses. Even after his retirement to Stratford, he fought on their behalf; indeed on one occasion he rushed back to London to struggle against some particularly cruel enclosures of common land. The story has a grain of truth. Shakespeare did concern himself with some enclosures in the early seventeenth century, but regrettably they were *his* enclosures, and he appears to have been trying to secure his own interests.

Moreover, it is never entirely clear that discussions of the past are just that – discussions of events and figures decisively removed from the conflicts of the present. There is an ancient tradition in China of conducting serious contemporary debate through the medium of historical argument and literary criticism. Recently, I was told, there was an official declaration that henceforth when history is discussed, the subject is to be understood as *really* history, not an indirect reflection on the present. But such a declaration only bears witness to the persistence of veiled debate and criticism. The principle extends to the choice of literary works to be studied or performed. For instance, the chief Shakespearean production in recent years in Beijing was *Measure for Measure*, a "problem play" far less frequently performed in the West than the major comedies and tragedies. It seems an odd choice until one reflects that its plot concerns the enigmatic withdrawal from authority of the rightful Duke, and the rise and fall of a fanatical, self-righteous, and corrupt lieutenant – in short, one version of recent Chinese history. In my own lectures I found myself drawn almost irresistibly into this oblique mode: when I recalled the plot of *King Lear* – the painful "retirement" of the absolute ruler and the demonic ascendancy of the four villains – there rippled through the huge audience waves of laughter and stifled comment. And when a student asked me if in *The Tempest* Shakespeare was weaving together art and power or insisting on their ultimate separation, I knew that the question did not only, or even principally, apply to early seventeenth-century England.

What did my audience want me to answer? What were they straining, with such eager attentiveness, to hear? What Zhang and his generation wanted to hear could be summed up in one word: formalism. They wanted me to talk about patterns of imagery, the interweaving of plot elements, the text's internal structure. They hoped for close readings, for a discussion of tradition and the individual talent, for an account of the inner "world" of a work of art, for a version of literary history purged of power. This was indeed the heart of my own critical training, but my work over the past fifteen years has pulled against this formalism. I could commend close reading, but only as an initial strategy. For to understand literature, and particularly Renaissance literature, one must, I had learned, grapple with social, political, and economic forces. Shakespeare's theater was subject to ideological scrutiny, censorship, state regulation; plays set in the distant past were widely perceived as veiled commentary on the present; the Byzantine politics of the Elizabethan and Jacobean court spilled over onto the stage, while the players were frequently commanded to perform before the monarch. No wonder Zhang's generation wanted formalism. They were not indifferent to the conditions in which Shakespeare's plays were written and performed; they were living those conditions.

And the younger generations? They too had experienced the Cultural Revolution, and even without such memories they live now in a society that closely regulates what can and cannot be written by artists. But they seemed less certain that formalism would provide a solution – how could it, constructed as it was by their elders out of a prewar access to Western high culture, the culture of Richards, Empson, and Eliot? It was to this younger group, to students and faculty who would never achieve the intimate command of English upon which the technique of close reading and hence formalism is based, that I principally spoke. I urged them to understand the subtle blend in Shakespeare of subversion and submission, accommodation and resistance; I described the experimental work of contemporary American poets and novelists; and I unsettled as far as I could the stark oppositions – "positive roles" versus "decadent fantasy," "serving socialism" versus "self-expression" – within which Chinese criticism has attempted to regiment all of literature.

Once, at the close of a lecture on *King Lear*, after the flood of questions had subsided and the crowd had thinned, a young woman in her early twenties came up to me and held out her hand. I took her hand in mine, though I did not at first understand her gesture, and then I saw that on her palm she had written something in English in tiny letters: a diagram in which she had attempted to chart the coordinated shifts in the structure of the family, the state, and human emotions from the Middle Ages to the present. An ambitious project for a small palm.

"It was better when the world was ruled by ritual and duty," she said with a touch of Confucian nostalgia, "but now, in the West at least, everything is confused, and men are torn apart." Then in the middle of the swarm of words – "absolutism," "deference," "love," "surface," "inner depth" – she drew, while I looked on, a single blue line and said, "There is Shakespeare at the center. He is the poet of this confusion."

Toward the end of my trip, I was invited to lecture at the Foreign Language Institute in Xi'an, the ancient capital of the early dynasties and the site of some of the greatest archaeological finds in modern China. An official of the English Department, Professor Bu Gu-Xin, met me at the airport with a sign "Welcome Professor Queensplatt." Professor Bu had taught Sanskrit until China broke off relations with India, Russian until China fell out with the Soviet Union; and now English. All conversations with him had time lags, as if conducted long distance.

I was led to the room where I was to give my lecture. It was very hot. Before I entered, I was asked to remove my shoes and put on straw sandals. The lecture was to be videotaped, and the cadre in charge was afraid that dust might contaminate the equipment. My entrance was applauded by a group of older men and women who were sitting in the room in their stocking feet. These were the senior professors.

Before the lecture I was again led down the hall to another room where again my entrance was applauded by a larger group. These were the junior professors. They would watch my lecture on a monitor. Then upstairs, where I was introduced to a still larger group who would also watch me on a monitor: these were the graduate students. Finally, up another floor, the heat ever more stifling, to the room with the undergraduates. I told the students that I would come to them at the end of the lecture to answer any questions and to talk with them. But when I finished speaking, the monitors were shut off. There were questions first from the professors, then from the junior faculty down the hall. When I got upstairs at last, the halls were dark, the classrooms completely empty.

I do not wish to close on so bleak a note. On my last night in China my wife Ellen, who had joined me for the latter half of the visit, and I decided to go to see an acrobatic troupe perform at a splendid new theater. (We had earlier booked tickets for the acrobatic troupe in Suzhou and were mightily pleased that, with our smattering of Chinese, we had done it all by ourselves – until we arrived at the theater and discovered, when the curtain rose, that we were at the opera.) On the evening of the performance in Shanghai we had gorged ourselves, as usual, and were a bit late, so we decided to take a taxi. The man booking a taxi after us in the hotel was also going to see the acrobats, and we offered him a lift. A German from Bremen, in his mid-forties, a buyer of leather, he complained that the Chinese leather industry was not nearly so well run as the one in South Korea. We managed to show some mild interest.

"What China needs is a good period of liberalism like we had in Germany in the 30s."

"Liberalism?" we gasped; "Do you mean the Nazis?"

"Oh yes, my father lived in Germany all during that period, of course, and knows first-hand how good it was. Don't believe everything the entertainment industry tells you."

I could not speak; my wife managed to say, "You might have felt otherwise were you a Jew, or a gypsy, or any number of other people."

"Oh yes, to be sure," laughed our affable taxi-mate, as if Ellen had made a witticism.

By now we had arrived at the theater. We settled down to watch the show. After the plate twirlers and leapers and magicians and bird-call makers, its climax was a small man who came out and balanced on the bridge of his nose a wine glass, from which the flat bottom of the stem had been cut off. The man must have been in his late sixties, perhaps older – a survivor of decades of imperialism, rival warlords, invasion, purges, war, revolution. From a crystal decanter, he filled the wine glass while it was still on his nose; we applauded. He put a glass tray on top of the wine glass; then four more wine glasses, filled like the first, on top of the glass tray; then small lamps between the glasses; then another glass tray; more glasses; more lamps. The lights in the theater dimmed; he was balancing a chandelier on his nose.

He was then brought two free-standing ladders (the kind you need to lean against something). And he was brought a clarinet. Somehow he managed to climb the ladders – one poised shakily on each side of him – with the clarinet in his mouth and the chandelier still on his nose. And at the top – to the astonishment and delight of the People's Liberation Army soldiers and the factory workers and the tourists and, somewhere in the crowd, the Nazi – he played the old Yiddish melody, "Bei mir bist du sheyn."

12

CHINA: VISITING RITES (II)

In 1961, when I was a freshman at Yale, I used to do most of my studying in the stacks of the Sterling Library, a vast cathedral-like pile whose grand portals, vaulted ceilings, and gargoyles declare that though the true, evangelical religion must be housed in the spare and disciplined space of the whitewashed chapel, the florid, expansive spirit of medieval Catholicism survives in the house of learning. One day, bored with whatever it was I was working on, I looked up at the books shelved above my tiny carrel and saw there a multi-volume set called the *Boston Register*. This turned out to be a late nineteenth-century record of the names, addresses, and occupations of the inhabitants of Boston. I took down the volume for 1892 (if I remember correctly) and looked up my grandfather. There he was, Morris Greenblatt, of such-and-such a street, occupation "ragpicker."

The occupation startled me, not because my father, a lawyer, had actively repressed his class origins – he had told me that his father had a horse and wagon and went around buying and selling old things – but because the word itself, like *lamplighter* or *iceman*, has fallen so completely from use that it exists only as a marker of that which no longer exists. The word is testimony to the social forces that rendered it obsolete: at first perhaps the power of euphemism, which replaced *ragpicker*, with its uncomfortably vivid suggestion of someone bending down to clutch a piece of soiled cloth, with a phrase like *used clothes merchant*; then the power of economic and technological change which engendered such complete obsolescence that the occupation itself vanished along with the name by which it was originally designated. (Berkeley has its share of used clothing stores, but no one would think to call the entrepreneurs "ragpickers;" indeed several of the stores are rather fancy and bear cute names.)

Literature is full of such ghostly words; indeed the only other time I had encountered "ragpicker" was when, as a high school sophomore, I had dazzled my immediate family with a spirited portrayal of the ragpicker in a school production of Giraudoux's *The Madwoman of Chaillot*. If my father found it amusing or disquieting to see his son strutting about in the borrowed garment of a ragpicker – a resurrection of the linguistic dead – he did not see fit to share

This chapter was first published in *Raritan* Vol. 4, No. 4 (Spring, 1985): 44–56.

his response. It seemed to me in any case very odd to discover that this was the official, bureaucratically sanctioned name for what my grandfather did for a living, and to discover this in the stacks of the Sterling Library.

Before I went to China I had thought I might tell this story sometime – in a seminar or even a lecture – in part, I must confess, as a kind of sly boast (where else could one exult quite so sincerely, I imagined, in one's humble origins?), and in part because the story said something in a personal way about family, institutions, and social mobility in America. The pattern, after all, is a common one, enacted with small variations in a large number of immigrant families: from lower-class trades – laborer, ragpicker, cobbler, tailor, seamstress, and the like – to business or the professions, then to the academy. My grandfather dealt in the refuse of society, my father in its judicial mechanisms, and I in its aesthetic representations.

Such an account naively assumes, of course, that I am the goal of a historical development, as if my family's whole project, in its escape from Russia, its immigrant struggles for survival, its gentrification, had as its final purpose the production of an English professor. But this narcissism is merely the condition of everyday consciousness; in unguarded moments, at least, we all regard ourselves as the end toward which things have been tending, and, of course, within the limited sphere of our own consciousness we are just that. I thought, at any rate, that my family story could serve for outsiders as an initiation into an American code that has helped to shape the profession of literary criticism in our country – the study of English literature as part of a pattern of assimilation, an element in what Norbert Elias in his study of table manners has called "the civilizing process."

Literary study functioned, in my own case, less as the active agent of cultural absorption than as the sign that this absorption had been successfully completed, just as it marked not the process but the secure completion of my gentrification. The crucial moves – from Europe to America, from Yiddish to English, from ragpicker to lawyer – had occurred in my grandfather's and father's generations; literary criticism appeared as a "free choice," a seemingly independent decision to pursue what interested, pleased, and moved me. I use terms like "seemingly" not because I doubt my motives – they were and remain potent forces – but because I recognize now that even free choices are shaped by overarching family and social strategies.

Even as a green freshman in 1961, I was not allowed to be completely unaware of the connection between cultural assimilation and literary study. In the same week that I discovered the official name of my grandfather's occupation, my splendid English teacher, no doubt perceiving in me the early, owlish signs of an academic vocation, told me that he needed a student assistant to help him finish assembling materials for the book he had been working on and encouraged me to apply for the position. In those days such jobs were assigned by the Financial Aid office, to which I dutifully trotted for a routine appointment with someone I will call Mr Spaulding. After the briefest exchange of formalities, Mr Spaulding leaned forward – I remember the large Yale class ring on his finger – and said, "You're Jewish, aren't you, Mr Greenblatt?" I said that I was. "Well, frankly,

we're sick and tired of the number of Jews who are coming into this office after
they're admitted and trying to wheedle money out of Yale University." I had no
idea what to say. Finally, sounding very much like the callow teenager I was, I
asked, "How can you make such a generalization?" "It's all in the statistics," he
replied. And then, "What do you think of Sicilians?" "I don't know any
Sicilians," I said. "Well, J. Edgar Hoover has statistics that show that Sicilians
have criminal tendencies. Do you get my point?" I do not remember a great deal
of the remainder of our conversation – I felt dizzy and close to tears; all I recall
clearly is Mr Spaulding's remark that "We could people this whole school with
graduates of the Bronx High School of Science" – I protested with very little
irony, I'm afraid, that I was from Newton – "but we choose not to."

My Mr Spaulding was no doubt a bizarre atavism at the enlightened Yale of
the early 1960s; he spoke, I suppose, for a world in which ragpickers and their
spawn would not be permitted to sully the genteel halls of learning, but that
world had already crumbled away. The attempt to ward off the likes of me had
been made at leading American universities throughout the 1920s and 1930s; the
exclusionary devices ranged from explicit racial and religious quotas to vague
tests of "character" to carefully crafted schemes of geographical distribution. In
this period the sentiments and "statistics" to which I had been treated would not
have been at all exceptional. *Too many Freshmen!* How many Jews among
them?" Frederick Jones, the Dean of Yale College, wrote to his colleague the
admissions director; "and are there any *Coons*?" The Dean was spending the
summer of 1922 on Cape Cod with his friend Henry Pennypacker, Harvard's
Dean of Admissions: "Pennypacker is here & much disturbed over the Jew
problem at Harvard. *Don't let any colored* transfers get *rooms* in College. I'm
having a big rest." (Quoted in Synott, *The Half-Opened Door*.) But the big rest
came to an end; the sheltering world of Jones and Pennypacker had crumbled
away, leaving poor, nasty Mr Spaulding exposed and impotent.

Eliot's "Gerontion," with its Jew squatting on the window sill, was taught as
part of a literary tradition to which I and my secret sharers from Bronx Science
had full and legitimate access. The slur was not a gate through which we could
not pass, but, as the footnotes say, "a symbol of deracinated man," and anyone
adept at finding a path through the forest of symbols could enter and flourish.
I may even have been writing a paper on "Gerontion" when I glanced up at the
Boston Register. At a safe distance from the great migrations of the late nineteenth
and early twentieth century, I studied English literature as my cultural birthright,
and my tiny personal history could exemplify the role of literary studies in the
lives of many of my contemporaries.

I never intended to tell anyone in China about Mr Spaulding; I felt the
particular ethnic code involved would have been too obscure. And, as it happened, I never told my Chinese colleagues and students about encountering my
grandfather's ghost in the Sterling Library. I held back for several different
reasons, none of which ever came quite clear to me but which persisted
nevertheless like a vague, inhibiting mist. Social origins in China are not a matter
of mere familial interest; they deeply affect your standing in society, your
opportunity for travel abroad, and your access to information, goods, and

services. During the Cultural Revolution a "bourgeois background" meant almost certain persecution and could easily mean death. Your class background was – and possibly remains – a permanent part of your record, a determining factor of your identity in the eyes of the state.

Most of the Chinese professors of English whom I met came from bourgeois backgrounds, and most had, in consequence, suffered during the Cultural Revolution. There were public humiliations ("large-character posters," denunciations, compulsory self-criticism), beatings, arrests, and prolonged exile to work camps and collective farms. Only recently had officials been urged to observe toward artists and intellectuals of undesirable class backgrounds the "Three Don'ts" – don't pull pigtails, don't place caps on people's heads, don't beat them with rods – and to follow instead the way of "gentle winds and mild rains." To proclaim before such people that my grandfather was a ragpicker suddenly seemed fatuous and absurd. What on earth would it mean? Would I be demonstrating American indifference to social background, since I had been admitted to a major university despite my humble origins? Would I be proving our extraordinary access to information, since even as a mere freshman I was permitted to study in the stacks of a great and vast library? Would I be providing an illustration of the extraordinary weakness of family tradition in America, since I learned the name of my grandfather's occupation only through a chance encounter with an old book in a library he himself would never have been permitted to enter? Would I be displaying the social mobility of America – from ragpicker to lawyer to scholar – or would the mobility not seem so striking after all? Perhaps a ragpicker who owned his own horse and cart and bought and sold things was considered bourgeois here. Or perhaps, alternatively, the social distance would seem vast, and I would appear to these people a brazen upstart, confessing something vaguely shameful. Besides, the longer I stayed the harder it was for me to grasp what attitude toward their own class background Chinese academics held; I understood the surface meanings, but the nuances continually escaped me.

For a moment once, at a dinner party in New York, I thought I had a glimpse of the truth. An eminent senior Chinese academic, Professor Ming, and his wife had come for a visit: the visit was itself surprising not only because it is unusual for married couples to be permitted to travel abroad together but also because, with the downfall of the Gang of Four, the professor had been in considerable disgrace and even danger. He had *not* suffered during the Cultural Revolution; on the contrary, he had prospered and had in effect determined (though not alone) who would be persecuted in his department. Moreover, to compound the mystery, he came from a very wealthy industrialist family, some of whose wealth he had been allowed to retain. His impeccable English reflected both his early education and a prolonged residence in the United States, when the outbreak of World War II prevented him from returning to China from Columbia University, where he was studying.

My wife and I were invited to dinner with this couple; also present was Han Ru-jie, one of the professor's former students, an engaging, almost toothless academic in his fifties, with poor English and a very nervous laugh. (The man, it was said, had been an executioner with the Red Army during the War of

Liberation.) To complete the company there were our hosts and a young woman who was a scholar of Sanskrit. The evening passed pleasantly and uneventfully until the young woman, who prided herself on her frankness, turned to the old Chinese professor and said, "I understand you collaborated with the Cultural Revolution; why was that?" There was a ghastly silence, punctuated by short, involuntary bursts of mirthless laughter from Han Ru-jie.

"I came from a wealthy, bourgeois background," Professor Ming replied, after a moment, "and I believed in the Chinese Revolution. I saw not only the abuses everywhere abundant in the old China, but the specific injustices caused by my own family. When in 1965 the Chairman told us that we were to purge the rightists in our midst and to rededicate ourselves to the Revolution, I believed him. I believed whatever the Chairman said, and I saw an opportunity to purge myself of a collective family guilt that had been haunting me."

We were quiet for a bit after this – even Han Ru-jie did not find occasion to laugh – then we talked among ourselves about whether it was possible any longer in the Western world to feel a "collective family guilt." Kinship ties – flattened out and impoverished in discourse by the deliberately schematic and abstract term "bourgeois," imposed for ideological reasons on a social system that bore little resemblance to the one for which the term was originally invented – had suddenly acquired a significance at once personal and historical. Professor Ming's family had, in his account, the force ascribed to the household, in Greek tragedy; it constituted a destiny enacted *through* individual lives but bearing a meaning transcending those lives. Yet the transcendence mattered only because the individual – in this case the bespectacled, elderly, guilt-ridden professor sitting at the table – conferred upon it the concrete immediacy and authenticity of his inner life. An official profession of collective guilt (at a purge trial, for example, or in a politician's harangue) would have made us all queasy or indignant; a private revelation, made in the protected intimacy of the dinner table and released only by a violation of decorum, seemed by contrast utterly convincing and moving.

All of us had been touched by the unusual frankness of the professor's reply, and I felt that I had been brought closer to an understanding of the mysterious note struck whenever the Chinese spoke of their family background. But the next morning our hostess asked Han Ru-jie if he thought the moment had been a terribly awkward one for Professor Ming. "Not a bit," he replied laughing; "he said exactly what the Party told him to say if asked such a question!"

Did the collective guilt exist then, or was it a convenient bureaucratic fiction? The answer is not at all clear, nor can we know whether more than a handful of the tens of thousands of men and women accused of bourgeois backgrounds were given the slightest opportunity to collaborate with the Red Guards, even had they the stomach to do so. We didn't, in any case, hear anything about collective guilt in China, though we did hear a great deal about stoical resignation and silence in the face of persecution. "Didn't you protest?" my wife asked the academics who would tell us their horror stories of beatings, humiliations, and forced labor. "No, never," came the inevitable reply. "But deep inside," she would continue to ask, "there, surely, you protested." And again there would be denials. "But did you feel then that in some sense the charges leveled against you

were just? Did you feel some guilt, some partial complicity with your tor-
mentors?" "I felt," said Xue Bao-Chai, whose family's ancient renown only
intensified the attacks upon her as a bourgeois intellectual during the Cultural
Revolution, "that it was beneath my dignity to protest."

"They could do with less dignity," remarked an American friend who had
lived in Peking all through the Cultural Revolution. For though they were
vilified for their "bourgeois" background and attitudes, the literary intellectuals
seemed to display during the years of crisis few of the responses that we would
associate with the bourgeois ideology in the West: an insistence upon those rights
due to them as members of civil society, a tenacious defense of private property
and a linked sense that personal identity is itself a kind of property, a conviction
that society is an aggregate of individuals and that individual experience, unique
and irreducible, is the core of existence. Perhaps there were intellectuals who
manifested these and similar qualities – they may have figured prominently
among those who were murdered – but those we met in China seemed, like
Xue Bao-Chai, to stand far more on their dignity than on their rights. And if this
dignity seemed magnificently impressive – something inalienable, unshakable, far
beyond the vulgarities of politics, the market place, and the court of law – it also
seemed bound up with a stoical passivity that I would have found unbearable.

"We were for centuries a feudal country," one old professor remarked at
dinner in Shanghai, "a people accustomed to obey and respect the wishes of
the ruler. Mao had done so much for the country – or so we thought at the time
[nervous laughter]. So we accepted his wishes, and criticized ourselves, and
believed that somehow we must have deserved our sufferings." "But didn't
you ever begin to doubt that the persecutions were just? After all, you must
have known that virtually all of the charges against you were untrue." The old
professor did not answer, but a younger man spoke up after a few moments:
"I did begin to doubt," he said, "after the fall of Lin Biao [the Defense Minister
who reportedly died in a plane crash in 1971 after allegedly attempting to
assassinate Mao]. But it wasn't until 1974, when I began to realize that there
was a split between Mao and Zhou Enlai, that I understood that the charges
against us were lies." Such remarks – and they were typical of many – seem to
indicate that the false charges were in effect accepted by many of those against
whom they were brought, as long as the full and united weight of the Chinese
state was behind them. Perhaps "accepted" is too strong; but such charges were,
at least, not actively or even inwardly denied. Only when the state showed
cracks, when factions appeared, and above all when a significant split emerged
between Mao and Zhou Enlai, could many intellectuals fully acknowledge to
themselves that they had been falsely accused.

"There was no choice," the department chairman, who had spent ten hard
years on a farm, told us; "what was the point of complaining?"

"Did you always dream of getting back to Shanghai? Did you think the
persecutions would stop?"

"I tried never to think about such questions," she answered; "I forced myself
to put out of my mind everything except the task immediately before me. That
way I was less miserable."

"The worst moments," she added, "were not when I thought about myself but when I thought about my children. During their first two years in school they did nothing but criticize themselves and their teachers, and shout slogans. Then even that stopped and there was no school at all."

This anxiety about children being denied an education was something we heard again and again during our visit to China, and always the expressions were charged with an intensity that made them stand out from the almost ritualized litany of stories of suffering during the time of the Gang of Four. "For myself," said Xue Bao-Chai, "I truly did not care; I had given up most of my privileges long before the last of them were taken away by the Red Guards; I had turned my back on my bourgeois upbringing when I joined the student movement in Peking in the 1930s. But I suffered for my children. Both of them were taken out of school, branded the children of criminals, and forced to work at the worst jobs. For ten years I watched helpless, while the time for their education passed. The peasants on the commune would come to them whenever there was something particularly dangerous to do and would say to them, 'You have no family; it's only fair that you do this.' All I could think to myself was, 'When they are old, the only thing they will be fit to do is to be gatekeepers.' "

For a brief, giddy moment I thought Xue Bao-Chai had said "ragpickers," but "gatekeepers" evoked a different social world, the world not of my past but of hers. Spoken in the concrete room amidst the clutter of other shacks half-built or half-ruined – it was, as usual, hard to tell which – the word "gatekeepers" called up the courtyard mansions of the imperial elite, houses within houses within houses, each marked off from the others by gates dutifully kept by family servants. It was not, Xue Bao-Chai insisted, the loss of such wealth that tormented her on her children's behalf – that loss had already occurred, and she had welcomed it – but a different kind of loss: a loss of status, a loss of access, and above all else a loss of education. To be a gatekeeper here was to have no education. This was the disaster that Xue Bao-Chai and her husband saw befalling their children and hence themselves during the Cultural Revolution – a familial fall into ignorance – and it was a disaster they felt helpless to prevent. They seemed, too, to be forced into a kind of complicity, for they had to hide their books from the Red Guards and by doing so they hid them away as well from their own children. When for brief periods their sons were allowed to return home from the farm or the oil fields, they begged for books, but their parents were afraid to comply. After all, it was precisely because of the books – the corrupt, "bourgeois" Western knowledge – that they were being attacked, publicly humiliated, "struggled against in the fields."

At this point, Xue Bao-Chai's twenty-eight-year-old younger son Lung-Wei, who had been listening quietly during most of the evening, spoke up. His years of education had been utterly disrupted, he had had almost ten years of political indoctrination, and he had been taught that his parents were corrupt precisely because of their Western knowledge, but – and this is probably the crucial point – he spoke in surprisingly fluent English. "I stole the books I needed," he said. "When my parents refused to give me any, I found where they were hidden and stole what I wanted." At night, after work in the oil fields, he lay by a kerosene lamp and memorized pages of a tattered English-Chinese dictionary. He was now, to be sure, still behind those younger students whose lives had not been torn apart by the Cultural Revolution – he had narrowly failed the competitive examination that would have placed him in a special training program for translators – but he was not a gatekeeper. And his older brother had been even more successful: he had won a scholarship to an American university, had been permitted to accept it, and was now attending. What had he chosen to study? English and American literature.

In spite of everything, then, the family had managed to reproduce itself where it most mattered – in education. And though such anecdotes are obviously of no statistical value, this reproduction seemed to be happening at every university and foreign language institute I visited. From this point of view, the Cultural Revolution appeared to be – among many other things – an astonishing, even desperate, national attempt to disrupt the intellectual line of succession, an attempt to shut off access that met with an equally astonishing, and apparently successful, resistance.

No doubt there are thousands of exceptions, but Chinese intellectuals seemed to have a truly ferocious determination to transmit their intangible heritage to their children; or better still, as the case of Xue Bao-Chai and her sons suggested, family forces were at work that triumphed over both political policy and the survival strategy of the parents themselves. Now with the fall of the Gang of Four, these forces have fewer impediments; the universities have been reopened with the professors whom the Red Guards had attacked and imprisoned; and the special schools that prepare students for the entrance examinations into universities and institutes are once again found for the most part in the cities, near the universities themselves. Since it is difficult for Chinese students to live away from home, it is now all the more unlikely for rural children, however intellectually endowed, to break away from the country, and all the more likely for intellectuals to reproduce their kind.

The strain that this system must put on a communist society is not necessarily grasped consciously: a professor (and a member of the Party) who once declared to me that in 1949 he had discovered the meaning of his life – to serve the communist revolution – also sweated out, in an agony of apprehension, the results of his only child's university entrance examinations. When the results proved successful, he proudly announced that his child would have a career in agricultural economics, and he added hastily, lest I misunderstood, that she would not be required to live in the countryside with the peasants.

Through these and similar conversations, I came to understand that it was not my ragpicker grandfather who would matter very much, if I were to speak in China of my own background. It was rather my maternal great-grandfather who would count, for in far-off Lithuania he had been a Talmudic scholar, an interpreter of texts. So had his father before him, and his grandfather too. All the ordinary work of the family – the raising of children, the making of money, the paying of bills, the daily decisions – was done by the overburdened, clever, anxious women. For my Chinese colleagues, I imagine, it would seem only that my family had passed through a dangerous and prolonged disruption – the cost of escape from Tsar Nicholas II's plan to "russify" the Jews by requiring twenty-five-year terms of military service – and had now returned to the natural order of things. To be sure, the texts had changed, the Mishna and Gemarah having given way to Shakespeare and Milton; but the intellectual vocation, the cultural position, the essential occupation, remained in a deep sense the same. Could I altogether deny it?

Yet it must make a difference that the texts are not sacred nor even commentaries on the sacred, that they do not compel obedience, that they are not the objects of veneration. Even as I make this disclaimer, however, I know that it is at most a half-truth. Last year an official delegation of Chinese humanists toured the United States; during their visit to Berkeley, they sat in on one of my classes, a large Humanities lecture course for freshmen, team-taught with an historian. The semester began with the New Testament and ended with Milton; on the day of their visit, I was lecturing on Dante. I could hardly claim great distance from the precinct of sacred texts. After class, the members of the delegation had several questions to ask my students and myself. "Why had we assigned 'original texts' (in translation) and not accurate summaries of them?" Because, we answered, our culture is uneasy about summaries, because we believe in unmediated encounters with the past, because we actively discourage our students from regurgitating stale ideas, because from the Renaissance onward Western humanism and Protestantism have insisted, like ancient Judaism, upon returning to the textual source. "But where do the texts come from?" the delegation asked. "From the bookstore," replied one of my students, with unwitting ideological profundity. "But how are the texts chosen? Are they assigned by a government ministry or by a university committee?" "The texts," said one of my colleagues, "are just there."

But, of course, they are not just there; they are constructed by a set of ideological choices that we constantly make. And if it is more difficult than it first seems to unmake these choices, we can at least reflect upon the sources of the cultural power that is embodied in our literary canon, and we can withhold from that power our unthinking assent. I do not wish to merge myself with the authors I study, nor do I seek to obey their imperatives. I am content to remain an outsider and to feel a strain of difference between myself and the texts I teach. And I admire the Chinese students of English and American literature precisely because they have pursued this project so much further than I have been willing or able to do.

One sweltering day in China, I climbed a holy mountain, Tai Shan, with a British friend who was an ardent enthusiast of Chinese Communism. We passed a laborer repairing a stone bridge; he was chipping away with a small chisel at a large granite rock. My friend said, "At least now he knows he's working on his own rock." What is my relationship, I wonder, to the objects at which I chip away? "At least," I may say of my Chinese colleagues, who struggle to interpret literature produced by an alien culture, "they know they're *not* working on their own rock."

13

LAOS IS OPEN

For your next vacation I do not recommend the River View Hotel in Vientiane, the capital of Laos. A large, dreary concrete block, converted with Soviet help from a warehouse, it is utterly without charm. At the entrance, to be sure, there is a welcoming gesture: two life-size cardboard figures of smiling Laotians in the prayerlike, palms-together posture of greeting, called a *wai*. But the colors are faded and the cardboard disintegrating, as if to signal what lies within. Whoever designed the bathrooms evidently had had little previous experience of indoor plumbing; how else to explain the quaint decision to place the toilet inside the shower? And I had no idea that electric bulbs of such low wattage could be produced – though the gloom had the advantage of keeping us from looking too carefully at the sheets or deciphering the ominous smudges on the walls. My wife Ellen and I took the liberty of grumbling a bit to Amkha, the Lao Tourism guide who had been assigned to our family of four, but he shamed us by finding our complaints incomprehensible. The hotel is excellent, he declared with manifest conviction, though he regretted that it was enormously expensive – about twenty dollars a night, or half the monthly salary of an office worker or a teacher.

Why the warehouse was converted to a hotel is something of a mystery, though perhaps no greater mystery than why the warehouse was built in the first place – commerce being not much more evident than tourism. There are some small shops now in Vientiane and, in the modest covered market, an unprecedented if still very tentative display of big-ticket items: a few washing machines, stereos, and televisions. But it is difficult to see where Laotians will get the money for such purchases. One of Laos's principal sources of foreign currency is the sale of air rights for overflights; another is the export of used US bomb casings dug up by peasants who frequently get blown up by the ones that failed to explode the first time round. There are, to be sure, unofficial sources of income: major opium production, stolen antiquities from the largely unguarded temples, the illegal cutting of timber, and – or so I was told by a Thai environmentalist – the illegal capture and export of exotic animals eaten as aphrodisiacs by wealthy Japanese. But there is almost no industry, no infrastruc-

This chapter was first published in *Confessions of the Critics* (H. Aramvesser (ed.), 1996, pp. 221–34).

ture, no sign of domestic manufactured goods. This is an unimaginably poor country.

On our first night in the River View Hotel, we dined entirely alone – not in the melancholy dining room which was darkened and empty, but on the rooftop, a huge, empty expanse of tar paper, lighted like a basketball court by a long row of glaring floruescent streetlamps. It was atrociously hot. Our meal was carried up four flights of stairs and served by a delicate young woman in a long wraparound skirt and embroidered blouse and an even more delicate young man with rings on his fingers, startlingly long fingernails, and a coy smile. Neither of them seemed to break a sweat.

Somewhere in the darkness flowed the Mekong, but there were no signs of life on the river, only a few lights on the Thai side, no cars or bicycles on the street below, and apparently no one else in the hotel. At breakfast the next morning, however, there were two other guests. The first was an American, paunchy, balding, and loud, in a sweat-stained polyester suit. He was a lawyer, he said, a "consultant" to the Lao government. What did he consult on?

"Anything they ask me to. Socialism is dead, they know that. But they don't know how to do anything different. The fault is the United Nations. Their bureaucrats are everywhere, and they give the Laotians endless money, so they have no incentive to develop their economy. It makes me sick. You see the bureaucrats – Indians mainly, who spend their lives shuffling forms – having dinner at the best restaurant in town, where they charge three times the price anywhere else. Their cars and drivers are sitting outside waiting for them. A little money gets through, of course, but 90 percent goes to pay their salaries. It makes me sick."

He had lived in Asia, he said, for more than twenty years – he arrived then, like so many of our other exports, with the Vietnam War – and "everyone knew him." But a few minutes later he said that he had lived for a year recently in Yugoslavia. And a few minutes later still he said he had been living in Florida where his daughter was in college. Had she grown up in Asia, we wondered. "No, on my yacht in Coral Gables."

The other guest at breakfast was a genial Indian who had listened with a smile to our compatriot's ramblings and who worked, he said, for Unilever. "What is Unilever doing in Laos?" we asked. He chuckled, "Having breakfast."

As we got up to leave, another foreigner hurried into the hotel, a lean American in his mid-thirties, with grease-slicked wiry hair and a loud Hawaiian shirt. He was carrying an attaché case and asked to see the manager. He was going to stay for a month, he said, and wanted a 50 percent reduction in the price of the room. He would have many visitors, he added, "my wife, my girlfriend, my father, my friends," and would have them all stay at the hotel. He spotted the "consultant" – "Am I glad to see you!" – and the two of them rushed off to a corner and began to talk earnestly in low tones. My younger son, Aaron, who used to be a great lover of Tintin comic books, looked at them with excitement: "Opium!" he whispered.

We didn't stay around to spy on the sinister pair, for it was time to see the sights of Vientiane, which is a capital largely without sights. A long history of defeat and domination – by the Thais, the Burmese, the Vietnamese, the Khmers, and the French – has taken a heavy toll on the dusty old city. There are a few Buddhist temple compounds, several quite lovely, but all of them on a modest and subdued scale compared to the glittering opulence of the *wats* of Bangkok. We resisted the temptation to pocket some fine old Buddha images in Wat Si Saket – there were thousands of them in dovecot-like niches along the cloister walls – but it was clear from the empty niches that others had not resisted. Everywhere there was an air of desolation, destruction, pillage: buildings razed in war, temples falling into ruin, melancholy reminders of famous treasures taken to Siam, murals flaking apart, headless and armless statues thrown in heaps. And the fact that we were alone at all of these sites intensified the poignancy and the sense of loss.

Thailand, just across the river, is overrun with tourists, but the Laotian government, though hard-pressed for foreign capital, is showing few signs of welcoming tourists. In fact it was remarkably difficult for our family of four, hard currency in hand, to get visas. We tried first in the United States, after we had heard from a friend of an anthropologist friend that Laos was "open" after so many years of being tightly "closed." For Americans who came of age during the Vietnam War, Laos has an extraordinary resonance: it conjures up a special outrage, for it was there, in the Annamite Mountains, along the Mekong Delta, and on the Plain of Jars, that the fatal combination of American arrogance, violence, and futility reached its zenith. The outrage, intensified by my generation's quaintly idealistic belief that the United States was supposed to behave justly, was oddly mingled with what Victorians must have felt at contemplating the implausible names of those whose faraway lands their empire was ravaging. For a few years our newspapers were filled with exotic characters – Prince Souphanouvong, the sinister General Phoumi Novasan, the Pathet Lao leader Kaysone Phomvihane, gallant, courageous Prince Souvanna Phouma, King Sisavang Vong and his son King Savang Vattana – who seemed to inhabit a Gilbert and Sullivan opera, even while our B-52 s bombed and bombed and bombed. At first the bombing was "secret" – the planes flew under different markings, and our government systemically lied about what it was doing – but even when we finally admitted what we were up to, there was not much of an explanation or excuse. Without a declaration of war, and hence without either congressional debate or legal authorization, the United States dropped more bombs per capita on remote, weak Laos than we did on Germany in World War II.

My family and I had been planning a trip to neighboring Thailand anyway, and something about this resonance, along with those words, "open" and "closed" – as if a country were a strongbox or a long-buried tomb – made us want to go to Laos. Memories of the devastation we visited on one of the poorest countries on earth were paradoxically intertwined with the tourist's dream of the unspoiled: if only you can get there, the *Lonely Planet Guide* declares, Laos offers you "an unparalleled glimpse of old South-East Asia." The world is full of places about which everyone says maddeningly, "You should have been here twenty years ago, before it was ruined": Chiang Mai, Rio, Berkeley. At last we would get to a place before it was ruined. We would be in on the ground floor of touristic spoliation. Years from now we could say to friends, "If only you had visited Laos when it was first opened to foreigners."

There is a Lao-American Tourist Association, in Elgin, Illinois. I imagine that it is located in Elgin because a bureaucrat in Vientiane looked at a map of the United States and put his finger down more or less in the middle. We had an elaborate and, in its odd way, warm exchange of letters with this office – I explaining to Ms Marla that we did not want a package tour, Ms Marla assuring me that we would be welcome on our own, that we would certainly receive visas, that we had only to fill out the applications in triplicate and tell them a bit more about ourselves and our reasons for wanting to visit. Applications duly sent; then long delays, more letters, more assurances, more delays, futile phone calls to Elgin and then to Washington, mumbled but evidently heartfelt apologies, still no visas – and then it was time to leave for Thailand.

In Bangkok we made our way to the Laotian embassy for another try. It took us almost two hours to get to the embassy through some of the worst traffic in the history of the world, the air insufferably heavy and full of exhaust fumes. We stood in line while two young Italians threw a prolonged histrionic tantrum at the demure young clerk behind the desk who was not giving them a visa. Finally, she relented, instructing them to leave their passports and return the next day. We had been told by the friend of the friend that the Laotians despised displays of anger, and valued gentleness and good humor: even after all we did, she said, they prefer Americans to the Russians, because we smile so much more. We approached the desk wreathed in forced smiles, a family of Malvolios. The clerk smiled in return and instructed us to fill out new applications. But when we presented these applications – duly filled out in triplicate, with grinning photographs – she quietly said that we would not receive visas. "Why not?" She only shrugged. "But why did the Italians get visas?" "They not get visas. I only tell them come back tomorrow. But no visas." So, in a way, our smiles had been rewarded.

Still we had wasted the better part of the day and had no visas to show for it, and we wandered around Bangkok's Chinatown disconsolately. It was amazingly hot and humid, and the traffic was hideous. We ducked into a warren of alleys to get out of the sun, but it was almost as hot back there in the dark, and it was difficult to walk, because the ground was thick with refuse and the space almost completely filled with cooling ducts, pipes, electric wires – the stuff of unregulated, uncontrolled construction. Out on the snarling street again, we looked for a taxi. My older son Josh cooled his hands in the melting ice of a fish stall; we pointed out to him that the water was of dubious cleanliness. He has the regrettable habit of biting his fingernails from time to time.

The next morning Josh fainted on the airport bus taking us to a flight to Chiang Mai. Admittedly, that bus was crowded and hot – I felt faint too – but we took his temperature and knew that when we landed we had to get him to a doctor. The same anthropologist friend who put Laos into our heads had given us the name of another friend of his, an American-born lawyer who had married a Thai woman, become a Buddhist, practiced law in Bangkok, and – crucial for our purposes – commuted to Chiang Mai where he and his family lived. His wife was at home when we phoned and said she would come immediately to the hotel: "I was just going to drive to that part of town anyway." In her mid-forties, Ti Garden was cheerful, soft-spoken, immensely kind, and – in a way immediately apparent though difficult to define – not completely of this world. Where does one get such an impression after ten minutes' conversation, preoccupied by a feverish child and constrained by the formality of a first meeting? From very obscure signals: a certain timbre in the voice, the way sentences take form and trail off, a posture that somehow conveys the indwelling of the spirit. This will sound absurd – doubly so when I add that Ti Garden had gone from high school in Chiang Mai to Radcliffe, drove a big Range Rover, and had two teenage children. Less sylphlike than sturdy, quick to laugh, and utterly unpretentious, she nonetheless immediately struck all of us as the native of a different planet.

We talked about what to do with the suffering Josh. Ti knew a Western-trained doctor in town, but she urged us to do first what she would do with her own children: go to a Buddhist healer in a forest monastery on the outskirts of town. "I happen to be going there this morning anyway, so it's not out of my way. I'll take you." Josh is sixteen and is developing a sense of irony as well as a capacity for despair. He groaned audibly.

We piled in the Range Rover, and Ti drove us to the monastery, our son swearing quietly in the backseat. The saffron-clad monk, sitting in front of a hut in the forest, wore wire-rimmed glasses, which was vaguely reassuring. He did not look at Josh – that was less reassuring – but listened attentively to a description of his symptoms, then brought out a glass of water and a paper packet of herbal pills and told him to take ten of them immediately. He noticed that we looked askance at the water and explained that it was rainwater. We evidently looked unconvinced, because he went inside the hut and brought out a glass of what he said was boiled rainwater. Fifteen minutes after Josh took the pills his fever was completely gone. There was no charge.

It was cool in the forest, and we walked around the monastery, listening to the crickets and the howling of a gibbon, hidden somewhere in the trees. Ti said she wanted us to meet someone. In a cell by a small pond she introduced us to a middle-aged German who had become a Buddhist monk, a coarse-featured, hairy-chested man, his shaved head nicked by his razor, with a big paunch under his saffron robe. He was from Hamburg, he said, and was raised as a Lutheran. He had run away from his mother and stepfather when he was sixteen; then lived a wild life in Sweden; then followed Rudolf Steiner; then found Buddhism. Even during his years sharing "the material affluence and sensuous gratification of Swedish youths" (which he pronounced unsettlingly like "Jews"), he had been seeking something. He had lived in the cell by the pond for seventeen years. Did he think that he would ever leave? Perhaps not, he answered, though he would like to go to Laos.

Ti also longed to go to Laos – "it's deeply Buddhist, very unspoiled." Back in the hotel, we saw an ad for a tourist agency in Chiang Mai – the aptly named Exotissimo Travel – that claimed it could book trips to Laos; a week later (for an extravagant sum that more than made up for the no-cost medical treatment) we had our visas.

At the River View Hotel we wondered whether we were missing the Buddhist epiphany that Ti and the German monk both associated with Laos. The capital certainly did not seem a notably mystical place. The temples, or *wats*, were empty; the only place where we saw worshipers was at the ugly, modern site of the city pillar – an ancient stone column set into the ground – where a handful of women knelt on the linoleum and made offerings to an image said to bring luck. We went to a forest temple just outside of town – a place with the imposing name of Wat Mahaphutthawongsa Pa Luang Pa Yai – where toothless nuns in white robes gave us herbal saunas and pleasant massages, but it all seemed more like Calistoga than Nirvana.

The most striking thing about Vientiane is not the aura of religious life but the sense of being in the provinces' provinces. In one direction along the river from our hotel, there were lots of young people sitting on small wooden decks built out on the banks. They were chatting and smoking and quietly laughing. They probably lived in the horribly squalid concrete apartment blocks behind us, with their glimpses through curtainless windows of bare rooms, lit by a single naked bulb or a long fluorescent light, cracking paint and plaster, with blotches of water stains, scraps of corroding metal. In the midst of these, there survived a few dilapidated French-style houses, with long shuttered windows, as if lifted from a town in Normandy. A small food shop or two were the only signs of commercial life, and even these seemed shut, so that a young couple could sit by their bicycle (a passenger seat cleverly fitted on to the frame) and hold hands and feel quite alone (until, that is, the girl noticed the unfamiliar sight of the American tourist strolling towards them). In the other direction from our hotel, the pavement gave out after a block or two, and the dirt lane was lined with bamboo houses on stilts, with pigs and chickens in the space below. There were woodcutters lopping off branches with machetes, fishermen casting graceful nets into the flooded rice fields to catch minnows, and farmers, plodding behind their water buffalos, turning the heavy mud. Here a few shops were open, selling tiny selections of fish and meat, and two or three vendors were making small rice cakes. But all was quiet, except for the crackling voice on the loudspeakers attached to concrete poles, broadcasting the news, I suppose, or the latest production figures from Savannakhet, or the Party's latest manifesto.

The loudspeakers were one of the very few signs of ideological life, though the Pathet Lao remains very much in power. We seemed to be the only visitors at the Lao Museum of the Revolution, in an old, faded mansion. The museum is an odd place. Its account of World War II completely suppresses the fact that the Americans fought the Japanese, who surrendered to "the Anti-Fascist Alliance." (But then the East German Museum at Buchenwald concentration camp, near Weimar, scarcely mentioned that Jews died there; and the Musée de l'Armée at the Invalides in Paris does an impressive job of minimizing the American role in the liberation of Europe, celebrating instead what it shamelessly pretends was a widespread French resistance to the Nazis.) There are news photographs of Johnson and MacNamara ordering the bombing of Laos and painful photographs of children burned by "U.S. imperialist napalm" and a few old rifles and charred pieces of American planes. Above all, there is much celebration, in the old

Maoist manner, of Comrade Kaysone: his heroic exhortations to the people, his life hidden in caves (one display case shows the exercise cables – just like I had as a kid! – with which he kept fit while in hiding), his surprise attacks, and his plans, as one caption rather nakedly put it, "to seize power." But outside the museum there were few signs of indoctrination – no elaborate posters, no flags and photographs, no parades. At the same time, there were virtually no books or magazines and very few televisions, and though there must have been newspapers somewhere, we never saw one. Perhaps indoctrination seemed beside the point.

There were some of the familiar signals of the police state at the airport, where we went to catch a plane to Luang Phabang: photography forbidden, papers stamped and counterstamped by sour-looking bureacrats and customs officials, a distinct sense of disapproval though no very clear indication of what any of us had done wrong. We would have preferred to go by bus or still better by boat. But the river in the summer months was too low, and the road, we were told, was impossible. "Why impossible?" "I don't know," said our guide, "Maybe mines, maybe Hmong guerillas." The Air Laos flight didn't seem much safer. The small twin-engine Chinese plane couldn't get much altitude, and we bumped along perilously close to the rugged mountaintops, skimming (within automatic weapons range, I thought) over the isolated Hmong villages where the CIA recruited its army and where much of Laos's opium is grown. The plane grew tremendously hot, the cabin filled with smoke – just normal condensation, we were told – and several passengers became violently ill. Then the mountains came still closer – they seemed about to scrape the bottom of the plane – and we were landing at Luang Phabang.

In the mid-nineteenth century a French naturalist, M. Henri Mouhot, travelled through Southeast Asia on behalf of the Geographical and Zoological Societies of London, collecting specimens, making scientific drawings, and writing reports. In July, 1861, after a nightmarish voyage on elephant, beset by mosquitoes, ox-flies, and leeches, he reached Luang Phabang. "It was a charming picture," he wrote in his journal, "reminding one of the beautiful lakes of Como and Geneva. Were it not for the constant blaze of a tropical sun, or if the mid-day heat were tempered by a gentle breeze, the place would be a little paradise"[1] I can corroborate both the torrid heat – two of the passengers collapsed on the short walk from the plane to the little shed that serves as the terminal – and the intense beauty, though the steep jungle cliffs and magnificent temples seem very far from the Alps.

Poor fever-ridden Mouhot! By the time he reached Luang Phabang, with his precious cases of beetles and butterflies, he must have been dreaming of lively Italians and yodelling Swiss peasants. The Laotians seemed to him disagreeably passive and withdrawn – not hostile, exactly, but indifferent, unhelpful, and lacking all normal curiosity. Before he set out, a Chinese merchant had warned him to carry a good stick, the longer the better: "Put all delicacy aside," the merchant advised, "Laos is not like a country of the whites." The somber words continue to echo weeks later in his journal entries. "I am getting tired of these people," he writes, "a race of children, heartless and unenergetic. I sigh and look everywhere for a man, and cannot find one; here all tremble at the stick, and the enervating climate makes them incredibly apathetic."

Though the king of Luang Phabang received him with great pomp, Mouhot's mood did not improve, even when he had the pleasure of watching the natives kill a rhinoceros. Despite his long stick, he could not seem to compel service; and even gifts, the kindler, gentler alternative to beatings, were not properly recompensed. The Laotians seemed to him ungrateful and egotistical: "they not only will give you nothing – one has no right to expect it – but after taking presents from you, they will make you no return whatever." From morning to night the priests continually made their "frightful noise," but everyone else seemed "indolent," cultivating only enough rice to survive and then – as Mouhot puts it with fine Victorian exasperation – "lounging about the woods." They weren't even picturesque: "I saw some pretty young girls with intelligent faces; but before the females attain the age of eighteen or twenty their features become coarse and they grow fat. At five-and-thirty they look like old witches." Only the elephants seemed to him entirely admirable in their patience, goodness, and intelligence.

Mouhot labored on to collect his specimens, but his wanderings in the mountains near Luang Phabang – his own purposeful version of lounging about the woods – broke his health. By September his journal entries have become little more than lists of place names, interrupted by complaints about the tormenting mosquitoes and leeches; by October they have become for the most part unreadable:.IP5,4/

15th October. 58 degress Fahr. – Set off for Louang Prabang.
16th. – .. .. ..
17th. – .. .. ..
18th. – Halted at H. ...
19th. – Attacked by fever.
29th. – Have pity on me, oh my God ...!

Mouhot died in delirium on November 10, 1861. A large beetle was named in his honor, *Mouhotia gloriosa*.

There was a *Mouhotia gloriosa*, or one of its close relations, in our hotel room in Luang Phabang. It was too big to squash – it would have been like smashing a squirrel – so I picked it up in my son's baseball hat and escorted it outside. This was our principal experience of the area's wildlife – the tigers and rhinoceroses are all gone – if you except the drowsy civet cat in a very small cage and a monkey on a very long chain in the hotel's garden. We did not try to find any leeches, and we wore enough repellant to ward off every mosquito in Southeast Asia. The incidence of malaria in the region is astonishingly high, as is the general level of disease that so dismayed (and finally killed) Mouhot.

Good as its word, Lao Tourism had sent a guide to the airport to meet us – a sweet, quiet, sad-eyed young man named Tongchan who spoke some French and a few words of English and had one exceptionally long, indeed finger-length fingernail on his pinky. I asked him why. "Useful," he said, and mimed cleaning his ears with it. He took us sightseeing – for the most part, *wat*-hopping. We were, as far as we could tell, the only tourists in Luang Phabang and were the sole visitors in all of the splendid temples and in the former royal palace at the center of town. On the second day we did, however, meet another American while we waited on the steps that led down to the Mekong for a long-tail boat that would take us about 30 kilometers upriver to caves with famous Buddhist carvings. Our compatriot was a somewhat brassy Laotian woman, originally from Luang Phabang. She had been in a refugee camp in Thailand, she said, then in the Philippines, and now in Oakland where she had become a US citizen and lived near 35th Avenue. She had the Laotian's ready smile, but all of the diffidence was gone: she was expansive, irrepressible, and above all loud. It was impossible for us to tell, of course, if she had left Laos because she was so loud, or if she had become loud in America: some are born loud, some have loudness thrust upon them. "You should take pictures where they tell you not to," she boomed at us. Tongchan looked away, as if lost in thought.

Along the river, in the event, we were not asked to refrain from photography. The long-tail boat swooped in close to a half-sunk US patrol boat, Vietnam War vintage, and stopped at a riverside village where rice wine – here called "Lao-Lao" – is brewed. This was, quite obviously, the standard tour. But in the village I was forcibly struck by something I had already noticed in Luang Phabang: no one was interested in selling us anything. Indeed there was virtually nothing for sale. I had wandered around the town for several hours looking for something to buy, even a postcard, and the best I could come up with was a small bamboo stick crudely decorated with an odd checkerboard design. I asked what the design was meant to signify, but I couldn't make out the answer. At the riverside distillery, similarly, there were no souvenirs for sale. Two large, rusted barrels were sitting over a wood fire on the bank; a woman was pouring river water into the barrels through a homemade strainer; a bamboo pipe dripped the wine into dark earthenware pots. I was invited not to buy but simply to taste: the cup was a Sprite can, with the top removed and the edges smoothed. Tongchan ladled some Lao-Lao into this cup by dipping what appeared to be the top of an old antifreeze container into the pot. Preferring death to dishonor, I gingerly drank some, but even then there was no hint that I might want to buy a bottle to take with me.

Laos was, I realized, the culture least oriented to selling anything that I have ever encountered. This restraint or, to use Mouhot's term, indifference extends to places where you would most expect a sales pitch: market stalls, shops, hotels, restaurants (where you are never urged to have any drink but water). There was, to be sure, the rapacity represented by the absurd sum that the government charged for a tourist visa, but that sum seemed largely to function as a device to discourage visitors and inhibit commerce. Indeed I never saw anyone in the country actively trying to make money. No one tried to interest us in commodities or sell us services; no one seemed eager to initiate exchange of any kind. Even in the handicraft village to which we were taken (and where again we were quite alone), the weavers did not display goods by their looms or urge them upon us; instead all of the women sat chatting with one another around the perimeter of an open-sided wooden shed and, if we happened to glance in their direction, held up their goods. Prices were rather high, and there seemed to be no interest

in bargaining, just as there seemed to be no frustration, anxiety, or disappointment at not making a sale. So too in the appallingly poor little villages along the
river at which we asked the boatman to stop, there was virtually no grasping after
us, even among the children. It is not that the children or, for that matter, the
adults were, to use Mead's and Bateson's famous term for the Balinese, "away."
No, the kids giggled and dared each other to approach us and say "Sa-bai-dii"
(hello); the adults smiled, and responded to our greetings; a few went further
and expressed some quiet amusement or interest in our presence. But the
villagers seemed to lack any of the familiar signs of social *desire* – to sell, to
acquire, to impress, to touch, to improve their lot, to signal their presence in the
world.

This was what it meant then to reach a place untouched by tourism, the place
that our acquaintance Ti and her friend the German Buddhist monk dreamed of
visiting: we had reached the Land of No Desire. Now and then there were signs
of activity: two young men cutting planks with a long saw, a few dugout canoes,
some villagers coming down to the river to fetch water. But the villages, though
full of people squatting by their bamboo huts, seemed oddly still, and the wide,
muddy river, flanked by jagged limestone cliffs and lush mountains, was empty
and silent. Was it beautiful? Yes, of course. But I found it strangely unsettling that
no one seemed to want anything from us. It is the intense mutual exploitation of
tourism – the sense of consuming and being consumed, the search for a "bargain"
and the fear of being ripped off – that conditions the dream of an escape from
tourism; without the exploitation, without a feverish climate of exchange, the
actual escape seemed unnerving. Moreover, I am more of a Victorian than I had
realized: it was impossible for me not to feel some half-repressed version of
Mouhot's horror, a version focused on the big-bellied children caked with mud
and mucus. We had read that Laos has one of the highest infant mortality rates in
the world: that was, in the villages along the Mekong, not an invisible statistic but
a graphic reality.

Tongchan took us to his village, one of the poorest we had seen on the river
and one of the most disheartening. But in the midst of the disorder, with huts
falling into ruin, pigs rooting about the midden, children wandering about naked
and coughing, there was a central meeting hall of sorts – a row of plank benches
under a thatch roof – and a small *wat* with simple, touching paintings of the life of
the Buddha. Tongchan led us to the hut where he was born and introduced us to
his parents. His mother was a thin, toothless woman with an elegant face. She
held her grandchild, the daughter of Tongchan's sister whose husband had been
killed while serving as a soldier. Tongchan's father, an emaciated seventy-year-
old, was a blacksmith; a fire grate, a small vat of water, and a few simple tools
were the signs of his trade. We drank tea. The old man cleared his throat and
remarked that the river was low. We agreed – as if we had some idea of its usual
height. He said it would rise later in the season. We agreed again. The conversation gave me the chance to look at the tattoos on his chest and arms. I realized
that they were the same odd checkerboard design that was on my stick, and I
asked what they signified. They keep the poisonous snakes in the river from
biting, he said. Mystery solved.

I was safe from snake bites, then, but not from the sadness that welled up from the great brown empty river and the ragged children and the sight, as we returned, of the sunken US patrol boat. Back in Luang Phabang the feeling was only intensified by a visit to the National Museum. This large, rather graceless building on the riverbank had served as the royal palace until the 1975 revolution. Then the king, who had made the mistake of backing the United States and counting on its support, was sent with his wife and five children to a "reeducation camp" in northern Laos. They have not been heard from since.

The museum's great treasure is the "Pha Bang" from which the town (Luang means "big") gets its name: this is a deeply venerated first-century standing Buddha, supposedly made of solid gold. Displayed in a cluttered room and seen through a locked grate, it looked rather unimpressive and, more to the point perhaps, fake. But who can tell? Perhaps it was simply cheapened by the surrounding elephant tusks and Chinese porcelein vats and small bronzes – second-rate loot in a well-traveled Edwardian gentleman's country house. No doubt it was more impressive when it was washed ritually every year by the king in a solemn temple ceremony; judging from the dust, it had not been washed since 1975. I looked dutifully for the requisite minutes, daydreaming that I was in Nabokov's Zembla, and then moved on to the rest of the palace.

The whole house – a succession of reception rooms, bedrooms, a modest bathroom, and a small library that contained only a single immensely large history of the Ming and Ching dynasties – had an air of desolation. King Savang Vattana may be officially the enemy of the people, but the guards in the museum gave the distinct sense of being in deep mourning. Why didn't the king try to escape? we asked, thinking of our South Vietnamese allies. "The king did not leave Laos because he decided to die with his people," came the answer. Perhaps. Or perhaps he was naively confident in the power of his allies. Among the array of official gifts to the royal family was a medal with Lyndon Johnson's picture on it, a piece of the moon given by Richard Nixon, and, in the place of honor, the key to the city of Los Angeles, presented by the mayor, Sam Yorty.

On our last morning in Luang Phabang, I awoke at 4:30 a.m., couldn't get back to sleep, and tiptoed out to have a last walk around the town. A line of monks was going on their alms round, each carrying a covered bowl and receiving offerings – a bit of meat, fish, or rice – from passersby. They turned into Wat Mai, the temple where the king used to wash the Pha Bang. I decided to climb to the top of Phu Si, the steep hill that dominates the town, so I scrambled over the locked gate and, in the very great solitude of a city filled with solitude, hiked up the path to the top, past the frangipani trees, the *bodhi* tree sent from India, the tangle of vines and palms and flowers. There was a strange birdcall and the cry of a gibbon.

From the foot of the *stupa* on the summit, I looked out at the mist-shrouded river and the temple roofs, but I couldn't bring myself to sit in solitary contemplation for very long, so I hiked down again and continued my walk through the largely deserted streets. Several small shops and tiny repair sheds were opening, a few parents were out with their children, and a solitary *samlor* pedaled by. Mostly there was emptiness and silence.

I reached Wat Xieng Thong, a marvelous seventeenth-century temple complex at the northern end of town. I hadn't realized that I had walked so far, and I suddenly felt tired. There was no one in sight, but the side door of the main *sim*, or chapel, was open a crack, and I took off my sandals and entered. There are no windows in the *sim* – the roof in the Luang Phabang style sweeps almost down to the ground – and very little light came through the door. Wats have neither the massive solidity of Romanesque nor the soaring, dazzling light of Gothic. Rather, and especially in Laos, they seem to be entirely about darkness, enclosure, withdrawal. Here it was almost pitch-dark, though I could just make out a glint of gold from the enormous Buddha at the end of the hall. At first all that was visible was part of the arm; then very gradually, as my eyes adjusted to the darkness, I deciphered more of the huge figure, along with the smaller figures standing in the strange, stiff "Calling for Rain" posture – arms held rigidly to the side, fingers down – characteristic of Laotian Buddhism. I tried, in a half-comic, half-serious way, to pray, or rather to clear my mind. If it was going to happen for me, whatever it was that Ti and the German monk longed for, it would happen here and now. But I was too preoccupied, worrying about whether Josh had been completely cured, about whether Ellen was enjoying herself, about my work, about the sick children in the villages, about the possibility of getting locked in the *sim*, about the flight back to Vientiane. As a Buddhist I was a complete failure. All that had happened was that my eyes had involuntarily adjusted to the darkness. And then I realized, with a flash that even my relentless irony couldn't entirely undermine, that adjusting to the darkness was the best I could hope for.

NOTE

1   M. Henri Mouhot, *Travels in the Central Parts of Indo-China, Cambodia, and Laos*, 2 vols. (London: John Murray, 1864).

14

STORY-TELLING

My earliest recollections of "having an identity" or "being a self" are bound up with story-telling – narrating my own life or having it narrated for me by my mother. I suppose that I usually used the personal pronoun "I" in telling my own stories and that my mother used my name, but the heart of the initial experience of selfhood lay in the stories, not in the unequivocal, unmediated possession of an identity. Indeed the stories need not have been directly about me for me to experience them as an expression of my identity: my mother was generously fond of telling me long stories I found irresistible about someone named Terrible Stanley, a child whom I superficially resembled but who made a series of disastrous life decisions – running into traffic, playing with matches, climbing out onto the window ledge, or trying to squeeze through the bars on the cast-iron railing that enclosed the back porch where my mother would hang the washing. We lived in Roxbury then – in those days one of Boston's main Jewish neighborhoods – and Terrible Stanley's worst, and most delicious, misadventures involved the nearby Franklin Park Zoo.

I am presumably one of the few Americans who woke regularly as a child to the sound of lions roaring in the distance. I can still remember pacing back and forth on the porch and imagining that I was a caged lion. My mother has a picture of me holding on to the bars and with my mouth open wide. I suppose I was roaring. Contrary to *his* mother's explicit warnings and his own solemn promises, Terrible Stanley would sneak away from Maple Court (where we also happened to live), walk down Wayne Street past the Garrison Public School (where my brother was caned in the early 1950s for refusing to recite the catechism), cross Blue Hill Avenue, and go to the zoo. On innumerable occasions, he narrowly escaped being eaten by the lions or crushed in the terrible embrace of the pythons. The zoo was hard to resist.

As I grew slightly older, the sense of identity as intertwined with narratives of the self and its doubles was confirmed by my father, who also had a penchant for story-telling – stories not so gratifyingly focused on my small being as my mother's were, but compelling and wonderfully well-told stories of himself and

This chapter was first published in *The Threepenny Review* 11 (1990): 23.

of a cousin, a few years younger than he, by whom he was virtually obsessed. My father and his cousin came from almost identical backgrounds: first-generation Americans born in Boston to poor Jewish immigrants from Lithuania. Like my father, the cousin had become a lawyer, and here began the story. My father was named Harry J. Greenblatt; his cousin Joseph H. Greenblatt. But when the latter became a lawyer, he moved into the same building in which my father had his office, and he began to call himself J. Harry Greenblatt. He managed, or so my father thought, to siphon off some clients from my father's already established practice. By itself this would have been enough to cause considerable tension, but over the years J. Harry compounded the offense by apparently becoming considerably richer than my father, Harry J. – wealth, as far as I can tell, being measured principally by the amount of money donated annually to local charities, the contributions printed annually in a small but well-perused booklet. There were, as I grew up, endless stories about J. Harry – chance encounters in the street, confusions of identity that always seemed to work to my father's disadvantage, tearful reconciliations that would quickly give way to renewed rancor, great potlatches of charitable contributions. This went on for decades and would, I suppose, have become intolerably boring had my father not possessed considerable comic gifts, along with a vast repertory of other stories.

But a few years before my father's death at eighty-six, the rivalry and doubling took a strange twist: J. Harry Greenblatt was indicted on charges of embezzlement; the charges were prominently reported in the newspapers; and the newspapers mistakenly printed the name of the culprit – convicted and sentenced to prison – as Harry J. Greenblatt. Busybodies phoned our house to offer their commiserations to my mother. The confusion was awkward, but it had at least one benefit: it enabled my father to tell a whole new set of stories about himself and his double. When you are in your eighties, new stories can be a precious commodity.

My father's narrative impulse, I can see from this distance, was a strategic way of turning disappointment, anger, rivalry, and a sense of menace into comic pleasure, a way of reestablishing the self on the site of its threatened loss. But there was an underside to this strategy that I have hinted at by calling his stories obsessive. For the stories in some sense *were* the loss of identity which they were meant to ward off – there was something compulsive about them, as if someone were standing outside of my father and insisting that he endlessly recite his tales. Near the end of his life, he would sometimes abandon the pretence of having a conversation, interrupt what was being said, and simply begin to tell one of his stories.

This sense of compulsiveness in the telling of stories is not simply a function of garrulous old age; it is, I think, a quality that attaches to narrative itself, a quality thematized in *The Arabian Nights* and *The Ancient Mariner*. In response to the compulsiveness there have arisen numerous social and aesthetic regulations – not only the rules that govern civil conversation but the rules, that govern the production and reception of narrative in books, on screen, on the stage. And there have arisen, too, less evident but powerful psychic regulations that govern how much narrative you are meant to experience, as it were, within your identity.

One of the worst times I have ever been through in my life was a period –
I cannot recall if it was a matter of days or weeks – when I could not rid my mind
of the impulse to narrate my being. I was a student at Cambridge, trying to
decide whether to return to America and go to law school or graduate school in
English. "He's sitting at his desk, trying to decide what to do with his life," a
voice – my voice, I suppose, but also not my voice – spoke within my head.
"Now he's putting his head on his hand; now he is furrowing his brow; and now
he is getting up to open the window." And on and on, with a slight tone of
derision through it all. I was split off from myself, J. Harry to my Harry J. (or
Terrible Stanley to my Stephen), in an unhappy reprise of my early sense of self as
story. It was unhappy, I suppose, because by my early twenties my identity had
been fashioned as a single being exactly corresponding to the personal pronoun
"I," and the unpleasantly ironic "he" sounding inside my head felt like an
internal violation of my internal space, an invasion of my privacy, an objectifi-
cation of what I least wished to objectify. I experienced the compulsive and
detached narrativizing voice as something that had seized me, that I could not
throw off, for even my attempts to do so were immediately turned into narrative.
It occurred to me that I might be going mad. When the voice left me, it did so
suddenly, inexplicably with the sound of something snapping.

If the experience I have just described intensified my interest in narrative, it
made me quite literally wish to get the narratives outside myself. Hence the
critical distance that I attempt to inscribe in and with the stories I tell, for the
narrative impulse in my writing is yoked to the service of literary and cultural
criticism; it pulls out and away from myself. Hence too, perhaps, my fascination
with figures of estrangement: I could not endure the compulsive estrangement of
my life, as if it belonged to someone else, but I could perhaps understand the
uncanny otherness of my own voice, make it comprehensible and bring it under
rational control by trying to understand the way in which all voices come to be
woven out of strands of ahen experience. I am committed to making strange
what has become familiar, to demonstrating that what seems an untroubling and
untroubled part of ourselves (for example, Shakespeare) is actually part of
something else, something different.

We spent last spring in Boston, and I wanted to take my wife to the apartment
house in Roxbury. My mother and everyone else in my family told us that we
shouldn't go back to the old neighborhood. I had lived in California too long,
they said, and didn't know what it was like. There are murders every night, said
my cousin Sherman; whites aren't welcome, said my cousin Ann; there is
nothing to see, said my cousin Eldon; the animals in the zoo have been killed
off one by one, with bb guns and poison, said my brother, and the park is a
nightmare, even in broad daylight. Of course, we went anyway. That is, after all,
the lesson of the Terrible Stanley stories.

There were lots of animals in the zoo – I don't know if the cages had been
restocked or if the story of the killings was merely a grim joke that had
eventually, in the tense and racist atmosphere of Boston, been received as
truth. The park, designed by Olmstead, looked beautiful, easily the loveliest

green space in the entire city. But my family was right that the neighborhood looked awful: the streets empty, shops boarded up, trash piled on the sidewalks, windows broken everywhere, graffiti spray-painted on walls. No landlord or bank had put any money into the buildings for years, probably for decades. We found the great old synagogue. Mishkan Tefilah, whose vast neo-classical bulk still dominates the area: it was torched, I don't know when, and stands in massive, burned-out desolation.

About half the windows of the apartment house on Maple Court were boarded up, but there were people living there, and I could see washing hanging from the porch where I used to practice my roaring. On the driveway below the porch, a young woman was waxing her car. She heard me say to my wife that that was the apartment we used to live in, and she beckoned to us, "Stand here for a few minutes and let people see that you're talking to me." She spoke in the tone of quiet urgency with which my mother used to enjoin me not to go to the zoo, not to wander off from the haven of the apartment. "Then get out quickly," she added. "It's not safe for you to be here."

STEPHEN GREENBLATT:
A BIBLIOGRAPHY (1965–2003)

This bibliography was prepared by Gustavo P. Secchi.

BOOKS

Three Modern Satirists: Waugh, Orwell, and Huxley (New Haven: Yale University Press, 1965).

Sir Walter Ralegh: The Renaissance Man and His Roles (New Haven: Yale University Press, 1973).

Renaissance Self-Fashioning: from More to Shakespeare (Chicago: University of Chicago Press, 1980).

Shakespearean Negotiations: The Circulation of Social Energy in Renaissance England (Berkeley: University of California Press, 1988; Oxford: Clarendon Press, 1988); German translation.

Learning to Curse: Essays in Early Modern Culture (New York and London: Routledge, 1990); German, Japanese translations.

Marvelous Possessions: The Wonder of the New World (Oxford: Clarendon Press, 1991; Chicago: University of Chicago Press, 1991); German, Japanese, Italian, and Portuguese translations.

New Historicism: Literaturgeschichte als Poetik der Kultur, ed. Moritz Bassler (Frankfurt: Fischer, 1995).

Practicing New Historicism [with Catherine Gallagher] (Chicago: University of Chicago Press, 2000).

Was ist Literaturgeschichte? trans. Reinhard Kaiser and Barbara Naumann (Frankfurt: Suhrkamp, 2000).

Hamlet in Purgatory (Princeton: Princeton University Press, 2001); Italian translation.

BOOKS (AS EDITOR)

"The New Historicism: Studies in Cultural Poetics" (series of volumes published by University of California Press), General Editor.

Allegory and Representation, Selected Papers from the English Institute, 1978–1980 (Baltimore: The Johns Hopkins University Press, 1981; paperback edition, 1986); Japanese translation.

The Power of Forms in the English Renaissance (Norman, Oklahoma: Pilgrim Books, 1982); also published as: *The Forms of Power and the Power of Forms*, a double issue of *Genre*, 1982.

Representing the English Renaissance (Berkeley and London: University of California Press, 1988).

Essays in Memory of Joel Fineman (special issue of *Representations*, 1989).

Redrawing the Boundaries: The Transformation of English and American Literary Studies [with Giles Gunn] (New York: MLA, 1992); Korean translation.

New World Encounters (Berkeley and London: University of California Press, 1993).

The Norton Shakespeare (New York: Norton, 1997), General Editor.

"The Sixteenth Century," in *The Norton Anthology of English Literature*, 7th edn, co-editor.

The Norton Anthology of English Literature, 7th edn, 2 vols. (New York: Norton, 1999), Associate General Editor.

ARTICLES

"Sidney's Arcadia and the Mixed Mode," in *Studies in Philology* 70 (1973): 269–78.

"Learning to Curse: Aspects of Linguistic Colonialism in the Sixteenth Century," in *First Images of America: The Impact of the New World on the Old*, ed. Fredi Chiappelli (Berkeley: University of California Press, 1976), 561–80.

"The False Ending in Volpone," in *Journal of English and Germanic Philology* 75 (1976): 90–104.

"Marlowe and Renaissance Self-Fashioning," in *Two Renaissance Mythmakers: Christopher Marlowe and Ben Jonson*, ed. Alvin B. Kernan (Baltimore: The Johns Hopkins University Press, 1977), 41–69.

"More and the Suburb," in *University Publishing* 5 (1977): 16–17.

"More, Role-Playing, and Utopia," in *The Yale Review* 67 (1978): 515–36.

"Marlowe, Marx, and Anti-Semitism," in *Critical Inquiry* 5 (1978): 291–307; German translation in *Christopher Marlowe, Der Jude von Malta*, trans. Erich Fried (Berlin: Wagenbach, 1991): 125–52.

"Improvisation and Power," in *Literature and Society*, ed. Edward Said (Baltimore: The Johns Hopkins University Press, 1980), pp. 57–99 (reprinted in *William Shakespeare's "Othello"*, ed.Harold Bloom (New York: Chelsea House, 1987); and in *Shakespearean Tragedy*, ed. John Drakakis (London and New York: Longman, 1992), pp. 153–93. (A brief, early version appeared as "The Improvisation of Power: The Power of Improvisation," in *University Publishing* 7 (1979): 17–18.)

"The Resonance of Renaissance Poetry," in *ADE Bulletin* 64 (1980): 7–10.

"Invisible Bullets: Renaissance Authority and Its Subversion," in *Glyph* 8 (1981): 40–61. Revised versions of this essay appear in *Political Shakespeare: New Essays in Cultural Materialism*, ed. Jonathan Dollimore and Alan Sinfield (Manchester: Manchester University Press, 1985), pp. 18–47 (reprinted in *William Shakespeare's "Henry IV, Part 2,"* ed. Harold Bloom (New York: Chelsea House, 1987), pp. 125–50); and *Shakespeare's "Rough Magic:" Renaissance Essays in Honor of C. L. Barber*, ed. Peter Erickson and

Coppelia Kahn (Newark, Delaware: University of Delaware Press, 1985), pp. 276–302.

"The Cultivation of Anxiety: King Lear and His Heirs," *Raritan* 2 (1982): 92–124. Reprinted in K. M. Newton, *Theory Into Practice: A Reader in Modern Literary Criticism* (London: Macmillan, 1992), pp. 256–74; *"King Lear": Contemporary Critical Essays*, ed. Kiernan Ryan (London: Macmillan, 1993), pp. 158–79.

"Filthy Rites," in *Daedalus* III (1982): 1–16 (a brief early version appeared in *University Publishing* 8 (1979): 5–6).

"King Lear and Harsnett's "Devil-Fiction," in *The Power of Forms in the English Renaissance*, ed. Stephen Greenblatt (Norman, Oklahoma: Pilgrim Books, 1982), pp. 239–42.

"Chinese English," in *The Threepenny Review* 12 (1983): 4–7; reprinted as "China: Visiting Rites," in *Raritan* 2 (1983): 1–23.

"Murdering Peasants: Status, Genre, and the Representation of Rebellion," in *Representations* 1 (1983): 1–29.

"China: Visiting Rites (II)," in *Raritan* 4 (1985): 44–56. Reprinted in *Cambridge Review* 108 (1987): 154–8.

"Shakespeare and the Exorcists," in *Shakespeare and the Question of Theory*, ed. Patricia Parker and Geoffrey Hartman (London: Methuen, 1985), pp. 163–87. Reprinted in *William Shakespeare's "King Lear"*, ed. Harold Bloom (New York: Chelsea House, 1987), pp. 97–119; in *Contemporary Literary Criticism: Literary and Cultural Studies*, 2nd edn, ed. Robert Con Davis and Ronald Schleifer (New York and London: Longman, 1989), pp. 428–47; and in *Shakespeare: King Lear*, ed. Frank Kermode (London: Macmillan, 1992), pp. 258–98. A slightly different version of this essay appears in *After Strange Texts: The Role of Theory in the Study of Literature*, ed. Gregory S. Jay and David L. Miller, Papers from the University of Alabama's Ninth Annual Symposium in English and American Literature, 1982 (University, Alabama: University of Alabama Press, 1985), pp. 101–23.

"Exorcism into Art," in *Representations* 12 (1985): 15–23.

"Loudun and London," in *Critical Inquiry* 12 (1986): 326–46.

"Fiction and Friction," in *Reconstructing Individualism: Autonomy, Individuality, and the Self in Western Thought*, ed. David Wellbery and Thomas Heller (Stanford: Stanford University Press, 1986), pp. 30–52.

"Psychoanalysis and Renaissance Culture," in *Literary Theory/Renaissance Texts*, ed. Patricia Parker and David Quint (Baltimore and London: Johns Hopkins University Press, 1986), pp. 210–24.

"Towards a Poetics of Culture," in *Southern Review* 20 (1987): 3–15. (Japanese translation, in *iichiko* 16 (1990): 111–26). A slightly different version of this essay appears as "Capitalist Culture and the Circulatory System," in *The Aims of Representation: Subject/Text/History*, ed. Murray Krieger (New York: Columbia University Press, 1987), pp. 257–73. Norwegian translation: "Mot en Kulturens Poetikk," in *Samtiden* (Oslo) 6 (1994): 53–62.

"Erotische Provokation im Elisabethanischen Theater," in *Shakespeare-Jahrbuch* (Berlin, 1988): 56–61.

"The Manipulation of Anxiety," in *Shakespeare-Jahrbuch* (Berlin, 1988): 163–9.

"Where Do We Go From Here?" in *The Village Voice Literary Supplement* (October, 1988): 21.

"Maravilhosas possessoes," in *Estudos Historicos* (Sao Paulo, Brazil) 3 (1989): 43–62.

"The King Retires," program essay for Old Vic production of *King Lear* (director: Jonathan Miller), spring, 1989.

"Anti-Dictator" (on Etienne de la Boetie), in *The Harvard History of French Literature*, ed. Denis Hollier (Cambridge: Harvard University Press, 1989), pp. 223–8.

"In Memory of Joel Fineman," *Representations* 28 (1989): 1–3.

"Identity" entry in *The Spenser Encyclopedia*.

"Culture," in *Critical Terms for Literary Study*, ed. Thomas McLaughlin and Frank Lentricchia (Chicago and London: University of Chicago Press: 1990), pp. 225–32.

"Resonance and Wonder," in *Bulletin of the American Academy of Arts and Sciences* 43 (1990): 11–34. Also in *Literary Theory Today*, ed. Peter Collier and Helga Geyer-Ryan (Cambridge: Polity, 1990), pp. 74–90; *Exhibiting Cultures: The Poetics and Politics of Museum Display*, ed. Ivan Karp and Steven D. Lavine (Washington and London: Smithsonian Institution Press, 1991), pp. 42–56; German translation, "Resonanz und Staunen," in *Freibeuter* 47 (1991): 14–30; Portuguese translation, "O novo historicismo," in *Estudos Hisoricos* 9 (1991): 243–61.

"Elizabeth I," *Encyclopaedia Britannica*, 15th edn (1990), 18: 243–47.

"Story-Telling," in *The Threepenny Review* 11 (1990): 23.

"Where Little Fyodor Played," in *London Review of Books* 13 (1991): 8–10.

"Joel Fineman's 'Will'," in Joel Fineman, *The Subjectivity Effect in Western Literary Tradition* (Cambridge, Mass.: MIT Press, 1991), pp. ix–xix.

"The Demand for Love," program essay for the American Repertory Theatre production of *King Lear* (spring, 1991).

"The Best Way to Kill Our Literary Inheritance ..." in *The Chronicle of Higher Education* 37 (June 12, 1991): B1–B3; reprinted in *The Council Chronicle* (November, 1991): 16.

"Varieties of Historicism" and "The Silence of the Criminal," in *Litteraria Pragensia: Studies in Literature and Culture* 1 (1991): 3–4, 57–60. (Czech translation in *Iricialy* 2 (May–June 1991): 31–4.)

" 'A passing marvellous thing...': Global Visions in the Age of Columbus," *Times Literary Supplement* (January 3, 1992): 14–15.

"Laos Is Open," *Threepenny Review* 51 (1992): 20–3; reprinted in H. Aram Veeser, ed., *Confessions of the Critics* (New York: Routledge, 1996), pp. 221–34.

"Utopian Desire," in *Litteraria Pragensia* 4 (1992): 30–41.

"The MLA on Trial," in *Profession* (1992): 39–41.

"The Emotion of Multitude" ("Pocit Nesmirneho Mnozstvi"), in *Svet Literatury* (Prague) (1992): 78–84.

"La souris mangeuse d'hostie: les miettes du repas eucharistique," in *Traverses* 5 (1993): 42–54.

"Shakespeare Bewitched," in *New Historical Literary Study: Essays on Reproducing Texts, Representing History*, ed. Jeffrey N. Cox and Larry J. Reynolds (Princeton: Princeton University Press, 1993), pp. 108–35; *Shakespeare and Cultural Traditions*, ed. Tetsui Kishi, Roger Pringle, and Stanley Wells (Newark, Delaware: University of Delaware Press, 1994), pp. 17–42.

"Utopian Desire," in *Surprised by Scenes*, ed. Yasunari Takada (Tokyo: Kenkysha, 1994), pp. 1–15.

"Toward a Universal Language of Motion: Reflections on a Seventeenth-Century Muscle Man," in *Linq* 21 (1994): 56–62; also in *Choreographing History*, ed. Susan Leigh Foster (Bloomington: Indiana University Press, 1995), pp. 25–31.

"The Eating of the Soul," in *Representations* 48 (1994): 97–116 (earlier version in *Intrecci e Contaminazioni*, ed. Valerio de Scarpis, Loretta Innocenti, Franco Marucci, and Armando Pajalich (Venice: Supernova, 1993), pp. 65–820.

"A Mark Morris Symposium" (on *L'Allegro, il Penseroso, ed il Moderato*), in *The Three-penny Review* 61 (1995): 20–1.

"The Interart Moment" ("Mote mellan konstarterna bar frukt"), in *Svenska Dagbladet* (Stockholm), May 15, 1995.

"Columbus Runs Aground: Christmas Eve, 1492," in *The Sheila Carmel Lectures, 1988–1993*, ed. Hana Wirth-Nesher (Tel Aviv: Tel Aviv University, 1995), pp. 125–47; *Counting and Recounting: Measuring Inner and Outer Space in the Renaissance*, ed. Paola Bottalla and Michela Calderaro (Trieste: Edizioni La Mongolfiera, 1995), pp. 13–40.

"Memory and Monumentality," in *The Threepenny Review* 64 (1996): 35–6; See also "Grounds for Remembering," in *Grounds for Remembering: Monuments, Memorials, Texts* (Townsend Center for the Humanities Occasional Papers, 1995), pp. 22–8.

"Martial Law in the Land of Cockaigne," in *Materialist Shakespeare*, ed. Ivo Kamps (London: Verso, 1995), pp. 108–41.

"What light through yonder Windows breaks?" (review of CD-ROM *Romeo and Juliet* and *Macbeth*), in *Civilization* 3 (1996): 78–9.

"Remnants of the Sacred in Early Modern England," in *Subject and Object in Renaissance Culture*, ed. Margreta de Grazia, Maureen Quilligan, and Peter Stallybrass (Cambridge: Cambridge University Press, 1996), pp. 337–45.

"Changelings: Mozart, Shakespeare, and the Art of Maurice Sendak," in *Townsend Center Occasional Papers* #5 (1996): 25–33. A shorter version appeared as "Maurice Sendak's Rabbis," in *The Threepenny Review* 66 (1996): 32–3.

"Warum reisen?," in *NZZ Folio* 6 (June, 1996): 7–11. Also in *Voyage: Jahrbuch fur Reise-& Tourismusforschung* (Cologne: DuMont, 1997), pp. 13–17.

"Best Books of 1995," in *Misuzu* (Tokyo) 418 (1996): 42–3.

"William Shakespeare drammaturgo elisabettiano," in *Storio della Civilita Letteraria Inglese*, ed. Franco Marenco, 4 vols. (Torino: UTET, 1996), 1:551–75.

"Mutilation and Meaning," in *Miscast: Negotiating the Presence of the Bushmen*, ed. Pippa Skotnes (Cape Town: University of Cape Town Press, 1996), pp. 25–39 [Hungarian translation in Cafe Babel (Budapest)].

"Die Macht des Als-ob," in *NZZ Folio* (December, 1996): 28–9.

"Miracles," in *The Threepenny Review* 69 (1997): 34.

"The Interart Moment," in *Interart Poetics: Essays on the Interrelations of the Arts and Media*, ed. Ulla-Britta Lagerroth, Hans Lund, and Erik Hedling (Amsterdam: Rodopi, 1997), pp. 13–15.

"Vom höchst Begabten bis zu dem, der eben lesen mag," *Frankfurther Allgemeine Zeitung* (November, 14, 1997): 48.

"Bildung als Uberlebensmittel," in *Berliner Zeitung*, Einstein Forum Supplement (December 3, 1997): VI–VII.

"Warum reisen?," in *Voyage: Jahrbuch für Reise- & Tourismusforschung 1997* (Cologne: DuMont, 1997), pp. 13–17.

"Il Nuovo Storicismo e il Futuro della Letteratura," in *Allegoria: Per uno Studio Materialistico della Letteratura* 8 (1996): 130–43.

"*Hamlet*: Interiority and Revenge," in *"Hamlet" ou le texte en question*, ed. Gilles Mathis and Pierre Sahel (Paris: Editions Messene, 1997), pp. 9–19.

"What Is the History of Literature? *Critical Inquiry* 23 (1997): 460–81. A version also appears as "Benefit of Clergy, Benefit of Literature," in *Stanford Humanities Review* 6

(1998): 11–25. Translation: "Ó que é a historia da literatura?," in *Interseções: Revista de Estudos Interdisciplinares* (Rio de Janeiro) 1:1 (1999): 13–32.

Foreword, *A New History of Early English Drama*, ed. John D. Cox and David Scott Kastan (New York: Columbia University Press, 1997).

"The Mousetrap: In Memory of Louis Marin," *Shakespeare Studies* (Japan) 35 (1997): 1–32. "Past Na Mysi," Czech translation in *Svêt Literatury* 17 (1999): 3–23.

"The Touch of the Real," in *Representations* 59 (1997) (Special Issue: "The Fate of 'Culture': Geertz and Beyond"): 14–29.

"The Use of Salutary Anxiety in *The Tempest*," in Shakespeare, *The Tempest*, ed. Robert Langbaum (New York: Signet, 1998), pp. 156–79 (adapted from *Shakespearen Negotiations*).

"Auerbach and New Historicism," in *Kyoto English Review* 2 (1998): pp. 1–20.

"America's Raciest Read," Op-Ed essay, *New York Times*, September 22, 1998 (on Starr Report).

"About That Romantic Sonnet …," OpEd essay, *New York Times*, June 2, 1999 (German trans. *Tages-Anzeiger; Theaterheute*).

"Hamlet in Fegefeuer," in *Rituale heute: Theorien-Kontroversen-Entwürfe*, ed. Corina Caduff and Joanna Pfaff-Czarnecka (Berlin: Reimer, 1999), pp. 99–125.

"*The Tempest*: Martial Law in the Land of Cockaigne," *Shakespeare: The Last Plays*, ed. Kiernan Ryan (London: Longman, 1999), pp. 206–44. (reprint).

"Ghosts of Berlin," OpEd essay, *New York Times*, May 28, 1999.

"Commentary I," in *Word and Image* 17 (2001): 62–4.

"Racial Memory and Literary History," in *PMLA* 116 (2001): 48–63.

"Scholars at Risk," President's Column, in *MLA Newsletter* 34:1 (2002): pp. 3–4.

"E-Mail Academy," President's Column, in *MLA Newsletter*, 34:2 (summer, 2002): p. 3.

"The MLA in the World," President's Column, in *MLA Newsletter*, 34:3 (fall, 2002):3–4.

"Keep Us Informed," President's Column, in *MLA Newsletter*, 34:4 (winter, 2002):3.

"A Eulogy," *Michigan Quarterly Review* (fall, 2002): 543–5.

"Psychoanalysis and Renaissance Culture," in *The Renaissance: Italy and Abroad*, ed. John Jeffries Martin (London: Routledge, 2003), pp. 124–38.

"Ghosts" (excerpt from MLA Presidential Address, December 2002), *The American Scholar*, 72:2 (spring, 2003): 160.

"Presidential Address 2002: 'Stay, Illusion' – On Receiving Messages from the Dead," in *PMLA* 118 (2003): 417–26.

REVIEWS AND INTERVIEWS

"Shakespeare," in *The Yale Review* 63 (1974): 447–53.

"Shakespeare as Magus, Psychiatrist, and Feminist," in *The Yale Review* 65 (1976): 443–50.

"Terrence Des Pres, *The Survivor: Life in the Death Camps*, in *San Francisco Review of Books* 2 (1976): 13–26.

"Bryan Little, *Sir Christopher Wren: A Historical Biography*," in *American Historical Review* (1977): 98.

"Roy Strong, The Cult of Elizabeth," in *Renaissance Quarterly* 31 (1978): 642–4.

"Dialectics of Being, Self, Family, and Society," in *CLIO* 8 (1979): 275–8.

"A Crisis of Poetic Faith" (review of Alvin B. Kernan, *The Imaginary Library*), in *The Yale Review* (1983): 455–7.

"Splenditello" (review of Judith Brown, *Immodest Acts*), in *The London Review of Books* 8 (June 19, 1986): 5–6.

"As They Like It" (review of Northrop Frye, *On Shakespeare*, and Terry Eagleton, *William Shakespeare*), in *The New Republic* (November 10, 1986): 42–7.

Review of Andre Thevet's *North America: A Sixteenth-Century View*, ed. and trans. Roger Schlesinger and Arthur Stabler, in *Renaissance Quarterly* 41 (1988): 164–7.

"That's America" (review article on Michael Rogin, *"Ronald Reagan," the Movie, and Other Episodes in Political Demonology*, in *London Review of Books* 10 (29 September, 1988): 6–7.

"Loitering in the Piazza" (review article on Giovanni Levi, *Inheriting Power: The Story of an Exorcist*), in *London Review of Books* 10 (27 October, 1988): 18–19.

"Kindly Visions" (review article on Catherine Lutz and Jane Collins, *Reading National Geographic*), in *The New Yorker* (October 11, 1993): 112–20.

" 'New Historicism': Interview med Stephen Greenblatt," in *Kultur og Klasse* (Denmark) 68 (1990): 8–20.

"Resonance et Etonnement," interview in *L'Ane: Le Magazine Freudien* 56 (1993): 30–2.

Review of William Empson, *Essays on Renaissance Literature*, vol. II, in *London Review of Books* 16 (1994): 31–2.

Review of Gary Wills, *Witches and Jesuits: Shakespeare's "Macbeth"*, in *The New Republic* 211 (November 14, 1994): 32–7.

"Nyhistorismens Tvisynte Far: Samtale med Stephen Greenblatt" (interview), in *Samtiden* (Oslo) 6 (1994): 47–52.

Review of Anthony Grafton, *New Worlds, Ancient Texts: The Power of Tradition and the Shock of Discovery*, in *History of European Ideas* 21 (1995): 92–4.

"The Truth About El Dorado" (review of Charles Nicholl, *The Creature in the Map*), in *Times Literary Supplement* (August 18, 1995): 3–4.

Review of Paul Theroux, *The Pillars of Hercules*, in *The New York Times Book Review* (November 5, 1995): 11.

Review of *The Jew in the Text: Modernity and the Construction of Identity*, ed. Linda Nochlin and Tamar Gelb, in *Tate: The Art Magazine* 8 (1996): 77.

Review of Adam Phillips, *The Beast in the Nursery*, in *New York Times Book Review* (February 22, 1998): 7.

Review of Jonathan Spence, *The Chan's Great Continent*, in *New York Times Book Review* (November 14, 1998).

"New Historicism," in *Cult* (Brazil) (December, 1998): 32–5.

Review of Lorraine Daston and Katharine Park, *Wonders and the Order of Nature, 1150–1750*, in *London Review of Books* 21 (January 7, 1999): 8–9.

Interview: in Mihaela Anghelescu Irimia, *Dialoguri Postmoderne* (Bucharest: Editura Fundatiei Culturale Române, 1999), pp. 170–82.

Review of John Updike, *Gertrude and Claudius*, in *The New Republic* (2000).

INDEX